THE GATEKEEPERS

Inside Israel's Internal Security Agency

DROR MOREH

THE GATEKEEPERS

Inside Israel's Internal Security Agency

DROR MOREH

Preface by Ambassador Dennis Ross

Editor: Shachar Alterman

Skyhorse Publishing
New York

Skyhorse Publishing books may be purchased in bulk at special discounts for sales promotion, corporate gifts, fund-raising, or educational purposes. Special editions can also be created to specifications. For details, contact the Special Sales Department, Skyhorse Publishing, 307 West 36th Street, 11th Floor, New York, NY 10018 or info@skyhorsepublishing.com.

Visit our website at www.skyhorsepublishing.com.

10 9 8 7 6 5 4 3 2 1

Library of Congress Cataloging-in-Publication Data is available on file.

Cover design by Brian Peterson
Cover photo credit: Doron Koren

ISBN: 978-1-63220-641-1
Ebook ISBN: 978-1-63220-807-1

Printed in the United States of America

For Amnon and Mika

Translator's Note

The General Security Service (Hebrew) or Israel Security Agency (English) is Israel's internal security service, charged with defending Israel against terrorism and espionage. It is usually referred to as the Shin Bet or the Shabak, based on the Hebrew acronym for its name. In this book, the agency is generally referred to as the Shin Bet or as the Service, based on the terms used by the book's interviewed subjects.

Table of Contents

Preface

By Ambassador Dennis Ross

Who would have thought that all the former heads of Israel's Shin Bet, the equivalent of the American FBI and Secret Service, would reveal their innermost thoughts about the dilemmas they faced? Yet in the film *The Gatekeepers*, we saw them express, poignantly, what they had to do to stop Palestinian terror in Israel. Preemptive arrests, extracting information to prevent bombings, using informants frequently by coercing them, and carrying out targeted killings were not abstract concepts to be tested but real actions taken to save the lives of Israeli's. In theory, it all seems straightforward. In reality, it is rarely so simple.

What the film *The Gatekeepers* made vivid visually, the book makes even more compelling. This should come as no surprise as the filmmaker Dror Moreh, who conducted the interviews with each of these former directors of Shin Bet, is able to present much more of what each of these men had to say in the book, and as the reader will see, they did not hold back. The hard choices, the tough recommendations, the need to live with the consequences of their decisions, and the frustrations with the political leadership, all combine to make a powerful statement not just about how to combat terror but also about the impact that continued occupation of the Palestinians has on Israel and its future.

For me, the film and the book have great meaning, intellectually and emotionally. I know five of the six former directors, and at times worked closely with four of them: Ya'akov Peri, Ami Ayalon, Avi Dichter, and Yuval Diskin. When I was the American negotiator on peace during the Clinton administration, I would always stop by Shin Bet headquarters to meet them and to get their assessments of what was going on with the Palestinians—the factors influencing Arafat, the mood on the street, what the Palestinian security forces were doing and not doing, the threats Israel was facing, the prospects for agreements, etc. At this point, and later during and after the worst of the Second Intifada, when I was outside the government and then when I was back in it, the assessments I heard were often not reflective of what I would hear from the Israeli prime ministers at the time.

Even then, I saw a readiness to speak truth to power and report to the prime minister—whether it was Rabin, Peres, Netanyahu, Barak, Sharon, Olmert, or Netanyahu again—about developments with the Palestinians and the consequences of different actions.

For those who reacted to the gatekeepers and wondered why some of their criticisms or doubts were never exposed publicly until after they left their positions, they should understand that they never pulled their punches in private. To do so in public would have been to betray their office and their responsibilities as they defined them.

In my conversations with each of these former heads of Shin Bet, I not only knew where they stood on different questions, but I also saw how they wrestled with some of the moral dilemmas they faced. It added to the respect I had for each of them. Their willingness to be so forthcoming in *The Gatekeepers* is a testament to their character and to the strength of the Israeli democracy. If anything, the readers of *The Gatekeepers* are likely to be even more impressed with these men and the country that produced them.

INTRODUCTION

November 4, 1995, is the date that shook up my life completely. Since that awful night when Prime Minister Yitzhak Rabin of Israel was murdered by a Jewish assassin, I've been plagued by a feeling of futility and hopelessness regarding our ability to create a better future for our children in the State of Israel. The emotion that Shimon Sheves, director general of the prime minister's office under Rabin, expressed so well when he cried out, "My country is over," echoes within me to this day. Some hope may have flickered faintly when Labor Party leader Ehud Barak was elected in 1999 and declared "the dawning of a new day," but this, too, soon faded.

Most of the people in my immediate environment have lived with a sense of fatalism and complete acceptance of our state of existence from that day to the current one. We are doomed to live by the sword for the foreseeable future, and must get used to the suffocating sensation of hopelessness. "One hand on the spear, and the other on the plow," as the forefathers of Zionism decreed—this is how we will live for the foreseeable future. Whole sectors of Israeli society have given up on the possibility that there is indeed a chance to ever resolve the conflict with our Palestinian neighbors. We have grown so accustomed to the terrible price that Israeli society pays in return for continuing to live by the sword that we nearly fail to see this cost. This feeling, and the desire to understand how we've arrived at this point, motivated me to make *The Gatekeepers*—my Academy Award–nominated 2012 documentary that offers revealing portraits of the men responsibe for Israel's national security.

The inspiration for *The Gatekeepers* came from several sources. One of them was the Oscar-winning documentary *The Fog of War*, by American director Errol Morris.

In the film, Morris interviews Robert McNamara, who was the United States secretary of defense between the years 1961 and 1968, and worked alongside President John F. Kennedy and his successor, Lyndon B. Johnson. When I watched the movie for the first time, I was awed by the power of first-hand testimony, testimony coming from the secret chambers of American strategic decision making.

I was amazed by the exposure of the ways in which decisions determining the fates of millions are made.

An additional catalyst for the creation of *The Gatekeepers* was a conversation conducted for a different movie of mine—*Sharon*. In that documentary, I tried to understand, through interviews with the people closest to the former Israeli prime minister, what led Ariel Sharon to the disengagement plan. What led the father of the Jewish settlements to uproot seventeen settlements in Gaza and four more in the West Bank, settlements which he himself initiated and established?

As Dov (Dubie) Weissglass, who was bureau chief for the prime minister between the years 2003 and 2006, explained in the film, it was only after a series of profound events in Israel that Sharon began to change his thinking. In 2003, Alex Fishman published an interview in the newpaper *Yediot Ahronot* with several Shin Bet directors, who warned that if Sharon continued to run the country in the same aggressive way, Israel would hit a dead end. In September of that same year, twenty-seven Israeli Air Force pilots published a letter objecting on moral and legal grounds to the air operations that they were being ordered to carry out in Gaza and the West Bank. And in December, thirteen Israeli soldiers publicly declared that they would refuse to serve in the Israel-occupied Palestinian territories. This series of highly publicized conscientious objections to Israeli policy, observed Weissglass, "This wasn't exactly protest[ed] by the traditional groups which we usually identify as objectors or as draft resisters or as the extreme left, to which, honestly, we don't pay much attention. From Arik's [Sharon's] perspective, this protest was a matter to contemplate seriously. He was familiar with some of the names, he knew these were people for whom not only was Israel's security precious, but who had also contributed to and made sacrifices for Israeli security, perhaps more than anyone else. All these things, juxtaposed, made him change his perspective, and see that the problem is not only a diplomatic one. It starts to build up as an internal problem."

I remember that when I heard these words from Dov Weissglass, the idea to bring together all the heads of the Israel Security Service (Shin Bet), to tell their story and, through them, the story of the Israeli-Palestinian conflict from 1967 on, began to come to life.

The heads of Shin Bet themselves asked me more than once, "Why us?" The answer is simple: because the Israeli-Palestinian conflict is the Shin Bet's area of expertise. This is its overwhelming focus, more than any other organization in the State of Israel. The heads of the Israel General Security Service have played a crucial role in shaping the history of the contemporary Middle East. They were always at the forefront of action, in on all the secrets, right there with the prime ministers. They led their people in the fight against terror and against threats upon Israeli democracy, from without and from within. Their opinions and assessments influenced government policy in the West Bank and in the Gaza Strip more than anyone else's. The decisions they made frequently determined who would live and who would die.

They were there when Israel conquered the Sinai Peninsula, the Golan Heights, Gaza, and the West Bank by storm in the Six Day War and became a regional power overnight. They were there when the right-wing activists of Gush Emunim ("The Bloc of the Faithful") started to settle in Sebastia in the north of the West Bank during Rabin's first term as prime minister, and with his government's support. They were there when the leaders of the Jewish Underground—which was attacking Arabs and which also planned to blow up the Temple Mount, bringing on the War of the Apocalypse—were captured. They were there when the First Intifada—the Palestinian uprising—broke out in 1987, while we were still thinking we would "break their bones." They were there, when the Oslo peace accords were ceremoniously signed but also when a death verdict based on the "Law of the Pursuer"* was invoked against Rabin, and when the prime minister was indeed murdered at a peace rally in Tel Aviv. They were there in 2000 when the Second Intifada broke out immediately after the Camp David summit, and when Prime Minister Ehud Barak did "everything" to resolve the conflict and discovered that "there's no partner." They were there when human bombs slew hundreds in Israeli cities, and when Shin Bet interrogators tortured

---

* In Hebrew, *Din Rodef*, a religious permit for bystanders to kill a person who is threatening to kill, or commit a grave crime against, another. Prime Minister Rabin was branded a Pursuer or *Rodef* by some religious authorities following the Oslo agreements, a decree which Rabin's assassin later cited as justification for the murder.

suspects termed "ticking bombs." They were there when Hamas took control of Gaza and turned the Gaza Strip into "the Iranian delegation 16 miles from Ashkelon." They were there when the Israel Defense Forces (IDF) tried "to brand the Palestinian consciousness" for the umpteenth time, and every time that helicopters took off for yet another "targeted prevention" in Gaza.

They were there, and they are still here today, as the numbing sensation sets in that nothing on the ground is going to change and that nothing is going to get better.

I conducted the *Gatekeepers* interviews with the heads of Shin Bet in the years 2009–2010. Many times, I was asked why these powerful and secretive men agreed to talk; how had I managed to bring six chiefs of Shin Bet, five of them retired and one active (I interviewed Yuval Diskin at Shin Bet headquarters while he was still in office), to speak in such an honest, direct, and open way?

The truth is that I never asked them why they consented to be interviewed. In retrospect, I think that maybe on a personal level, they put their faith in me since I approached them as professionals, experts in their field. I did not have a hidden agenda: I was simply someone who asked to hear their story and their honest opinion. But, more important, I think they understood, certainly before I did, that our window of opportunity to resolve the conflict is gradually and ominously closing.

My journey started with Ami Ayalon—who was brought in as Shin Bet chief in 1996 to rehabilitate the service, after its disastrous failure to protect Rabin. My conversation with Ayalon opened some doors for me with the other men who ran Shin Bet. I met each of them several times, during which they often turned the tables and interrogated me at length. Even though I prepared dozens of questions in advance for each filmed interview—which were generally conducted at their homes—the conversations quickly took their own course. Mostly, I wanted to understand. I felt lucky in many respects to have the opportunity to explore the most dramatic moments of the recent decades in Israeli history, from the point of view of the heads of such an important agency.

After most of the interviews, I had a hard time falling asleep. I was haunted by the complex challenges that the State of Israel confronts each day, hour by hour, and by how these challenges require an extraordinarily talented leadership. I was also struck by how large the gap is between the ideal and the reality when it comes to the leadership that has led us and leads us.

During the interviews, the heads of Shin Bet were often asked difficult, painful questions, which forced them to confront their past and the worst errors of their career. Some of them bear deep scars from their period of service, and have paid a heavy price, which is reflected in every expression on their faces. I was left speechless when Avraham Shalom broke a silence that had lasted nearly thirty years and started to unfold his version of the Bus 300 Affair, after having informed me firmly in the first interview that he would not do so. (The notorious 1984 incident, involving the summary execution of two Palesntinian bus hijackers, blackened Shin Bet's name and became Shalom's own private mark of Cain.) I cringed in sympathy when Carmi Gillon, with his appealing directness, said that after Rabin's murder, with the whole weight of the failure on his shoulders, his wife Sari was mainly busy with the attempt to keep him alive. My jaw dropped when Avi Dichter described how the famous assassination operation against Hamas bomb-maker Yahya Ayyash, using a booby-trapped cell phone, actually failed the first time—and was successfully re-executed only a week later. And my eyes opened wide when Yuval Diskin, while still on active duty, told me how he discharged his feelings of torment after targeting enemies, no matter how successful and "clean" the operations.

After the movie was released, I was asked many times what was the most painful aspect of the history to which I was exposed while interviewing the Shin Bet directors. My answer was the number of opportunities for peace that were missed—mostly due to short-sighted leadership that preferred its personal, petty, temporary agenda over creating a better strategic reality for the future. I was filled with a grim recognition of how many thousands of casualties, how many horribly scarred families—on both sides—had resulted from this ineptitude.

As all heads of Shin Bet emphasized, the Palestinian side—also bears equal responsibility, at the least, for this tragic state of affairs. However, *The Gatekeepers* enables us, as Israelis, to gaze directly at ourselves and to see with devastating clarity where we've been, where we are now, and where we continue going with our eyes wide shut.

In March 2013, after President Barack Obama's stirring speech to young Israelis in Jerusalem, Ami Ayalon phoned me and asked me what I thought about Obama's call for young people to bypass their leaders and stand up for peace. Ayalon reminded me that he had made the exact same invocation during his interview for *The Gatekeepers.*

I'll quote here the relevant portion of Obama's wonderful speech:

> "Four years ago, I stood in Cairo in front of an audience of young people. Politically, religiously, they must seem a world away. But the things they want, they're not so different from what the young people here want. They want the ability to make their own decisions and to get an education, get a good job; to worship God in their own way; to get married; to raise a family. The same is true of those young Palestinians that I met in Ramallah this morning. The same is true for young Palestinians who yearn for a better life in Gaza.
>
> "That's where peace begins—not just in the plans of leaders, but in the hearts of people. Not just in some carefully designed process, but in the daily connections—that sense of empathy that takes place among those who live together in this land, and in this sacred city of Jerusalem. And let me say this as a politician—I can promise you this: *political leaders will never take risks if the people do not push them to take some risks. You must create the change that you want to see.* [My emphasis.]
>
> "I know this is possible."

Obama's words imbued momentary hope in many people here in Israel, but then quickly sank in the swamp of reality.

In the interview Ayalon told me:

> "When I meet young people, and I do it a lot, I tell them the following—when I was born in Jordan Valley, I had a wonderful childhood, and I knew that in Jerusalem there was a house and on the second floor there's a long corridor and at the end of the corridor there's a door and behind the door there's a wise man who decides, who makes decisions. He's a thinker. My parents called him 'the Old Man.' And years later,

> after the Yom Kippur War, I came to Jerusalem, and I went to that building, and I was on the second floor, and I saw that at the end of the corridor, there was no door. And behind the no-door there's no one who thinks for me.
>
> "Now the question is, what do we do with that. I have to admit that for me, something happened that in retrospect I see as very positive. I suddenly understood that if there was no one there, the responsibility placed on me is multiplied numerous times. I know the weakness of the leadership and also, to a great extent, the impotence limiting the ability to lead in taking action even when you already know it's necessary. And we have a role, we have to get up every morning, and realize we have the capacity for change, we have the tools for change, and in moments of crisis we have the duty of initiating change.
>
> "This is an understanding that began with the Yom Kippur War for me, but that's something personal. It's possible that for my children it began, I don't know, maybe for one of them after Rabin's assassination, and for the third one in the Second Lebanon War. Every one has a moment in which they understand that they bear extra responsibility."

This chronic feeling of hopelessness is all too familiar to me. During the course of the very long work on *The Gatekeepers*, I was filled with a growing sense of despair that we would ever be able to live a sane, normal life here in Israel. I watched more than a thousand hours of archival materials documenting the Israeli-Palestinian conflict over the years. The years flew by, as the film images went from black and white to color, but the images remained remarkably the same as one generation after the next of young Israeli soldiers continued to patrol the casbahs of the West Bank and to stand guard at the checkpoints. The grandchildren of yesterday's IDF soldiers continue the grim work of occupation.

The great majority of the Israeli public likes to believe that something different is still possible—but they do their wishful thinking mostly in their TV armchairs and in living-room conversations with friends. That's what we did when hundreds of hard-liners confronted Yitzhak and Leah Rabin every Friday as they returned to their home, shouting for them to be hung in the town square as traitors. And that's what we have done every day since then. We prefer to live in a bubble, ignoring what's taking place just outside our door.

Or, in the words of Avraham Shalom: "For the first time, I see the question of the State of Israel's existence as an issue. Up till now, it wasn't an issue. Citizens see it, too. They just aren't willing to admit it. Most of the citizens hide behind the morning yogurt and the lunch-time steak."

But something broke in me as I spoke on the phone with Ami Ayalon, following President Obama's Jerusalem speech. Ayalon's words made it clear to me once again that resignation and despair are not an option. That every one of us has the duty to act, each according to his or her own way.

For me, the *Gatekeepers* project, of which this book is perhaps the fullest and most complex version, constitutes one step in fulfilling that duty. Here, then, are Israel's watchmen, in their own words. We fail to heed their words, or learn from their bitter experience, at our own peril.

Avraham Shalom

Avraham Shalom (1980–86)

It all happened in one day. I think it was March 13, 1938. I was almost nine and a half. The walls of my room were entirely covered in maps. Maps of trains, maps of roads, maps of mountains and hills—that was always my hobby. When the Germans came in, I looked every time to see where they were coming from, why they were coming, what they were planning. And then the German army arrived. First the air force planes in the sky, and then the army in the streets. I was all excited, like a kid.

On the night when the Germans entered Vienna, our live-in maid didn't come home. In the morning she arrived and told us, "I got married." Mother asked to whom, and she answered, "A German pilot." To intimidate the Viennese, the Germans arrived in many dozens of planes, and then went wild in the bars, and one of them took a liking to our maid. So he took her along and came to us, the Jews, to ask permission to marry her. We said, please, take her. She thanked us wholeheartedly and the next day left with him for Germany. She didn't ask her parents. She asked us. It's strange, but that's what the relationship between us was like.

We lived in the center of Vienna. My father was a partner in textile factories in Germany. My parents didn't have a grasp of religion or politics. They weren't interested in those topics. I didn't even know that Hebrew was written from right to left. I wasn't familiar with the sound of the language. I hadn't always been aware of the fact that I was Jewish. When the priest came to our first-grade class to teach the first religion lesson, he chose me to read the verses, and complimented me after the reading was over. When I came home, and bragged to Mother, she didn't say a word, but went to my homeroom teacher, and told him I wasn't a part of this business. He immediately took me out of religion lessons, but didn't transfer me to the Jewish class. In that class were ten Jews who were registered with the community. We weren't registered with the community—to this day I don't understand why. Along with me, two Protestants remained outside, a pair of twins—a boy and a girl. Since we had no religion lessons, every time this lesson took place, we played ball in the yard. All the kids envied us.

And then, when the Germans entered Austria, I went to my friends, who were sitting on the balcony across from the hotel in which Hitler was giving a speech. I watched it. As a kid, it doesn't leave the same historic impression on you. He congratulated them for the unification of Germany and Austria. He wasn't much of a genius, but he was insane enough to drive the whole world crazy. You're sitting down there, he's up there on the balcony, and down there the masses are screaming with flags and saluting with raised arms. When I came home, my mother said, "What, you saw Hitler, you weren't scared? Why were you sitting on the balcony?" But the Germans didn't do anything against Jews on the first day. The Austrians did. All of a sudden, they got the courage.

The day after *Kristallnacht*, Mother sent me to school. It was a day in which all the Jewish kids knew they shouldn't go to school, but Mother said to me, "No, you have to go to school, what are you talking about?" I don't know if my parents were worried before the German invasion. If they were, they didn't reveal it to me. My relationship with my parents was a German sort of relationship, not the "Yiddishe Mama" kind. Whatever I didn't need to know, they didn't tell me; they had a formal, "square" way of thinking. That was also the reason Mother sent me to school on that day.

I was the only Jew in class, because all the other Jewish students didn't come. They had brains. I was harassed in various ways, and getting pummeled quite a bit, until the teacher came to separate me from the other students. I was laid up at home for about two weeks. They dropped me on the central heating radiator, and I was seriously banged up. One of them had a father who was a policeman, so he led the group. After the war, I looked him up in the Vienna phone book. His name was Hubert Leitner.

Why did you remember his name?

Avraham Shalom: Because he was the rottenest. A bad pupil, a stupid father. A cop. The police weren't real geniuses in Austria, either. He yelled the most. He didn't hit me himself because he was scared, but he led others.

After those two weeks in which I was bedridden at home, I didn't go to school anymore. Mother was afraid to send me.

We had one relative who had just graduated high school. He was ten years older than me. One day he disappeared. His mother called my mother, and my mother said, "Don't worry." Six weeks later he returned, completely wrecked. He stuttered, talked nonsense, his face was battered, the bones broken and the skin hanging off. He didn't look like a human being. His eyes kept leaking blood, something awful. He couldn't talk and he didn't want to talk, of course, about what he'd gone through in Buchenwald. At that time they were sending young Jews to concentration camps, but not killing them. Instead they returned them to scare the others, because the Germans wanted the Jews to leave. And the Jews weren't leaving.

At the time, my father was in Germany. Then he escaped from there and called home. I remember that Mother told him, "Don't come. It's no good here." And he started making inquiries where he could move us. One morning, out of the blue, the police came and said that within two weeks, we had to vacate the apartment. We had nowhere to go. After we were kicked out of the apartment, we stayed in a pension that was open only to Jews. I started going to Jewish school. Actually, it was the Nazis who revealed to me that I was Jewish.

The most humiliating thing isn't being beaten up, it's the contempt. The contempt was overwhelming. Even the butcher and the doctor—everyone was contemptuous of you. If you stood in line, you always had to be last. People who came after you went in before you. All kinds of little things like that. You'd see Jews in front of their store, washing the sidewalk or the road. JUDEN was written on the shop window. Or a sign in a coffee shop: NO ENTRY TO JEWS AND DOGS. Those were the humiliating things. You're constantly viewed as sub-human. And that reminds me of the situation here [in Israel].

It's not similar, but it is similar. The Arabs are treated like second-class citizens. And I'm talking about Israeli Arabs. To be an Arab here is like being Catholic in England; they're also a minority. If I had to pick whether to be a Jew or an Arab here, I wouldn't want to be an Arab. Or a Jew in Austria on the eve of the war. It's very hard to make a comparison, but it's reminiscent. And I left Austria before the really big trouble started.

We left Austria for Italy in March 1939. Meanwhile, my father arrived in Tel Aviv, and, through a friend, obtained money for a Certificate, the British visa. In August, the long-awaited Certificate arrived, and my father came to Italy and took us. We arrived in Haifa on the day World War II broke out. September 1, 1939.

Father rented us a room on Ben Yehuda Street in Tel Aviv. This city was like a foreign country to me. I didn't understand a word. My parents said, "Language or no language—first of all, start school." They enrolled me in Shalva School in north Tel Aviv. They told my parents that all the Germans go there. And I did find some students who spoke to me in German mixed with Hebrew, but I didn't connect with them. I learned Hebrew every evening with a private tutor, and it took me a year to open my mouth. Here, when you make a mistake, they attack you immediately—so I didn't talk. On the other hand, I was good at English, while they didn't know anything, and geography and math, too. Anywhere where I didn't have to know Hebrew, I was okay there. In the last week of fifth grade, I opened my mouth because I felt that I could participate in the dodgeball game. Since then I've talked with no issues.

Very quickly I grew acclimated to my surroundings. At the end of World War II, my parents wanted to go back to Austria, and I didn't. I'd already put down roots. I told them, "If you want to go back, go back. I'm not going." My mother said, "If he's not going back, I'm not going back, either." So my father didn't return, either. It was only because of me that he didn't go back to Austria. My father, till the day he died, didn't know Hebrew. He couldn't write, read—nothing. Being a refugee doesn't enhance your life. He couldn't manage here. All the guys he talked to spoke German to him, and when he needed to make deals with Israelis, they cheated him, and he didn't catch on. My father died of sorrow when he was sixty-four. He had five heart attacks in one week and died.

I joined the Palmach* in '46 when I was 17. Before that I was in the [youth battalions of the] Hagana,** and then we joined the Palmach, a whole group of us. I felt that I was an Israeli in every way. If in Vienna I had maps on my walls, I had them here, too. In high school I'd go on lots of hikes. Once I walked from Yagur to Beit Ha'arava. And I grew to know the country. I really loved walking from village to village. There wasn't a village I didn't know, Jewish or Arab.

The War of Independence caught us during the settlement training period in the Palmach. Our platoon commander was "Gandhi," Rehavam Ze'evi.*** We fought in every front. We started in Mishmar Ha'emek, then in Galilee, then in the Lod-Ramla area, all over what is Road 6 today, and then in the Negev Desert. Even in the War of Independence, I couldn't watch Arabs being killed for no good reason, but I didn't do anything, because I was a kid. Gandhi never called the Arabs "Arabs." He called them "Ishmaelites." It was out of contempt, not an historical or biblical point of view. But I didn't understand that at the time. I thought it was formal Hebrew.

On November 29, I sat by the radio in Kibbutz Maoz, and I heard the results of the vote on the proposal to divide the country and establish the State of Israel. But nothing was going through my mind. We were so tired from the activity and the patrols that it didn't affect us. What's more, the state hadn't been declared yet. This was only the UN vote.

The declaration of the State of Israel on May 14, 1948, found us in the north, in Malkia. The whole Lebanese army swarmed our hill, and for me, that was the most horrible day in the war. I thought I wouldn't get out of there. Three thousand Lebanese soldiers attacked us in armored vehicles. We, on the other hand, had nothing. I had a tiny two-inch mortar, and I shot it like a pistol. They attacked us and conquered meter after meter after meter. Most of the guys from

---

* The Palmach, an acronym meaning "strike forces," were the elite battle units of the Hagana, the Zionist Jewish underground in British Mandate–era Palestine.

** The Hagana (meaning "defense") was the Zionist Jewish underground during the British Mandate in Palestine before the establishment of the State of Israel.

*** Following his military career, Ze'evi became a right-wing politician and founder of the nationalist Moledet party. He was assassinated by the Popular Front for the Liberation of Palestine in 2001.

our platoon, which was also my settlement training group, died in Malkia. They conquered it from us, and we ran. I remember I ran with the mortar on my back after I couldn't see anyone alive next to me, just dead people, and I ran into the valley below. When I got to the bottom, I fainted.

Two weeks later, we had to conquer it back. After that defeat, considering the differences in force, when they send you to conquer it again, you're a little apprehensive. Not really scared. We had no fear, because we were young. But this time we advanced, and after two shots, all the Arabs ran away. We stormed uphill, and discovered that their coffee was still hot. The escapees left documents behind, and we found out that it wasn't the Lebanese army. During those two weeks, the Lebanese army had left, and was replaced by an army of Palestinian gangs.

The chief of command was Yigal Alon,* and the battalion commander was Dan Laner. They came to marvel at the great victory, and by chance I was around, so they said, "Come on, Avrum, tell us what it was like." So I said, "Last time, it was the Lebanese army. This time it was Palestinians without much training. The minute we started shooting at them, they ran off. Here are their documents." Then Yigal Alon grew very angry and said, "What are you talking about, this is the Lebanese army, these aren't Palestinian gangs!" Apparently, being a commander who wins a battle against "gurnischts" [good-for-nothings] doesn't come with a whole lot of glory.

I was a reconnaissance squad commander. We conquered village after village without meeting a lot of resistance. We didn't ask them to stay, to phrase it delicately. I remember someone conquered Lod and Ramla. We were at the periphery of it; we saw caravans of Arabs walking on foot to Ramallah. So I don't know if we displaced them or if they left by themselves, but there's no doubt the Arabs made a strategic mistake by conveying to their friends, "Never mind, let the Jews advance. We'll come back along with Egypt, Sudan, all the Arab armies, and conquer it all back." I don't remember receiving

---

* Yigal Alon was an Israeli military leader and politician. He was the architect of the Alon Plan, a proposal to end the Israeli occupation of the West Bank by dividing its territory between Israel and the Palestinians.

an instruction to displace the Arabs. They didn't let the Palmach do that. Things like that were done, but I know that only from hearing about it.

After the War of Independence ended, I looked for work. For two months, I was at Kibbutz Revivim. I realized that it wasn't for me, went back to Tel Aviv, worked on a tractor in olive orchards for a month or two, then I drove a pickup for some farmer growing oranges, and then I met Rafi Eitan.* He asked me what I was doing. I told him, "Nothing." So he said, "Why don't you work for the Security Service?" I asked what that was. He told me, "They catch spies, all kinds of people, it's a blast. Counter-espionage."

I didn't understand what that was at all, but I liked the word. I told him, "Okay." They gave me a form to fill out, and nothing happened. After three months, I asked him, "So, what's happening with that?" So he went and looked into it, and the next day someone came with a form and said, "Sign here, you start work tomorrow morning." I asked why it had taken so long. They said I came from Kibbutz Revivim, which was "a kibbutz affiliated with Ahdut Ha'avoda" [a left-leaning political party], so I wasn't trustworthy. I didn't understand that, but eventually I got in, and they gave me work I didn't like.

I left and got my matriculation certificate, because I didn't do my senior year in high school due to joining the Palmach at the end of my junior year. Then I went back to the Service, and they gave me operational work around Arabe, in Galilee. I didn't like that, either. I screwed around there. Information-gathering tasks about uninteresting objects. So I joined the army's officer course, and then came back, and that time they let me be an operational commander in Jerusalem. I carried out operations on this side of the border and on the other side.

We had an operation across the border in Jerusalem in the fifties. At that time it was Jordan. We had to pick up written material, photograph it, and return it. You had to cross the border and stay there, hiding in a car and all kinds of tricks like that. If you got caught, they'd kill you or return you through the Mandelbaum Gate [the border checkpoint between Jordan and Israel] with half

---

* A prominent figure in the Shin Bet and the Mossad.

an ear. I was responsible for operations in Jerusalem, and I chose the people who participated in the operation. I chose someone who was an expert on locks, because some locks needed to be picked, I chose someone whom I trusted to help me if I was in trouble—that was Rafi Eitan—and someone who stood by the border fence with a car in case of trouble, so we could run to him, get into the car, and get out of there. And we did it. It was the first intelligence operation across the border.

A month later, we did it again, and then Isser Harel, the head of the Mossad, who was also in charge of the Service, called me and wanted me to tell him what it had been like, because it was my plan. He said, "If you can do something like that across the border, do it in Europe." And so I established the Mossad's operations unit.

Isser told me, "Go to Europe and suggest to me what can be done operationally against the Arab countries." He gave me about half a year to get to know the territory. I had a ball. I traveled from country to country, looking for surveillance objects. I speak three languages, but understand and get along in five or six. So I didn't have to ask where this was and what that was. After six months, I came back to Israel and made a plan, which I brought to Isser for confirmation. I was told, "Okay, a group of people need to be recruited." That's how we began the Mossad's operational work in Europe.

The Capture of Eichmann

> *Prime Minister Ben Gurion's announcement yesterday from the Knesset podium, regarding the capture of the Nazi mass-murderer Adolf Eichmann and his impending trial in Israel, came as a complete surprise. The deep silence which spread in the Knesset testified like a hundred witnesses to the immense impression which the announcement, both laconic and dramatic, created among the people's elected representatives.*
>
> (S. Svislotski, *Yediot Ahronot*, May 24, 1960)*

---

* The Mossad, meaning "The Institution," is Israel's national security agency, responsible for covert operations, gathering intelligence, counter-terrorism, and protecting Jewish communities abroad.

Avraham Shalom: When I came back from one of my trips abroad, Isser called me and more or less took me off the plane straight to the Mossad. "How would you feel in a Spanish-speaking country?" he asked. I told him I didn't know anything. He said, "So go to Argentina. We might have a chance to catch Eichmann* there." I knew they'd been looking for him for a long time with no results, but we had sent a Service man named Zvi Aharoni, who had a really persitent ability to find something he was looking for. Isser showed me a photo and told me, "Let me know if we can conduct an operation. To bring him here, to abduct him. Send me just a word or two—possible, impossible."

So I went.

In the meantime, Rafi Eitan, head of the unit, prepared the people and the equipment here. We had put the crew together previously. We needed multilingual people, people with physical strength. Physical strength wasn't me, but multilingual was.

I had two mishaps on the way. Since I was constantly switching passports, in the end I apparently got a little confused. I had to fly from Paris to Buenos Aires through Lisbon. In Lisbon they took us off the plane, told us we had to wait in transit, and took our passports. The Portuguese soldier who collected the passports went to the connecting flight and started calling out to people: "You, come here, what's your name? Give, give me your passport." When he got to me, the alias flew out of my head, and I didn't know what to say. I remembered that I didn't remember. In the end, I remembered that I had a German passport, which was green at the time. I located my passport in the pile he was holding and told him, there's my passport. I opened it and showed him the photo, and he didn't notice anything suspicious. I got on the plane and heaved a sigh of relief.

When I checked into the hotel in Buenos Aires and gave the German passport to the desk clerk, he said, "Oh, you're from Hamburg?" I told him that I was from this-and-that village, going by the cover story. "Yes? I'm from that village, too!" he said. I felt ill. I didn't know anything about his village, I barely knew that it

---

* A top administrator of the Holocaust, who fled Germany after the war, ending up in Argentina in 1950.

existed, and here I am meeting someone from that same village. . . . I told him, "Listen, I'm in a hurry," and he said, "Don't worry, you just sign, I'll fill out the questionnaire." He gave me the questionnaire, but I'd forgotten the name again, and he had the passport. I didn't know which name to sign. So he asked, "What's the problem?" and I said, "Listen, I forgot my money inside the passport." So he said, "Really?" He opened the passport, and there was no money there. I said, "Oh, no, that's scary, show me for a minute!" and I took the passport. I looked at the name, and since then I remember it to this day. Waltznofer.

It has no meaning in German. Nothing. That's why I didn't remember it.

Then I met Zvi Aharoni and Ya'akov Gat. We drove to the area, I saw a man in the dark walking with a flashlight, and even from a distance I could see that it was the man in the photo. I said, "There he is!" And Zvi Aharoni hit the brakes. I told him, "Don't brake, because he might get agitated and run away." We dropped Ya'akov Gat off, and told him, "Follow him." He followed him for about 200 meters (650 feet), till the man arrived at the same house where Zvi had covertly photographed him earlier. That was a sign that this was indeed the man in the photo. I looked around; it was pitch black, no street lights, no houses, nothing. A swampy area. I decided it wasn't going to get any better than that. That same night, I telegraphed Isser the code word through a contact person to the Mossad in Tel Aviv: "Possible."

After a week, they arrived, Isser and Rafi and all those guys. And we got settled. Until they arrived, we stood, Ya'akov Gat and me, every evening by the handrails of some train to see if Eichmann would arrive at the same hour. Eighteen days we conducted surveillance on him, to see if he didn't change his habits. He didn't. He always walked with a flashlight with white light on the front and red light on the back, like a car. And he walked against traffic because it was safer. That man didn't fit into the Argentinian scene, definitely not the lower-class one. It turned out he had switched apartments three or four times in Buenos Aires, and each time he moved to a worse apartment. That's how he planned to disappear.

We rehearsed the operation itself three hundred times on a sand table in some yard. We worked on it and did abduction exercises in all kinds of safe houses. I think it took two or three weeks. Rafi practiced with the team, and I practiced with Rafi, and in the end we put together two teams. One team which actually picked up Eichmann and another team driving behind them in case the car breaks down and diverting suspicion to themselves in case we ran into one of the many police blockades.

Every night he'd arrive on the same bus, but on the night of the operation he didn't come. We waited for the next bus, and then he did arrive. Two people jumped him, pulled him into the ditch, and got him in the car. They took off, with me following them. His first sentence was in the car I wasn't in. He told them, "I'm already resigned to my fate." He understood these were Israelis or Jews. The next sentence he said to us was, "*Bereshit bara Elohim et hashamaim ve'et ha'aretz.*" [Hebrew for "In the beginning, God created the heavens and the earth."] We were frightened. We thought he spoke Hebrew. But he only knew one sentence, taught to him by the chief rabbi of Budapest. From then on, they barely spoke to him.

We drove in a car with fake diplomatic plates and got to a safe house, and there the interrogation began. Only Zvi and I spoke German. Zvi interrogated him and interrogated him, and in the end he admitted to his name. He gave three other names first, and in the end he said his name was Adolf Eichmann. Now we needed to get him out of there.

In that same period, a big delegation came on an El Al plane for the 150-year anniversary of the Argentinian Republic. Abba Eban [an Israeli politician and diplomat] was on that plane, without knowing why. El Al still wasn't running flights to Argentina, and just for the delegation, they brought a plane with the company's senior pilot. We parked the plane in the technical repairs hangar, and wanted to load Eichmann on it. I practiced walking back through the turnstile, where a soldier was standing, checking papers. I wanted him to get to know me and let me walk through without papers. So I practiced this exercise about ten times, until he really knew me. And then I told him, "I'm coming with my friends." And I did that a few times, too. In the end, on the critical evening, I came with Eichmann, in an El Al uniform, and another three or four people, and he already let us in that way. We had a doctor who injected him with a sedative in advance. We laid him down and said it was an El Al pilot who was sick. No one asked us anything. It went smoothly. They saw me and let us pass. We got him on the plane half woozy.

Did you feel that you were on an historic operation that would become a milestone?

The motion of history's wings? That's not my nature. My nature is to make sure the operation ticks along smoothly, and that he goes and arrives in court. That's my nature. I didn't see history kissing my back the whole time. I have to admit, though, when he finally said, "My name is Adolf Eichmann"—I felt relief. I shook Zvi's hand, and we drove off immediately to tell Isser. Isser was happy, but he didn't say anything. He was already preoccupied with something else. He already wanted to catch Mengele.

1967—The Palestinian State Was Our Idea

"Latrun and Jenin have been conquered. Tonight the IDF completed the capture of North Sinai."

Rafah, Arish, Khan Yunis, Deir al-Balah, and al-Auja have been conquered. Many enemy losses. The IDF has captured a multitude of loot. Our losses are relatively light.

(*Yediot Ahronot*, June 6, 1967)

"What will you give the Arabs and what will you take from them?" the minister of defense, Lieutenant General Moshe Dayan, was asked yesterday, and replied:

"We will give peace, and we will take peace."

(Yohanan Lahav, *Yediot Ahronot*, June 8, 1967)

Avraham Shalom: Until 1967, our problem wasn't the Arabs of Gaza and the West Bank of Transjordan. IDF, not us, was the one handling those targets. In the Service we acted mainly against espionage attempts from the East Bloc countries. We had some very nice success stories, like Prof. Kurt Sitte, Aharon Cohen, Israel Bar, and Marcus Klingberg, who was only caught in the eighties, but we knew of him before then as well. Suddenly, in '67, all these targets disappeared, because they were operated by the personnel of the communist bloc countries' consulates and embassies, and they all left Israel following the war.

It's an amazing thing. I was in the Service for seventeen years, and I worked the whole time against Russians, against Arab intelligence, against non-Arab intelligence, and suddenly you're left without an enemy. The Arabs surrendered, and you're left like the dog in the dog race looking for the rabbit. The rabbit burrows in the ground, and the dogs look for him and can't find him. So we were like that, too.

After '67, I started going into Arab territory a little more, to see where I could help with my unit. I was head of the Operations Division then, and the Arabs weren't such a hot topic for us. When I started to poke around, I saw things I didn't like. But I didn't make a fuss because I thought that apparently that was the way you had to work opposite Arabs. I didn't speak Arabic, and I fed off the explanations which the managers under me provided me. The Service managers themselves had learned for forty to fifty years how to talk to Arabs in Arabic. They do know Arabic, but they don't know how to talk to people as equals.

We started working in the Gaza Strip and in the West Bank, in the anti-terror field, without knowing exactly what it was because terrorism still wasn't an issue. The population wasn't hostile. In the Bank we had replaced the Jordanian conqueror, who was more brutal than us. I remember after the Six Day War, the first thing Anwar Nuseibeh [a Jerusalem-born Jordanian politician and diplomat] told me was, "Listen, you have wonderful soldiers. They're not like the Jordanian soldiers who go to the grocery store and take ten crates of Coca Cola without paying. You do pay. You don't rape women or anything."

Meanwhile, in the Service, we had a group of people who went from Arab to Arab in the West Bank and talked to them. The goal was to understand what motivates this business, the Palestinians. Originally we wanted to make peace with Jordan, not with the Palestinians, because who thought the Jordanians weren't coming back? Noel Khatib was the West Bank governor on behalf of Jordan. You came to his house, and he'd host you like he was the king of England. He sat on this armchair, he was fatter than me, and he talked like he was the ruler on behalf of the king, and I'd sit opposite him like a clerk.

And then the idea of a Palestinian state popped up. The Arabs didn't come up with the idea. It was us. Like we invented Hamas and Hezbollah. We didn't actually invent them. We contributed to it happening, thanks to all kinds of "Arab experts." There's actually no such thing as an expert on Arabs, just like there are no experts on Jews. Maybe the Arabs are experts on Arabs; the Jews aren't.

I got enthusiastic about it, even though it wasn't in my occupational turf as head of the Operations Department. I gradually caught the Palestinian State bug, without being aware of it. I was convinced it was a part of the solution we could live with. Why did the idea of a Palestinian state grab me? I don't know, but I thought it was more logical than conquering them. What did we want to achieve? We didn't know ourselves, because we didn't get any guidance from upstairs. When you're not getting guidance from the political echelon, you're also—just like with the rabbit—you're looking.

But, like the cynics say, "lucky for us," terrorism gradually increased. Until '72, there was terrorist activity here and there, but in '72, it started getting serious. Both in Gaza and in the West Bank. Suddenly we had work. The minute you're dealing with specific things, you forget about strategy. So we stopped messing around with the Palestinian state. The minute we stopped messing around with the Palestinian state and started dealing with terrorism, terrorism got more sophisticated, and we got more sophisticated, and suddenly there was lots of work. In Gaza, in the West Bank, and abroad. And we forgot about the Palestinian subject. In the seventies there was terrorist activity on a scale that required all our energy, and we said, "There's no one to talk to on our side, anyway, so let's leave it alone."

In those years we had to catch dozens of terrorist squads. We had to provide the intelligence, because without that you can't do anything. And I think the Service was successful at it, because it worked with kid gloves and relatively gently. The army had operatives, and we had operatives. And the operatives liked to work with us, because the army was rigid and we talked to them in their own language. And so we had lots of operatives and lots of success and, generally, we controlled the war on terror. We could contain the flame at such a level that the country could do whatever it wanted to, which is important. But it didn't solve the problem of the occupation. It only made it so that instead of twenty terror incidents a week, there'd be twenty incidents a year. And that's a big difference.

Israeli politicians were thinking in terms of a strong nation, which would not let the Arabs have a foothold in areas that might harm the security of the individual Israeli, and it's true to this day. Once, in '74, I was at some meeting at the Ministry of Defense, and they were talking about Hebron. A day earlier, they had declared it "the City of Our Forefathers." So, I said, "Guys, how can it be 'the City of Our Forefathers' when there are a hundred thousand Arabs there and not one Jew?" Rabbi Moshe Levinger [a leader of Gush Emunim, the settler movement] was already in the city of Hebron, and I thought letting him in there was a mistake, but after they'd made that mistake, we had to get out of it somehow. I also said it was impossible for one people to control another people in the long term; it's a waste of effort. They looked at me like I was crazy, like I was betraying the Jewish legacy, and since then, I've learned my lesson.

And you didn't say it to the political echelon anymore?

I said it all the time, to anyone who wanted to listen. [Yitzhak] Shamir [right-wing politician and Israeli prime minister, 1983–84 and 1986–92] wanted to listen, but not so he could do what I say, but to let me let off steam. [Menachem] Begin [founder of the right-wing Likud party and prime minister between 1977 and 1983, when he signed Israel's peace treaty with Egypt]—the Arabs didn't interest him. The Christians in Lebanon interested him. [Egyptian leader Anwar] Sadat interested him. But did the Arabs in Nablus interest him? Did he know where Nablus was? . . . On the map. Maybe. He'd never been to an Arab village, not even in Israel.

Shimon Peres [longtime Labor Party leader, prime minister and co-winner of the 2007 Nobel Peace Prize for his role in the Oslo Accords]—I told him many times, but he supposedly shared my opinion. Supposedly. You can't share my opinion and allow Levinger to settle in Hebron. You can't think that one people can't control another, and on the other hand, you go and build settlements.

I realized that there was no one to talk to. During Peres's time, the atmosphere changed—he wasn't vulgar in his references to Arabs—but he did the same thing his predecessors had done. For Shimon Peres, it was important that things be heard and seen, but not done.

But it started even before them. Golda [Meir, prime minister between 1969 and 1974, including during the Yom Kippur War] was a Jew from Russia, from America. Arabs didn't interest her as residents of Palestine. She was interested in a Jew who did or didn't immigrate to Israel, and how much money he was bringing with him. The same for [Levi] Eshkol [prime minister from 1963 until his death in 1969]. Eshkol didn't really see the Arabs, but at least he spoke to them politely. Of the prime ministers, [David] Ben Gurion [the legendary Zionist leader and Israel's first prime minister] was the only one who impressed me as at least respecting the Arabs, because he also had Arab friends, but he wasn't around long enough.

All in all, the prime ministers of Israel over the years, regardless of their party affiliation, didn't pay attention to the Palestinian people. Not within the borders of '67 and not outside the borders of '67. They saw that we were overcoming terrorism on a short-term basis, and that was enough for them.

From the field, I'm getting specific impressions that told me the Arabs didn't like the occupation, but were putting up with it and were living with it, and that, during my term, at least, there was no risk of general uprising. We maintained the situation so that the government didn't have any immediate concerns. There was no reason to rush and pull out of the Territories because of this.

That's what politicians always want, in England, in Norway, and in Israel. To be left alone. So that they can conduct their internal affairs, without dealing with all the complaints and comments of all kinds of minorities. If you can solve it your own way, go ahead and solve it, and good for you.

Every time, [Ya'akov] Peri [Shin Bet director from 1988 to 1995] would show us this chart as head of district—how many people were caught, how many operatives we have, how many attacks we prevented, how many attacks we didn't prevent—and every time, it was a pretty optimistic portrait. But it was short-term. There was no strategy there. Only tactics.

The Head-Chopper from the Security Division

"The Israeli delegation leaves Munich; A manhunt in Germany after the 15 terrorists."

"When the shooting commenced, the Israelis trapped in the helicopters made a desperate attempt to break free of their constraints."

Depressed and solemn, 17 members of the Israeli Olympic Delegation are taking off from Munich this morning in a special El Al plane which arrived from Israel yesterday. At 8 a.m. Israel time, the coffins of the 11 murder victims were brought on the plane. . . . The information I've gathered in the last 24 hours indicates almost without a shadow of a doubt that the nine hostages were killed by three of the five terrorists who were on the airstrip. They debarked, as reported, from three helicopters to examine the Boeing plane placed at their disposal to fly to an Arab country, along with the hostages. The snipers and the German police force opened fire at the five, but only managed to hit two of them.

(Dov Atzmon, *Yediot Ahronot*, September 7, 1972)

Avraham Shalom: In '72, after the massacre at the Munich Olympics, they fired the previous head of the Security Division, and appointed me. When they gave me the division, I'm ashamed to say this, but I didn't leave a lot of people there. I asked the head of the Service to remove most of them. Before that, there were people there who didn't know what "security" means. From the Service director on down. Yosef Harmelin, head of the Service, couldn't tell left from right when it came to security. At every stage, at every rank of command and management, were people who don't understand security. It was definitely because of them that what happened in Munich happened. Today the head of the Service would certainly go down for that. It's like the prime minister being murdered. Same thing.

When I started the job, I chose thirty to forty people I knew within the Service whom I thought were the right people, and we started doing staff work. Building security. The classic operational rationale of waging war is actually also good for security. We built a whole staff apparatus in Israel, a separate staff for El Al, a separate staff for naval activity, a separate staff for the Ministry of Foreign Affairs, and all within the Service. We placed combat soldiers in all those positions, and also supervisors who were ex-combat soldiers. Not sixty-year-old old guys but thirty-year-old old guys. That's how it started working. There were about ten incidents in the two and a half years since I got the job when they tried to target us, and we won all of them. Today half the world follows our methods.

What are our methods? First of all, you choose good people, with brains, disciplined. When you tell them to do something, they do it—and don't just stand there on the sidelines when someone shoots Rabin. Actually, you take and build the whole theory of security operation abroad and in Israel—VIP security, delegation security. You're constantly under total stress. If you fall asleep for a minute—that's the minute when it happens. That's why you conduct drills, you talk to people, and if one of them screws up, you tell him, "Go home." No games. During that period, I threw out dozens. I established discipline. They all hated me. They'd say that every time I go abroad, I come back with some security guy's head under my armpit. . . . It was a joke, but it was also half true. The truth is, I personally didn't come back with any security guys' heads under my armpit. When I came, they'd be good. I had to send other inspectors, and they'd be the ones who returned with the head. . . .

Security is based first of all on discipline and on common sense. You don't need to study medicine to work in security, but you do have to carry out 100 percent of your responsibilities. Not ninety-nine.

A security officer has to be extraordinarily alert. It's very hard to be alert one hour, two, three. You have to relieve them. The whole secret is not to demand something that's beyond human capacity from them. You have to be so alert that you can fire the second shot. Only rarely do you get to fire the first one—when the other guy makes a mistake, takes out his gun and doesn't shoot. But you have to have extraordinary, brutal discipline.

We had a lot of incidents in Munich and Vienna and Brussels where we were the second shooter. I remember that in Brussels there was an attack at the airport, and the security officer there took care of the incident. Or Leila Khaled in the plane,* which was a very difficult event. She or her boyfriend was already holding a hand grenade. Think for a minute of a hand grenade exploding in a plane in midflight. So we invented methods that let you toss a hand grenade into a reinforced box in the plane, and when it exploded, nothing would happen.

To maintain alertness and discipline, you conduct drills all the time. That's basic stuff. How can you maintain the tension within such a complex system, involving thousands of people, when you're

* Khaled and her accomplice, members of the Popular Front for the Liberation of Palestine, hijacked a TWA flight from Rome to Tel Aviv in August 1969, forcing the plane to land in Damascus. The following year, Israeli sky marshals captured her in the middle of another hijacking attempt and handed her over to British authorities.

alone, sitting in some chair in Tel Aviv? Only through simulations and drills, and more drills. I fly a lot and I see [the security precautions at Tel Aviv's Ben Gurion International Airport].

In Tel Aviv, it's excessive. Suddenly you suspect someone, and then he's done for, he won't extract himself for an hour. Especially if he's Arab. I don't understand how they take it; I wouldn't get through it. It's humiliating. But what can you do? Once you have to protect a prime minister with twenty to thirty people simultaneously, it's a lost cause.

The Appointment

After three years as head of the Security Division (1972–75), Avraham Shalom was simultaneously appointed as second to Shin Bet Director Yosef Harmelin. Shortly thereafter, Harmelin was replaced by Avraham Ahituv, with whom Shalom had a difficult relationship. Despite this, and despite Shalom's utter lack of experience in the Arab sphere, Ahituv recommended to the prime minister that Shalom replace him once he retires.

Avraham Shalom: When Ahituv was about to retire, Begin asked him for two candidates. He told him, "You, don't tell me who the next head of the Service will be. I want two candidates. I'll choose." So Ahituv game him my name and another name. Begin brought us in for an interview, each of us separately. He was sick, greeted me in pajamas, and really enjoyed the conversation with me, but I think he'd already decided previously. The other candidate, I think, also told him, "Take Avrum." That's what I found out. Anyway, the next day I was told he had picked me.

I'm trying to understand how you were appointed Shin Bet director when you say you had no knowledge on the Arab topic.

I'd only dealt with the Arab sphere through the operational, terrorist perspective, not from an intelligence perspective. Not even indirectly. Ahituv asked me not to touch this subject because he dealt with it. It's true that for two months I was in charge of the Gaza Strip, but that was temporary, because the person in charge was sick. When I was appointed to head of the Service in '80, every day, after working in the office for half the day, I'd go out for a day and a half in the field, and talk to coordinators and investigators and observe the Arabs. It took me three to four months until I understood how things work.

Yuval Diskin: Avrum didn't inspire awe, he inspired fear. Even we were afraid of him. He was a powerful, authoritative man, smart, very sharp. Really stubborn, uncompromising, and really tough on others. When he didn't like something, heads would roll. He would sometimes come to visit the units, and he'd always have questions that you had no chance of answering. For example, he'd sit there and ask how many lecturers there were at An-Najah University in Nablus. How do I know how many lecturers they have? Come on, do I count them every day? And then Yankale [Ya'akov] Peri, who was head of the district then, would kick me, and he said, "Avrum, there are sixty lecturers at the university." So Avrum says to me, "What, you didn't know there were sixty?" I'd say, "No." After the discussion ends, Peri grabs me: "Don't you understand? When Avrum asks, answer! Say something! Otherwise he won't leave us alone here. . . ."

Carmi Gillon: Avrum was head of the Shin Bet at a very difficult period for the State of Israel. He was appointed in '80. A year and a half later, the Peace for Galilee war* broke out. IDF is in Lebanon, occupying areas to the north up to Aley and north of Beirut. The Shin Bet, whose domain was the Territories, was instantly tasked with the entire internal security of our forces in Lebanon, and IDF asked the Shin Bet to start securing the safety of its forces. Within a very short time, the Service, headed by Avrum, established sub-districts throughout Lebanon, in Tyre, in Sidon, in Beirut, in Aley, in Nabatieh, throughout Lebanon, recruits operatives, and in no time, the Shin Bet is controlling Lebanon like it's controlling the West Bank. By the way, the Service also suffered losses [in Lebanon] during this time.

Avraham Shalom: The Service shouldn't even have been in Lebanon. It's just, Begin woke up one morning, I think because of his military secretary, Efraim (Froyke) Poran, saying, "Soldiers are being killed here, bring in the Service to clean things up." Something like that. So Begin called me and said, "Froyke wants you to be there." Something like that.

---

* Operation Peace for Galilee, later referred to as the First Lebanon War, commenced on June 6, 1982, when the Israeli army invaded southern Lebanon, and continued until June 1985.

Meaning it wasn't his idea. So I said, "I can allocate ten people for that, that's nothing." So he said, "Get started, we'll see what happens."

In Lebanon, we encountered a reality that was unfamiliar to us. We thought we were dealing with the Shiites from the south, who wanted to get rid of Fatah and initially greeted us with rice and candy. Terrorism began, and then we had the two disasters in Tyre.* That hit us very hard. We lost twenty good people. The Service couldn't take it.

If there was something that devastated Begin, it was the Lebanon war. He couldn't forgive himself for that, and I don't know if he understood that he was led there, by Ariel Sharon [then minister of defense] and Raful [Rafael Eitan, Israel's chief of staff]. He believed in them, and they saw that he believed in them. So they each took him by the hand and slowly led him until he found himself secured and surrounded on all sides by people who wanted a war, so he wanted a war, too. He didn't understand all this. When Begin understood that he went to war on the basis of bad intelligence, it consumed him. Sharon and Raful misled him. I think he suspected it near the end of his life. Before he retired, we talked about it a little. He said he was sorry. He didn't understand that there would be so many casualties. He didn't realize it. They told him thirty casualties. I told him three hundred. In the end there were six hundred. It consumed him.

You, as head of the Service, didn't have a say regarding the Lebanon War?

No. At that stage we weren't operating in Lebanon. The Mossad was operating in Lebanon, and they believed the Christians. That's a mistake by people who don't understand human nature. The Lebanese Christians are about the last race I'd trust. I was once invited to a dinner by [Phalange party leader] Bachir Gemayel [who was elected president of Lebanon in 1982 and later assassinated], along with his entourage and the Mossad. Begin told me, "I want you to come, too, see these people, even though it's not your business." So I came along. The next day he asked me, "So, what was your impression? Did you see how they eat? Like Europeans." I told him,

---

* In Novermber 1982, the Israeli Military Administration building in Tyre collapsed, killing seventy-six Israelis and twenty-seven Lebanese. In November 1983, sixty Israelis were killed by a terrorist explosion of a car next to the IDF and Border Patrol headquarters in Tyre.

"Right, Europeans. . . . These are gangsters with a French education." He said, "That's no way to talk!" and I told him, "Listen, that's my impression."

I sat down with Bachir Gemayel and he was bragging: "I'm sitting next to the head of the Israeli Security Service, me, Bachir Gemayel. In two weeks I'll be president of Lebanon!" Two weeks later he was already dead. I was asked who I thought would win the war. I said, "The Shiite Arabs, of course." They asked why. "Because they're more determined," I said. "These Christians aren't determined people, they don't like to fight, they won't fight anything."

And how did they not listen to you? I heard that you were one of the most powerful people in government meetings.

That's ridiculous.

I was told that when Avraham Shalom got up to speak at government meetings, the room would go silent.

Because when I talked and someone else would talk, I'd stop talking. I don't think that's true.

The story was that you had immense power, that your opinion prevailed on any security matter you spoke about.

My opinion prevailed because sometimes they agreed with me, sometimes they didn't. I didn't always state my opinion. That's a gross exaggeration.

You didn't have that kind of power?

No. I attended government meetings more than my predecessors. Yosef Harmelin attended government meetings maybe twice a year. I went twice and three times a week. Because of the prime ministers, they summoned me. I never volunteered. They counted on me. I had no political ambitions, I didn't want to be in the Likud [Israel's major center-right party, founded in 1973 by Begin] or in the Ma'arach [Israel's left-leaning Labor Alignment party]. So it's convenient to listen to a person like that, because it doesn't hurt them, doesn't threaten them.

When you come to convey topics that are close to your world, was there an in-depth discussion in the government of these things?

No. Usually I'd agree on it in advance with the prime minister, or sometimes not, and they'd pass it on. I'm trying to recall cases where they didn't accept my opinion. I think one of them was

Demjanjuk.* I was opposed to bringing him here. And who won? The party. They wanted the Likud's Eichmannn.

Carmi Gillon: I think that as a prime minister, Begin, and Shamir after him, considered Avrum to be the most important member of their security entourage. I'd say that during Avrum's year—after years in which the Mossad was the leading intelligence apparatus—the Shin Bet became the leading apparatus. And I think what happened to Avrum was that he felt he could do whatever he wanted. Avrum's career is extraordinarily impressive. In my humble opinion, he amassed personal power which no head of Shin Bet had historically until Yuval Diskin. And this personal power brought about his great slip-up in regard to Bus 300. And that, I think, is what happens to a person who loses his own brakes.

The Bus 300 Affair

"The minister of defense has appointed an investigative committee in the hijacked bus affair."

Minister of Defense Moshe Arens appointed an investigative committee yesterday to look into the circumstances of the death of two terrorists taken off a bus hijacked two weeks ago on its way to Ashkelon. The committee is headed by Major General (Ret.) Meir Zorea, who has until recently served as the Defense Establishment Comptroller. The committee will investigate the events which happened approximately two hours after IDF soldiers gained control of the hijacked bus. As reported earlier, western publications reported, based on the testimony of Israeli journalists who were at the scene, that two of the terrorists appeared to be alive when they were taken off the bus. The speaker for the minister of defense said yesterday that the committee's conclusions would be released after they were presented to the minister of defense.

(*Hadashot*, April 27, 1984)

---

* John (Ivan) Demjanjuk was deported by the United States to Israel in 1986 to stand trial for war crimes, after being identified by eleven Holocaust survivors as "Ivan the Terrible," a notorious guard at the Treblinka death camp. In 1988, he was convicted of crimes against humanity and sentenced to death, but the verdict was overturned by the Israeli Supreme Court in 1993.

Ya'akov Peri: The Bus 300 affair catches me out of the blue one afternoon when I'm going back to my apartment in Jerusalem, and I get a call on the secure line from Chief of Central Command Ory Or, and he tells me a bus was hijacked on its way from Tel Aviv to Ashkelon, roadblocks had been set up, the bus managed to evade the roadblocks, some of those pursuing it shot at it, and the bus was on its way to the Gaza Strip, already being chased, including by helicopters, etc. I hung up the phone. When I hung up the phone, I told myself, why should you go there? There's a district commander, there's a head of Service, there's a chief of Southern Command, this is not in your sector of responsibility, and I didn't go there.

Later, some claimed that that's what earned me the crown of Service director.

Avi Dichter: With Bus 300, the hijacked bus stopped in the Deir al-Balah area, which is under the jurisdiction of my sub-district. That night I was vacationing in Eilat with my family, and they called me near morning, told me about the incident. I got ready to travel from Eilat, and they told me, "No need, your guys, Sayeret Matkal [an elite Israeli Special Forces unit], are just about to break into the bus." Then they told me, "Listen, they broke into the bus, and two terrorists were taken for interrogation." I turn on the news and hear, "All terrorists were killed." I remember telling my wife, "Something smells very bad."

Avraham Shalom: When the bus was hijacked, I was in Haifa. They told me, "Get over here." So I came. When I arrive, I see the bus with four hijackers. They seemed like amateurs to me. One of them was holding some kind of liquid, and he was threatening others with the liquid. You can't tell if the liquid was gasoline or distilled water.

Then the army dealt with it. They killed two, and two apparently emerged unharmed. And they beat the crap out of them. The whole army attacked them. When we got them, they didn't look like in the famous photo anymore. The photo was taken before the beating. I was told that when we got them, they already looked like they were done for. Some people thought they were no longer alive. They broke their bones, I don't know. It was a lynching.

You didn't see them in person, these people?

Shalom: I didn't see them. Later I authorized executing them, after they'd already almost been beaten to death. I had general authorization from Prime Minister Shamir, giving me the authority to decide myself whether to do a thing like that or not. I said to Ehud Yatom, who was then head of the Operations Division, "What condition are they in?" They told me, "They're almost dead," or the soldiers said, "almost dead." I said, "So hit them one more time and that's it." But that's not what he did. He did what he described, which I found out maybe a year later. If I had known what he was going to do, I wouldn't have approved it, but that's wisdom in retrospect.

What did he do?

I don't know. I think he just took a rock and broke their heads open. But they weren't conscious. I don't know what state they were in. If I'd known he was doing it like that, I wouldn't have authorized it. But he was the head of a department. He should have known himself what to do and what not to do. He also could have said no. If he didn't agree. There were a few more heads of departments there, and no one said a word.

To this day, I debate this question with Ehud. I asked him, "Why, Ehud, why, when you saw they were alive, I didn't see them, you saw them, you're a department head, you're not a kid." Apparently Ehud got all fired up and gave an order to himself, because he was riding in the van with them. With Nachman Tal [at the time, head of Shin Bet's Arab affairs division] and another two or three people. Two months later, the Zorea Committee interrogated him, so he described the way he killed them, and I fell out of my seat, because I had no idea that's what he was like. If he saw they were alive, why did you people kill them? "You told me they were dead, so you don't need to kill dead people twice." So he stuck to his version that they were already dead and there was nothing to be done. A year later, he changed his mind. I really didn't like it, because I didn't know how to explain it. To this day, I don't know whether they were dead or not. But when you take an unconscious person, his whole head is blown up, and you hit him again, punch him, that doesn't make him deader.

You gave the command to kill them.

But I gave that after I was told they were already dead.

What's with you, Avrum? That doesn't make sense. You wouldn't give a command to kill them after they were already dead.

No, I'm saying they were already dead using their language, you can't, you can't interrogate them. That's how you should understand it.

You mean, they were already almost done for physically, like that?

Yes. I found out about the fiasco only the next day, when I saw the photos in the paper. And then I said, "How does that happen?" So one of the guys in the photo told me he had said to me in the field that he'd been photographed. But I didn't realize that he'd been photographed with the terrorists. And there's that photo where they're leading one terrorist who's alive.

Why did you instruct that they be killed, anyway?

I didn't want them to get out alive. This was the first terrorism incident within Israel after a long time. Instead of killing all four, the army only killed two. They screwed up. I didn't want more live terrorists in court. It would increase terrorism. There was no longer any terrorism. Almost. Excluding Lebanon, hardly any. There were no intelligence subjects. No one standing trial. Nothing. They were only in jails. But with two people like that, you stir up a trial like that, you get two more heroes. And that stirs up a whole new wave. We didn't want that. I didn't want that. So I thought we should finish the job. And I had no accomplices other than Prime Minister Shamir. The prime minister was a full-fledged accomplice. And him, I was acting according to his orders. He gave me authorization to kill them, a year in advance.

What do you mean? What did the authorization say?

That terrorists, if I saw fit that they should be made to disappear, they disappeared.

The prime minister gave you authorization?

Yes, not for this, generally speaking.

There was a general authorization that any terrorist—if he was caught—could be killed?

No. Not that. If I assessed that it served us well, he could be killed. I reported to Shamir how it happened, so he told me, "Great, it's a good thing you did it. A good Arab is a dead Arab." He had this slogan, "It's a good thing we did it." He conveyed to me that he was very pleased with this outcome, and I forgot about it.

In the beginning, Shamir wasn't too upset by this whole business. He just said, "Damn, you were photographed. We have to get you out of this business." And he worked hard. Him and Peres together. And Rabin. The three of them worked hard so that it wouldn't leak out, but they were unsuccessful. Ultimately, each of them also thought about himself and his party. That's two different parties. Shamir approached Peres and Rabin, who was minister of defense, and said to them, "You've also granted authorizations like that, so if you abandon us, the Likud, we'll drag you down with us." So they proceeded together, and didn't trust the army or the attorney general or anyone else. They kept telling me what to do and how to react. I didn't do anything without coordinating with them. I was sure they'd support me. And they did support me. For a year. And it didn't leak out until the three Shin Bet retirees publicized it by force through the attorney general. Through Dorit Beinisch [Israel's state attorney and later president of the Supreme Court]. I never imagined that after a year of coordination, the politicians would disengage and say, "We didn't know."

Ya'akov Peri: I think for Avrum, the boundaries may have blurred a little, what was under his authority, what he needed to request authorization for. That's the way I can explain it, but that's just my assessment. Avrum never sat down, definitely not with me, and opened his heart and explained exactly what happened. That happens when a Service director achieves a very, very dominant status within the political system. You have to watch out for that, because the lines really can get blurred. There are very clear things in the system of responsibility between the political echelon, between a head of state, and between the head of the Service. And for every action that's not in the routine course of events, in the Service's routine circumstances, you need to receive advance authorization.

Such as taking a life?

Of course. And things much simpler than that.

But according to what Avraham Shalom claims, he had authorization from the prime minister.

No. There's no sweeping authorization. Take for example the subject of targeted preventions. For every targeted prevention, you need authorization from the political echelon. There's no such thing as the administrative echelon taking matters into its own hands. It's also like that on the topic of covert audio surveillance, it's like that on the topic of special operations, and there's no reason why it should have been any different in the case of Bus 300. It may be, sometimes, when you're serving as Service director, you can interpret and predict in advance what the prime minister's or some minister's reply will be, but that doesn't grant you the authority.

Could a situation occur in which, in November, the head of the Service and the prime minister meet and they have a database of names, and then in March, there's no need for renewed authorization?

But you have to give notice when these things happen, because they can occur when there's a different diplomatic background, a different political environment. Maybe when there's the possibility of an operation, it's not politically convenient for the prime minister. You've got to present these things to the prime minister. That's even truer in regard to Bus 300, when it's an ongoing event, where there was time to consult, to ask, to report, to say. Things are completely clear here. There can be no room for error here, certainly not on the subject of taking a life.

Why didn't you call Shamir that evening, for example?

Avraham Shalom: I called his bureau chief. I don't call the prime minister at midnight and tell him the terrorists are dead. That's not . . .

But didn't you have to ask him for authorization for this?

No, not in my opinion. He didn't think so, either.

Do you mean that your agreement with Shamir was actually that whenever you assess that killing is necessary. . . .

And it's an inconvenient hour and it's. . . .

You don't need to call him, you do it, you can decide on your own.

Yes, everyone knew I could decide on my own, me, when he gave me that authorization. The next morning I held a staff meeting, and I explained to the whole staff that Shamir gave the authorization; everyone remembers that. Why did I tell them that? That was six months or a year before Bus 300.

Under what circumstances did Shamir give you the authorization?

The circumstances were terrorists in Lebanon and terrorists in Israel. There was an incident or two when I couldn't find him. When it had to be done. When Arabs who were about to carry out a terrorist attack, or who had done it, needed to be dealt with. And he told me, "If you can't find me, decide on your own." I said, "So you're giving me the okay?" He said, "Yes, I'm giving you the authorization to do it." And I used it and then he changed his mind. He didn't support me all the way.

Were there cases where you called Shamir, asked to shoot a terrorist, and he told you, "Yes, do it"?

Yes.

Before Bus 300?

Before and after.

Within Israel, too?

That I don't remember.

But you remember everything. Did it happen in Lebanon? Bus 300 was the first incident in Israel?

No, no. I don't remember. It's too many things. When it doesn't make headlines, you don't remember. It's very possible that it was.

You don't remember?

I don't remember. I'd be very surprised if nothing happened. Yitzhak Shamir's opinion on terrorism was very similar to mine. He and I had a close working relationship, it's like, I come from the Palmach and he's from Lehi [Israel Freedom Fighters, a militant underground organization active during the British Mandate], and he talked to me in terms of brothers in arms, even though we were from two ends of the political spectrum. But that didn't bother me and it didn't bother him. We knew each other back in the Mossad.

And he left it up to your discretion? Based on what?

My reasoning had to be such that I could explain. For example, that I didn't want terrorism to win a local victory. In Gaza. If those two were to live, later the trial would last a year, if not three, and they'd say we were like this and we were like that. This way you bury them and call it a day.

So your reasoning was—I don't want there to be bargaining terrorist attacks, that they be portrayed as martyrs.

Exactly. We still had hostages in Lebanon, I think. That was my consideration. When you're dealing with a terrorist you can finish off, finish him off. That makes sense. They trusted me not to abuse it. And I screwed up in this case, because I didn't see the photographers. I didn't know. If I had known they were being photographed, I wouldn't have given the instruction. I have no compunctions regarding the moral implications of killing two terrorists who were already dead, almost.

People who put their hands up in the air . . . terrorists who had surrendered.

A terrorist who puts his hands up, his feet up, I don't care about that. They'd already wanted to kill them earlier. The army doesn't know how to shoot well. If they had given it to the Yamam [the Special Central Unit, an anti-terrorist department established by the Israel Police], they'd be dead.

In retrospect, Shamir made all kinds of statements like, "I knew what a prime minister has to know." What's that? He determines what he needs to know? I had told him! I looked for a witness to say that Shamir was in the picture, because I said this could destroy the Service, and we'd done plenty of things like that before, not with a rock, but we'd done them.

What do you mean, "we'd done plenty of things like that before"?

We killed Arabs. Like in that film you're making.

How? Not drone attacks.

No, but there were similar things, each based on the technology of the period. They did worse things, before I became head of the Service. And I kept looking for someone who would tell Shamir, "Look, you approved it for him."

And this authorization you say Shamir gave you—did it apply to Lebanon?

No. I didn't even mention Lebanon.

So that means that as far as you were concerned, that authorization applied to everything.

Yes.

And what you told me you did, executing more terrorists during that period, was that in Israel, too, or just in Lebanon?

That was just in the Territories.

The West Bank and Gaza.

And Lebanon.

So you did it?

We did it.

So how come Reuven Hazak, deputy Shin Bet director, comes out and says, "I thought it was just Lebanon"?

He said that then, but ask him a year later, and he wasn't saying it anymore. That's what we understood, that's what he said, that's what we understood.

But you killed Palestinians in the Territories, not like that, maybe in a different way, I don't know how you killed them, but you did it?

We did similar things.

Avi Dichter: The subject of Bus 300 is an example demonstrating a chain of events which ends with someone thinking he has the authority to beat someone else to death. It's hard for me to say what the Service director's instruction was, but it's perfectly clear that it's excessive when no one stops and says, "I'm not carrying out this command, because it's clearly illegal and is sporting a black flag."

Ami Ayalon: What did we do with Bus 300? We killed a terrorist whose hands were tied, who was no longer threatening us. What right did we have? But in the General Security Service of those years, there was no such term as a "blatantly illegal command." That term was born in IDF after the murders in Kafr Qasim [a massacre of Arab civilians carried out by the Israel Border Police in October 1956]. Meaning, [in that case] forty-eight civilians—old people, women and children—had to be murdered in order for us to understand there's a limit to obedience, and translate it from theory to fact, that there's a stage where not only are you entitled to refuse a command, but that it's your duty to refuse to obey. But all that didn't reach the General Security Service, decades after Kafr Qasim. We're in the mid-eighties. The General Security Service leads the fight against terrorism. And terrorism is brutal. In the Gaza Strip, in the West Bank. And the mistakes the Service made, it's not because Service people are built differently genetically. The General Security Service, for defense purposes, crossed the line permitted in a democracy. The endless commitment to protecting the citizens of the State of Israel caused Service members to do things which are unacceptable. These discussions didn't take place in the Service during the eighties, and these were the discussions we should have had. You've got to understand that in the General Security Service, opening up the wound of Bus 300, which caused the resignation of a Service head, is not a trivial thing.

Avi Dichter: As head of Shin Bet, I arranged a conference and brought in all the main characters of Bus 300, including Avrum. Avrum initially didn't agree to come, and I talked him into it. It was one of the most important moves I made to bring an end to this affair. I brought them all to a meeting in Kibbutz Tzova, and there was a very meaningful discussion there. Really. A cleansing process for an organization. To sit down and analyze Bus 300. And Avrum actually admitted, "I was wrong." I made a point of insisting that Bus 300 be taught in courses. I think anyone who was present at Bus 300 understood it was a mistake, that they had done things they were not permitted to do, except for one person, who I believe to this day isn't convinced Bus 300 was a mishap. All the rest already understand the mistake, and mostly understand how it could take an organization and throw it in the wrong ditch. It is, without a doubt, the Service's most severe trauma, as an organization for which the decision-making process, from the head of the Service on down, was simply impaired.

Until Bus 300, the Service didn't acknowledge the concept of "an illegal command"?

Avraham Shalom: I couldn't answer that definitively. That's a bad question.

Why?

Because it can't be answered honestly.

I don't understand your answer.

It's . . . That's your problem. I'm done explaining.

Does that mean the concept of "an illegal command" didn't exist?

No, I don't remember anything like that. I believe these things happened, and weren't exposed. That's why they didn't make the headlines. That's all.

But you also told me that actually, during that year you carried out . . .

Why that year?

Before?

Both before and after.

But it just wasn't exposed.

Yes.

But it happened. And if it happened, people weren't disciplined?

I'm not answering that. You're asking questions that are harmful to the State of Israel; I'm not answering them.

Bus 300: The Cover-Up

"Contradictions between Shamir's testimony and the testimony of the head of Shin Bet."

The exiting head of Shin Bet, Avraham Shalom, said in his testimony to the police that Yitzhak Shamir was in contact with the Shin Bet to ensure the people involved in killing the terrorists on Bus 300 would not disclose details to the Zorea Committee. Shalom said in his investigation that several days after the incident on the bus, he personally reported the details of the event to Shamir, including the killing of the terrorists. He reported that before the bus incident, he had received a general instruction according to which terrorists should not emerge alive from such incidents.

(Orly Azulai Katz, *Yediot Ahronot*, September 4, 1986)

Avi Dichter: In 1986, when the investigative committees started working, some young guys who had to testify came to my home and told me, "Look, we have to testify before the committee, and there's a preparation meeting." I understood what a preparation meeting was, that it's a coordination meeting, to instruct them and to guide them. And I told two of them, "Look, ultimately you can't lie to an external committee. If you lie, you'll have to stand in front of the mirror and shave by yourselves, and there's no reason for you to cut yourselves because you decided to lie to the committee." I had a feeling I'd convinced them; in retrospect, it turned out I hadn't. They went and perjured themselves to the committee according to the instructions they'd gotten. And by the way, ever since then, those two, when they see me, they always cross over to the other side of the road.

Ya'akov Peri: I always asked myself, if Avrum, the head of the Service, had summoned me, and asked me to convey to the investigating committee a certain version, which I knew wasn't accurate or complete, would I agree or not, and I had a hard time answering myself. When you're inside the system, and the head of the Service is the ultimate authority, and the system is a greenhouse, it's a closed system, it's a nurturing system, very intense, I don't know who among us would stand up, find the courage and tell him, "I refuse to go," or "I refuse to say that."

Ultimately, each one of us, the head of the Service, or a police officer, or a simple soldier in Golani [one of IDF's most highly decorated infantry units], also ends up alone with himself. And I estimate that's what also happened to the people dealing with the Bus 300 affair. These were ultimately people who understood that if they didn't take manipulative action, and I'm talking especially from Avrum's perspective, he'd be on trial for murder tomorrow. When you're being sentenced for murder, the judge doesn't have the option of giving you community service.

Do you believe Avraham Shalom should have been indicted for murder?

No. Unequivocally, no. I don't think there was murderous intent here, in the criminal sense of the word. If you're asking for my opinion, he made an error in judgment. There's no doubt about that. A judgment that cost a life . . . in this case the life of terrorists, but a life in every sense. They're flesh and blood.

Judgment?

But a wrong judgment.

Not because it was exposed, you mean.

No. The action itself.

When the affair exploded, and the photos of the live terrorists were published, you claimed in the investigative committees that Yitzhak Mordechai, chief of Southern Command, was the one who beat them up.

Avraham Shalom: It's not true that we wanted to incriminate Yitzhak Mordechai. We didn't recount things that never happened before the investigative committees. What the Service people, the army people, testified there was all exactly what happened there. There was no false testimony. We just didn't say that I'd instructed to give them one last blow so that they wouldn't get to the hospital alive.

So the entire claim that the Shin Bet withheld evidence and gave false testimony isn't true?

You're talking about something different. You're talking about the Zorea Committee. There we didn't say we'd acted under the prime minister's instruction. We said we admit everything except for killing them. Why? Because then we'd have had to say that it was systematic. And that's what we were told both by our legal advisors, who were no good, and by the prime minister, with whom I was in contact on this matter three, four, or five times a day. Since he'd been the one who'd given me the instruction to kill them. A year previously. I had authorization to do it. But that authorization was valid, and he also said he would continue to acknowledge it, and that didn't happen.

And what about the claims that the Service coordinated testimonies, and that Yossi Ginossar [a senior Shin Bet official] was a mole within the Zorea Committee, reporting to you?

Because of Shamir.

What do you mean, "Because of Shamir"?

Shamir wanted Ginossar to tell him what he was doing. I was with him there.

Yossi Ginossar came to Shamir and told him what was going on?

Not all the time, once or twice. Shamir said, "Don't worry, and have no doubt, we'll protect you to the end." So everyone calmed down. But in the meantime, a clique came together within the Service, organized by Reuven Hazak, to sacrifice me at the altar of international justice. And that I can't stand.

Reuven Hazak did that to bring you down? But he was already your successor. Didn't you ask yourself why he was doing it?

Yes.

But?

I don't know.

You weren't interested?

I was interested.

Did you talk to him?

Naturally.

What did he say?

What I said was that I had to go because that would serve justice, and not just me, but him, too. You can't emerge clean from this business. But he wanted to emerge completely clean. You take all this crap and you fling it at your neighbor.

I don't understand what you're claiming. What do you mean, "You take all this crap and fling it at your neighbor"? He only lost out by coming out against you.

He made a mistake. It's a fact that if he had kept his mouth shut, he would have been Service director. I told him, "Wait two more months, I'm leaving anyway." Then he said, "No." That was after he'd spoken with Dorit Beinisch and with [Yitzhak] Zamir [Israel's attorney general at the time], and these are things I wasn't sure of, because

I wasn't monitoring them. They thought I had surveillance on them. That's bull. I don't do things like that. When I told Shamir he would replace me, Shamir said, "A traitor isn't replacing you."

Ya'akov Peri: Why Reuven Hazak, Rafi Malka, and Peleg Radai decided to do what they did, I can, to this day, only try and understand. But I don't accept their motives as they explain them. Reuven Hazak, who was the natural, sole, and clear candidate, without a doubt, to become the next head of Service, after Avrum, came to Avrum and told him, "You betrayed the trust of Service employees. You statements weren't accurate, to phrase it diplomatically, and you better get up and leave." Avrum was already at the end of the affair, and he said to Reuven, "You go home!" So Reuven Hazak and Rafi Malka and Peleg Radai decided to go to Dorit Beinisch and to Yitzhak Zamir. At the end of this story, of course, Avrum handed in his resignation. But that was after those three's coup attempt. Rafi Malka, Reuven Hazak, and Peleg Radai, they were among the cornerstones of the Service, they were also among the most solid elements professionally, as well as in the admiration they evoked in the Service, in regard to their capabilities, and in regard to what they did. It would be as if a quarter of the IDF General Staff got up today, tried to pull off a mini-revolution, and ended up going home.

Avraham Shalom: Those three guys—Reuven Hazak, Rafi Malka, and Peleg Radai—opened up the Service to the press. And then the attorney general's office took this dowry and made a Roman banquet out of it. They went to the prime minister and wanted to "make a deal," and the prime minister threw them out of the room several times. And the attorney general never went alone, he always went with the state attorney. And Shamir couldn't stand that. Shimon Peres also got sick of the whole business, and Rabin was also impatient about it. He wanted them to let it go. To forget it. And he wanted to convince the attorney general, who was ready to forgive, but then the state attorney came and she exerted pressure on him not to forgive. I'm not that fluent in the details, I didn't deal with it much. Because I naively assumed it was the politicians' problem to get us out of the mud. I'm very disappointed with people who, in the beginning, when they need you, stand behind you and next to you and above you and below you, and when it starts to touch them or their party, then they abandon all their principles and everything they'd said before and forget everything. It's awful.

To this day, in the history of the State of Israel, there hasn't been a political echelon that devoted itself so fiercely to getting the operational echelon out of the mud the way Shamir and Peres did in regard to Bus 300. They replaced the state's attorney general, fought to prevent the affair from getting more complicated, misled the Court of High Justice, granted a pardon before the case even came to court. Do you think they were scared that if you opened your mouth in court, they'd be accused, too, and would stand trial?

I wouldn't have opened my mouth.

What do you mean? They would have accused you of murder.

If I'd have been accused alone, I wouldn't have fought with such desperation. But they tried to accuse eleven people from the Service, and that I couldn't allow.

Do you mean that if they had accused only you of inciting for murder, you'd just give up?

I wouldn't admit it, but I wouldn't have fought from minister to minister, opposition to coalition.

When did you understand you had to resign?

On the first day, I proposed to Shamir that I resign. He said, "Don't you dare." For half a year or a year, he supported me. It's not that he abandoned me immediately. But when he saw that the attorney general was beating him, then his princes—Dan Meridor and Ehud Olmert – came, and told him, "If you don't give up on Avrum, then the Likud will topple." And that convinced him. He didn't want me to resign at all, he thought I'd switch from one government position to another after the whole affair. He offered me an ambassador position. I told him, "I'm not interested, I can't, and it wouldn't do any good." I didn't want to stay in a position where the government pays my salary. Meanwhile, the attorney general passed it on to the police, and the police investigated it in a very amateurish way and also said untrue things. And then came the genius idea of the pardon, which to this day I don't know if we did the right thing by accepting it or not. At that stage I wasn't treating politicians seriously.

Because?

Because I saw that these were not trustworthy people. They leave a wounded man in the field. Not for me.

You're the wounded man?

Not just me. The whole Service.

Ya'akov Peri: The Service personnel said . . . We get sent, evening after evening, morning after morning, day by day, to missions which are sometimes at the outskirts of the law, sometimes adjacent to the law, sometimes legal; no one supports us. If we get caught, there's no one to protect us. Yossi Ginossar said it well when he said, "We get sent to the gutter, we poke around in the gutter, we come out covered with what the gutter delivers, and no one bothers to rinse us off, or to offer us a warm shoulder. We're alone in the battle. We're orphans."

Yuval Diskin: I didn't know what happened with 300. I think most people, except those who actually participated in the incident, didn't know what happened. Till one day all the coordinators in the West Bank were told to come to a meeting with the head of the district at the Qalqilya dump. Apparently, it was appropriate for the situation. . . . And we sat there, not far from the dump, and Yankale Peri, who was head of the district, gave us some kind of version. I don't even remember word for word what it was, but I believe it was still an edited version of the events. But we understood it was a major event.

I have to say I learned much more about the story from the media than from the Service at the time. My real experience of Bus 300 actually resulted from the details that emerged further down the road in the media, when you start to understand what really happened there, what certain people from the Service did. The whole story of taking captives and killing them—which is inconceivable. It was also inconceivable in the Service during those years. And the cover-up that happened around the affair, which was also inconceivable. You come to an organization where they educate you from day one, explaining how different you are, how unusual, how honest we are, how we maintain standards, and suddenly you discover that something like that happens in your organization. Personally, I experienced very deep disappointment. This wasn't the organization I had understood I was joining.

And then the internal debate begins, should we protect those people who took part in that? Did they have permission or proper authority to do what they did, or not? Do they deserve a pardon or not? And other things like that. Today, from the perspective of a Service director, I think about it more. About what the relationship was between Yitzhak Shamir, as prime minister, and Avrum, as head of the Service in those years, and whether the claim made by Avrum and other senior people in the Service was correct, that actually what was done was done with proper authority and with permission, or according to some agreement between Avrum and the prime minister. I claim that today it couldn't happen. Today there are things that I believe can't be agreed upon in that way between a prime minister and a Service director. That's something that's changed dramatically. But I think it's possible that back then there was more of a feeling, say, with Avrum or other senior personnel, that the end did justify the means a little.

Today I try to explain it to young managers in the Service as well—that the end is very important, we are a mission-based organization, we have to produce results, but if you attain the goal in an unworthy way, you end up destroying yourself as an organization. When things have no clear moral framework, ultimately you get hurt as an organization, as a person, and even if you attained that goal, it's not worth it.

Bus 300: "The Cleanest People"

In 1980, a new Service director (Avraham Shalom) stepped into office, and served in this position until late 1986. Even as he was appointed, he discovered a well-established norm (of perjury in court) which has existed for many years. But while his predecessor was aware of the problem, was discomforted by it, and therefore repressed it, this Service director no longer felt there was a problem at all. "When I think about fighting terrorists," he told us, "I don't think in the context of an Israeli court. To me, it's important that the guilty terrorist is punished." As part of his testimony, we asked him whether he, like his predecessor, had repressed the problem. His reply was illuminating. "It's not a matter of repression," he said. "You repress something when you're aware of it. This wasn't even on my radar." The committee sees him, too, as one of the people responsible for the illicit system discussed here, and for its longevity till it exploded so violently.

(From the report by the Landau Commission, a governmental investigative committee headed by the former Head of the Supreme Court, judge Moshe Landau, to look into the Shin Bet investigations. The commission was established after Shalom's resignation, and its report was published in November 1987.)

You told me that when you were appointed as head of the Service, you canceled some of the permits the interrogation division had previously had for irregular methods of interrogation.

Avraham Shalom: They had all kinds of tricks, like the Americans have in Iraq. I don't know if they listened to my instructions, because you couldn't be at every interrogation, but it was a problematic division. They did more than they were allowed to do, the interrogators, and we stopped it. We also threw out, I think, one or two of the interrogators. They'd hit. Hitting was prohibited; you could slap them on the cheek.

Explain to me how you reconcile this—on the one hand, they can't hit, on the other hand, killing terrorists who had surrendered.

It's like on the one hand, you can support Meretz [an Israeli left-wing party that advocates human rights and a two-state solution to the Israeli-Palestinian conflict], and on the other hand, be a soldier in Sayeret Matkal. How can you do that? It's a fact that it happens.

But in this case, on the one hand, there's a Service director who forbids his people from hitting, but then says, "Kill people who surrender."

These things aren't related to one another. That's exactly the point with a commander—to know how to distinguish between things you can do, should do, have to do, and can't do.

Killing the Bus 300 terrorists was something you should do?

Based on the result, no.

Only based on the result?

Only based on the result.

Meaning if there hadn't been a reporter there, it would have been okay?

If he hadn't come, we wouldn't even know about it.

And the moral aspect of the thing?

There's no morality in terrorism. First of all, look for morality in the terrorist.

And if he puts his hands up and surrenders?

That's not a moral problem.

So what kind of problem is it?

It's actually a tactical problem. Not strategic.

Explain it to me.

I don't know how to explain it any better. You need an intelligent enough person to distinguish between something that to you supposedly looks like a cruel thing, compared with the same person who, the next morning, or five minutes later, releases a long line of Arabs because they . . . they have kids at home. What do I know? Something like that. Anyone who's responsible for something faces dilemmas like that every day, if he thinks about them. It's the same thing with us.

So from your perspective, the decision to kill the two terrorists . . .

You always phrase it as black or white. There are decisions that . . .

Two captured terrorists were killed.

But why are you hung up on that?

I'm trying to understand the morality of it.

There is no morality in this case! In the war on terror, forget morality. If you're dealing with a one-ton bomb, forget morality. There is no morality. What's your idea of morality? You're asking questions which I think are immoral because they harm Israel.

Why do they harm Israel? Explain that statement to me.

You, when you're listing things where you think the moral element is questionable, that certainly ultimately harms our country. The answers harm it. The questions do, too. Because you have to answer like this. . . . I'm not answering you straight, I'm answering you like this.

Yeah, I noticed that.

So stop asking. I made a mistake with those two terrorists. I don't think it was a smart thing to do. I made a mistake, I shouldn't have done it, and I paid. I had collaborators, it's true, but I pulled them out of the holes, and that's that.

But you're saying that the mistake was that you did it in front of press cameras.

No, the mistake was that I did it at all. Not because of the press, but as a matter of principle.

A moral error or an operational error?

Both.

So why did you say to me, "Terrorists who get caught, I believe they should be killed"?

I believe they should be killed because they'll come back again and again and again. Their children, their cousins. But not every terrorist, and not in every case. I think terrorists—who are the scum of the Earth, all the ones who commit suicide—can't live alongside normal society. So I don't want to help them.

There's a saying Ben Gurion told us once: "You do the country's dirtiest jobs because you're the cleanest people."

What does that mean?

That you can do things that are a bit on the edge of the law, not killing, but we're the only ones who can do that because our hands are clean—we don't take bribes; we don't gain any kind of personal benefits from it. They still say that in the Service to this day, I think. I don't know if it's still true today; I hope so.

Avi Dichter: It's not just the head of the Service; it's a whole set of managers who thought they could conduct activities in the gray zone. Ultimately, very high-level people, who were given commands and relayed commands to others, were involved with Bus 300. There was no situation where the Service director gave an instruction and a senior official blocked his instruction; the commands carried on. Later, when I was Service director, I remember that at one of the professional meetings, a very senior minister said to me, "Look, Avi, this shouldn't be under discussion, this is in the gray zone." I said to him, "I beg your pardon, I refuse to have the Service working in the gray zone. I don't know any gray zone. There's black, which is prohibited. There's white, which is permitted. And that's it."

Bus 300: The Day After

He was once the strongest man in the country, with a weak minister of defense (Moshe Arens), and an apathetic prime minister

(Yitzhak Shamir). A man who controlled people's fates. Who could move villages from their locations, spies from their mistresses, prime ministers to action. The man who was sitting on the largest information bank in the Middle East. The strongest man in the country. And then, one day, came the fall. Within less than two years, the man left his job, his friends, and in essence, his country and homeland. Since then he's been wandering the world. Less poetically, you can say: the man didn't find appropriate work in Israel, so he traveled abroad. He tried his luck in New York, in London and in other European capitals. And there he works and wanders and lives alone.

(Ronit Vardi, *Ma'ariv*, 1992)

How do you get through a period like that?

Avraham Shalom: For me it went by easily. Really easily. From day to night.

I'm talking about the period where you're still head of the Service and everyone around you is talking, and there are constant revelations in the press.

I learned not to read it. It didn't bother me that much. It bothered me, but it didn't cause me to have a psychological crisis or anything like that.

With whom do you discharge the pain? The frustration and the anger?

[Avraham Shalom points at himself.]

Only internally?

Yes. I only discharge my mistakes internally. I also discharge my successes internally.

Did your family not suffer as a result of this? Your wife, the kids? How did they deal with Bus 300, for example?

We didn't talk about it at all.

But it has to be one of the hardest periods in your life.

Yes, but it didn't make me faint; I knew I was right.

Do you talk to your wife? Do you let off steam somewhere?

No.

Alone with yourself?

Yes, that's healthiest. Why should I harm others?

When I'm having a hard time, I call my girlfriend to share it with her.

I've never had a girlfriend, I had a very intelligent wife.

Who understood you without talking?

Without talking. Once I flew in a plane with Eli Zeira [IDF major general and head of Aman, Israel's military intelligence, during the Yom Kippur War]. He was a pilot. And we crashed, in Sinai, before there were roads. This was after the Six Day War. We flew back from Sharm, six people in a little plane. Midway between Sharm and Eilat, the engine went still; no engine. Zeira was a pretty talented pilot. I don't know if a young Air Force pilot would have done better than him. A [single-engine] Cessna like that has gliding capability, limited, but it's there. He kept trying to go down as if he were landing, but very fast. In one minute we descended 4,500 feet. Eventually the plane got stuck with its nose in the ground, but we weren't injured. It was a miracle, but we lost contact with the world. Eli broadcasted a distress call, but no one heard him. After about two hours, some Arkia plane went by, I don't know where from. We had a mirror, we signaled it with the sun, and the pilot reported to the Air Force that he'd found us. After fifteen minutes two combat planes arrived, flew over us, and after two hours two helicopters came to rescue us. At Sde Dov airport, they gave us champagne in honor of the fact we weren't killed. I was supposed to have come home at six or seven, and I arrived at ten. My wife said, "Where have you been?" So I said, "Listen, we crashed in Eli's plane." Eli lives here, two houses away from us. She said, "That's no reason to be late." And that was the end of the story. So you ask me if she understood me? She understood.

You told me you were remembered for the Bus 300 affair, and not for what you did before then.

That's true.

Why?

I don't know. It's the most prominent thing. They also remembered me a bit for Eichmann, but that passed. Because there's no "news" there. It's not a "news item."

Does it hurt?

No. I don't even think about it. It wasn't especially difficult. I actually came out of it okay. I was glad I didn't transition to the semi-governmental sector but to the private sector, and that's it. You need controls, you need discipline, and you need to tell yourself, this is prohibited and this is permitted, and you have to pay the price. I paid the price for my stupidity. It happened to me. That's life.

Ya'akov Peri

Ya'akov Peri (1988–94)

I was born in 1944, in Nachlat Yehuda, near Rishon LeZion. My parents emigrated from Poland in the thirties. I'm the grandson of a well-known writer named Druyanov, after whom a street and a school in Tel Aviv are named, a writer who lived many years later in Odessa, a friend to Bialik* and Ravnitski.** I grew up in their laps in Melchet Street in Tel Aviv. My parents left for Netanya, where I was educated and graduated from high school.

In my youth, I distinguished myself through my musical talent, and I was expected to have a significant musical future. That was my intention, too. From the age of thirteen, I was already helping to support my family by playing what's called "moonlighting" gigs, and aiming to be a musician. At age sixteen and a half or seventeen I also won a scholarship to the Julliard School in New York, and I planned to go there immediately after my military service to study music.

At first [the military] didn't want to recruit me because of a systolic heart murmur, and I appealed the decision, and eventually my appeal was accepted. I wrote a letter to Ben Gurion at the time, and they let me enlist. I joined the Paratroopers. I did part of my service doing HQ duty, but most of it in operational roles. Towards the end

---

* Chaim Nahman Bialik (1873–1934) was one of the pioneers of modern Hebrew poetry and is considered to be Israel's national poet.

** Yehoshua Ravnitski (1859–1944) was a prominent Jewish writer, publisher, and educator.

of my service I broke my leg, I received early release because of the injury, and until my studies in Julliard began, I decided to study at the Hebrew University of Jerusalem. At first I signed up for civics and statistics. Then I realized it wasn't exactly my field, and switched to studying history of the Middle East.

I arrived in Jerusalem in the sixties, and spent three wondrous years there. Jerusalem in the early sixties was small, bohemian, insulated, and lots of fun. Thanks to my musical ability, I immediately joined the Hebrew University student band, along with Ehud Manor,* Rivka Michaeli,** and Dan Biron,*** who remained my good friends from then on. I made a living playing in the Kol Israel**** orchestra of those days and in Bacchus, the well-known student club.

At some point, director Giora Godik approached me and invited me to play in *My Fair Lady* at HaBima Theater. They'd brought in two trumpeters from Scotland, and they needed a quality local trumpeter. For a few months, I'd drive each night from Jerusalem to Tel Aviv, to perform at HaBima. I had a really rich life, and so I decided to pass on the scholarship to Julliard and to complete my academic degree.

In 1966, I transferred to Tel Aviv University. That year might have been the most difficult one in terms of the economic recession in Israel, and my father, who was an impoverished construction worker, appealed to me in an emotional way and said, "Listen, music is a great thing, and I also see how much fun you're having. And since you're an only son and I worry, and my ability to help you doesn't look promising in the near future, you should find work that leads to a monthly salary, something permanent, something steady. You can always make music, with any job."

My father's appeal apparently affected me, and I looked for work. What can you do? One day, I see an ad on Tel Aviv University's bulletin board stating, "Young people with a combat military record who are interested in work involving security challenges, political challenges," something like that, "are invited to reception committees

---

* A prominent Israeli songwriter.

** A well-known Israeli actress.

*** A musician, director, and reporter.

**** "The Voice of Israel," the official Israeli broadcast authority.

at the Armament Branch of the Ministry of Defense in Tel Aviv." During that period, I was a bohemian—a real bohemian. Long hair, flip-flops, a chain with a medallion, a proper hippie. I lived in a rented apartment over the Cassit Café, and I was a "Dizengoffian" at the time when Dizengoff was Dizengoff.* My first actual encounter with the Security Service was through the weekly *HaOlam Haze*, which maligned it and called it "the apparatus of darkness." Beyond poring over the last page of *HaOlam Haze*, which always featured photos of girls in bathing suits, I'd read about the "apparatus of darkness," and that was actually the first time I grew aware of the fact that there was a covert intelligence organization in Israel.

I went to the reception committee dressed casually and uncombed, as was my custom. I didn't treat the subject very solemnly. I didn't prepare myself. I said, "we'll see." Inside I was greeted by people wearing suits and serious expressions, and they asked me to tell them my life story, asked a few questions, and said they'd send me to a few tests. They didn't tell me what it was all about, just said it was a covert organization, but they would tell me the details if they decided I was worthy. For half a year, I ran around for all kinds of aptitude tests and personal interviews.

What appealed to you about it? You were a musician, which is completely an opposite sort of world.

Look, I think anyone, even today, if they made him an offer and took care of him like they took care of me during that six-month period, the curiosity would kill him. You tell yourself—I've got to try, and later we'll see. Beyond that, you know, the time was a little different. The nature of life in Israel, I'd say even the subject of Zionism, was a lot stronger.

And then, in February 1968, they informed me that I'd been accepted to the General Security Service, and instructed me to come on March 1 to the clock tower in Jaffa. They told me to hold a newspaper under my arm, and that some lady would come and take me. A lady who was actually nice did arrive, took me a few hundred meters from there to a building that sat right across from the flea market.

---

* In the sixties and seventies, Dizengoff Street in Tel Aviv was the center of the city's counterculture scene.

And that was Service headquarters. That's how I started working in the General Security Service, without meaning to.

For a day or two, they buried me in forms and sent me to the archives. And the archives didn't have a computer in those days, they'd file manually with iron hole-punches. I'd find myself returning home every day, all injured from filing the papers, but then they didn't really designate me to be an archives employee. They said, "This is a stage in your professional training." During that time, unlike today in the Service, they employed the apprentice method. They assigned me to someone who would teach me the profession, like a shoemaker or a carpenter in Eastern Europe, and I became the apprentice of some dear people.

The basis for the Service's Arab branch was comprised at the time of people from Shai, the Palmach's Information Service, or of people from Arab countries, who spoke the language as their mother tongue. I sat with some of them, and in addition to my technical work as an archivist, they taught me what intelligence work was, what an agent was, what a "live source" was, what collection was, how the material was processed, how to be a handler, all gradually.

After a few months, they decided we, the three new recruits, would travel to Arab villages in which there were Service operatives, we'd stay with them, live in the houses there, experience the milieu for a few months, and also brush up on our Arabic. I came with some Arabic, a little from high school and a lot from university, but it was poetic, literary language. I had to practice the spoken language and the customs.

The year was 1966, about a year before the Six Day War. They assigned me to the home of the head of Baqa al-Gharbiyye regional council. I slept in his living room. He'd put down about eight mattresses for me, so I'd be comfortable—when I'd sleep, there'd be about half a meter (twenty inches) between me and the ceiling—and walk around the house at night with a hunting rifle to protect me. It was amazing.

At that stage there was still martial law in the Arab villages within the state of Israel, and every large area also had a military governor, usually a lieutenant colonel or a major. And when martial regime personnel would come to Baqa al-Gharbiyye, to the head of the council, I'd serve them coffee, translate what the host was saying into Hebrew, and so on. And I guess I blended in. I blended in so much that later, after I'd already passed the apprenticeship period in the Arab village, and after I'd finished the basic intelligence course, I came to a conference the military governorate was conducting, with the participation of police personnel and Shin Bet personnel, and the military governor of Baqa al-Gharbiyye saw me there. Everyone called me Ya'akov Abisat then, after my host. He took one of the senior Service people aside and asked, "What's that Arab doing here?"

During my apprenticeship, I discovered I liked the atmosphere; I sometimes even like that type of thinking, the mentality. I discovered I could connect a bit, that I have some quality of being liked, of creating connections that eventually turned out to be very valuable, when you have to recruit agents, handle them, create very strong relationships of trust. But what fascinated me, I'd say almost on the level of a drug, was intelligence activity. I was also very swept up in the importance of the role I attributed to the Security Service in strengthening and stabilizing Israel's security. Very much so.

I had some "screw-ups" in the first year. They kept asking me why I hadn't reported that I dated this Finnish girl and that Irish girl and so on. And every time, ultimately, they told me they thought my potential and talent and ability to make connections—both working as a lone wolf and working in a team—were very promising, and they believed the training I would undergo would convey me to the right "Service-y" arenas. But I was never a conservative Service man.

After three months in Baqa al-Gharbiyye, I took an Arabic language lab. We'd study from early Sunday morning till Thursday late at night, leave for Friday-Saturday, and come back Sunday. We studied, very intensively, spoken Arabic, literary Arabic, reading articles, reading handwriting. People who graduated from the Service's language lab, and did it seriously, know Arabic. Know how to listen to Arabic, know how to read between the lines, know how to read a note from an operative. And these things are an asset. There were periods when I'd identify very accurately which city or which area a person came from, based on hearing alone. In the last seventeen to eighteen years, it's eroded a little.

When I started work after the Six Day War, my territory was the mountain areas besides the Jordan Valley. "Land of Pursuit."*

* A nickname for the Jordan Valley in the period following the Six Day War, due to the frequent chases after terrorists conducted in the area.

I started working with the Valley Brigade, running in manhunts in the mornings, and handling agents in the afternoons and at night. You come home once every two weeks. I was living with my wife and my little son in Netanya at the time. I'd arrive on Friday, at four or five in the afternoon, after a week or two when I hadn't been home, and half an hour later there'd be a phone call and I'd be back in Nablus. Your personal, private life disappears completely, and you begin to try and recruit. It's not easy in the beginning, but gradually you build a network of connections. The intelligence connections aren't only covert. You also start to travel to the homes of local leaders, of informants, as their guest. The whole village knows you're a Shin Bet coordinator.

That's not scary?

It didn't scare me at the time. The fact is, we survived it. Unfortunately, there were those who didn't survive. The first surprise I ran into was when, as a very young coordinator, at the end of 1967, I recruited an agent from a village in the Jordan Valley. After two or three meetings, I came to the conclusion that this was a traitorous, unreliable source. One night, I had to conduct a covert meeting with him at the outskirts of his village. I prepared a Border Police force, and at the last minute I decided, based on a gut feeling, that I wasn't showing up for the meeting. A few hours later, it was reported that they'd shot at a white Mercedes there at the outskirts of the village, and people were wounded. We'd ride in these white Susita Carmel cars then. It turned out he'd ambushed me.

The work is very intense. You make arrests, you handle sources, go over information, get to know the territory, take part in all IDF pursuit activities, and locate terrorist bands. When IDF can't eliminate them on the waterfront, you have to conduct a chase. Arik Regev, Gadi Manela, and Tzvika Ofer, rest in peace, all of them are no longer with us. I have a photo of my second son's Brith ceremony.* In the photo, everyone except my son and me, they're all no longer with us. You lose lots of friends, lots of friends lose their lives.

The first citation I got in the Service was for a chase in 1968, with a resident of Beit Furik. Beit Furik was a village teeming with terrorists, which produced all the guides who would leave for Jordan,

* Brith Milah is the ritual circumcision ceremony, performed when a baby boy is eight days old.

lead the band of terrorists in, and guide them on the trails into the West Bank. It was Passover Eve. We were on a chase in the Jordan Valley, and we'd lost the terrorist band. And then, close to Beit Furik at night, there was an altercation, and some of the band members were killed, some of them were injured and captured, and we lost a sergeant from the Paratroopers.

We laid a siege around Beit Furik and started looking for the guide. We asked, "What's the guide's name?" They didn't know. "What does he look like?" They didn't know. And then I remember I had some info that the man should have a scar, and I stood behind the Susita Carmel and the village residents passed by, and some Arab who I thought had some mole or bump or something like that arrived. I asked, "What's your name?" He told me his name. I said, "Come with me." I went with him behind the house, started talking to him, and after about an hour or an hour and a half he admitted he was the guide. For that identification, I got a citation from Yehuda Arbel. He and Uzi Narkiss, chief of Central Command, arrived in Beit Furik in a helicopter.

Is there hatred in this war?

Without a doubt. Not on our side. I can say we have educated and still educate Shin Bet personnel not to hate. I think that the minute you feel true hatred toward your rival, your senses get blurred. Meaning, you're not acting in a professional, balanced way like you should. There's a large distance between love and hate. But I think that in the thirty years I've spent in the Service, I've learned to generally like the Palestinian population. I think they might be "the Arabs' Jews." . . . Talented people, including the refugees. They're nice people, they're people who like to live well, to eat well, to kick back and relax. I'm generalizing here, of course. There are menaces among them. No doubt. The Palestinian movement, from the day it was established to this day, including the whole Yasser Arafat saga, is a massive Palestinian mistake. They've had countless opportunities to improve their situation, in every way, politically and financially, and they missed out on them. On the other hand, we're not complete saints, either.

I want to go back to the topic of hate. Are there manhunts that are very personal?

I remember the period when there was a trend of murdering couples who were sitting in the woods. They'd go off to make love in the woods close to Jerusalem, Beit Shemesh and Bethlehem, and a majority of these couple murderers would emerge from the village of Beit Surif, in the Bethlehem sector. I remember Amnon Lipkin-Shahak,* and I drove out there in the morning to organize a curfew there. He was chief of Central Command at the time, and we caught two or three of these couple murderers. I think that was the only time I went into the interrogation room and felt like strangling them on my own. It's a rage you have to put a stop to, since you have to be level-headed, cold, a tactician. In some way, you have to continue tending to collection and investigations and gathering information. And the minute you cross that line, and you become a vengeful hater, you can't do it anymore. Certainly not effectively. So you stop the rage. Neutralize it. You tell yourself, "This is my job, they have their motivation." I don't respect them, and if I could, I'd even stick a knife in them myself, but you can't think like that.

You pay a heavy price, I suppose.

The manhunt period was a very intense period. Endless adrenaline. I couldn't shake off the adrenaline even in much later stages of my career. I'd come home, and I couldn't fall asleep. Your blood pressure level is so high that you can't fall asleep. So what I'd try to do is create some kind of break. I'd watch movies on the VCR, and fall asleep about when the subtitles started. Every movie like that took me six to seven days to finish.

The personal cost is very high. You actually have no life. We were all completely dedicated to the cause. Everything else was less important. But the cost, when it hits you, you become aware of it. When you begin divorce proceedings. When you start to see you don't know your children, when you start to pay the price health-wise. There are complicated costs.

Since I've retired in '95, I've madc an attempt at rehab procedures. I actually came to know my children, my three children, intimately for the first time only when they were already pretty big. My daughter was a little younger. The divorce I went through, the first one for sure, was also a result of failing to develop a life as a couple. There wasn't any kind of crisis I could report to the nation. But I think those are the results. I was injured very badly in a serious accident close to Ramallah. I was hospitalized in Hadassah for almost a year and a half.

* IDF Chief of General Staff (1995–1998), as well as, later, a member of the Knesset and minister of tourism.

I limp a little, I was breathing through here. . . . All these things aren't easy, but, believe me, they're trivial. All in all, when I sum up those years, I'd repeat them in the exact same way, without a doubt.

Why?

Because first of all, you're doing the most important thing, the most Zionist, the truest, the one with the highest values. It's not that I look down on the business community, and I can't complain, I've succeeded in the business world. When I retired, Cellcom [Israel's largest telecommunications company] was good to me in every possible way—but you can't even compare decisions you have to make regarding human life to decisions you have to make in regard to money. However important money is, and however important the economy is in the life of a state and in moving the gears of a kingdom, there's nothing more important than protecting citizens' security, and locking up those that really want to kill you.

Handling Agents—The Art of Persuasion to Betray

"The Katyusha rockets were dismantled only ten minutes before their planned launch."

"The alertness of three Arabs prevented a major disaster in Jerusalem."

. . . the police officer who arrived at the scene discovered a frightening sight: three launchers containing Katyusha rockets, aimed like three threatening fingers at Jerusalem. The targets at which the rockets were aimed were unmistakable: the Western Wall area, the city's southern neighborhoods, and the King David Hotel, at which the American Secretary of State, Dr. Henry Kissinger, was already up at an early hour.

(*Yediot Ahronot*, April 1976)

You were dropped into the field as a young coordinator. How do you know who to recruit?

Ya'akov Peri: You start to implement everything you've learned in the courses, and everything you've learned in the limited experiences of the previous year. You're assigned an office in the Military

Governorate in Nablus, and start doing what's called "basic coverage" of that territory. First of all you're assigned a territorial area, and start to learn it village by village, mountain by mountain, trail by trail. Whether through area patrols, or through lots of interviews with the people who arrive in masses at the Military Governorate. You sit down with people and ask, "Tell me about the village, tell me about the clans, tell me everything . . . "—from the number of village residents, through the division into clans, through the institutions in the village, through its access roads.

You take an area cell—a village or a town or a neighborhood—and you analyze it street by street, house by house, character by character. You look at the negative security elements there, who the marked targets are. In the Service, you eventually get to marking who you want to recruit. You don't walk down the street saying, "Guys, who's with us and who's against us?" After you locate the person or the group that you want to use as a source of information, you do the work. You inquire about him, you check up on him. Eventually, you know you want X, since you assess that X's status, his ability to infiltrate the places you want to keep an eye on, make him the person you want to recruit.

Avi Dichter: Basic coverage gives you a life routine and the misfits, and you single out the misfits and start to handle them. We remember the terrorist who hit the "Maksim" restaurant, for example. She was a young woman, twenty-nine years old, single, a lawyer. In their culture, in Jenin, a twenty-nine-year-old single woman lawyer is almost a whore. What do you mean, "Twenty-nine years old, not married yet, and a lawyer on top of that!" It's an irregular event, which for us would not attract any attention. And then you know to take these cases and try and hone in on these misfits. That's the role of basic coverage. And if coordinators do basic coverage well, they can stay on top of these incidents.

Sometimes you can get a smidgen of information, practically nothing, and ultimately you have to connect these things correctly, and to constantly know how to link them quickly, so as to relay it to whoever needs to take action—to whoever needs to make an arrest or a hit. These short lines are a very significant advantage of the Shin Bet. For example, you get a report about John Doe, who's a pretty pathetic character, down and out, walking around with a beard. You get a report that John Doe suddenly looks like he walked out of a billboard, which is a very problematic indicator. When you're in a wave of suicide bombers, you understand it's an indicator. It doesn't mean he's a suicide bomber yet, but it's an indicator. You say—let's hang a balloon over him and make sure it floats. We won't lose him until we dispel the suspicions. For example, if it turns out he's getting married, we understand why he cut his hair.

If the suspicion persists, you can start at the end of that thread to make progress, and to know first of all to input his name at the roadblocks, because he's walking around with his ID card, and then you can assign targeted coverage and find out what's really going on with him. You get someone close to him, and you can get the story. And if you know the person he's associating with is a Hamas man, the story's more or less closed. That's one example of many. You can suddenly see that someone whom people would never pick up if he tried to hitchhike is suddenly picked up by a vehicle when he hitchhikes. You see him sitting in a restaurant, things that didn't happen before. These are the things that basic coverage exposes and makes you notice.

Yuval Diskin: Ultimately, you're working within a population, and you can't allocate an agent to every person. So there were all kinds of approaches that developed, and some of the first were basic coverage approaches—how do you approach an area cell, how do you approach the population in an area cell, how do you study it, how do you determine where you want to have agents. Over time, it became more sophisticated, and we switched to a combination of basic coverage of the geography and the demographics of a certain area cell, and more targeted coverage, where you work only according to targets. Meaning, a target is the Hamas organization, a target is the Islamic Jihad organization, Global Jihad. You have a target somewhere, in a specific area, and your role is to infiltrate that target, or to introduce agents into that target, or to recruit an agent from that target and handle him.

And the agents, what motivates them?

Ya'akov Peri: There are several kinds of agents. First of all there's the volunteer kind, whom you always have to watch out for, because he's an intelligence addict or he has some agenda, or he was sent by the target organization. But there are also good volunteers. There are a great many volunteers who volunteered, both here and abroad, came and said, here's my motivation, here's what I want, here's the information, this is the money I want, or this is what I want in return in this case, and you can check it out and sometimes it also comes out okay, but it's a type that requires a bit of caution.

The trick on the topic of handling sources is cross-referencing. If you have a single piece of information that's a doozy, you need to try and cross-reference and verify it. You can't run around from morning to evening arresting people and interrogating people. In certain periods, the Service would interrogate tens of thousands of people. You can't sustain that. To hit the mark, you have to verify that the intelligence you got from X is reliable.

Ultimately, when you collect information from a live agent, it's not just about what he said, but also about trying to uncover, both along with him and after he leaves, "what was the poet's intent" and constructing your own assessment of whether the report is trustworthy. That's true of any information a handler receives from an agent. What's the chain of relay? From whom did he hear the information? Is it "S.W.S."—Some Woman Said—is it a rumor on the street, or did a terrorist, recruited by some band of terrorists we're supposed to capture, tell him personally? Does he belong to the same cell? There are whole books about handling live sources. You study them and you acquire experience over time, because there's no substitute for experience in these subjects.

As a handler, you want to milk your sources of information, you direct them toward people about whom you want to hear what they did, where they met, how they expressed themselves, and so on. All this material, along with your assessments and recommendations, you send to your desk person—that's the "back office," which is usually located in the districts, at HQs. They read the information and respond back to the field with instructions, requests for expansions, questions, clarifications. And what's called the "collection cycle" is carried out.

There are many cases where the operations unit has to be activated, because you need surveillance, monitoring, photographs, before you carry out arrests. Of course, there's a commander who has to make the decision whom to arrest, whom do you arrest first, how the arrests happen. You involve the enforcing powers in it—the army, the police, the Border Police, the Yamam, Duvdevan.* The coordinator usually heads out at the head of this unit along with the force commander. The detainees receive a respectful welcome in the Service's interrogation branch, where the interrogation unit starts to question them, and then "roll up the carpet," as it's called, go out later to collect weapons of war in their possession, arrest additional people, and write interrogation reports. Interrogation reports are also distributed to desk people and to research units, and that's how you know how Hamas is built. It's a massive collection system, a giant warehouse of information, and the trick is not to lose yourself inside it.

To a certain extent, the intelligence profession is not insulated. It's not mathematics. It's far from precise, and so your analysis and assessment capability is critical. The experience amassed is critical. The more you recruit, the more you fail at recruiting, the more sources you handle, the more meetings you attend, the more you experience what happened as a result of the information you brought in, that's how you become a better intelligence professional, and your assessment capability improves. I define this work as an art. The art of making a connection, creating trust, ultimately convincing a person to become a traitor. Betray his surroundings, his friends, sometimes even his family. That's not a trivial thing.

How do you actually convince them?

Peri: You have to locate the motivation that will cause him to tell you the real, important things. Sometimes it's ongoing motivation, or momentary motivation. Many Arabs who needed medical treatment for their wives or for themselves in an Israeli hospital would come to the Military Governorate HQ. Seemingly, these are people with motivation, but it's not ongoing motivation, because the minute he's got the permit and his wife, or his son, was treated in Hadassah or in another hospital, the motivation is gone.

Avi Dichter: Look, people are a spectrum of weaknesses. And a spectrum of weaknesses is what you're dealing with. I remember in Lebanon there was an Imam of a mosque who, at the time, had

---

* An elite IDF special forces unit operating in the West Bank, known for its undercover and counter-surveillance activity.

to lead us to a very large weapon arsenal. An Imam like that who's "iron," there's no chance he'd talk in the interrogation. One report said he had a stash of pornographic material. And, indeed, the interrogator who came to him—an exceptional guy, by the way, who'd one day head the interrogation branch—came with this shred of information, searched the house thoroughly, found the stash, took out the pornographic material, and from that moment the interrogation took a different turn. They loaded him on a helicopter and took him to the place where the arsenal was. And at the last minute he got cold feet and decided not to point out where the weapons were. So you take out a magazine and another magazine, and you keep the incriminating magazine till the end—he had very incriminating magazines that linked him to the story—and you saw that even a big Imam knows how to report on little things.

It's always most convenient to handle on a monetary basis. Monetary compensation is always more convenient. There's a saying: "A source that doesn't want silver wants gold." Gold in the sense of benefits which you later have to provide. I once made a mistake as a handler. A source who was responsible for an exceptional operation, we wanted to give him a monetary bonus, and he said, "I prefer a driver's license." We went with his preference, and we wanted to give him a license. Since in Gaza he'd driven his whole life without a license, he had no problems on the practical driving test, but the hard part was the written test, because, unfortunately, the guy hadn't mastered reading and writing. So we brought a special tester for people who don't read and write, and he tested him on traffic signs. After the test, the officer from the Civil Administration calls and informs me that he failed. How could that happen? He says, "Look, there were traffic signs where the tester went easy on him. A sign where the road gradually converges, becomes narrower, and then he says, 'The future is still distant from us.' Never mind, he passed. A sign where the road twists, so he says, 'There are snakes on the road.' The tester could somehow let it all pass, but when he saw the sign showing a hand, he said, 'Hitchhiking station.' You can't overlook that one."

The toughest recruitment I remember was a female activist in a terrorist organization, on one of the fronts. A very prominent figure. They trusted her because she was a woman. It was clear that if she became an operative, we'd arrive at a lot of things we hadn't known before. It took a whole lot of stages and meetings and summons and area patrols. At every one of those meetings, you're building something new, a new stage of trust, and then another slightly deeper stage of trust. She had some motive, some treatment for a very difficult personal problem. And through this you provide help gradually, very reliably, and she did indeed receive the treatment for her problem. And then you see you're slowly moving her over to your side. And I remember the conversation when she understood that now the transfer of information begins. It starts with phone numbers or another form of communication. We sat in some room and conducted a conversation like that for a few hours, and at the end we'd actually set up the methods of communication, and she gets up to leave and looks at me, finally clears her throat a little, and says to me, "But don't ever seat me across from that thing again." And I look back, wondering how I didn't notice, it was a room which contained a human skeleton for study purposes, and she'd sat for those few hours facing that skeleton! I didn't see it at all, and I can only imagine what was going through her mind for those four hours, and to what extent it completely unknowingly contributed something to her willingness to consent.

What are the required traits for a handler?

Dichter: Look, I'm saying something that sounds a little paradoxical, but as a handler, first and foremost, you have to be a trustworthy person and be perceived as a trustworthy person. By the way, those two traits don't always go hand in hand. You can be trustworthy and not be perceived as trustworthy, or vice versa. If you're not perceived as trustworthy, or if indeed you aren't trustworthy, you'll just fail sooner or later. After that come all the other traits. First of all you have to know how to talk to a person at eye level, even when you're sitting across from the biggest killer and the most despicable person, and you know that you're talking to someone who yesterday or just a moment ago carried out a horrible terrorist attack, or sent others to commit such an attack. If you know you have to get him to tell you who the people who carried it out were, or, God forbid, who are the people who are going to carry it out, and you're at the stage of preventing the attack, you've got to be very focused on your goal. Not let any emotion influence you or take over you. If, to get the information from him on where the explosive charge was hidden, you have to joke around with him, give him a pat on the shoulder, and eat with him, that's exactly what you need to do.

You can be sitting with a source who you know has betrayed you. You know he's a member of a terrorist cell which carried out attacks, and when he came to meet you, before or after that, he himself was involved in a terrorist attack. And you sit across from him and you know that when he leaves the meeting with you, our operations guys will follow him to get to the others, and he must under no circumstances leave the meeting with you feeling that it was different from the previous meeting. Listen, it's like being a stage actor in real life. You don't finish the play after two hours and that's that, you get applause. You can sit with a source for hours and days, and he cannot under any circumstances sense that you don't believe him or that you're pulling one over on him.

Only when you really experience a traitorous source—and there's no serious handler who hasn't experienced a traitorous source—do you understand your own limits. Until then, you think it won't happen to you. There was a very significant source who worked with us on a few very serious operations and gave very good information. It was a source I'd recruited, so I thought I knew him literally from the ground up. He was a young guy and we had good chemistry, and, really, he was a source with an exceptional level of information, who took extraordinary risks upon himself. But apparently I didn't notice his fluctuations.

Eventually, we took him out to some terrorist HQ, and he came back and sold us a story, and it was actually the desk person who took the material who said, "Listen, I'm not buying this story, we have to have a source interrogation." And then you're usually offended and say, "What do you mean, a 'source interrogation'? This is my source. Come on, you don't believe me?" And he says, "No, I believe you, I don't believe the source." He showed it to me in a professional way, and then it was clear that something was really up. And we actually took him in for interrogation.

An interrogation can start in a neutral location, in a hotel or somewhere else, and end in jail. That's what happened. And actually, in jail you pass him on to interrogators who arrive completely fresh, they're not his handlers, there's no connection between them, and, gradually, through all kinds of investigation tricks that are something completely different, they actually cause him to admit that he lied about this and he was wrong about that. After that, you still have to continue the handling, because he's a quality source.

And you've got to get past this hurdle, go into the jail, and know you have to keep handling him. And you know he pulled one over on you, and he knows he pulled one over on you, and you keep on playing the game and continue to handle him from that point onward. Ultimately, it's not a difficult crisis. I've always said that sometimes, when you're debating which of two people you want to promote, and if both are equal in terms of qualities, abilities, personality, it's better to promote the one who's already known failure. He'll always be more experienced.

Yuval Diskin: To identify when a person is lying, it's much more than language. It's reading the whole human being. You need to read his body language. A person doesn't only speak with his mouth. A person speaks in a lot of ways. He has body language, his eyes talk, his body postures talk, his hands talk, his pose talks—there are a lot of things that talk in a person. His reactions, his sweat, there are lots of little things that you learn to read. Sometimes you make a kind of "checklist" for yourself, sometimes it works automatically. Some kind of traffic signal jumps up for you—"Something seems off, not like usual. . . . " There are a lot of situations like that on the job.

Ya'akov Peri: An agent handler has to know how to socialize but not go over the line. Some handlers have become "more Arab than their operatives." You can't go overboard. On the other hand, you can't create the kind of distance that would stop the other side from wanting to "be your friend." He won't agree to have covert meetings with you, put himself at risk, get into an adventure that's certainly not simple and that involves the risk of death.

You have to be respectful. Talk at eye level. No agent likes a condescending handler. It's true that he works for the State of Israel and supplies essential information and you save human lives, and he may be contributing to an ultimate reconciliation between us and the Palestinians—all those slogans are ultimately true—but when you're sitting with him in the meeting room, or when you're in a car tossed off somewhere on the mountains in Jordan Valley, in the middle of the night, he's working for you and he wants to please you, he wants a good word from you, recompense from you. And if you know how to behave and fulfill those needs without, God forbid, groveling, you usually achieve a lot more as a handler than the condescending ones, the masters, those who order people around.

But you also have to develop a certain chill, as much as possible. A kind of detachment despite all that. Since you can't get emotionally attached, and it happens. We're all people, after all, we're flesh and blood, and it happens sometimes that you get attached to a certain source and you like him. He almost becomes your friend, in this limited sense of these meetings.

Yuval Diskin: Recruiting people means taking a person who generally doesn't really like you, and making him do things he wouldn't have believed he'd be willing to do. You need very deeply rooted integrity for this thing, since you're living in a world where there are quite a few lies. As part of this deal, you also sometimes pull the wool over the other party's eyes. There's a certain amount of hypocrisy on both sides. You constantly have to remind yourself why you're doing it, and to know that from the minute that meeting or the activation is over, and you're sitting with your friends, you have to disengage from that world and switch to this world. And in this world we don't lie to one another. We have different norms. We don't bullshit our colleagues, and we don't bullshit our superiors, we report what happened fully and precisely. That's something you have to work on constantly. You have to imbue people with these values. You have to educate them all the time. If you don't do that, mishaps happen. And they have happened.

How do you deal with life within a space of lies?

Ya'akov Peri: I don't think the concept of lies is correct. I think it's a double life. It's not lies. Because if the system is essentially one of falsehood, it doesn't bring results. If you get into handling very deeply, you understand you're working with people who lead double lives. It's Dr. Jekyll and Mr. Hyde. On the one hand, those around him can't know, God forbid, that he's an agent of the Israeli intelligence; on the other hand, he has to relay true information and true data, and he lives with a kind of split personality.

I actually meant on the side of the handler who works within an area of lies and fabrications opposite the agent.

I've recruited and handled a great many agents, and I've never lived with a feeling that I was lying to myself or that I was conning them.

It's true that sometimes, in order to create a certain atmosphere, to soothe, you need to make promises that you alone know won't all be fulfilled. But I think that's true for a major part of the way we live. Sometimes you also tell your significant other, your family, or your friends, "People, calm down, it'll be okay, we'll get it under control," when privately you're not convinced you could bring about those results. So I'm not saying it's exactly like that, but there are parallels.

Do you fear for your sources sometimes?

Sure. Not sometimes, you're fearful all the time. The safety of your sources is among the most important topics. You drill him from morning to evening on how to maintain normative behavior that won't bring him under suspicion. How not to ask questions that are too invasive. The targets are very sensitive to traitors and agents, and you constantly have to conduct conversations about preventive behavior with him. There's a very well-known story about an agent of the Mossad in an Arab country who, the minute he received the first payment after a meeting in Europe, bought himself a red sports car, and that was his funeral. Our brothers the Arabs are very suspicious by nature. Although there are obvious distinctions, it's similar to the way Internal Revenue examines us—how did he get that car, how exactly did he buy that house.

If, heaven forbid, some suspicion was raised, and you receive it from other intelligence sources, you must maintain maximal awareness, and you're obligated to immediately brief the source himself on how not to increase suspicion. If, God forbid, all these precautions don't help and he is exposed, I think it's the moral duty of the organization and the handler to get him out of there and save him and his family.

In '89, some villagers attacked a collaborator's house. They dragged him from the house and hung him in the village square. Something like that causes a pretty severe crisis. These aren't pretty images, and they can certainly shock a collection apparatus to the point of a source abandoning you. On the other hand, there were thousands of incidents, and I stand behind that number, where the suspicion of collaboration had no connection to reality. It was a way of getting even in local conflicts, ancient conflicts, by shaming someone as a collaborator. But there were also executions and harassment of real collaborators, and there were cases where we had to get them and their families away.

Usually, the man under suspicion doesn't cooperate with you to save his skin. He's actually among those soothing you and telling you, "Yes, it's an old conflict between the X family and the Y family, don't worry, I'm okay, I'm in control." And sometimes you almost have to force him to uproot from his home or from his village with his family and move to a protected place.

Are you in contact today with your former agents?

No. I have one good quality, among other qualities. I know how to disengage.

Did agents try to get in touch with you?

Yes, of course. People contact me a lot as a result of the fact that I've become a relatively famous person. I try to deal with them, but I don't maintain social relationships.

Have you ever experienced a dilemma because you received a piece of intelligence, the exposure of which could save lives, but would endanger your source?

It happens constantly. Almost any information which an agent brings you, which results in operational activity, endangers the agent's life. The smaller the terrorist cell is, the more using the agent's information becomes problematic, more dangerous, and more likely to expose him. We had an operation that received a lot of media coverage. The Malabi brothers from Jerusalem tried to launch missiles from a town called Beit Fajjar, close to the King David Hotel when Kissinger was here, along with Mrs. Nancy Kissinger, when he was mediating between us and the Syrians and Egyptians after the Yom Kippur War. We were informed of a person who brought the missiles themselves to the Malabi family and helped them set them up. We had to arrest these people, and it was totally clear that if we arrest them, within seconds they'd understand who turned them in.

In cases like that, there are plenty of methods to ensure the agent's safety. One of the most popular methods is to arrest the agent along with them. There are a lot of other methods, but let's be honest with ourselves, you don't succeed in all cases. There are a lot of cases where you understand there's a high risk to the agent's life. It's your duty and the organization's duty to ensure his safety, but the consideration here is a very easy one, since exposing or blocking terrorist activity always justifies endangering the life of an agent. You can't put Jews at risk just because there's an agent involved in the matter. The agent knows this, too, in his heart or in his gut, when he starts working with you. He knows there might come a stage where he might have to either be exposed or run or be arrested, or something like that. With good agents, it could happen any day. Not all sources have a short shelf life, but, generally speaking, it's true that the professional life of a good source gets proportionally shorter the better he is.

I won't talk about specific sources, but I can say that in my lifetime, I and others subordinate to me recruited sources who were part of the target. So much a part of the target that the source arrives at a meeting with his handler and says, "I was assigned to throw a hand grenade," or, "I was assigned to place a demolition charge. What should I do?" And it's inconceivable that we'd let our source throw a hand grenade at our forces. So you're entering an immense system of dilemmas here. Usually, in these cases, we'll expose the cell to prevent the attack, since you're acting on the assumption that if he doesn't carry out the attack, one of his friends will. But how to stop that cell or that activity without exposing the source? And here comes the Security Service's art of war, which we won't expose.

Tell me a little.

No.

Why?

Because I think these are purely operational topics of how the Security Service copes with this war, and if the current head of the Service wants to tell you, that's his prerogative. I don't.

No, but look, you gave me the example of someone who comes and says, "I was assigned to throw a hand grenade." What happens in a case like that, do you arrest the cell?

One of the possibilities is arresting the cell.

What other possibilities are there?

I told you, my lips are sealed.

Can you explain to me how the Israeli intelligence, the Shin Bet, manages to recruit so many collaborators or sources among the Palestinians? I don't know if there's any parallel to something like that.

First of all, we're talented people. . . .

Okay. . . . But beyond the talented people. . . .

Look, it's a system that's very well-oiled and highly planned and very efficient. And I don't know how to assess the failures, but there are probably more failures than successes. You work according to a system. It's not improvised work, where you wake up in the morning and say, "Oh, we need some kind of agent here. . . . Let's go see how we get out of this one."

Do you think if the situation was reversed, if we were under occupation, they'd be able to obtain so many sources from us?

Look, that question isn't fair to the Israeli people, but I want to tell you that the Arab intelligence service organizations—for example, the Jordanian Service, parts of the Syrian Service and the Egyptian Security Service—are intelligence organizations that should not be underestimated. They know how to conduct work which is certainly professional, worthy, with different methods, of course.

Avi Dichter: I suggest we be very careful with generalization. I didn't thoroughly investigate how Yair Stern* was captured, and what the story was behind quite a few events that happened to us under the British mandate. And I think that if you sit down with people who lived in the former USSR, they'll tell you stories which aren't simple about how Jews were also employed to report on other Jews. So I suggest we don't think it could never happen to us and can only happen "on their side." It probably happens to everyone. And, unfortunately, I know a few hard-core traitors in the State of Israel over the years—part of this was made public, part wasn't—who make our hair stand on end when we think of them.

Ya'akov Peri: I estimate they'd have a slightly harder time with us, since we're a "thick-necked," stubborn people. We're also a little more difficult, both with each other and with the outside world. I think the only thing I can think of as a parallel is the extent of the Service's success in recruiting agents from Gush Emunim, from among the settlers. It's very difficult, almost impossible, because of their ideological core. By the way, without making a comparison, God forbid, it's also very hard in the Hamas organization. It's very hard to recruit agents from the Islamic Jihad. They're suffused with ideology, fanaticism, motivation. It's very hard for them to talk about any kind of

---

* Avraham Stern, known by the alias Yair, was the founder of the militant Zionist group Lehi, also called the "Stern Gang," during the British mandate over Palestine. Stern was shot dead in Tel Aviv in 1942 by the British police, under unresolved circumstances.

betrayal. Nevertheless, we can recruit there, too, but not with the same ease in which we could recruit from Fatah, from the Popular Front, from the Democratic Front, and from the other organizations.

You mean that our occupation of the Territories helps us recruit a lot more agents than if, say, you had to handle or locate an agent in Jordan.

The minute you control the daily routines of the citizen in Nablus, in Hebron, or in Ramallah, you're present at the scene. That's the practical essence of occupation, our presence there. The moment you get out of there, like we got out of Gaza and like we got out of other areas in the West Bank, handling live sources becomes a lot more difficult, and naturally dwindles.

Is there a moment where you face an area cell you're responsible for and say, "That's enough, I've gotten all I can here"?

It doesn't work in an "I've gotten all I can here" way, since life, especially the life of terrorist and underground organizations, has a certain dynamic. There are always secondary circles of families, of fans, of those who feel the pain of their arrest; you need levels of supervision. It's like throwing a stone in the water and getting ripples. You need to track these ripples until they really disappear. You can't talk at all in terms of total elimination. It's endless. The Security Service is actually known among world intelligence organizations as an organization that successfully prevents terrorist attacks. Meaning, in the sense that you clean out the terrorist cell almost completely. But there were periods, especially in the early '90s, when the amount of wanted fugitives on the Security Service's list might have been the largest that any intelligence organization in the world has ever had. Dozens in any area. Hundreds in any area. Thousands. And fugitives are the product or the result of failing to close the circle you asked about.

What you're saying is that actually, the organization continues to dry out the swamp, but the swamp refills constantly.

That's the nature of terror. That's the nature of guerrilla warfare. Even the largest nations in the world, which actively work and try to eliminate terrorist organizations, can never declare victory, except for those countries where the terrorist organizations became the country itself. And it's Sisyphean work that never ends, unless there's a political treaty. And even then there are always buds of opposition by those who object to the treaty. The good thing about it is that once you establish a state entity, then dealing with it is the state entity's own problem, as the opposition is against it. But based on the nature of our lives here in the Middle East, Israel will always be a target as well. The arrows will always be aimed at us as well, and not only at themselves.

The Bus 300 Affair: The Take-Off Point

"I made a mistake when I didn't depose those who were pardoned after Bus 300."

Ya'akov Peri regrets that he didn't impose early retirement on the Shin Bet senior personnel who transgressed in the Bus 300 affair. Not because they had killed the two terrorists and had falsified evidence in the investigation, but due to the damage their vindictiveness caused the Shin Bet, and him personally.

(Alex Fishman, *Yediot Ahronot*, June 4, 1999)

To a great extent, Ya'akov Peri owes his meteoric rise to Shin Bet director to the Bus 300 affair. The affair, which resulted in Avraham Shalom's departure and in the early retirement of Deputy Shin Bet Director Reuven Hazak and two heads of departments, Rafi Malka and Peleg Radai, chopped off the organization's tallest branches in one fell swoop. Yosef Harmelin, the previous head of the Service, who was at the time head of security in the state comptroller's office, was called in to temporarily fill Shalom's role, in order to stabilize the shaken-up Service, which had had its wings clipped, and started the search for an appropriate successor. Peri, who had served successfully for years as head of the Jerusalem and West Bank district, the most important district in the Shin Bet, was the only candidate from the organization who had not been harmed by the affair.

In 2004, Dorit Beinisch says, "The amazing thing which the affair revealed is the Shin Bet's unlimited power. Only when we handled the affair did we understand that that power could be directed at anyone, including at the legal system, and if necessary, at the political echelon as well. We found ourselves maligned, vulnerable and threatened. We thought that if we could explain this to the prime minister during the examination of facts, it would be possible to also cleanse the Service of practices of whitewashing facts

and evading the truth. Peres explained to us, in utter seriousness, that there should be another law in effect for the Shin Bet, which should not be subject to the usual rules."

Ya'akov Peri: Look, Dorit Beinisch is speaking out of her own personal distress and from the situation in which she found herself in the Bus 300 affair, and I don't resent her for it. But that's certainly her personal perspective. There's no doubt that the Service is an incredibly powerful instrument. You can't ignore it, and it's a good thing you can't. You just have to take those powers and those strengths and control them, supervise them. Activate them wisely and not as an implement of destruction.

When there was a mass exodus—including Reuven Hazak, Rafi Malka, and Peleg Radai, and later the legal advisors Ron Shalev and Shlomo Wertheim, and finally Avrum—the Service underwent a very deep crisis, forcing the prime minister at the time to summon former Service directors, and appoint Yosef Harmelin, who was head of the Service for fourteen years, then was in the state comptroller office, and was also the Israeli ambassador in South Africa and in Iran, and task him, among other things, with recommending to the prime minister who the next Service director will be.

Yosef Harmelin was already an older man, it had been quite a while since he'd retired from the Service, and the Service did enter what was a period of relative quiet, but it was beaten down. And when Yitzhak Shamir appointed me as Service director following Yosef Harmelin's recommendation in April 1987, I found a bruised Service, characterized both by internal lack of trust and by a lack of trust with external agencies like IDF, the state attorney, the political echelon. And I, along with my colleagues at Service headquarters, started the work of rehabilitation, which was very quick, since the Service is an institution that gets back on its feet immediately.

I decided in advance not to conduct a discussion on the lessons of Bus 300; such a discussion only took place in 2004, and I wasn't even invited to take part in it. I decided in advance not to touch that painful wound, to expel it, to go back to operational work, and that work towed us forward and the Service eventually rehabilitated itself, until the next blow, which was Rabin's assasination.

One of my intense deliberations was what to do with some of the pardoned who were Service headquarter members. I wavered between asking them to depart for educational training and then retire, or retire without educational training, and between leaving them in the Service. And my decision was to leave them, since I felt that when someone was harmed in the course of his operational service, he deserved to be protected by the system, to be cared for by the system. And I was wrong because those who later tried to chop off my head or peel off part of my skin were actually among those people that I decided to protect.

Actually, after the Bus 300 affair, all Service rules are being established, everything that had been in darkness till then becomes more and more regulated and organized with the Shin Bet Law.*

I felt that as part of the rehabilitation, it's good for things to be regulated, written and unequivocally clear, with no room for interpretation, whether it's on the subject of interrogations, operational topics, or the relationship between the political echelon and the Service. The first thing I decided to do was initiate a Shin Bet law. I found a retired district court judge, and I assigned him to start working on this subject. The law passed four or five years after I retired. I think it's right that in a democratic country there would also be a law for an institution like the Security Service. Even within that law, you can't include every topic, since the DNA of a security service contains things that can't be legislated. But once there's a legal framework, you know what's allowed and what's prohibited.

Simultaneously to rehabilitation and to arranging these matters, and of course parallel to the Service's operational work, I understood we'd also have to pay a certain price in regard to openness. With Bus 300, the Service was already quite open. There was a pretty heavy amount of leaks, of relationships with reporters, and I needed some kind of answer to that, too. Avrum was once asked by the Foreign Affairs and Defense Committee if he was considering appointing a spokesperson for the Service, and he answered, "Yes, of course. As long as he's a deaf-mute . . . " I considered appointing a spokesperson for the Service, and finally decided not to appoint one. Because you can't, for every arrest made, for every investigation, for every action, present an account to every reporter from

---

* Passed in 2002 by the Knesset, the law defined Shin Bet's scope of operations and the mechanisms for its supervision and regulation.

the Kiryat Haim local paper, for example, who wants to know why Muhamed Abdallah from the Ein Mahil village in the Nazareth district was arrested. That's problematic. But I understood that between not appointing a spokesperson and opening some sort of channel of understanding, of communication, with the sane and responsible elements in the media, there's still some distance that I had to traverse. Those who wanted to criticize my actions said I opened up the Service too much. If you look at what's happening in the Security Service today, and if I paved the way there, I can only be proud of that.

Death in the Interrogation Room

"Serious violations in Shin Bet interrogations; senior officials fumbled, investigators lied."

"Shin Bet leaders failed severely at their role of conducting the organization's activity within a legal framework"—so states the state comptroller's report regarding the interrogation methods of the General Security Service during the years '88–'92. . . . The Comptroller [Miriam Ben Porat] places the blame on the chain of command and on the Shin Bet's director during those years, Ya'akov Peri. "The examination showed that all levels of command and staff share a role in this situation. The critical report reflects the existence of a double standard in the Service, both in regard to diverting from authorization and to failing to faithfully adhere to truthful reporting."

(*Ma'ariv*, February 10, 2000)

Ya'akov Peri: The Security Service's interrogation apparatus is one of the main elements in the collection system. A terrorist's or terror cell member's interrogation report is first-class collection material, not only for the purpose of carrying out additional arrests. Tens of thousands were interrogated in the Security Service, if it hasn't already surpassed the hundreds of thousands. That's a huge apparatus.

The Service has a system of first-class professional interrogators. A sophisticated, creative system that knows its work, that knows how to plan. Every interrogation involves planning an operation. It's not some kind of slapped-together thing where someone comes in the morning and says, "You've got misters A, B, and Z today. Go in, they're waiting for you." When you get to a Security Service interrogation, you're stepping into a very professional, very determined, and dedicated interrogation system. They work for hours non-stop. The interrogators know their job well. All that notwithstanding, there are interrogees who to this day have apparently not told us everything.

This is a battle of the minds, which is among the most sophisticated ones I know. You have to bring the interrogee to a state in which he understands you know he's guilty. You don't always have the information he has, but you have to convince him that you possess that information anyway. You also have to cause him to experience some sort of stress, some pressure, some mental state in which he understands that eventually he'll have to hand over the information he has, and the sooner he does it, the better off he'll be.

There's no torture in the General Security Service, but there's definitely employment of methods such as sleep deprivation, such as using expressions which are very far from diplomatic. The Israeli people have to understand that the atmosphere in the interrogation room is not that of a luxury hotel like Mizpe Hayamim or Yearot HaCarmel. These are little rooms within prisons, full of interrogees, and the interrogators who ultimately have to expose terrorists, including the most vicious and brutal terrorists we've ever known. And the atmosphere isn't one of mutual appreciation where one person pats another on the shoulder and waits till he sings for him.

When Begin was appointed prime minister, he wanted to cleanse himself from the image of a Jewish terrorist, as the British used to see him. His primary agenda was to ensure that interrogations were carried out cleanly, appropriately, in an orderly way, and in a way that preserves human dignity and freedom. He forbade slapping an interrogee, even with authorization.

Jews or Palestinians?

Palestinians, Jews, all interrogations.

So the Service didn't slap?

You weren't allowed to slap without authorization from the head of the Interrogation Branch. Avraham Ahituv told him he accepted it in general, but there could be cases where there was a ticking bomb out there, and there's a certain urgency and you have to use methods such as the famous shaking and things like that to wake up the interrogee and cause him to confess more quickly, and they had whole arguments about that. Today, in the Security Service, to slap someone you need authorization from the head of the Service.

And all the external testimony of torture?

Look, in the system I was a part of for almost thirty years, I knew tens of thousands of interrogees, and there isn't one who didn't complain to the Red Cross that he was tortured till he expired. Even when not only did no one touch him, but that immediately upon his arrival, they brought him a bouquet of flowers, two cups of coffee, and packs of cigarettes to smoke and enjoy. Since the first thing in any interrogee's DNA is that he has to justify why he confessed. And the best excuse is, "They tortured me till I stopped breathing." That's something that's completely clear.

There are complaints by interrogees that they weren't allowed to sleep, and complaints that they weren't allowed to urinate, and I assume that some of them are also true. I'm not naïve, and I don't cover my eyes with some sort of mask. It's true that with some methods there are very thin lines, which sometimes also get blurred, between what the Palestinian sees as physical torture, and what we see as a method enhancing the interrogation. Look, I think laying someone under a table with their hands tied reaches the level of physical torture. I'm not playing it down or trying to prettify things. I think sleep deprivation is also something in the physical realm, but, ultimately, the damage that can be caused by it physically to the body is lower, is controlled.

In addition, the role of the Red Cross and the role of the international system is to condemn the Israeli occupation. This is a whole, very sophisticated system. I once called its activists "bleeding hearts." Today, when I'm on the outside, I understand that some of those people do it out of genuine belief, out of a wish to help Palestinian society and to help in resolving the conflict, and I don't make light of that. But part of this apparatus is a system which has no relation whatsoever to the facts, while another part or a minority of this system publishes some facts which are true and worthy of attention. I read the reports by Amnesty and by the Human Rights Committee in Geneva on a regular basis. Part of what's said there has a legitimate basis, part of it is assessments built on limited facts, and part is just lies and built-in libel.

The Israeli or Palestinian organizations that deal with the subject—the Public Committee Against Torture in Israel, "B'Tselem" organization, and other forms of wildlife—are institutions trying to do their job. I have to say, and you can't suspect me of being objective on this subject, that some of them are a lot more than bleeding hearts. Some of these people completely ignore Israel's security situation, and the fact that you're dealing with terrorists who kill or aim to kill innocent people, kids riding the bus. With all the existing criticism about this method or a different method used, I have yet to see the state of Israel use methods like that.

If [left-leaning Ha'aretz columnist] Gideon Levi thinks there's room for comparison between the tractor attack in Jerusalem, where a terrorist seats himself in a bulldozer and injures and even kills Jews with forethought and intention, and the tractors of the Israeli occupation, which since 1967 have been destroying the West Bank, I think he's acting demagogically and not dealing with the matter at hand. On the other hand, when he writes about the distress of a Palestinian family which can't get to Tel Hashomer Hospital, or that there's an injustice or a wrong that the Israeli regime causes to a particular family or to a specific person, sometimes I even sympathize, but, generally speaking, those organizations should do their jobs. In a democratic country, everyone's allowed to express their opinion, and it's good that everyone feels free to do it. The Service has to carry out its job faithfully, and they should carry out their jobs faithfully, and ultimately, everyone will be content with their mission.

Avraham Shalom: In interrogations, you have to decide if you want to live in the West or in the East. In the Netherlands, when a suspect doesn't confess, the interrogator leaves the room and comes back after about a week and says the same thing, and comes back again after a week, and it goes on like that for a year. Over here, we slap him on the cheek and he talks; that's the whole difference. To slap him on the cheek takes five minutes, and to get the Netherlands answer, you need a year or two. And then one of them explodes and dies and they're all over you. Why? Because you didn't hit him and prevent a terrorist attack by doing it. So that's the dilemma.

I remember that I, as head of the Service, canceled most of the authorizations. When I was deputy director, Ahituv wouldn't let me touch the Arab realm, but one day they took me to the jail in Hebron.

I went into one interrogation room, and there was an Arab there who looked old to me. He was fifty-five then, the Arab, but he looked a lot older. And our guy, who spoke Arabic, yelled at him, "Why are you lying!" And this Arab was shriveled up, old, pathetic, and I started to feel sorry for him. I asked, "Why's he yelling at him?" And finally the interrogator took a chair, broke the chair on the floor, took the chair leg, and broke his hand. He said, "Place your hand on the table," and broke all his fingers. I went immediately to the head of the Service, and I have to say I was appalled, I got all green. I was head of the operations branch then. Yosef Harmelin was the head of the Service, and I considered him a "goodie two-shoes." I told him, "Listen, you allow that kind of thing? You know about this?!" He looked at me with Buddha eyes. Didn't say a word. I said, "Listen, stop it. You can't authorize that. You're just turning our guys into killers!" So he says to me, "You must be wrong." I'm not wrong. Politically, he wanted to tell me that I was wrong so that it wouldn't be documented. And then I understood that he was a coward, too. But I could see that the interrogators' cruelty was completely excessive.

I once saw an interrogator kill an Arab. Not by beating him. He was throwing him from wall to wall, from wall to wall, from wall to wall. I was in Operations, and I said, "Guys, you're breaking his head!" So he grabbed his head and almost broke the wall with this Arab's head. And I said, "Stop it," and Yehuda Arbel stopped it. They're both dead. Both Yehuda Arbel and the guy supposedly conducting the interrogation. He wasn't conducting an interrogation, he just hit him so he'd talk. A week later, the Arab died from a brain hemorrhage. It got covered up. So Bus 300 is nothing in comparison with these things. And this was a vegetarian head of Service who has a street named after him in Tzahala. Harmelin.* Everybody did it. It's impossible that I go into a room and they're breaking some guy's fingers there, and go into another room—maybe a year later—and they're breaking somebody's head and he dies later. It got covered up. You won't find mention of it. I remember which village he was from.

Avraham Shalom told me that he personally witnessed torture, beatings, hands being broken, even death.

---

* A neighborhood in northeast Tel Aviv, initially designed to house army and security personnel.

Ya'akov Peri: I didn't. Look, the fact that there were irregularities . . . Listen, when you're interrogating the killers of an Israeli couple, and you catch them forty-eight hours later, their impudence can't leave anyone indifferent. So there were interrogators who were more hot-headed, and interrogators who were less hot-headed, but all in all, if you look at the big picture, this business was generally conducted by the book and according to instructions. Not that there weren't deviations here and there, not that there weren't mishaps here and there, and interrogators have paid the price, interrogators were relieved of their duties and investigative committees were formed and things like that, I assume there were irregularities here and there.

And trials-within-a-trial due to confessions given under pressure of physical torture?

That was mainly before Landau. I'm telling you the percentage of false confessions in which people confessed to things they didn't do is minimal, if it exists. It almost never happened.

How do you know?

You've got proof for everything. When a person comes and says, "There's a weapon arsenal here," or when you prevented that terrorist attack, or when you caught organizations in progress. These aren't confessions of a person regarding himself, but of networks, recruitments. You have tools to assess whether the confession is true or not. When a person confesses only in regard to himself, then you can say maybe he also took upon himself things he didn't do. But in ninety percent of the cases, there's proof regarding these confessions. So you have a basis for checking how many false confessions happened. And the percent of false confessions in the Service in my time, and I believe that after my time as well, was close to zero. Close to zero doesn't mean zero. Ultimately, the media always deals with cases where the irregularities and the divergences happened, and the state attorney does the same thing.

So why was there uproar?

Because this is a democratic country, and within it, there are a lot of fighters for human rights, who, on some level, guard human rights and guard moral standards. Which is just fine. I've got nothing against it. But the Service had contact with that sector of Israeli society with the most despicable murderers, the terrorists. You're dealing with this scum. . . . By the way, it also happened in the Jewish sector. The minute the Jewish department was established in the Shin Bet, then all those Arab haters who to this day want to banish them off the face of the earth started complaining about Service interrogations, that they weren't conducted in a way that was—how do they say it—liberal enough, legal, things like that. In both cases, it wasn't entirely accurate.

Avi Dichter: Interrogations with displays of aggressive force, not always in a controlled way, not always in a systematic way, not always in an approved way, that was good for the era of the '60s and the '70s, but we in the Service didn't read the map correctly. We thought the '60s and the '70s continued into the '80s and the '90s. We got clobbered with Bus 300. We got clobbered later with the case of Khalid Sheikh Ali, who died in an interrogation. He was a member of the Islamic Jihad. He was interrogated following a terrorist attack in which four soldiers were killed in Gaza, and died during the interrogation as a result of being beaten, and the people who interrogated him were sentenced to six months in prison. That was in Peri's term.

This was a chain of things that began back in the '70s, with false testimonies in trials-within-trials of interrogees, conducted around an interrogee's complaint that he was subject to illegal measures. And then in the '70s you'd go to a trial-within-a-trial, and the interrogee would say, "They beat me," and the interrogator would come and say, "He wasn't beaten." Everyone knew it was a lie, that the interrogator was lying. The military prosecutor knew he was lying, because he knew he was being manipulated, the judge knew he was being lied to, and it was a kind of closed-circuit game. Everyone knew the testimony was perjury and the man had been beaten up during the interrogation. But you know, they went on like that. When this story of perjury in trials-within-trials blew up, of course the judges said, "We weren't aware of that." The prosecution said, "We didn't know they were giving false testimony!" And ultimately the Service man is the one who has to do the work. He perjures himself. It was convenient for everyone to run away at the last minute. That was also the Bus 300 affair, with coordination of testimony and false testimony to the committee. A general security service can't work within a framework of lies. Period. No matter for what purpose. You can't take a Service employee and tell him, "Lie to the committee, and tell the Service director the truth." There's no such animal.

Ya'akov Peri: Avi Dichter and everyone else are over-simplifying the matter. If I could come out and say, "Listen, there was a period when a culture of lies ruled the Service," it would be relatively easy. That really wasn't the case. It's not that interrogators were sent to lie in court, but there were things that the Service internalized, unjustly, by the way. It's a kind of culture that formed over years. Because until the Landau Commission, the whole subject of interrogations in the Service was a separate, closed-off territory. No one came in, no one went out. And I know interrogators were never instructed from above to lie in court. But there were some things they didn't disclose, and not always awful things. Ultimately, the Landau Commission took all the testimony and compared it to the actual cases, and the question asked was, you, the man who was deprived of sleep for three days, came to court and didn't say anything for three days. . . . You can't over-simplify that, call it a "culture of lies," but the truth also wasn't stated sincerely, precisely, purely, like a Service man is expected to state it. We've actually thrown people out of the Service for simpler things. When a person cheated on his living expenses by a hundred lira [the Israeli currency preceding the shekel], he'd be thrown out of the Service immediately and with no compensation! Even in my era, I threw out people who were inaccurate in reporting their hours and exaggerated, for example. I threw them out of the Service with no compensation, after years of service. So the discrepancy is between that, between maintaining truth and accuracy and sincerity and purity and humility, and between going to court and not telling the honorable judge, "This and that happened, from A to Z. . . ."

The judges also say, "We knew the interrogators were lying." The prosecutors knew they were lying.

Listen, the excuse of national security and the sacred work done here is effective with everyone, except the state attorney. Everyone understands that you're dealing with slightly different material here. It's not the neighborhood thief.

So you come and see that you're lying and the judge is also lying and so is the prosecutor, and the effect of all this filters in, and then nothing happens to you, either. Does it change something in you? Does it affect your personality, the fact that you did something you weren't supposed to do and got away with it?

You're amplifying the story to a large extent. It's true that it received a lot of momentum with the Landau Commission, but it wasn't such a significant event. It wasn't a whole system that went to lie in court. It wasn't like that, it really wasn't. There was a series of trials-within-trials in which interrogators didn't tell the whole truth. You can call it lying. That's okay. But it wasn't a system. . . . There wasn't a battery of attorneys and interrogation experts sitting in the Service and telling the interrogator, "Don't mention that statement." The occurrences were a natural consequence of the way the Service was managed. And I'm not saying the Service was managed well. It's not right. But security needs overshadowed the need to be completely transparent, real. It's an atmosphere, and you're amplifying it in a way that I think is exaggerated. The media blew it up and called it "perjury." It wasn't perjury, but let's put it like this: some of the testimonies didn't state the whole truth.

Ami Ayalon: I can't break a law in the State of Israel because I'm a member of the Shin Bet. In the '80s, when Shin Bet employees gave false testimony under oath in courts, and violated the law in the State of Israel, they didn't understand this simple thing, that there's no law you can violate in order to attain the Service's goals. Not only did they not understand it, but the state attorney didn't understand it and the cabinet didn't understand it and the prime minister didn't understand it. This was the reality of a different State of Israel.

When the state attorney's people came to Shimon Peres during the Bus 300 affair, he said, "The Shin Bet should be subject to different laws."

Ayalon: That's legitimate. So legislate them. That's exactly it. But you don't even have the courage to pass a law. It's very easy to come and say, "The Shin Bet should operate under a different set of laws" without legislating the law. There were cases where Service interrogators served prison time because they failed at what's permitted and what's prohibited during an interrogation. The people who should be serving time, if anyone should, are not only them, but more senior people. But that's a discussion that didn't really take place in the General Security Service. Shin Bet interrogators served time in prison because they violated Service procedures. . . .

A man was killed with punches.

They didn't kill a man with punches. He left the interrogation facility alive. But he apparently died because of the interrogations he underwent. No one knows which one of the blows he received killed him, so when you decide that these two are going to prison and not the whole team and not the head of the team, you're actually saying—these two will pay the price for the whole Service.

Ya'akov Peri: There was a time, before the '70s, when behavior in interrogation rooms was less formal and less based on an authorization system. Following countless conflicts between the Service and law enforcement elements, especially the state attorney, due to the treatment interrogees received from the Service, the Landau Commission was finally established in '84 or '85. It was a state investigative committee headed by the retired president of the Superior Court, Justice Landau, and I prepared the material on behalf of the Service for the committee. I can say unequivocally that there were indeed irregularities. These irregularities were publicized and they were all handled, even at the level of prosecuting interrogators and having them serve prison time. But these are isolated incidents. In testing results, the percentage of true confessions in General Security Service interrogations is among the highest in the world. When I say true confessions, it's not that I confessed to killing Kennedy because I was beaten or tortured.

And all the claims in the report about torture that the Service employs?

There wasn't actual torture. There was a regulation board of what was permitted and what was prohibited. If, for example, sleep deprivation was permitted, forty-eight hours later you needed to receive authorization for another ten hours, another twelve hours, and if authorization wasn't granted, they'd still extend the sleep deprivation to a lot more than the permitted time, and violate regulations. It was regulated, but was not dealt with in a regulated manner.

But there was torture?

No.

So what's with the Izat Nafsu affair?

In the Izat Nafsu affair, I wasn't the head of the Service. I was head of the northern district at the time, and the investigation was then an investigation by the National Investigation Division. Nafsu was an IDF officer in the south Lebanon area, a Circassian officer from Kfar Kama, and we received intelligence about his connections with Fatah. He was arrested for interrogation, and there was a very, very convoluted interrogation, conducted by Yossi Ginossar. There wasn't actual torture, but more psychological methods. The man had all sorts of problems, and Ginossar was playing on his psychological issues there. He brought him a psychologist and all kinds of stories like that, and tried to get the man to open up one way or another. I don't remember physical torture in regard to Nafsu.

He wasn't allowed to sleep for a long time, he was cuffed.

Sleep deprivation, cuffs, head covers, these things are methods that the Landau Commission agreed were not problematic, if done in moderation, in cases that concern "life and death." The term "moderate physical pressure" became prevalent at that time, and moderate physical pressure doesn't mean you take a person, beat him to within an inch of his life or something like that, but when you deprive him of sleep for a really long time, you seat him cuffed and with the head cover, and you isolate him that way. There were media stories at the time that in the interrogation rooms they'd play classical music; those are legends, it doesn't matter. If the interrogators had, what's the term, classical music CDs, then they wouldn't have been interrogators. . . .

But it's very oppressive. Listen, you're under mental stress, and they won't let you sleep, and you're cuffed and so on, and then there was the whole subject of shaking, they wrote that an interrogator can hold the interrogee by both shoulders and shake him to demonstrate authority or something like that. With Izat Nafsu, I believe the problem wasn't so much actual torture, but the effect of those methods, which finally brought about a false confession, according to his lawyers' claims.

What do you mean, "according to his lawyers' claims"? The court accepted it.

No. There's one section for which the court did convict him, but in regard to all kinds of stories he told about transporting weapons from southern Lebanon, it was determined that these were things that were forced out of him, and it was a false confession, so the court decided to free him. They did discipline him in some way. There was a conviction, but the conviction got swallowed up. . . .

Did it have immense meaning, as far as the Service was concerned?

Yes, Izat Nafsu created an earthquake in the interrogators' branch.

In what sense? This is already the period in which you were head of the Service, right? What were the consequences?

The consequences were that the interrogators' branch took care to follow the authorization system. For example, you couldn't slap without authorization from the head of the Service. And I remember I'd sometimes go to the prime minister and I'd tell him, "This month we gave two slaps." That was fun. It became absurd.

You told that to Rabin?

No, to Shamir. He'd look at me like I was. . . .

"This month we gave two slaps"?

Yes. We got into insane meticulousness, and then a detainee in Jenin died on us, and the person who I'd designated to be head of the Interrogation Division, I sent him home. Not because of the torture, but because he didn't tell the whole truth. I threw him out of the Service, and he was an excellent person. There was total hysteria then about sticking to procedures, and there were massive quantities of detainees. It was the beginning of the Intifada, and we were dealing with the question of whether someone had or hadn't deprived him of sleep for thirty-two hours. . . . It was something else. It neutralized the Interrogation Division for two or three years, but got us on a course which I believe works well to this day. It was a major shake-up.

Landau, even if it wasn't official, functioned as a follow-up committee. He'd call up the prime minister every time and tell him, "The Service is doing okay," or, "The Service isn't okay. . . ." especially to Dan Meridor, who would go to Prime Minister Shamir and report to him immediately. There were all kinds of mishaps, of course. There was an awful mishap in Gaza. Two interrogators punched an interrogee, who ultimately hemorrhaged and died. None of the interrogators wanted to reveal who was responsible for the punching. So one night I summoned the whole interrogation crew to me, and said, "You're endangering the entire Service. You'll ruin this organization. Get out of my room, go to the parking lot, and come back to me with an answer: who were the interrogators responsible for the punching?" They came back to me with the two names. I called Dorit Beinisch at 2 a.m. and she told me, "Go to the head of the Interrogation Department in the Central District." The two interrogators were sentenced to a year in prison, something like that.

This is the story of Khaled Sheikh Ali, which caused the tension between you and Dorit Beinisch.

Yes. But there was always tension between me and Dorit Beinisch.

Why?

Because they played the bleeding hearts, the holier-than-thou. The Service's claim had always been that we work in the gutter. "You prevent terrorist attacks, and we'll sit in the Ministry of Justice. . . ." On the one hand, you have to supply the merchandise, prevent terrorist attacks, expose hazards—and we're talking about the Intifada period. There were dozens if not hundreds of detainees a day. The work is intensive, twenty-four hours a day, and judges and attorneys are coming at you, and each of them is dictating his own proedures by the book, while sitting in an office. It's a very intense conflict. There's a lot of resentment—you resent them and they resent you. And as head of the Service, you have to a) make sure the machine functions, and b) work according to state laws and not violate them. It was a rough period, but, eventually, it benefited the Service. Landau, too, in retrospect, which was like the parting of the Red Sea while it was going on. Listen, it shakes up the Service.

Were you an interrogator?

No. I interrogated, but I was never an interrogator.

So tell me about that tension that's really at the heart of the Service's work, between the need to catch killers and the limitations on interrogations.

The interrogator is sometimes in an impossible situation, because he receives, based on intelligence collected for the investigation, people to whom sometimes really heinous crimes are attributed. Some of them sit down in the room and say, "Give me some paper, I'll write down the whole story for you," and some of them sit down and say, "I don't know what you're talking about." And between this kind and that kind there's an enormous range of interrogee behavior, but here you're really dealing with child killers and killers of innocent people, and people who plant bombs on buses and kill, actually slaughter, Israeli couples who went to make out a little in the woods.

Now, the interrogator's alone with the interrogee in the interrogation room. On the one hand, he has all the limitations that the Service places upon him. On the other hand, he has an interrogee who isn't confessing of his own free will, and, additionally, he has to ensure that the interrogation or the results of the interrogation will be true results. He wants to expose the cell, create true prevention, and obviously you can't have someone confessing to killing Kennedy without having killed him. It's not a simple story. Now, for anything that's done in interrogation rooms, ultimately there's someone in the media or at this or that organization, or, to make a very clear distinction, in the state attorney's office, who's sitting and searching, not maliciously, to see where the Service went wrong, or where the Service distorted or where the Service didn't precisely follow the rules.

The pressure on the Service, generally speaking, when there's a period of terrorist attacks or disorder, isn't applied by the political echelon. The political echelon isn't saying, "Listen, why are there so many terrorist attacks?" But there's internal pressure on the Service. I always tell my subordinates that I see every terrorist attack as a failure by the Service. Every explosion, every grenade, every Molotov cocktail is a failure of the Service, which didn't succeed in preventing it in advance. Now that's the attitude in the Service, and that's a good thing. That's why the organization is so top-notch and successful. Listen, all in all, the Service has succeeded in decreasing the waves of terror dramatically. If the Service didn't exist, the political echelon couldn't reach any decision in the State of Israel, on almost any topic. The Service, since it first existed and to this day, enables the political echelon to run a normal state. There could have been a bloodbath here, or total anarchy. Not just in regard to the Palestinians. In any realm related to preserving the state's security. There's no lack of all kinds of anarchists here. . . .

So the Service is constantly under the sort of pressure that can be called positive tension, but this positive tension creates pressure on the interrogator. Now shift to the perspective of an interrogator alone in the interrogation room, at 2 a.m., and usually you're dealing with young people here. This one just had a child three months ago, and he has to focus on his mission 100 percent, and his wife called an hour ago and said, "The kid's not sleeping, just not sleeping." Or his head of department just called and told him, "Hell, you've been sitting on this for four days, what's going on here?" Things aren't simple, and then, unfortunately, all kinds of incidents can happen, including extreme ones, where he suddenly says, "I'll take your head and stick it in a bucket." Maybe you can understand why it happens. You can't justify it, you can't allow it, you have to deal with it immediately.

What are you personally going through when you hear about the death of Khaled Sheikh Ali?

First of all, you get very angry, because you understand you're now facing a period of hostile media and arguments with the state attorney. Your first step is to find out what happened there and fix it immediately and make sure it doesn't happen again. Suddenly you have an irregular event that attracts all the attention, and it doesn't matter what the Service does and what the Service has achieved and how many terrorist attacks the Service has prevented and foiled. It's all eclipsed, as if it never happened. The whole world's dealing with the fact that the Service killed some detainee.

When confronted with the Khaled Sheikh Ali case, you say, "I have fires to put out now."

It's not just putting out fires. It's tackling the roots of the problem. It's finding out what happened, who did it, dealing with those people. Facing the state attorney's office and explaining, and you also can't abandon your people. You're a commander, you can't. . . . Something happened to these people while they were fighting a battle in the interrogation room. Not like fighting [a battle] in the Yom Kippur War, but still fighting a battle. . . .

But ultimately they served time in prison.

Of course, I wouldn't compromise. They went to prison because I thought it was also right for the Service to deal with this all the way.

What do the interrogators tell you when they come to you?

They tell me what happened there. I don't exactly remember the details. Someone punched him in the stomach, and then he didn't feel well, and they didn't report it, and then did report it . . . the usual stuff. It was a tragedy with those two guys. A real tragedy. One of them was previously in VIP Protection with Arik Sharon. Arik would invite me over and say to me, "What happened to you, why are you prosecuting them?"

But it wasn't up to you, right? It was the state attorney.

It wasn't up to me, but I could have also "engineered" the story differently. I decided to expose it after those two came and confessed to me. I could have gone there and said I was going to sleep on it and in the morning "we'll see what we can do." That's not what I did, and I'm glad I didn't. I think it contributed to the Service's health.

You said that as a commander, you couldn't abandon. . . .

That's not abandoning. Ultimately, people violated the law, and they knew they'd violated the law. The fact was, they didn't come tell me on their own. This was after the Service had been pummeled from every direction on subjects like these. If you want to continue operating an interrogation branch, and you want to continue operating a Service that's healthy and legal and pure, you have to pay the price. That's the bottom line. These aren't easy leadership decisions, and sometimes you have to make the call. I think if I hadn't acted the way I had, I'd have harmed the Service more than I helped it. So the fact that people paid the price . . . that's not exactly like leaving them behind in combat. After Landau and after all the stories, after everything we've been through, it was unacceptable that an interrogator could come and take the law into his hands, even if he was pissed off and even if the guy was a son of a bitch. You have to make a decision that has implications, and you have to stand by it.

And what was the reaction?

They didn't like my decision in the Service, but they knew to accept it, like the Service knows how to accept things.

Ami Ayalon: Shin Bet investigators weren't born with the genetics of people who like to produce suffering. That's far from true. It's not that a Shin Bet interrogator goes into an interrogation room and starts throwing a fit. Do you know that a Shin Bet interrogator, if an interrogee spits at him, has to leave the room, think, count to ten, and only then come back? And if he wants to slap him in return, he has to pick up the phone and receive authorization at least from the head of a branch. Now it's true, Shin Bet interrogees were slapped. But these aren't things done in the heat of anger. These aren't things that were done in my time. During my era, no Shin Bet interrogee was killed, and no one went to the hospital. But the question was, what can we do in interrogations to obtain intelligence to thwart or neutralize a ticking bomb, meaning a terrorist who we know is about to carry out an attack?

Avi Dichter: Sometimes you're forced to take dramatic shortcuts. There was a case in Petach Tikva. We received unequivocal information, sometime around 2 a.m., that a terrorist from Nablus was in central Israel, and was supposed to place an explosive device in a bus station. The device was supposed to be activated by cell phone from Nablus when the buses start running. Now, you begin your work with that, go out there, look for someone who fits the profile who's out and about at those hours. There aren't a lot of people out on the streets. Some time around 4 a.m., we arrest the man who, according to the information, placed the explosive charge. The buses start running at six in the morning, and now you have to find out at which station he placed the charge. Between four and six in the morning, that's the time you have to deal with the interrogee. You have to get to a point where you take the man, define him as an "interrogee under necessity protection," which, in common speech is a "ticking bomb," and allow the interrogators to conduct the interrogation in a slightly more aggressive way. Slightly. You don't hang him with his feet up and his head down, but interrogate him in a slightly more aggressive way, to get to a point where he gives up the location of the bomb. And there's no term that ticks as urgently as this ticking bomb.

If the interrogee comes to you and says, "Listen, I was wrong, I've sinned and transgressed, the explosive device is at this and that location. . . ." that's fine, but unfortunately, that's not the situation. He knows that if he hangs in there for two hours, the device will be activated, and he'll look very good to his handlers. He's going to be charged with planting the charge anyway. So he starts to play games with you. He doesn't reveal the place where the device was planted. You think he should be interrogated with kisses? Go ahead, interrogate him with kisses. As an interrogator, your role is to save lives. There's no difference between that interrogator and the person who sees someone holding a gun to your head and planning to shoot you. He's entitled to shoot the man who's about to shoot you.

At this stage, a very specific set of methods is introduced into the interrogation. A special, approved set, presented to the state attorney general, presented to the Foreign Affairs and Defense Committee. The Service director is the only one permitted to authorize use of methods as a part of necessity protection. For any interrogee. That authority is limited to the Service director only.

Let me into an interrogation like that.

Dichter: Look, I don't want to go into specific measures, but it's a set that's supposed to apply deterrence measures upon the person, because he doesn't know exactly how far your set of measures can extend. He understands that the nature of the interrogation is changing. In most cases, by the way, when the interrogation begins, the interrogee understands that it's a different interrogation, and they usually already open up at this stage. Usually, not always.

In this case, I think that within an hour into the interrogation, they started to utilize some physical measures, not significant ones, not dramatic ones, but some physical measures. The interrogee understood that this wasn't going to be the usual sort of game, and did lead them to the explosive device half an hour before the buses started running, and lives were saved that way. I can't even say how many. There are cases where they employed these methods and didn't obtain the information. It's only a few cases, but the interrogees kept their mouths shut.

In a case like this, do you request authorization from the attorney general in advance?

No. I don't request authorization from the attorney general to employ these measures. I inform them retroactively. There's a periodic report. You come to the attorney general and tell him, "In the previous three months, special measures were employed against twenty interrogees as a part of necessity protection. Following is the specification. . . ." What the reasons were, which measures were employed, how much it advanced the investigation, a proper professional discussion. Sometimes you pinch yourself to remind yourself you're in a meeting on thwarting terror, it looks like a yoga class sometimes.

Why?

Because you have to sit there and describe it. But there's no other choice, those are the rules of the game. I told the people there, "Guys, we have to understand that if we want these measures, we have to display transparency." I'm willing to provide a lot of transparency to get more measures.

Ami Ayalon: Eventually, the High Court of Justice ruled in September '99 that a general security service may not interrogate preventively, and may only conduct a police-type interrogation. But the police investigate to bring people to justice after the crime was committed. A general security service is supposed to operate in an opposite way—to investigate in order to thwart terror. That's why the General Security Service actually constructed a completely different method of interrogation, until the High Court of Justice came and said, in very simple words, "Gentlemen, you want to interrogate using different tools? You want to employ physical pressure? Mental pressure? Enact a law." My central complaint is not against the High Court of Justice. It was entirely clear to me before September that the High Court of Justice was going to reach the ruling it reached. Most of the state attorney people didn't agree with me. But from the day the Basic Laws were enacted in 1992, the Supreme Court has told us for years, "Gentlemen, what was previously permitted, according to the Landau Commission report, i.e., moderate physical pressure, doesn't exist anymore." It's been telling us that in a thousand and one ways, without cementing it in a ruling. And it said, "The only way in which you can continue to try and cope with this reality is to try and enact a law." The State of Israel, all its prime ministers since 1992, all its Shin Bet directors, all the pertinent ministers, the minister of justice, senior personnel in the state attorney's office, come and promise the Supreme Court—we're enacting a law. And the State of Israel doesn't enact a law.

We're brazenly lying to the High Court of Justice. And I've been saying that first to [Benjamin] "Bibi" Netanyahu [prime minister from 1996 to 1999, as well as from 2009 to the present], and then to Ehud Barak [prime minster from 1999 to 2001]—gentlemen, what's going on here? Eventually, the High Court of Justice is going to get it. One day, the High Court of Justice will tell us, "How many times do we have to tell you until you understand? We'll just come and inform you—you're no longer allowed to interrogate with authorizations." Why don't we have the guts to come to the international community and say, "Gentlemen, we have no other way to fight terror, this is what we have to give Shin Bet interrogators as a protection in order to neutralize a ticking bomb?" The State of Israel didn't do it, and the High Court of Justice did the obvious thing. From that moment, the General Security Service stopped employing authorizations. After the High Court of Justice ruling, I can't promise a Shin Bet interrogator protection in advance, every time, God forbid, things go wrong, a person gets hurt, or, God forbid, a person dies in the course of an investigation. So I go through all Shin Bet interrogators, and I tell them, "I promise you only one thing: none of you will go to prison alone. I'll go to prison with any one of you, if and providing that you act according to regulations." That protection they wanted in advance, I can't give it to them. I'm just consoling them that they won't sit in the cell alone. How much of a consolation it is to sit in a cell with me, I'm not sure; maybe it's better to sit alone . . . but that's the most I can do.

Yuval Diskin: In the year between the High Court of Justice ruling on authorizations and the second Intifada, we faced a "ticking bomb situation," as Justice [Aharon] Barak [Israel's former Supreme Court president] defined it, once or twice. One of them was the first time we detained a Hamas activist who we knew was probably holding dozens of kilograms of TNT meant to detonate a car bomb. We got to him after a very complex operation, and we were facing the dilemma, is this a "ticking bomb" or not, and whether we could employ the special measures against him.

Since we had conducted very complex discussions with the state attorney and the attorney general after the High Court of Justice ruling, we asked what happens when an interrogator reaches a "ticking bomb" situation; is he now supposed to employ some special measure to save lives? Would that interrogator face legal charges, and could he be put behind bars? And we didn't get a good enough answer from the attorney general at the time and from the state attorney. I sat with our interrogation directors, with Ami Ayalon, we were in a very intense meeting with the attorney general at the time, Elyakim Rubinstein, and with the state attorney, and we left with unclear answers. And if it turns out that there was a ticking bomb, and, God forbid, something goes wrong, who gets blamed? The interrogator sitting across from the interrogee, or the person who instructed him to handle the situation? Is the responsibility of the senior echelon the determining one, and they bear the responsibility, which is what we thought would be right, or is it the interrogator's responsibility?

There was a harsh argument with Ami Ayalon, who was head of the Service at the time. As far as Ayalon was concerned, it was a hundred percent clear to him that it's the Service director's responsibility. Period. And if anyone bears responsibility, it's only the Service director. We told him that he hadn't convinced us. And then Ayalon calls me the morning after the man was arrested and says to me, "What's happening, are you already interrogating this man as a 'ticking bomb'?" and I tell him, "No." So he tells me, "But I gave the instruction." I told him, "I understood your instruction, but your instruction is inadmissible, as far as I'm concerned, since you can't guarantee with certainty that the interrogator would not bear responsibility for a situation like that." So he says, "But I'm instructing you." So I told him, "You can instruct, but I don't accept the instruction, because I think it's an impossible situation." He said to me, "What are you going to do?" I said, "I'm on my way to the facility and I'll see what the situation is over there, and, if necessary, I and the head of the interrogation department will employ the required measures and take responsibility. But I don't intend to instruct one of my interrogators to do it, and I don't think you can order me to do something like that."

Ami Ayalon understood that it was a complex situation from a leadership, a managerial, and an essential perspective. So he said, "Okay, we'll meet at the interrogation facility." He got in the car, we were all on our way, we got to the interrogation facility, and went into the room of the head of the interrogation team, and an argument broke out there. The ceiling and walls almost blew out from the yelling going on there, everyone yelling at everyone else, and at the same time, the head of the interrogation branch also arrived to take part in this essential discussion. He left for a second and went to the other room in which the interrogee was sitting. Meanwhile we were still yelling and the argument was not decided, of course. Each of us was convinced that he was right, and then he comes in and says, "Guys, what are you screaming about? The man already confessed, everything's okay. We went in, we talked, and he confessed. End of story."

What was the argument about?

Diskin: Whether we would instruct the interrogator to employ what we call "special authorizations" in view of the situation of a "ticking bomb," and who would bear responsibility for the incident, if ultimately the court doesn't accept our judgment and decides that the action was illegal. Would the interrogator actually face the court himself, or would the head of the Service or the head of the district face the court, and be examined in regard to their judgment?

But there's no risk to the interrogee's life.

No.

So what's the fear?

That the interrogee would complain that certain things were done to him, the court would instruct opening an investigation, people would be charged, and finally the guy who's last in the chain of command pays the price.

What are you permitted to do in interrogations today?

They don't authorize us in advance to do anything. It's our judgment that must stand the test retroactively. According to our agreement with the attorney general, every case is reported in great detail, in writing, and later in a face-to-face meeting between us and the attorney general. He examines both the judgment that guided us and our action, the proportionality of it.

Explain to me what's permitted with authorization.

I won't specify.

We've heard of shaking, of cuffing.

There's no shaking.

Try to let me into an interrogation with authorization. What's an interrogation with authorization?

Ami Ayalon: Most of the discussions on this subject focused on shaking. But what went into the "physical pressure basket" was withholding hours of sleep, sitting while cuffed in a painful, humiliating, exhausting position. Things like that. I don't intend to go into a discussion beyond that. Don't waste your time.

Why?

Ayalon: Because. It's not relevant, and that's that.

I wanted to understand from which aspect you don't want to go into it. From the moral perspective of the thing?

Moral debate is always very elusive. What is morality? People don't understand that any one of us, and I'm speaking as a head of Shin Bet and as commander of Shayetet 13 [the Israeli Navy's special forces unit] and as commander of the navy, as someone who's taken part in dozens of operations and fired endless rounds of ammunition and killed in many operations—when we go to sleep at night, we need to go to sleep with everything we carry with us. We need to go to sleep with the fact that we employed pressure on an interrogee which the High Court of Justice thinks is unjustified and inappropriate. But, no less than that, we have to go to sleep with those cases in which we decided not to employ pressure, and as a result Israeli citizens were killed. Any one of us can point out those moments. I'm not sure I'd include them in my memoir, and I probably won't exactly tell you about those moments now, but you know and I know that they exist.

So, if you ask me with which of those I'd rather go to sleep, I'll tell you—if I could erase some moments from my personal history, I'd erase the moments where I didn't do enough, and as a result Israeli citizens died. So if we've decided, if I've decided, that this or that Shin Bet interrogee will suffer more so that we can save Israeli citizens from death, I have no problem with that. I can go to sleep peacefully.

How We Didn't Foresee the First Intifada

"The chief of general staff: The government will be the one to determine when and where IDF will attack the terrorists."

IDF is taking steps to prevent deterioration in the Gaza Strip. Two students from Jabalia refugee camp were killed, and 16 others were injured in demonstrations yesterday.

(The first item on the outbreak of the Intifada,
Yediot Ahronot, December 10, 1987)

Ya'akov Peri: I was appointed to the position of Service director in April 1988, when the First Intifada was about six months old. During this time, the Service was transformed from an institution thwarting targeted terror attacks to an institution which had to thwart what's called disturbers of the peace, who couldn't be termed terrorists in the classic sense of the word. First of all, these are very young people, and the options for dealing with them are limited. We didn't detain kids who were eleven or twelve, and a large part of the rock throwing and the massive disturbances of the peace were carried out by children like that. It became a sort of national pastime, throwing rocks at settler vehicles, at IDF vehicles. The intelligence network changes, too, under these circumstances. You need to recruit and handle live sources that are not from the same cells you dealt with before.

Previously you've described a grand intelligence apparatus that controls almost all aspects of Palestinian life, that knows everything, that manages to control how high the flames go. But the Intifada caught you by complete surprise. How does that happen?

First of all, almost all intelligence organizations worldwide have failed at predicting major historical events. Which major intelligence organization in the world predicted the fall of the Berlin Wall? So to complain today and say, "The Service should have predicted. . . ." In a formal, hypothetical way—yes, that's the expectation. That's why you pay systems, you pay people, you maintain huge information warehouses. That's true. It's possible that if the Security Service had massively expanded its collection efforts, it might have received signals indicating the breakout of the Intifada. But even then, I doubt if we could have received a focused warning that on a certain date a popular uprising would break out. There's no intelligence organization for spontaneous events; no security service in the world can anticipate them.

The First Intifada was a true protest, a street protest, villages protesting, youth protesting. Against the occupation, against the fact that we're under an occupier, under a foreign regime. And no one's coming to save us, and maybe we'll take the stick we're holding and try to chase off, in quotation marks or without quotation marks, the Israeli regime. A people rises and tries to start a revolution. What's a revolution? Running us off. Which also has positive aspects. It's an indication of maturity, of maturation. You ask yourself, where did I go wrong? Where did I go wrong, not in the very fact of ruling there, but should I have let this happen, or should I already have not been there before they told me—go away? But these are questions that are more philosophical than practical.

The great majority of the uprising originated in educational institutions, including universities, which the state of Israel encouraged, wanting to improve basic and higher education in the West Bank. An-Najah University in Nablus and the Islamic University in Hebron and Al-Azhar University in Gaza eventually became centers of resistance bearing the First Intifada on their backs, and later terror cells also originated there. There's a large peer group of young men and women emerging, who, on the one hand, want to abolish the Israeli army and establish their own state, and on the other hand, there's no element directing them. No one directed it, not the PLO and not the State of Israel.

Every initiative like that, every volunteer activity, every youth organization, whether it's by a terrorist organization or by the village or by a charity organization or by the water society or what have you, became a sack or a bag of explosives. And over the years, lots of sacks of explosives became stacked up in the same room. All that was needed was a detonator. The First Intifada was the detonator that blew up that room with all the sacks full of explosives. Because it was a spontaneous uprising. It was disturbances of the peace. And a people's uprising lives up to its name. The PLO was just as surprised by it as the State of Israel, IDF, and certain parts of the Service. In retrospect, by taking the correct steps, we could have postponed the outbreak of the Intifada, but it would have broken out. If not at the end of 1987, it would have happened in the middle of 1988. If not then, then half a year later. Because the potential was there, the sacks were stacked up and just waiting for the detonator.

When you say, "There's a room with lots of sacks of explosives," how did we not see that?

We saw the explosives all along, but there wasn't anyone who could dismantle those sacks, since your hands are tied. Here and there you can dismantle some society or some volunteer organization, but all in all, the law isn't on your side. If a group of young people comes together in an Arab village in Samaria and sets out to clean the mosque, clear up access roads to the village, help the residents pick their olives, what can you do? And these are the youths who carried the First Intifada on their backs.

During these years, we had thousands of terrorist attacks, if not tens of thousands—from throwing rocks, through Molotov cocktails, blocking roads, knifing, and up to shooting attacks, which were the smaller portion. A new era in the relationship between the State of Israel and its security system and the Palestinian population was initiated. IDF needed to construct a different kind of activity for itself, and, actually, significant parts of IDF as a whole were transformed into a security police. There were periods, particularly in the early '90s, when the amount of fugitives the Security Service was searching for might have been the largest amount any intelligence organization in the world has ever dealt with. Dozens, in every area. Hundreds in every area. Thousands.

Avi Dichter: A wave of mass events on a scale we really hadn't seen previously erupted. Hundreds and thousands marching and being blocked only by live fire. At the time rubber bullets and other things really weren't an option. The whole development of means of dispersing rallies and no-kill weapons came later. Only fire stopped them from attacking the regime headquarters in Khan Yunis, from storming in the direction of Gush Katif.* The amount of casualties

---

* A bloc of twenty-one Israeli settlements in the southern Gaza Strip, evacuated in August 2005 as part of Israel's disengagement from the Gaza Strip.

was an actual generator that pushed more and more people into the Intifada's sphere. It started in Gaza, and later developed in the West Bank. The number of casualties just created a wheel that became unstoppable.

And you, the people in the field, didn't foresee it.

Dichter: I think that any institution, any state, has to understand that there are processes that you can't read. You don't have the tools to read them in advance. Definitely not on this scale. I think the Soviet Union couldn't predict its own dismantlement, and Germany couldn't predict what happened there. I think we couldn't predict in advance the First Intifada and the Second Intifada in the version in which they developed and grew to such awful proportions.

Carmi Gillon: We have to be more humble. Shimon Peres said, and he's right about this, that the intelligence service didn't predict the revolution in the Soviet Union, and the intelligence service didn't predict the revolution in Iran. A lot of things. Why? These are political processes, public processes, they don't take place in the dark, they happen in sunlight. The ones with the best intelligence are politicians, or journalists. A serious journalist covering, say, Iran for years, who has sources within the parties there, he could tell you what the trend was.

But you're also supposed to collect and identify public sentiments. The Intifada broke out on a background of people being fed up with the occupation which, supposedly, could have been identified.

Avi Dichter: No. The "No More Occupation" sentiment existed before this as well. In '79, when the peace treaty with Egypt was signed, one of the items dealt with autonomy in Gaza, and the Gazians were very preoccupied with it. Fatah brought in a lot of weapons, intending to get organized in time for '82, when the peace treaty would be in effect. They wanted to take control of the Strip. Sheikh Yassin* started organizing Hamas, then still called Mujama al-Islamiya, as an alternative or opposition to Fatah. There was terri-

* Sheikh Ahmed Yassin was a founder and leader of Hamas, killed in an Israeli attack in 2004.

ble frustration there about the fact that autonomy was not going to happen, and it didn't transform into an Intifada. That's why you can't put together all the public sentiments and say, "We're heading for an Intifada."

But do you identify the other side as a people? Do you suddenly see that there's a people that's starting to rise to its feet?

Dichter: Look, I don't think the test of a people is whether it's willing to swarm en masse and throw rocks to let out its anger. I think that, to me, they were a people before this. They're not some shrinking violet.

What's the meaning of the First Intifada, as far as the Service is concerned? What does it cause? I'll read you what journalists Ze'ev Schiff and Ehud Ya'ari wrote: "In only one month, Israel lost its control over the Palestinian population. The tools of the occupation were broken. The habits of submission and obedient resignation to the regime's arbitrariness melted in the atmosphere of rebellion. It was a sharp psychological reversal by a collective. IDF stood helpless before this unfamiliar phenomenon. In late 1989, the Shin Bet's intelligence network disintegrated, and its entire method of operating within the occupied territories effectively collapsed. The population was more wary of the rebels than of the Israelis. Cooperation with the regime ceased, and the Shin Bet's sources of information, which enabled Israel to easily manage the occupation, ran dry."

Dichter: Look, I think there's a baseless exaggeration here with no basis in reality. What does "ran dry" mean? I remember prevention actions on an unprecedented scale taking place in the years up to the Oslo Accord and after the Oslo Accord. Arrests of 150 to 250 people in an operation throughout the Strip. And listen, we weren't getting lists of names from the Red Cross. So talking in terms of sources of information running dry, that has no basis in reality. However, a population shedding its almost blind obedience is definitely the most significant indicator. The era where you could drive through Gaza or the West Bank in a vehicle with just one other guy as your security backup was over. It disappeared off the face of the earth.

Ya'akov Peri: I know of many crossroads since 1967 when, in my opinion—and that was more or less my opinion even back then—we should have signed an agreement and run out of there, gotten out of there. We've been sitting there too many years, and the first uprising actually happened not long after we went in. From 1967 till 1987, that's exactly twenty years, which is the time span of a generation. A generation born into the Six Day War, which grew up, was educated, and those are the fourteen-, fifteen-, sixteen-, seventeen-, eighteen-, twenty-year-old youths who bore the First Intifada on their backs. And this generation is a generation we raised. And I think we shouldn't have raised that generation, certainly not to bring it to maturity.

This period where we've been occupying the Territories, to this very day, is not something that's benefited the State of Israel. And I'm not just talking about buses being blown up or suicide attacks or rock throwing or multiple people injured. I think that ultimately we attained a brilliant victory in 1967. We should have kept those parts, such as Jerusalem, that I assume there's more consensus over, and we should have pulled out of all the other territories relatively quickly, within a year, two years, three, four. And there were opportunities. The first years were opportunities to return it to Jordan. Because Jordan still hadn't disclaimed all responsibility for the West Bank. We had a much larger problem with Gaza, because there were no buyers for Gaza, and there aren't any buyers today. But with the West Bank, we could have come to an agreement with King Hussein. We didn't do it when [Moshe] Dayan was minister of defense, and I think one or two years after the Six Day War, he had a golden opportunity to do it with the Jordanians. We didn't do it before the Intifada when the Palestinians were signaling to us that they were ready on some level to rejoin Jordan, as part of a Confederation offer. And some of the Palestinians, who were then on the level of mayors, actually took the political burden on themselves and said they were willing to sit and discuss it. Those are the historical missed opportunities.

Can you describe the change in your opinions from the moment you start to get exposed to the Palestinians, the Arabs, and until the end of your term?

Peri: I think that with me, it's the result of a process. I can't claim I was a perfect "Arabist" when I got to the Service and to the Territories in 1966. Over the years, I got to know them very intimately, from all angles and all corners. Those on the outside and those on the inside. The bad ones and the good ones. There's definitely development.

There's learning that happens over time, and wonder at the mistakes they make and the misguided things they do. But once you develop and get to the senior levels, and become a part of the Israeli political establishment—not as a politician, but at a head of the Service who takes part in all government and cabinet meetings and is subordinate to the prime minister—you see how this country operates, start to make comparisons, and start to get perspective on both sides. And then you also get your fair share of disappointments.

Where did this happen to you for the first time?

I think it happened for the first time when I was appointed in 1980 as commander of the West Bank district. I started to get exposed in a massive way to the political echelons, beyond the minister of defense. You start to look and you pretty much wonder who's running this business, how the business is run. As a government official you can't do much, but when you retire, you can start yelling. You see displays of hypocrisy. You sometimes see even indecency. Sometimes you have comments on the degree of depth, on the level of reasoning. I'm talking about our side, not to mention their side, where things are completely wild and wide open.

Let's stay with our side for the moment.

You won't hear sharp specific criticism against people from me, even though I could write you a whole book.

Why not?

Because I don't think that's right.

But that's the only way we can learn to change things.

Okay, the Israeli people will learn from someone else. Look, I have lots of criticism. But I won't expose it. What I had to say, I said openly. Sometimes maybe even too openly. There weren't always factions in the government or in the cabinet that really loved what I was saying, but I think they respected my opinions and listened to them. A Service man also has limitations on what he's allowed to say and in which forums he's allowed to say it. But the pluralism regarding intelligence organizations in the State of Israel dictates letting the head of Aman [IDF's military intelligence unit], the head of the Mossad, and the head of the Shin Bet state their opinion and their assessments honestly, and they are listened to. Unfortunately, the spirit of their words is not always followed, but that's a different matter.

I think we did miss opportunities. I'm willing to say that. For quite a few years we could have taken steps that possibly—and there's a big question mark there—could have changed the situation a bit. This isn't a result of malice. It's sometimes a result of lack of talent or inattention, or incorrect priorities, or assigning inappropriate people to manage the negotiations. An array of everything. I know those people I worked with and who were my superiors, whether it's Yitzhak Shamir, then later Yitzhak Rabin and Shimon Peres in the middle, and then Bibi Netanyahu, when I'd coordinate an action on the subject of POWs and MIAs, all of them were serious people and all of them had good intentions, each, of course, according to his political point of origin.

The way Yitzhak Shamir ran the country was different from all other prime ministers. As far as management style, he was still working by the standards of an underground movement, of the Lehi. What do I mean? He didn't have one piece of paper on his desk. He ran the whole country off one little note he had in the jacket of his Bar Mitzvah suit. The note was divided into these tables. It said: Peri, Ehud—Ehud Barak was the chief of general staff—Shabtai, who was head of the Mossad then, and a list of ministers. If I'd remind him of a topic he needed to discuss with me, he'd write "Peri" and the subject. Before every weekly work meeting, he'd tell me, "Just a minute," take out the note and look to see if there was anything under the heading "Peri." If it said "Dror," he'd say to me, "What's happening with Dror?" I'd tell him, "Dror's okay, being monitored, nothing new." He'd erase, put the note in his pocket, and we'd carry on.

Shamir really loved the Service and the Mossad. He was in the Mossad for ten years. He'd come visit me a lot at my headquarters in Tel Aviv and see my desk overflowing—stacks, telegrams, a crazy mess. He'd say, "How are you managing the business?" I told him, "What do you mean, managing the business? I try to read, go over almost any information or telegram going out, at least skim it, and I sit here at night and read and work." He said, "Take my advice: take everything you've received today and put it away, don't touch it for a week. Urgent, not urgent—leave it, don't touch it. Come back to it after seven days, ten days. This is what you'll see—ninety percent will take care of itself, and the ten percent that didn't—that's probably what you need to deal with." And that's the way he ran the country, too.

In the first period of the Intifada, Yitzhak Shamir said, "Throwing rocks? They'll calm down." The man didn't believe that we could ultimately come to some kind of arrangement with them that would preserve even part of his values. It was also like that on the subject of the 1991 Madrid peace conference [co-sponsored by the United States and the Soviet Union]. When they told him, "Yitzhak, you have to go there," he said, "That doesn't interest me, nothing's going to come of it." They told him, "Yes, but there's pressure, America and Europe, and everyone came and took part. . . ." And then he asked me to go there first. He hoped maybe I would tell him, "Yitzhak, don't come, there's no need." Which, of course, didn't happen. And then he arrived like a man acting against his will. I think that to the end of his term, he didn't believe that an agreement with "the Arabs"—there were no "Palestinians" for him—that an arrangement with the Arabs was even a possibility. Israel's eternal heritage, Greater Israel, faith in our power, in our ability, in our control over own faith, those were the determining factors, and the rest would be sorted out according to those things. And not the other way around.

Was that frustrating to you as the head of the Service?

To a certain extent it's undoubtedly frustrating. When you're head of the Service, you're busy with a thousand fateful things a minute. You don't have too much time to sit and tell yourself, this is a missed opportunity, that's a missed opportunity. You're running like crazy. But in those moments when I was by myself, or, for example, when I'd come back from meetings, from government sessions, from Jerusalem, traveling and thinking on the way since the chauffeur was the one doing the driving, and I'd nod off for a bit. Yes, you're frustrated, you're saying on some level—where is this heading? What's the direction? You see the triviality, the lack of initiative, the rolling of . . . letting things roll without you ultimately sticking your finger in and saying, "That's enough! This direction or that direction." And of course that's frustrating to a certain extent. When you're Service director, your time is so limited and your brain is so overloaded that it really is just a few minutes, but, eventually, after you retire and you look back, it's on the level of what's called "bloopers."

Yes, only it's our lives, it's not "bloopers."

Listen, it is all our lives, but we're alive, the people of Israel are alive, don't forget that for a moment. Your life isn't bad, either.

Why didn't you say anything to Shamir?

It's forbidden, in a democratic country, for the Service director to tell the prime minister what to do. It should be the other way around. What a Service director can and should do is state his opinion. Say what he thinks was the right thing to do. And the minute the prime minister, or the government under which he operates, doesn't do it, he has only one choice, and that's resigning. And I don't think resignations are an advisable step, not for the Service and not for the country.

The role of the Service director, the role of Service staff, is to state their opinions, to say what the expected repercussions are, to give assessments and provide recommendations for action. The political echelon accepts them? Great. It doesn't accept them? It has its own set of considerations. Shimon Peres said, "The Service sees through the keyhole, I see the whole room. I add your recommendations to the pot, I have other things I have to cook, and the cake I bake is the cake I'm responsible for. You're a part of it." The Service does not ultimately control the State of Israel, and that's for the best. God help us if the Service ran the State of Israel. We all have criticism, that's obvious, but it's not a part of a Service director's role to convince the prime minister to go or not to go to the Palestinians.

It also depends on the people handling the topic. Yitzhak Rabin, I had deep conversations with him on the subject of what should be done with the Palestinians. And I think the ideas of separating us from them were raised in those conversations, and he really liked the idea. Then there were similar conversations with Ehud Barak, too. Yitzhak Shamir didn't handle "little things" like that. I got a lot of appreciation from him both for the operational work and for the thinking, but, ultimately, he didn't want to act.

On some level I have to assess whether it's critical, whether action on my part—resigning, a press conference in which I'd say something like, Yitzhak Shamir or Yitzhak Rabin or Menachem Begin or Arik Sharon are taking the wrong political and diplomatic path, they're leading us to disaster, I can't continue carrying out my position—whether that would be the right thing to do. They'd ask me, straight away—maybe you're right, but how is this the Service director's business? Catch terrorists, prevent terrorist attacks, clean up the spies, and secure our institutions so we can fly quietly. That's your job. Anything beyond that, maybe you should report, maybe you should assess, maybe you should advise because you might see the bigger picture. But it's not part of your objectives, not part of your job. If you want to do what you're saying, go be prime minister, go be a politician and do it.

Did you think about it?

God forbid.

Does the Service serve the Israeli people or the Israeli government?

The Israeli people. The Israeli government is its board of executives.

If it serves the Israeli people, and if the head of the Service who serves the Israeli people sees that the Israeli government, in this matter. . . .

He can get up and resign, and say, "I think this government isn't fulfilling its function, or its mission, so I don't want to continue serving in my position." That's always legitimate, but it won't happen, since when you join the Security Service, you join to maintain the security of this nation, its wholeness, and let the political echelon do its job.

But if you see that on the Palestinian side there are people who are willing to pursue peace, and on the Israeli side there's a government that doesn't want to pursue peace?

Then resign.

Oslo Days

"Peres: The Palestinians accept the proposal for autonomy 'in Gaza and Jericho first.'"

"Currently there is greater agreement between us and the Palestinians than ever before; this enables a breakthrough in the Washington talks next week." A PLO senior member: "There's a secret agreement with Israel regarding establishing an autonomous regime in Gaza and Jericho first." The senior official, a member of the PLO's Executive Committee, Salah Rafat, presented the agreement's items: complete and simultaneous Israeli withdrawal from the Gaza Strip and Jericho, and transfer of command over these areas to the PLO. The withdrawal from "Gaza and Jericho first" is only an intermediate stage to the implementation of UN resolutions 242 and 338 over the Territories as a whole. Peres: "Let it be clear. We're talking about self government and not about the establishment of another state. Security will remain under Israel's responsibility." The agreement was achieved following contact between state officials in the Israeli government and senior PLO officials; the assessment is that this refers to secret meetings Shimon Peres recently conducted in Europe. Arafat's advisor: "After Israel withdraws from Jericho and Gaza, Arafat and PLO leadership will move into the cleared areas." The Likud demands a special assembly of the Knesset.

(Shimon Schiffer, *Yediot Ahronot,* August 27, 1993)

Ya'akov Peri: When he started his second term as prime minister, Yitzhak Rabin was actually pretty extreme in his views on how the Palestinian population should be handled. He was fairly cautious and fairly measured, almost to the point of paralysis, on the subject of political negotiations. Rabin really liked to talk, to argue, to discuss, and to listen on all aspects of the Palestinian topic beyond the clear missions of terror and thwarting terror. The topic of the Gush Emunim settlements really depressed him, and he liked to conduct these conversations with people who he thought also had an understanding of the topic. Usually, almost in any personal meeting and almost in any social meeting, and if it was Saturday morning at his place, in his home in Neve Avivim, we'd talk a lot about this subject. And I wasn't the only one. Chief of General Staff Ehud Barak would talk to him about it a lot, Aman Director Uri Sagi would talk to him about it a lot. He used to really exhaust the topic. We started to talk about the necessity of a separation between us and the Palestinians, as part of some agreement, but he expressed a lot of suspicion about Arafat's intentions. I think Yitzhak Rabin, almost to the day he died, didn't believe that any sort of agreement could be made with Arafat. By the way, neither did I. But he believed we had to start making progress on the diplomatic track, simultaneously to the military and intelligence tracks.

He didn't like to meet Palestinian leaders, because Yitzhak was very practical, and the moment he understood the talks would be idle or just polite chit-chat, he wasn't the classic type for that kind of communication. But he really liked to understand various processes in depth, and try to dissect them analytically. Why are they like that, why aren't they different, why does a certain personality go in direction X while a different personality goes in direction Y. And just like he was very open, very intelligent, and a pleasant conversationalist, especially on these topics, he was also very determined and extreme about dealing with those hatching plots against us. Meaning, things were very defined and clear for him.

Shimon Peres, in contrast, from the first moment he had the possibility to do so, believed that the way of diplomatic negotiation was the right way, and anything done in other channels was only an obstacle. Peres thought we should be a lot more open, more flexible, take more risks. Ultimately, those two ends met. They met out of acknowledgment and understanding that the diplomatic path was the right one, and Shimon Peres, in his wisdom, knew to initiate the Oslo process in a truly confidential way, where only a precious few knew about it. To his full credit, let it be said that this was with Yitzhak Rabin's full agreement and knowledge, but Shimon Peres knew not to wear him out with the small details.

I wasn't immersed in everything that was going on. I knew some course of action was taking place, and then one of Shimon Peres's security people called me and said to me, "You know there's a signing this evening?" I said, "Signing of what?" And he said, "We sign with the Palestinians this evening in Oslo. Do you think I need to, you know, do something?" I said, "You? You shouldn't have even reported to me." Because as far as the extent of the security team's authority and responsibility, they're not allowed to report to me what this or that member of the political echelon is doing. I said, "Thanks a lot for the phone call," and I called Yitzhak Rabin. He told me, "Don't worry, I know, I'm in the picture." And then the Oslo Accords were signed in Norway.

Does that mean Rabin leaves the Shin Bet out of the picture until Oslo is signed?

Yes.

Why?

Since they didn't need our input at that stage; they needed our input after the signing, and after the signing Yitzhak Rabin called Amnon Lipkin-Shahak, who was IDF's deputy chief of general staff and me, as head of the Shin Bet, and asked us to start taking care of all the security arrangements.

How do you feel personally? A new era? Suddenly a new horizon?

Without a doubt. The era of Yitzhak Rabin, as experienced both in the Security Service and also, I think, on the street, was a short period I miss, since it was a time of hope. Hope and optimism. I'd travel almost every Friday-Saturday to meet Jibril Rajoub* and Mohammed Dahlan** in hotels all over Europe, and we conducted a very intensive set of talks. They'd consult with Yasser Arafat in the next room, and we'd consult in the next room with Rabin by phone. It was amazing.

The first meeting was in Geneva. We got there, Amnon Lipkin-Shahak and me, in civilian clothes, using false names, and in the lobby sat Jibril Rajoub, and I—not me personally, but the Service—we put him in jail when he was sixteen, and he served eighteen to twenty years in prison. Mohammed Dahlan also served a few years in prison. You're meeting people who were definitely part of the other side for the first time. It's a shock. But when both sides come truly meaning to try and reach an agreement, guided by the most senior echelons, the feeling is that it's possible and that there's a huge responsibility on your shoulders. You really feel the rush of history's wings.

The first thing that really shocked me was Jibril Rajoub's fluency in the little bits of gossip that circulate around the country. He knew exactly what party I'd attended lately, and when Amnon got married and what my wife's name was; amazing stuff. He had the ability to break the ice with little stories and things that showed that all in all, we might be on different sides of the line, but his knowledge of us and our knowledge of them—I'm speaking in a sense beyond the professional intelligence apparatus—is amazing. And you see you're ultimately meeting human beings whose desire for peace, whose desire for quiet, whose desire for an agreement, equal yours. That there is a partner for discussion.

Things that ultimately went down the drain. As of today.

Yuval Diskin: In 1993, on the eve of Oslo, I was already serving as a head of department at Shin Bet headquarters, and then Ya'akov Peri called me and appointed me to establish the connection with the Palestinians on the security angle. It looked fascinating to me, but I approached it with mixed feelings. You understand that you're going to be meeting people who, until this day, would show up on our

---

* A senior Fatah member, as well as, later, head of the Palestinians' Preventive Security Force in the West Bank and an elected member of the Fatah Central Committee.

** A Fatah leader and prominent Palestinian politician, appointed as head of the Preventive Security Force in Gaza after the signing of the Oslo Accords.

lists of terror activists abroad, and those are our real enemies. People with a respectable history of terrorist activity. Let's say I've met with people who had a background and a connection to the Munich massacre. We sat in some country, mediated by a third party, because there was a fear we wouldn't be able to talk. I believe we were there three days. On the first day we only talked through the third party. We sat in the same room, but you could just about cut the air with a knife. It was the first time I understood the meaning of that expression. A feeling of immense tension. Lots of cigarette smoke. We're sitting and not even shaking hands. Lots of hostility on both sides' faces. I couldn't see my own face but I saw their faces and apparently we looked like that, too.* We're sitting in the room and looking for a way to start talking, and it's very hard when you arrive with such negative emotional baggage toward the other side. So, one day goes by, and the engine just won't start. The second day starts in a pretty similar way, and then we understand that there's no other choice, we have to break the ice somehow, but no one's brave enough to jump in the water. And then I start smoking again.

The person leading the Palestinian delegation was a heavy smoker, and to break the ice, I said to him at some stage, "Can I take one of your cigarettes?" He answered immediately, "Sure!" I took a cigarette and it broke the ice, immediately. He lit my cigarette and I explained to him that I'd stopped smoking, and now he's gone and made me start smoking again. Some human, interpersonal interaction started, and it began to melt the ice a little. There was still a lot of ice, of course, but a real conversation started. It ended with our hosts taking us to dinner at some restaurant. I had a very hard time with it. It seemed to me like I was doing something I couldn't be doing. Up to this day I'd been pursuing these people, how can I suddenly sit down with terrorists? They murdered people, how can I sit down with them? Now to them, for them, I was a terrorist, too. And then you understand that "one man's terrorist is another man's freedom fighter," as they say.

Over time, throughout establishing this connection with the Palestinians from '93 and on, you get to situations where personal

---

* In September 1972, eleven members of the Israeli delegation to the Munich Olympics were murdered by terrorists belonging to the Black September organization.

friendships are formed, beyond the professional level. There's some kind of empathy sometimes, or sympathy. It's inevitable, when one person's with another person, feelings are formed, too. Some of them you like, some of them you don't like. I assume they feel the same way about us.

Are you still in touch with those guys you met?

With some of them I am.

Did it turn into a friendship?

With some of them more, with others it didn't.

Avi Dichter: Oslo broke out in one day for us. We weren't part of the process, so we didn't know about it. I was head of a district, Peri was head of the Service then, he updated me and told me, "Avi, listen, we have to start very quickly to talk to Fatah's people in the field, to sort out the whole subject of fugitives, because we can't keep chasing them after the signing in Washington." The signing in Washington was supposed to take place literally within a few days.

We decided that we'd let the "heavy" killers leave for Egypt, because pursuing them would mean starting to conduct operations, arrests, casualties, shooting, and you don't know how to end it. With the other fugitives, it was decided to reach agreements, to get them to the Governorate HQ and send them home. On our side, it was quite an event to sit down with them. These are people who were terrorists and now they're supposed to be official representatives. I remember in one of the meetings where we first sat with them, someone took a note and did the calculation. There were seventy-five years of prison time around the table. It was amazing. For some of our people it was simply a crisis—to call in a major fugitive, seat him down and afterwards walk him out of the Governorate building on his feet to go home. Not in a squad car and not in a "Zinzana" [a nickname for a police vehicle that transports prisoners] and without handcuffs. For some of the people it was traumatic, but it was clear that there was no other way.

By the way, it didn't stop the terrorism. September 12, '93, the day of signing, was one of the worst terrorism days I remember. It was a Sunday. In the morning they attacked a jeep in Shuja'iyya, in the eastern part of Gaza. Three soldiers were killed. They abused the bodies, photographed them. The three soldiers were Druze. I remember I brought the photographs to one of the soldiers' brother. Very brutal photographs. He was a senior officer, a brigadier general. And on that same day there was an attack in Holon Junction, an attack by the Islamic Jihad. To make a long story short, there were very brutal terrorist attacks. But at least you knew that opposite Fatah's people, you had an understanding that they would fight terrorism.

Carmi Gillon: We tend to forget, but I want to note first and foremost the most important achievement of the Gaza-Jericho agreement. The State of Israel's "number one" terrorist enemy, until the day Arafat entered Gaza, was Fatah. Fatah is the largest organization, with the largest infrastructure, which produced thousands of terrorist attacks. A mass of attacks which were not suicide attacks, but for those who remember the First Intifada—stabbings in Kfar Saba or shooting attacks throughout the country. And all at once, Fatah exited the cycle of terror, and it's lasted to this day. Later, the Tanzim and other organizations which may be products of Fatah were established, but the Fatah itself, in '93, abruptly exits the cycle of terror. Hamas and the Islamic Jihad were attracted to this vacuum.

However, we initially saw Arafat as an ally against Hamas. We thought he had a clear political agenda, but pretty quickly it turned out he was a liar by nature. Our maligners would say he pulled one over on us. He didn't pull one over on us. Anything he said, we could verify with ten other intelligence measures. It's not like we sat across from him, and whatever he said, we said, "Amen." You have to remember that Rabin himself was very suspicious toward Arafat. I think Rabin's attitude toward Arafat is best reflected in a very famous photo from September 13, '93, when Clinton compels Rabin to shake Arafat's hand. Maybe the most famous photo in the context of the Israeli-Palestinian peace, or "no peace." You can see Rabin's expression of revulsion, even disgust when he's shaking the hand. And that reflected, I believe, Rabin's true attitude toward Arafat.

So why did he decide to go for it?

Gillon: I think he went primarily so as not to miss a potential opportunity. He felt that we were heading toward a dead end. As far as the Palestinians were concerned, the Intifada could continue for another hundred years. The Israeli price was too high, and even if the chances were low, he felt we had to give it a chance. Maybe initially he was dragged against his will. Peres was a slightly more dominant and leading element, but later, Rabin becomes the deciding factor. He leads the process, and he went to give it a chance.

But he has a partner who wasn't a partner.

True. It may very well be that history as a whole would have unfolded differently if Rabin had stayed alive. I think he was waiting for the '96 elections to see the extent of the legitimacy and support he was receiving from the Israeli public to continue the process, and according to that, he would have navigated the rest of the way. What he did in the Oslo Accords themselves, which were the agreement to pull out from the cities, was to proceed gradually at a relatively low cost in terms of security, and to decide he'd test it over time. It was clear to him that it wouldn't abide by a short-term itinerary, it wouldn't be like the treaty with Jordan, which was an "instant" treaty.

The other thing about which Rabin was undoubtedly right was what the State of Israel would gain from this agreement. At this point it's good to remember that a treaty with Jordan would never have come about if we hadn't signed the Oslo Accords. Hussein would never have gone for a treaty like that. He expected that later there would also be agreements with Lebanon and with Syria. Israel won the world's support, he got $10 billion of guarantees from Clinton. You always hear about the "financial boom" during Rabin's administration; it was facilitated by those guarantees. He brought about an extraordinary upgrade of Israel's status in Europe, including a financial upgrade, tariff walls, and so on. Like a symphony conductor, he saw all the elements at work, and he saw that ultimately there was immediate profit here for Israel, and maybe in the long term, some kind of agreement with the Palestinians.

I don't think he was that naïve. Many here in Israel went around with doves in their pockets. There was a kind of euphoric feeling, peace has come and we're all about the peace, and how lovely. Rabin certainly wasn't caught up in this euphoria. His failure at public relations was that he didn't know how to explain, "Guys, it's a long process, and you have to continue with the diplomatic process as if there's no terror, and to fight terror as if there were no diplomatic process," as he did say later. The Israeli public didn't understand that. And that's how the public sentiment that we were tricked was created. I don't think we were tricked, I think we were very realistic. Rabin was certainly realistic.

Avi Dichter: At the beginning of '95, Rabin asked Yasser Arafat to meet with the Palestinian heads of security. Arafat gave his blessing, and Rabin met them in an apartment in Tel Aviv. I was there as head of the Southern District. The head of the Service then was Carmi Gillon. Unfortunately, they brought everything to that meeting except one thing—they forgot to bring a translator. . . . And then, very quickly, I found myself acting as translator. Rabin, as was his style, talked in very long sentences that had to be translated from Hebrew to Arabic, which was very difficult, and they were speaking literary Arabic, in honor of Rabin. Very high Arabic. Nasser Yousef, the senior representative there on behalf of Arafat, went even further and talked in especially elevated literary Arabic. To make a long story short, a very embarrassing situation.

But ultimately, Rabin's tactic in this meeting was intended to convey to them the insight of what it means in a state, or a state-in-formation, when the regime allows other elements to act in parallel with it. Or, in other words, to let Hamas do in Gaza what Hezbollah was doing in Lebanon. He gave them the example of the ship *Altalena** on our side, of Ben Gurion's orders and the ultimate shooting and sinking of the *Altalena*, so as not to enable any institution that was not a proper state institution to arm itself. He said, "One day you'll have your own *Altalena*, and the way you act opposite your *Altalena*, that will be how you know whether you're on your way to statehood, or whether you're still terrorist organizations." This meeting was a very powerful one, but, unfortunately, everything stated there evaporated in later periods.

Yuval Diskin: When they entered the Oslo process, there was some optimism, some kind of hope, that maybe the historical course of events was about to change. Very comprehensive staff work was performed in the Service, regarding how to prepare and what would happen when we transfer the Territories to the Palestinians' responsibility. It was also very hard for us to determine in advance how

---

* A ship purchased by the Irgun, the Zionist paramilitary group operating in Palestine during the British mandate, which reached Israel's shores loaded with weapons five weeks after the State of Israel was established. After the Irgun command refused to hand over the weapons to the IDF, the *Altalena* was bombed and sunk by Palmach fighters.

the political echelon would behave once the Palestinians entered the territory, how much freedom we would receive to act, how much we would insist on the things agreed upon during the preliminary debates of the Oslo process, how stubborn we would be, to what extent the Palestinians would do what they had committed to doing. We were guessing at a lot of things.

We finished the staff work, we invested a lot of resources in it to build up the Service for this new, dramatic situation here in the area, but then came May '94, we start to transfer Gaza and Jericho first, and all these things, alas, shattered. We find out that reality isn't exactly cooperating with the staff work we did. The Service didn't manage to prepare itself properly. The Service did prevent lots of terrorist attacks during those years, but it didn't manage to prevent some brutal ones. The effect was disastrous. Everything collapsed in the organization.

The wave of suicide attacks started as early as May '93, and increased even more in '94, with the attack on Bus 5 [in Tel Aviv, killing twenty-two people], and continued in January '95, in the awful attack at the Beit Lid junction [a double suicide attack that killed twenty-two and wounded sixty-six], and in July '95 by [a suicide attack on a bus near] the Stock Exchange [in Ramat Gan] and [by two suicide attacks] on the Bus 18 line in Jerusalem [in February and March 1996, killing a total of forty-five and injuring dozens]. And you find out the Palestinians aren't really preventing terror. They don't really understand their role. And slowly, we start to sober up from our previous immense optimism. You find out that there's a long way to go between us and peace.

Rabin coined the phrase: "I'll fight terrorism as if there are no negotiations, and negotiate as if there's no terror." What do you think of that statement?

Ya'akov Peri: I think it's a true statement. He knew how to differentiate between what's necessary in order to create the conditions for a diplomatic process, and an uncompromising fight against terrorism. I don't think there's a contradiction there.

But a statement like that doesn't motivate Arafat to fight Hamas. Hamas sends suicide terrorists, while he continues with the diplomatic negotiation.

Peri: Here you're more focused on leaders' hidden agenda, that if they didn't want the diplomatic process to be completed, terrorist activity assisted them. That's definitely an option. I'm not dismissing it. But I think what caused the diplomatic process to collapse was actually the system of terrorist attacks. If both sides had been unequivocally determined to reach an agreement, even terrorist activity, even if it was heavy terrorist activity, couldn't have ultimately disrupted it. Ultimately, if you look back, we never reached such stages in negotiations with the Palestinians where we were actually on the threshold of an agreement. We were constantly in the beginning stages, or making very little, very fragile, progress. We didn't get to serious negotiation where we only had to solve a few basic problems like Jerusalem or things that are at the crux of our differences. Ultimately, this is in the hands of the leaders. And just like there was a fierce desire and a pretty determined decision and a real intention by Shimon Peres and Yitzhak Rabin to reach an agreement, so, after Rabin's disappearance, the Israeli desire or intention to create a real agreement or to reach a real agreement gradually decreased, to use an understatement.

I also think Yasser Arafat reached a strategic decision that there wouldn't be an agreement or that he wouldn't sign an agreement with the State of Israel in his lifetime. Yasser Arafat lived in caves all his life. He hadn't slept in a bed for one night since he could remember. He was a haunted man. A man at odds with himself, with a very problematic relationship with himself and with others. Arafat came to the realization that he was a flag, a banner. He raised the Palestinian problem all over the world, transformed the Palestinian issue from an "underdog" to an entity for which the whole world supported independent status, and with that he fulfilled his historic destiny. Not that he told me that, but my impression was that he had internalized that he shouldn't be the one to forge the agreement, and if anyone should, it should be his successor. Let others bring in the agreement and cope with the criticism it draws. Because any treaty signed, whenever it happens, will draw criticism. I could see, from long conversations I had with him, that his "zigzagging" was a result of his not wanting the negotiations to be consummated.

And you don't think Rabin's murder, and the subsequent rise of Bibi Netanyahu and Ehud Barak, also create some kind of dynamic with Yasser Arafat?

Peri: The Oslo Accords were, in my view, a reasonable treaty, a good treaty, since it was based on several steps, so that at any point you could retreat, change your mind, or change direction. But Rabin's assassination cut off hope. It showed in the clearest way that a little pissant assassin, with a gun that barely shoots, can cut off an entire hope, a whole process. On the other hand, I think that if Rabin's murder hadn't happened, and I wish it hadn't, it wouldn't change Arafat's stance. I think Arafat did not want, in his lifetime, to reach an agreement with the Israelis. Eventually, Ehud Barak is sitting there and offering him 96 percent, 97 percent of the Territories—take it, just sign—and Yasser Arafat doesn't sign.

I saw Yasser Arafat during the signing of the agreement with the Palestinians in Cairo, when he was sitting and his hand was shaking, he couldn't sign, and he went out, behind the stage, and [Egyptian president Hosni] Mubarak, so rumor says, called out to him, "You dog, get in there and sign!" And then he signed under some kind of pressure or awe or fear. And that ultimately reinforces the fact that he didn't want to arrive at a situation where he signed any sort of treaty—intermediate, permanent, it doesn't matter how you call it—with the State of Israel.

Now, when you have one partner who's really interested, and one partner's who's not interested, it doesn't work. When you have two partners who aren't interested, it certainly doesn't work. All the rest is gravy. The terrorist attacks, and the political conflicts among us, among the Israeli people, and the right versus left, and Rabin's murder, and then the time of Ehud Barak's government. . . . I also don't think that today anyone could look into Benjamin Netanyahu's heart and say whether he really wants an agreement, or whether he wants to kill time. Our leaders are lucky that today there's no partner. The West Bank is flourishing, all in all there's order and governance there, a relative financial thriving, but until the Palestinians reach a peace among themselves, we have no partner. We need both the Gaza Strip and the West Bank, and so do they, ultimately. And so long as that separation exists, our leaders are getting off easy. You can't blame them.

We have no partner?

Yes, we have no partner. There are some very talented people among the Palestinian leadership, but there has never arisen a Palestinian leadership that could ultimately reach a decision.

Everyone there fears for his life, or fears what they'll say about him. Abu-Mazen [Mahmoud Abbas, a founding member of Fatah and chairman of the Palestinian Authority] is a charming man, practical, definitely worldly, sociable, but apparently he doesn't have the ability to make historical decisions, and since Hamas conquered the Gaza Strip, both sides now have a kind of "excuse." The Israelis say, "Maybe we can reach an agreement with Abu-Mazen, but that's not the whole Palestinian state. We also need Gaza, and Gaza won't play ball." Abu-Mazen says, until I reach some kind of agreement, even if just a tactical one, with the Gaza side, I don't have the whole Palestinian people." So the whole business is stuck.

But ultimately, to try and reach some kind of end or the beginning of an end to the conflict, and an end to the deep-rooted hatred and so on, we also have to try and stop making mistakes, and they have to try and stop making mistakes. I think the great majority of those who have served—whether it's in the Service, whether it's in the Mossad, whether it's in IDF or in other intelligence organizations—ultimately reach the conclusion that you can't win this conflict or kill off this conflict through Shin Bet-ian or military means. It will have to be eliminated by diplomatic and political means, by means of talking, of trust, of awareness, of concessions, of compromise. Bigger and better people than me, including Yitzhak Rabin, Shimon Peres, Arik Sharon, and others, came to the exact same conclusion. Unfortunately, we didn't succeed, but you can't lose your optimism.

Carmi Gillon

Carmi Gillon (1994–96)

I think I grew up in a very special home. I was born and raised in the Rehavia neighborhood in Jerusalem. My mother was a sixth-generation Israeli. Her father was the only Jewish Supreme Court judge during the British Mandate period, and she was named Sa'ada since he studied law in Constantinople, also known as Istanbul, during the Ottoman reign, and "Sa'ada" means "happiness" in Turkish. It also means "happiness" in Arabic. And that name gave her a lot of grief.

My grandfather himself was also born in Jerusalem. His father established the first Hebrew paper—*Havatselet*. If I have one childhood memory of my grandfather, it's that he had a kind of nightcap head cover, and he was maybe one of the only Jews who spoke Turkish. He translated the Majalah, the Turkish book of laws, which until '61 was in use in Israel and in the faculty of law, from Turkish to Hebrew. When I started to work at the university, they told me no one knew if he really translated it from Turkish to Hebrew or just made it up. Grandfather was the president of the Friends of the Hebrew University, and took on all kinds of public roles. He was the first chairman of the state investigative committee established in the country regarding the Yemenite Children* affair. My grandmother

* The alleged disappearance of hundreds of infants of new Israeli immigrants, primarily from Yemen, between 1948 and 1954.

was the daughter of a Biluyim* family who arrived in 1882 and were among the founders of the city of Rehovot. To make a long story short, we were "Mayflower" from that side.

My father immigrated to Israel from South Africa in 1936 because he couldn't stand the apartheid regime. He arrived in Israel, met my mother, and they got married here. Throughout World War II, he served in the British army, was discharged as an officer with a rank of major, returned to Israel, was a member of the Hagana [the Zionist underground during the British Mandate], and then served in IDF and attained the rank of lieutenant colonel. He was the first governor of Abu Gosh. Later, in 1952, he was appointed as state attorney. My mother was deputy attorney general. To make a long story short, you could say I was a privileged kid in the Rehavia neighborhood, although my father, the state attorney, got to work by bus at the time, or walked. We had no car at home. He never dreamt of getting his own vehicle. Different times. Today I wouldn't agree to work as a department head without a company car.

We lived comfortably, but not extravagantly. They lived like a pair of salaried employees of the State of Israel in the fifties. The other children in Rehavia were like me. This neighborhood produced some familiar people like Bibi Netanyahu, who was in the same age group in my school, [Reuven] "Ruby" Rivlin [Likud politician and Israel's current president], Dan Meridor. "The Fighting Family" [a nickname given by Menachem Begin to a close-knit group of Irgun veterans] lived in Rehavia, and so did a lot of loyal members of Mapai [the left-wing Workers Party, which merged into the Labor Party in 1968].

With my parents, public service was a value. My parents left Kupat Holim [Israel's state-sponsored system of health maintenance clinics] and transferred to private medicine so that, God forbid, they weren't linked with any political affiliation. The HMOs at the time had a clear party affiliation. They paid out of their own pockets just so no one would say, "Colin Gillon, state attorney, is in the Clalit HMO, identified with the Histadrut [a socialist-affiliated labor union]." So, after

* Members of the Bilu Movement, whose goal was the agricultural settlement of the land of Israel. Many arrived in Ottoman Palestine following the pogroms in Russia in the late nineteenth century.

my parents passed away when I was very young—my father passed away when I was eleven, and my mother was also ill and passed away at a very young age—we were left almost penniless. All their money was actually spent on medical treatment. So I grew up as an orphan most of my life. An orphan in a supportive environment, but it's definitely very hard to grow up without a father.

My first encounter with the Shin Bet was through my father. My father served as prosecutor in some very well-known espionage trials during that period. One of the incidents is remembered positively because they caught the spy; his name was Kurt Sitte, he was a professor at the Technion [Israel Institute of Technology], spying for Czechoslovakia, although of course it was for the Soviet Union. I was ten at the time. My father was already very ill, so he worked from home, and all kinds of strange people would come see him all the time. They never said what their names were, and they ignored me as a little boy. One day a big American car arrived, with a giant antenna, and my curiosity was, of course, immense. Even more important, I thought I could improve my social status if I brought my friends over to touch the car and the antenna and all that. And when I asked my father who these people were, he told me, "Those are detectives." Eventually I learned that the person who came to our house was the head of the Shin Bet at the time, Amos Manor, along with the heads of the interrogation branch at the time. They came to prepare the Kurt Sitte trial.

In '52, when my father was appointed as state attorney, I was only two years old. So I found out about the next story with Isser Harel only when I'd already joined the Shin Bet and I had the security clearance to hear it. My father was a very unusual man. Along with being state attorney, he was a stage actor, a chess champion, and mostly he liked to solve crossword puzzles. Since he walked to his job at the Ministry of Justice, so as not to waste time, he'd walk and do crosswords or play with a little chessboard, solving chess puzzles. After he passed away, I found seven hundred books of chess puzzles, and he also subscribed to all kinds of newspapers that came from overseas with crossword puzzles. His mother tongue was English, and one of the papers, *The New Statesman*, was associated with the left in England. When they wanted to appoint my father as state attorney, Isser Harel dropped in to see Ben Gurion and told him, "You can't appoint that guy, he's a communist, he has a subscription to a communist paper!" They didn't know what to do, so they sent Isser to talk to him. My father explained that the only reason he received *New Statesman* was that their crossword puzzles were the best. . . .

How did Isser know about the newspaper?

They ran a security check on Dad, I assume, like we run security checks to this day; I've also run security checks on people. I was shocked to read that the Shin Bet managed to convince the Judicial Selection Committee to run security checks on judges. That didn't happen at any point in the State of Israel's existence. I was shocked to see that.

As a child, I didn't like studying. I had a certain legitimacy for it because I had lost my father, and my mother was very sick, as I said, hospitalized most of the time, but that was just an excuse. I don't even remember how I managed to pass the Survey Test [a general knowledge test administered to Israeli eighth graders from 1955 to 1972] and get accepted to the Rehavia Hebrew Gymnasia. I was the black sheep of the family. My brother, who's a judge today, was also a black sheep. There was intense competition between the two of us. I was held back a grade, and then they decided to expel me from school and the principal invited my mother, who was chairperson of the PTA, to the dismissal talk. The whole conversation was actually about how sorry he was that she couldn't be chairperson of the PTA anymore.

But I gained something great from it. I went to the Jerusalem Music Academy, which had just been established. Refugees from all kinds of good schools all over the country ended up there. I started playing an instrument from age six, and I played a pretty good clarinet. No one thought I'd turn into a big star, but I was okay. Yaacov Peri is a much better trumpeter than I am a clarinet player. He played professionally during his military service. I wasn't that talented, even though I got an "eight out of ten" in my music matriculation exam.

I think if there's something I eventually used in the Service and in other things I did in my life, it's the ability to think harmonically about things. The first thing a head of Service actually has to do is take this great machine with its extraordinary strengths, and in effect conduct an orchestra. He needs very precise, sharp hearing, to immediately detect false notes. And mainly to ensure this body, which is a lean, muscular body, focused on its mission, doesn't stray. For that you need harmonic thinking. And I got that from music.

I got to the Service through friends. I'm talking about '71, '72. It was a period of "one friend brings another." A bunch of us were sitting at the house of a good friend who had passed away, Yair Snapiri, and Snapiri's big brother, who worked in the Service, came over and asked, "Any of you want to work for the Ministry of Defense?" Everyone else had already mapped out a future career, but I really wasn't a serious person at the time. I worked in security for Brink's, transporting money to Ben Gurion Airport in the morning, and going to school later. Then I was a school librarian for a while, all kinds of things that could certainly have indicated the direction in which I'd develop eventually. I didn't have anything better to do, so I told him, "I'll do it." That was it.

It took three months of security checks, interviews, all kinds of weeding, aptitude tests, and on November 1, 1972, I started working. Two months later, the Israeli delegation at the Munich Olympics was attacked and killed. There was an investigative committee, a lot of people were dismissed, the head of the Service's security branch, the Service's security director, the director of delegation security, and additional people. I had just been admitted to work in that vacuum. I hadn't had time to finish my first course, and on my twenty-sixth day at work, the Israeli embassy in Bangkok was seized, and the ambassador and the other employees were taken hostage. El Al was already subject to intense security at the time, and I was already an old hand, I had twenty-six days of seniority at work, so straight away I get a promotion, and they even made me a supervisor; I had one employee. Deputy commander of a quarter of a squad. . . . Eventually, I find myself in the security branch.

What are the important traits for a security person?

A security person is, first and foremost, a very technical role. First of all you have to become a fighting machine. Mostly using a pistol or a submachine gun. You have to know how to shoot quickly and accurately. That's the basic condition. The second trait you need is discernment. If, for example, you're working the El Al check-in line, there are thousands of people walking around in the airport. Out of all of them, you're supposed to identify the suspicious person who might attack your passengers. Or, on the other hand, if you're VIP security, you're supposed to identify the possible threat to the VIP you're securing. So you need discernment that can be exercised endlessly, but it's an inherent trait you have to possess. And the third thing, which isn't talked about but that you also need, is actually the willingness to place the object you're protecting above your own life. A VIP security person is supposed to shield the secured person with his own body. Take bullets for them. And there were a lot of cases like that. That's the kind of thing that isn't taught, isn't talked about, but it goes without saying.

I'd say those three traits are important. But what happens is you actually have to take instinctive action. The chance that a security person can act before the opponent is relatively low. There were very few cases where the security people opened fire first, but the second shot has to come from the security person, which means, of course, a very, very high reaction speed. Any bullet beyond the second one is already reason to look into what wasn't working right there.

How do you train for something like that? How were you trained?

When I was taking the course, there was a legendary man named Dave Beckerman. His ability to stress you out was so high that. . . . I'll give you an example: you shoot and shoot, you think you're doing great, then he comes over, looks at the results along with you, and then says something like, "You're not worth the oxygen you're taking away from me. . . ." Or he'd come in his van to pick up trainees at Arlosoroff station in Tel Aviv, and he'd weed them out right there. He'd say, "You, you, you—get on the van," and to the others, "I don't even know why you're here." Psychological pressure.

Avi Dichter: Dave Beckerman really was an extraordinary character. He emigrated from the United States. An American who lived the Wild West and the Westerns. He also spoke Hebrew with a heavy American accent, and he taught very basic things about the pistol. I remember that for hours and hours, we'd draw and shoot. Because with a pistol, a small mistake shooting—from a distance of ten, twenty, and thirty meters (thirty-three, sixty-six, ninety-nine feet)—that's already missing the target by a long shot, or killing—heaven help us—an innocent bystander. Over the entrance to the training facility, he hung a great sign with the famous saying by Samuel Colt, developer and builder of the mythic Colt 45 pistol, and the sign says,

"Fear no man, no matter size, count on me—I'll equalize." And later, every time I had to use a gun, and, unfortunately, or fortunately in certain cases, I did use a gun, you find out exactly how effective it is if you really know how to use it.

Carmi Gillon: In the training course, you shoot and shoot. Endlessly. You shoot thousands of bullets. There's no economy there. And you have to reach drawing standards, a speed of drawing, of getting the first bullet out. These are mathematical standards, it's not a matter of impression. Other traits really are more related to impressions. You're constantly under the instructors' magnifying glass. You practice ten to twelve hours straight, and they observe you all the time. I was head of the instruction branch in the Service, and I was in charge of dismissing trainees. That was after years when that authority was given to the instructors, and then Avrum Shalom decided at some stage that he was taking it away from them and transferring it to senior personnel. But eventually, you manufacture fighting machines.

You said it was something mathematical. How does math factor in?

There's reaction time. I don't exactly remember the numbers. But in my time, the first bullet on the target had to be in 2.2 seconds. By the way, these systems have grown a lot more sophisticated since then. We'd shoot in IDF ranges, and then the instructor would look at his watch and decide if it was 2.2 or 2.3. Go figure. Anyway, it was done in a very professional way. In my time, when I was head of the instruction branch, I'd constantly be approached by special units in IDF and other institutions that wanted to come and practice in our facility. Our combat practice was the best.

In '81, I completed three years in Europe. I was in Europe. It's a very important reference point in my life, because I got married there. My two elder daughters were born there. And I got all that done between '79 and '82. I was in a fairly senior position, deputy to the person responsible for all of Europe. These were years of terrorist attacks and warnings. For example, there was the attack in Orly airport in Paris. Terrorists armed with Kalashnikovs attacked an El Al flight, and were eliminated by our security people there. There was a terrorist attack in Brussels. A girl tried to smuggle in a record player with an explosive charge that she'd gotten from her Arab boyfriend. There was an attempted terrorist attack in Zurich.

The security apparatus worked very hard. For example, I was at all of Maccabi Tel Aviv's games in Europe during those three years, and I never knew how they'd ended. Including the games against CSKA [Moscow, the Soviet baskbetball team, which played several memorable games against Israeli team Maccabi Tel Aviv]. I was just so stressed that I wasn't even watching the game. After the team members were already safe in their hotel, I'd ask about the final score. And I love basketball; basketball is my hobby.

In '81, Maccabi was playing in Strasburg, in the finals for the Eurocup championship for the second time, so I asked Rafi Malka, who was responsible for Europe, to give me some off-duty time. For once, I want to go watch a game. I took my wife there, and I sat, let's say, in the fifteenth row, and Maccabi won the cup by one point. And I jump from the fifteenth row to the field, straight on the parquet floor. Dancing and joy and all of that, I don't feel anything, then it turns out I'd sprained my leg by jumping. That's the only game I watched, and it also ended with my being laid out at home for two more weeks.

The Jewish Division

"Security forces at highest alert: a strike in the West Bank and in East Jerusalem."

"The assessment is that a small underground group of Jews carried out assassination attempts."

"However, a theory that the perpetrators were Arabs is being investigated. Bassam Shakaa is still in serious condition; the Arabs will demand in the U.N. that sanctions be instituted against Israel and that it be suspended from the General Assembly."

Intense investigation by security forces, among both Jews and Arabs, has yet to reveal who is behind the assassination attempt on the mayors in the West Bank. What is already clear is that the level of operational sophistication evident in the explosive charges was at a very high professional level which has yet to be employed in past terrorist attacks. In at least one incident, the explosives originated from IDF.

(*Yediot Ahronot*, June 3, 1980)

"30 containers of explosives were prepared for blowing up the Temple Mount mosques."

An indictment was brought against 25 of the Underground's detainees—and two more will be brought today or tomorrow. Gush Emunim protests against "further public judgment of these precious people" and against the term "underground."

(Ronnie Shaked, *Yediot Ahronot*, May 24, 1984)

Carmi Gillon: In '82, I returned to Israel. I was promised a position I wanted very much, I can't specify which one. I was really preparing myself for it, and then, a month beforehand, I was notified that I was being assigned to a different position—head of branch—and they couldn't tell me what the job was. I felt very insulted. I tried to inquire with Rafi Malka, since as head of the Operations Division, he knew all the Service's secrets, but his lips were sealed.

I came back to Israel very bummed. I'd already served in two head-of-branch roles. A head of branch is something like a lieutenant colonel in the army, and I was sure I deserved a colonel. Since I had decided that in any case I was leaving security in favor of intelligence, I was willing to pay the price, but at least for a position I wanted. Intelligence proper. Real intelligence-intelligence. Enough, I couldn't hear "security people" any more, I was sick to death of it. And then, when they offered me a different position from the one I'd been promised, I was very angry and decided I wouldn't continue in the Service. I sulked for a month or two. Avrum really wanted me to take the job, and then he called Ya'akov Peri, who was head of the Jerusalem and West Bank district, and was supposed to be my boss.

I came to the meeting with Peri, who really didn't want me for the position. He didn't know me and thought I was one of those security-guy types, and he didn't like that, but he'd received an order, so he met with me. He wouldn't tell me what the position was, and told me, "I can tell you that I'm the head of district here, I've got lots of units under me, and I meet the head of branch responsible for this subject relatively more times than with anyone else. But I can't tell you what the position is. First you have to say you want it, and then we'll tell you." I said, "If it's like that, then no deal." I went back home, and continued my vacation. And then they sent over the man currently filling the position, who transferred from that job to be the Service director's bureau chief. From that I understood that it was an important role. He received authorization to tell me a little. Eventually it was revealed that I'd been offered the position of head of the branch dealing with the extreme right and extreme left in the Jerusalem and West Bank district, which includes the settlers on the right and includes the very intensive activity of the radical left. I didn't even know there was Jewish subversive activity. It's not a subject that was taught in courses or talked about. I had no idea the Service deals with subversive activity, and suddenly I find out there's real action.

Until that period, our activity was very minor, and what mainly occupied us was the extreme left. During that period, immediately after the Lebanon War, movements like Yesh Gvul [founded in 1982 by Israeli combat veterans], which opposed the war in Lebanon or IDF's presence in Lebanon, and called for insubordination, were established here. That, for example, was one of the Service's dilemmas: do you dedicate intelligence coverage to movements encouraging refusal of military service in Lebanon? And there was also the extreme, anti-Zionist left—like Matzpen, the Revolutionary Communist League, Derech Hanitzotz, and other groups. Eventually I had the honor of putting all of them in jail as head of the unit.

When we arrested the Derech Hanitzotz group, which was a bunch of very extreme people, who think a Palestinian state should be established here, period, and who assisted no less than the Democratic Front in Damascus by relaying information and so on, or the group led by "Mikado," Michel Warschawski, the Revolutionary Communist League, which is one of the more radical factions to originate from Matzpen, meaning Matzpen wasn't extreme enough for him, who cooperated with George Habash's Popular Front—they went to jail, and we were denounced in the streets. My unit and I were accused of blocking the freedom of expression. Meaning the left can cooperate with terrorist organizations because it's freedom of expression, the right to incorporate, and so on. As long as the Shin Bet catches Arabs, everything's okay. The minute the Shin Bet deals with Jewish topics, it gets delegitimized, both by the right and by the left.

I can give you an example from Arab Israelis. Between the years '90 and '94, the Islamic Movement in Israel [which advocates Islam among Israeli Arabs] published a newspaper that's published to this day, called *Sawt al-Haq*, which is a paper comprised totally of sedition and incitement against the State of Israel. Hamas couldn't write a paper better than that. I, as head of Shin Bet North, fought like

Don Quixote against the windmills, of course, with support from Peri, who was then head of the Service, to shut down that newspaper. And you come to the state attorney or to the Ministry of Interior, and they tell you, "That will never happen. You can't shut down a newspaper in the State of Israel. It's not democratic. He'll go to the High Court of Justice, and he's sure to win." Today we have factions and Knesset members we never dreamt we'd see in the eighties. There are people sitting in the Knesset today who not only do not acknowledge the State of Israel's existence, they don't acknowledge the existence of the Jewish people in the holy land that is Palestinian land in their eyes. We're constantly playing a pretty hypocritical game here.

About the left—the B'Tselem [which advocates human rights in the Territories], Ta'ayush [which promotes Arab-Jewish solidarity], and Anarchists Against the Wall organizations [anti-authoritarians who oppose the construction of the Gaza Strip and West Bank security barriers]—are these organizations that the Shin Bet would try to infiltrate?

Gillon: B'Tselem—no. But it's possible that the answer for Ta'ayush is yes. In the eighties, of course. These are actually the organizations that have replaced Yesh Gvul today, or are even to the left of Yesh Gvul, and I assume that at the time we'd have dealt with them. Today, I don't know.

How do you collect information in organizations like that?

There are different levels of collection. If we take as an example an organization like Ta'ayush, all their activity is out in the open. You don't need agents, you don't need phones, I read the papers. I read their posters, and I know what's going on. If they're going to Na'alin [a West Bank village that was the site of protests against the West Bank barrier] or not going to Na'alin.You don't need very sophisticated intelligence for that. The reasons you still need some kind of supervision over them is that the whole organization, ninety-five percent of it, is law-abiding and legitimate—maybe not entirely law-abiding, but let's say legitimate. But out of those grow the harmful weeds, the very extreme people. And here a very difficult question arises: is it okay to infiltrate a legitimate organization because you estimate that it will sprout harmful weeds? There's a very serious dilemma here.

Who decides the limits of your activity in the Jewish population?

I'll give you an example that's related to Rabin's murder. Immediately after the murder, when it was discovered that [Rabin assassin] Yigal Amir studied in Bar Ilan University, a great public outcry broke out, how is it that the Shin Bet has no intelligence coverage at Bar Ilan University, and they didn't know that a Yigal Amir like that was over there. An excellent question. But when you're spewing rhetoric—and the media usually spews rhetoric, and then people follow it and spew rhetoric, too—you don't ask the next question: would you want that within Bar Ilan University, where thousands of people study, religious, secular, normative people—do we want our universities to have Shin Bet presence, like in China? If so, by the way, you'd have to expand the Shin Bet by maybe ten thousand degrees so it would be capable of doing that. There are countries where that certainly exists, they happen to be totalitarian countries, but it does exist. So I remember that at the time I tried to withstand the surge and tried to explain, still as head of the Service, why the Service doesn't place an agent in every classroom in Bar Ilan, and microphones in the cafeterias. No one listened to me. People said, "That's bull, if you had microphones in the cafeterias, maybe you'd have heard Yigal Amir planning the murder!"

The State of Israel exists here as a democracy. But on the other hand, we have to understand that a democracy—and here I'm quoting Justice Barak—a democracy is not a prescription for suicide. He also coined the phrase "defensive democracy." A democracy can defend itself. There's a rift on the right, a rift on the left, which exists to this day, of course, around our relations with the Palestinians, and the Shin Bet is in the middle. Trying to maneuver all the time. This is the ultimate problem we have regarding Shin Bet legitimacy. By the way, the Mossad doesn't have problems like that at all. I, for example, deal with the question of what the Shin Bet's objectives are in the extreme right and the extreme left.

Not the prime minister?

No. He wouldn't dare. There's an element of political decision there. So, who ultimately decides? The head of the Shin Bet. And then you see that Avraham Ahituv decides like this, Avrum Shalom decides like that, Ya'akov Peri decides like this, Carmi Gillon decides like that, Ami Ayalon decides like this. I can say one thing in defense of all the heads of Shin Bet I know, that they are all without exception upstanding people, straight arrows. They approach everything with a pragmatic attitude, and I think none of them vote for the same party. . . .

Avraham Shalom: My first goal when I was appointed as Shin Bet director was the Jewish Underground. I talked about it in a lecture at the Ministry of Foreign Affairs two days after I was appointed as head of the Service. I told them, "I have to catch them, like I catch Arab terrorists. There's no difference on my end. Pray to Muhammad or pray to Moses, it's the same thing." At the end of the day, he kills people. The enemy that's hardest to catch is the one who comes from within. That's the one that can cause the greatest harm, because it's a cancer that eats you from the inside.

I saw the buds of the Jewish Underground back when they allowed Rabbi Levinger to enter the Park Hotel in Hebron. We started to enclose them. This is Hadassah's house, this is that one's house, this is another person's house, and they closed off the whole street and children started yelling, "Nazis!"

Do you understand? Jewish children started to yell "Nazis" at our soldiers because the soldiers set up fences so they wouldn't move from one side to the other. They got cocky. I remember it. I was sitting in some meeting, and they were talking about Hebron. Just a day before or something like that they'd declared it "the city of our forefathers." You know how they'd talk. So I told them, "Guys, there are a hundred thousand Arabs there and not one Jew. One people can't control another people. Don't waste your efforts." So they looked at me like I was crazy, like I was betraying Israel's eternal heritage. I've learned my lesson since then.

What Peres allowed Levinger to do is inconceivable. And he's not a right-winger, Peres. He's not a left-winger, but he's not right-wing. And he allowed it out of weakness. To settle in Hebron, in the Park Hotel? He should have thrown him out of there along with his nineteen kids. Thrown him out. There and in Sebastia [where a settlement was built in 1975].* They should have killed it while it was still small, because later you can't control it. The fact is, today there are

---

* Rabbi Levinger and others rented the Park Hotel in Hebron when their attempts to rent houses in Hebron in order to establish a Jewish settlement failed. A Passover ceremony was held at the hotel in 1968.

400,000 settlers, and 250,000 settlers in the settlements I call illegal. But you can't throw them out. How can you throw them out? You can't. So how can you make peace? You can't.

Ya'akov Peri: When Gush Emunim was established, in '74, the Security Service didn't just nod in response to their organization. But a decision was reached which the Service actually maintains to this day, that Gush Emunim, as an entity, is not an object for coverage. Illegal settlements were created despite the government's decisions, or in opposition to the government's decisions, but there's no prime minister and no government in Israel that didn't agree to them, that didn't resign itself to them. That's true since that time and to this day.

The fact is that since the settlements began, all of Israel's governments have been dragged along, and didn't take care to regulate the settlements' establishment and their expansion, and gave the settlers, or at least some of them, the impression that they were slowly becoming masters. That impression also caused them to decide to take control of law and order activities, such as vengeance campaigns against Arabs, whether physically or by vindictive actions against property, orchards, olives, taking over lands. The minute these people found legitimacy for taking action the government hadn't approved, some of them concluded they had to take the law into their own hands and execute justice and punishment themselves.

Carmi Gillon: In 1980, a Fatah cell attacked worshippers leaving a synagogue in Hebron on Friday after a Friday night prayer in the Cave of the Patriarchs, and the settlers, on the thirtieth day, carried out a vengeance attack and hurt the mayors—Bassam Shakaa in Nablus and Karim Hallaf in Ramallah. In al-Bireh, an explosive charge is discovered, explodes, and blinds a Border Patrol bomb disposal expert, in the home of mayor Ibrahim Tawil. It was clear that someone did that of their own initiative, even though [left-wing Israeli politician] Yossi Sarid thought maybe Sayeret Matkal [an elite Israeli Special Forces unit] or Shin Bet people had done it. There were all kinds of strange suspicions regarding that. And the Service doesn't even have the tools to start looking.

Ya'akov Peri: We knew Jews had done it, we didn't think for a moment that some competing organization blew the legs off Karim

Hallaf from Ramallah and Bassam Shakaa from Nabulus. You check within the Jewish material, and you find out you don't have a clue, and you understand you've got a problem, that you're facing intelligence failure.

Carmi Gillon: You've got to understand, the topic of the extreme right was hardly handled by the Service during that period because of an informed decision made by Avraham Ahituv, head of the Service before Avrum. Ahituv came to the conclusion in '77, following [the triumph of the Likud-led right-wing coalition in the Knesset], that the right in Israel is attaining satisfaction. The illegal settlement movement would become the legal settlement movement, settlement in the West Bank and the Gaza Strip would be completely legitimate, backed by the government, and really, the extreme right has nothing to complain about, and in view of that, he effectively shut down this unit.

Avraham Shalom: I remember that when they blew off the legs of the West Bank mayors, no one believed that Jews had done it. Only Jews could have done it, but they didn't want to believe. They told me, "Leave it alone, it's not that!" I told them, "Leave it alone? That's what we'll focus on." We arrested fifty–sixty people, but it took us three years to crack that organization.

I appointed Carmi Gillon, who was in security then, to investigate the Underground. I thought he was a guy with brains. I was right. Reuven Hazak was Carmi's HQ man, and it worked out well, because you really had to incorporate all possible non-Arab minds. You couldn't appoint a religious Jew there, and you couldn't appoint an "Arabist," because it's different material. And it was very interesting to watch Carmi's development within that milieu. He flourished there. Otherwise, he wouldn't have become head of the Service. I think he did a good job there.

Ya'akov Peri: We established a team and started scanning person by person, clue by clue, detail by detail. It took us about two years to get to clues indicating that maybe we had some kind of direction. But you still couldn't deduce serious intelligence conclusions from them. And then we activated the whole technological apparatus, and the Service's Operations unit. The Operations unit worked tens of thousands of hours, if not more, and we started to cover, in both the intelligence and the operational sense, those people who, according to the indications we'd received, might be involved. We worked like that for a whole year, day and night.

And when the clue came, it was completely circumstantial information from which we eventually attained an initial lead. An explosive charge wrapped in newspapers was found in a fuse box in Kiryat Arba. The Service tracked down the place where those newspapers were sold—it was either *La'Isha* or *At* [two Hebrew-language periodicals aimed at women]—found the newspaper salesman, and checked with him who was buying them. That's how we got to "Zambish" [Ze'ev Hever, one of the leaders of the settlement movement].

Carmi Gillon: The Underground's great mistake was that they carried out the attack against the mayors, but they didn't stop there. In July '83, Aharon Gross, a Yeshiva student, may he rest in peace, was murdered in Hebron. And again, on the thirtieth day, a vengeance attack takes place at the Islamic College of Hebron. Masked men break into the college and kill three and injure others with shooting and grenades. And that's where we actually realize we're dealing with a group.

Now, the Jewish Underground members were the most normative people in the world. People who would never cross on a red light. People who contribute to society, who served in elite units, who actually toil day and night for the people of Israel in the most legitimate way. Moreover, some of them are even leaders of the public in which they reside, and in that capacity they, for example, have contact with the prime minister, are friends with ministers. They're part of the respected establishment in the State of Israel. But simultaneously, there's a niche in their life they don't share with anyone.

Menachem Livni, one of the Underground's leaders, was under surveillance. He'd come once a week for a meeting with the prime minister. What does the surveillance team do? That team was used to following Muhammad who goes to meet Ahmed, but now they have this suspect. They follow him, he arrives at the gate of the prime minister's bureau, the gate opens, he goes in, he goes up, he passes the glass doors and goes in to see the prime minister. And what's the surveillance team supposed to do? Go in after him? Not go in after him? "Zambish" comes to a political party meeting, or to a Knesset committee meeting. Does the surveillance team follow him into the Knesset? Muhammad never goes into the Knesset, believe me.

These are completely legitimate people, which is definitely problematic. One of them goes on reserve duty, and gets to Lebanon that way, and he's told, "You'll provide security for the Shin Bet." And I don't even know it! I'm so compartmentalized within the Service, that the Tire sub-district doesn't know that when Haim Ben David arrives from Keshet to secure one of the coordinators or interrogators there, they should ask me. Why would they ask me? What is he, a criminal? One of the people arrested from the Jewish Underground, his father worked in the Shin Bet in the same corridor where I sat.

In the dead of night, these people go and place an explosive charge in the mayor of Nablus's or the mayor of Ramallah's car, and the next morning one of them, for example, journalist Hagai Segal, goes to the *Nekuda* journal, where he's assistant editor. Nathan Nathanson goes to his job as head of the Gush Emunim settlement movement, "Zambish" is head of the Kiryat Arba council. All extraordinary people, and at night they do what they do.

Ya'akov Peri: We understood that if we didn't catch them red-handed, we'd never crack that bunch. And then they planned a new terrorist attack—to place explosive charges in buses of Palestinian vacationers in a Jerusalem parking lot.

Carmi Gillon: The attack they planned was a crazy one. They intended to blow up five buses on Friday and kill 250 Arabs simultaneously, as retaliation for the attacks on buses that were happening in Jerusalem at the time—still not suicide attacks. But initially we only knew they were going to do something, we didn't know what, and we tracked them through the Operations unit. Night in Jerusalem, 2 a.m., it's not at all easy to track someone. There was a stage where we lost them, and then we found them again.

You're in the field?

Gillon: I'm at the operational HQ, I'm in a command post with Avrum and with Peri.

And you hear that you've lost them?

Of course. What happened was that Avrum wanted to go up to Jerusalem; we didn't have cell phones and all that then, like we do today. So he was stuck with the phone in his bedroom, and I kept reporting to him what was going on. There were moments of immense tension there.

You see them placing explosives on one of the buses, and then they disappear on you?

And then they go from bus to bus. Look, none of those buses would have exploded, because we wouldn't have let them move, but at some point they just disappeared.

What's going through your mind when they disappear?

Anxiety. There's no other word. A feeling of anxiety, what happens if something blows up on us and we don't know. And an immense feeling of missed opportunity. You've been working for almost two years focusing on this. And I'm not alone. I'm with a lot of good people who worked days and nights to crack this thing.

Avraham Shalom: I came at the last minute to tell them, "Don't catch them until I say so." They wanted to catch them before they planted the bomb, and I said, "Wait till it's proven that the bomb is a bomb and that they want to plant it there." You have to wait till the last minute. You need nerve for that, and they didn't have it. I got in the car and flew to Jerusalem, and they caught them after I arrived.

Ya'akov Peri: We arrested them at four-thirty in the morning, while they were placing the explosives in the buses. Then we got out of the cars and told them, "Come join us. If you don't want something to happen to the Jerusalem Police bomb disposal team, come defuse the bombs you've planted," and then one of the Nir brothers told us, "Damn, you're the best intelligence agency in the world." They went, defused the bombs, and then we made the first wave of arrests, including seventeen members. Then we dug deeper and found out that as of 1978 or 1979, they've been planning an attack in the Temple Mount. Blowing up the Dome of the Rock.

Carmi Gillon: Eventually, thirty people are arrested, twenty-seven of whom established the Jewish Underground. They included Shaul Nir, Menachem Livni, Barak Nir, Shaul's brother, and Uzi Sharback, Rabbi Levinger's son-in-law. In the course of the investigation, the story of the planned attack on the Temple Mount was revealed, as well as additional attacks we didn't know about, and we effectively clear the table. The investigation unfolded a lot more simply than we'd thought. Everyone confessed.

The person who opened up the Temple Mount story was Yeshua Ben Shushan, who simply said to the interrogators, "You're dealing with small change here, a few Arabs died here, a few Arabs died there, big deal. Us, we've got something way more serious, but I'm not willing to tell you, you're not senior enough. I'm willing to tell [Israeli military leader and politician] Fuad [Ben Eliezer]." Fuad was Yeshua Ben Shushan's commander in Sayeret Shaked [a former IDF Southern Command special forces unit], and was activity coordinator in the Territories at the time. In the end he compromised on Peri, as head of district. By the way, he knew Peri. Like I said, he was part of the system, he was an officer in the Central District.

Then he tells Peri the Temple Mount story of his own free will. He doesn't name any names, but he tells the story and tries to convince Peri of the ideological justification for the deed. That's what was important to him. That we think he's not just a criminal, but a serious thinker. And he explains the whole process. The idea was based on the thought that so long as "the abomination," meaning the Dome of the Rock mosque, remains in place of the Holy of Holies, there would be no redemption for the people of Israel, so that dome had to be eliminated. In '77, it became a practical plan after Sadat visited in Israel and the evacuation of the Sinai Peninsula began. So they also came to a political conclusion, that there's no doubt the Egyptians would halt the peace process the minute the Dome of the Rock was blown up. And they were right. There's no doubt they were right about that.

In the beginning, they approached mainstream rabbis. They didn't ask them, "What's your opinion about us blowing up the Dome of the Rock?" but they tried to understand if redemption can be speeded up through human actions, and they got a negative answer from the rabbis of Mercaz HaRav Yeshiva, which is the stream almost all of them belong to. Both because it could cause a world war between Jews and Muslims, and because the hearts of the people of Israel are still not ready for the arrival of the Messiah. They then approached Kabbalah-oriented rabbis, who are more messianic by nature, and they did receive an authorization from them. One of them, for that matter, was Yeshua Ben Shushan himself, who was not an ordained rabbi, but was a man of spirit and religious learning, and was perceived by them as a rabbi.

Operationally, they had everything ready. They went up to the Temple Mount a few times to collect OI—operational intelligence. They prepared the explosive charges. The explosives were prepared in a factory in Rishon LeZion that didn't know what it was making. This was planned by Menachem Livni, who was no doubt a genius in the field of sabotage. He was once a very well-known figure in IDF. David Laskov [a celebrated military engineer] said he was one of the geniuses in that field. The idea was to build explosive containers, fill them with a very sensitive explosive, Semtex, and cause the whole volume of the explosion to go toward the pillars and the posts, which would cause the dome to collapse. The reason they went for such a sophisticated plan was an attempt to prevent injuries in the Western Wall. It really was an exceptional plan. After we caught him, Menachem Livni asked to meet with old Laskov, who was already eighty-something years old, to explain the plan to him. Meaning they also had professional pride. They weren't just criminals.

To buy these containers, which are made of titanium and are very, very expensive, Menachem Livni used severance pay from his wife, who was a retired teacher, and spent about 200,000 shekels, which at the time was a lot of money, a fortune. At some point they also needed the explosives. Since they were all military men—there was also one pilot among them—they know one IDF device which contains a large amount of Semtex, and they infiltrate the Emergency Warehouse Unit in the Golan Heights and simply empty out the explosives. One of the things that bothered them was what if a war broke out, and the weapons are actually useless, so they assigned one of them, Gilad Peli, to call the division commander and warn him, "You should know your weapons are worthless."

How do they gather intelligence about the Dome of the Rock?

They go up, climb the Temple Mount, get in under this or that cover. One of them, Dan Be'eri, was a convert to Judaism who used to be a priest. So he dresses up as a priest, he has no problem maintaining his cover, and he infiltrates the Temple Mount and says he's conducting some kind of research. He's dressed like a priest, and one of the [Muslim] Waqf guards [responsible for guarding the Temple Mount] even grabs one end of the measuring tape for him, he grabs the other side, and they measure the distance between the pillars, between the posts. They had no problems. They just made incursions into the Temple Mount and saw what security procedures were in place. One of the problems they had was that there was an Israeli police station on the Temple Mount, and it was clear they'd go flying, too, but that's the price of messianic belief.

How did you feel when you understood what they were planning?

When Emil Grunzweig* was killed, I didn't sleep all night. I was looking for leads to locate the person who'd tossed the grenade. At seven in the morning I pop home to shave, change, and go back to work, and my wife tells me, "Did you hear? Emil Grunzweig was killed." And I tell her, "What? Where?" She says, "There was a terrorist attack, you didn't hear? They threw a grenade at a Peace Now rally!" I knew Emil Grunzweig personally. My wife's brother lives in Revivim, and Emil was from Revivim, a good friend of his. I wasn't aware of it. I didn't care who had been murdered. Do you understand how far that professional numbness goes? So I can't tell you I grabbed my hair and pulled it and said, "Such great luck that we were spared that," and so on; that looks good in a movie, but it's not the truth. At the time, I can't tell you I was blown away by this; I just kept on working. When we got that story, we still hadn't cracked the attack against the mayors, we still had a lot of work to do. But later, the deeper you delve into it, the deeper your anxiety gets. And it threatens me. I really feel it physically. Even today, many years after I left the system.

If, God forbid, someone shoots a missile at the Dome of the Rock, or at the al-Aqsa mosque, and blows up that dome, I don't know if we're not screwed. I'm intentionally using non-standard language so that every single person understands me. If something happens to the Temple Mount, I wouldn't want to be a Jew in Paris, and I certainly wouldn't want to be a Jew in Israel.

Ya'akov Peri: Can you imagine if, God forbid, it had happened, even if it had failed? Even if the bomb would have dropped and not gone

---

* An Israeli activist affiliated with the Peace Now movement, killed by a grenade thrown at a peace rally in Jerusalem in 1983.

off. It's the end of the world for you. Success in blowing up the Dome of the Rock mosque is initiating a world war between us and the Muslim world. And the planning was operational. The people who prevented it, absurdly enough, were the rabbis, who said the people of Israel's "hearts are not yet prepared for such action." There were a few smart rabbis who found the solution, and that's how it was prevented. But Boaz Heneman, who was an Israeli Air Force pilot, had already made reconnaissance flights over the Temple Mount, and all the weapons were ready. It was just one more step between doing it and not doing it. What saved the thing was first of all their consultation with the rabbis, but you also can't underestimate their intelligence, and I think they understood that even then. It was one step between this business and the whole Islamic world declaring war on us.

Did you interrogate the rabbis who talked to them?

Peri: Of course. We talked, we met, we tried to understand. Over the years, even before Rabin's murder. Carmi and others met with many rabbis, and we tried to understand. I'm not saying we got added value from those meetings. The rabbis were quite leery about opening up to us. Some of them renounced it, and some of them maintained their extreme views. Remember, during the time the Jewish Underground was exposed, the Shin Bet which was "the good Shin Bet" for the West Bank settlers, the Shin Bet that prevents terrorist attacks, the Shin Bet that arrests Arabs, became the bad Shin Bet, which arrests our sons, arrests our people and listens in on us and tracks us.

If someone comes to me and says he's going to blow up. . . .

It's your duty to go and report to the police, or else you'll be prosecuted for failing to prevent a crime.

Why wasn't that done to the rabbis?

They tried to do it; there wasn't enough evidence. They claim they didn't know. Ultimately, we couldn't prosecute or produce conclusive evidence which would enable us to prosecute a rabbi.

Avraham Shalom: Even back in '67, there were people who wanted to blow up the Temple Mount, who weren't religious extremists. How can you deal with a person whose witness is God? What are you going to do? You've got no dialogue with him. The Underground members themselves were terrorists who hate Arabs. They thought that by bombing al-Aqsa, you could save the people of Israel. Crazy people. There's no talking with people like that. You hurt people, women and children, and you call it ideology? You should catch them like you catch the others and throw them in jail. It's simple. Anyone who thinks you can discriminate in the way you treat Jews and Arabs shouldn't be the head of the Service.

How did the political system react to the exposure of the Underground?

Carmi Gillon: The political system reacted in a very positive way. Like it always reacts. It gets all enthusiastic about elegant operations. Prime Minister Shamir defines my unit as "the jewel in the crown." We get praise and sympathy from all directions. After the arrest, there was very broad condemnation. Even the journal *Nekuda*, the settlers' publication, published condemning editorials, mostly about the Temple Mount story. That's where they crossed the line, as far as the settlers were concerned. But very quickly, people started getting swept up. Ultimately, these are the darlings of the West Bank settlement movement, and a public movement to release them is formed. It was called "For My Brothers and Friends"—"Laor."

And then the advocacy groups start working, and I find myself dealing with this one's Brith ceremony, and that one's prison leave, because they were classified as security prisoners, and I had to give my opinion—yes or no. It was awful. I was in the Service body and soul, one of the most secret positions, even within the Service, and I start to get phone calls from [Orthodox] Rabbi Drukman [a former leader of Israeli religious parties], and phone calls from [prominent, religious, right-wing politician] Hanan Porat. It starts to get completely crazy, and then Avrum decides that he's no longer responsible for the Underground. They're transferred to regular treatment by the Israel Prison Service and the state attorney, stand trial, and are sentenced to terms of three years to life. Three of them were sentenced to life, but they all left prison very quickly through the Pardon Law. Since the Ministry of Justice refused to support such an early pardon, the Knesset enacted a special Pardon Law for the Jewish Underground.

Avraham Shalom: Yuval Ne'eman [a scientist, politician, and member of the right-wing Tehiya party] comes to me, and another one, and another one. All kinds of rabbis whose names I'd never heard before, they were all Knesset members. Came to me in a convoy. And I told them, "Guys, don't come to me. You're wasting your time." They asked not to prosecute them at all. In that period the Underground members were already in custody, but weren't serving jail time. But it wasn't an option. The minute that happens, we've got a real problem with the Security Service. But I don't think it's happened to this day.

In the end they let them out after two years. If I'd have been head of the Service, I would have fought that like you'd fight a fire. [Chaim] Herzog [Israeli president from 1983 to 1993] did it. Shamir tried to do it even in my time. He told me, "This one, I was his godfather, and this one's a friend of my friend." I told him, "I don't care about that. When you were his godfather, he was eight days old. What do you know about him?" The minute he came to me begging with the godfather story, I was done with him. I told him, "Listen, don't interfere here. I'm head of the Service. Do you want me to be head of the Service? Let me do my work."

When Yitzhak Shamir effectively signs the pardon request, what message does that send out?

Carmi Gillon: It's very frustrating, but I can't tell you I stopped working as a result of it.

And what's the effect on them, the Underground members?

Gillon: It gives them legitimacy. Are you kidding? They feel wonderful. Maybe they're even right. Although I have to say that in the Jewish Underground, at least as far as I know, they left their evil ways behind. There were people among them like Uri Meir from the Golan Heights who really dedicated their time, went from yeshiva to yeshiva and from school to school to explain what a mistake they'd made. I think that most of them have real remorse. Not all of them, it's true, but most of them.

Ya'akov Peri: Avraham Ahituv, who was head of the Service between 1974 and 1980, wrote an interesting article in *Davar* newspaper on August 19, 1983, and I'm quoting a section that reflects my opinion on the matter, too: "The failure to capture those responsible for the amputation of the legs of the West Bank mayors reflects primarily an intelligence failure which has no justification. The question arises whether security authorities didn't miss an opportunity to track a certain population group in advance. Most of the unauthorized settlements came as no surprise to the senior political echelon. Those who were resigned to them not only legitimized them, but also precluded any practical basis and intelligence justification for an investigative intelligence presence among this population."

Now, this was written by a Service director, who served in the role six years. A man who comes from a religious background, from a yeshiva. That's very meaningful. There's a very subtle but very cutting criticism here of the political echelon, which resigns itself to the establishment of illegal settlements, meaning to a violation of the law, and law violations begin with establishing a settlement or with beating up an Arab. Things that may be considered "lightweight" prepare some members, maybe just a minority, of that population to get to where the Underground members eventually got. And this article, of course, evoked the wrath of Menachem Begin, the prime minister. At the time it wasn't acceptable for a former head of the Service to openly criticize the political echelon.

Carmi Gillon: He was completely right, Ahituv. All the first settlements, Shavei Shomron or Sebastia, Alon More, Beit El, Ofra, Shiloh—they were all established as illegal settlements under this or that cover. And the political echelon couldn't justify it, so it winked. The Service suddenly found itself in a zone, as far as Ahituv was concerned, where it actually treated illegal activity as illegal activity, while its bosses were legitimizing it. The same thing actually happened with the Jewish Underground. In the beginning, "Oh no, they violated the law, they killed people, they wanted to blow up the whole country," and so on. But later, "They're all flesh of our flesh. . . ." And then the Shin Bet is the one that gets delegitimized. I was personally delegitimized by the extreme right, including when I was appointed as Service director. They found a master's thesis I'd written at the University of Haifa about ideological criminality in the extreme right in Israel, and said, "That man can't be head of the Shin Bet because he's opposed to the extreme right in Israel." I had very firm opinions about that underground. All in view of the damage to the State of Israel. It has nothing to do with worldview or politics. It has to do with the damage an ideological criminal could cause us.

In your master's thesis you wrote, "Law violations for ideological reasons by the extreme right threaten the democratic values

of society. There's a process of escalation in ideological criminality by the extreme right, both in terms of activity volume and in terms of activity intensity. This will also lead to a concrete threat on the state's existence. Society in Israel exhibits tolerance toward this criminality by the extreme right, and bestows a retroactive legitimacy upon this activity." You nearly predicted the future, and this was in 1990.

Gillon: That part, by the way, I'd already written in '88. I wrote a paper for the National Defense College, but I copied that sentence into my master's thesis in '90. Yes. That's my prophecy. It came true in its entirety, unfortunately.

Yaa'kov Peri: The Jewish Underground affair ultimately really shook up the Service. It brought about the establishment of the intelligence apparatus that since then has been watching over those suspects in the West Bank. But as reality shows you, you supervise and you act, and then you get someone like Yigal Amir, who was never on an actual list of "Service suspects" and one morning shoots the prime minister.

The Appointment

"He got the life sucked out of him before Rabin said yes."

In the Shin Bet, they'd already wondered whether the prime minister had forgotten that in a week, the old Service director was going home, and a successor had yet to be appointed. The nerves of C., the leading candidate, were worn thin with every speculation launched, until at last Yitzhak Rabin informed him that he was the man who would lead the Shin Bet during the difficult period awaiting us soon. . . .

(*Ma'ariv*, February 20, 1995)

Carmi Gillon: My appointment as Service director was not that obvious. I was C., but opposing me was G., who was Gideon Ezra, and there were others who saw themselves as worthy to be head of the Service. There were major generals, there were lieutenant generals, the stock market of names was bustling. It got constant attention. Ultimately, Ya'akov Peri, who was head of the Service, actually skipped a generation. Gideon Ezra was from Peri's generation, more or less, even more senior than him. He was the most senior of the department heads. The appointment was conveyed to the sole determination of Prime Minister Rabin, and it took him a very long time to decide. Even within his office, there were supporters and opponents, but ultimately he chose me. He invited me to a meeting, and informed me in a one-on-one conversation that he was appointing me to Service director. He also tried to give me all kinds of suggestions about appointments and so on, and I asked him not to interfere, of course using diplomatic language.

What I can say is that in the short period when I was head of Service under him, I'd wish a boss like that on anyone. There was one case where the Service screwed up, I can't specify, but the Service screwed up. Things got messed up, a coordinator didn't grasp what he was dealing with, and a serious mishap happened. Rabin called me and demolished me. Really demolished me. But I left the room and it was over. He didn't mention it again, and anyone who tried to say one bad word about the Service suffered his wrath, not mine.

I assumed the role in the midst of a crisis over the question of who was in charge of diplomatic intelligence following the Oslo Accords. This argument was conducted in the prime minister's office, and he ultimately decided that the Shin Bet would be the leading agency in the whole Palestinian topic, in regard to both terror and political aspects. From that moment, the Shin Bet attained intelligence primacy. You become the right hand of the prime minister almost daily. The Service developed a very high volume as a national assessor. In accordance with the fact that the subject with which the prime minister was involved more than any other was terror, and the Service has always had the lead there.

Do you emphasize your weight opposite Rabin regarding your political assessments of what Arafat was thinking and where he wanted to take this conflict?

Gillon: Look, the one who holds the knowledge is the one who holds the power in this case. The Shin Bet was the agency in charge of intelligence collection, including on Arafat. So, obviously, I had the knowledge. Usually, there's positive competition between the three intelligence entities in the State of Israel—Aman, the Mossad, and the Shin Bet. We do meet in the Service Directors' Committee, but there were periods when the head of the Mossad and the head of Aman weren't speaking to each other, and I was the mediator. There are prestige wars here, which are harmless. I'll give you an example. Every entity puts out a daily intelligence report. Who are they addressed to? The prime minister. The prime minister comes to work in the morning, sits down at his desk. What's the first thing he reads?

The daily intelligence report.

You're wrong. *Ha'aretz* newspaper. Then comes the question, which daily intelligence report will he read, the Shin Bet's, the Mossad's, or Aman's? Now, we all have human frailties, right? We prefer to pick up high-quality paper, well spaced out, with large-font letters. The Shin Bet is a modest, Spartan institution. Our intelligence reports looked like stencil pages. For those who don't remember, those were pages on which you put ink, and a big stain was formed, with small-font letters, on an electrical typewriter; it was horrendous. In contrast, Aman, the Mossad, they're rich, they've got plenty of resources. . . . One of the things I did as head of the Shin Bet was to go out and contact an advertising executive. I said, "Design a page for me that would make someone want to read it." And I sat him down with the head of the Arab department at the time, Yuval Diskin, and they designed an intelligence report—without the content, just the layout, the way it should look to be the first report. You understand, that's how far the competition goes.

How do you obtain information from Arafat's vicinity?

Look, first of all, during this period, we're still present in the Gaza Strip. The Shin Bet is on its way out, but we still have high accessibility in the field, the settlements exist in the strip, IDF is sitting in the Strip, and we manage.

[Likud party official] Uri Shani told me, "We knew what Arafat's health status was. People would say, he'll live another thirty years. . . ."

Let me tell you, when it comes to health matters, the entire Israeli intelligence community failed. Assad Senior died an intelligence death thirty years before the date he actually died. Hussein executed him once a week. We're not good at health, and when we try to act on health matters, like with Khaled Mashal,* we don't always succeed.

---

* A senior member of Hamas and the organization's leader since 2004. In September 1997, the Mossad tried to poison Mashal while he was in Jordan, but ultimately ended up supplying the Jordanians with an antidote to save his life.

You're head of the Service on the day Arafat enters Gaza?

Yes. It's a day that, the more you prepare for it, the more it surprises you. He came to the Gaza Strip first, then also moved into Jericho. He got settled in a villa on the beach that some millionaire gave him, and of course he's received with much applause and with demonstrations of support, and those are the moments where you feel, like when terrorists are released—this feeling of frustration, when you see the gloating. There, Arafat has won and he's here. Very quickly he was subsumed in street fights with Hamas, and a lot of tension formed there, politically and practically. By the way, if we're talking about moderation, that wasn't a trait he excelled in. In a demonstration there they killed about twenty Hamas demonstrators. Major upheaval.

Are you aware of the fact that when he goes in, he brings weapons with him?

We weren't aware of that. I also don't think this story's entirely true, but it's a good story, it would be a shame to spoil it. Look, Arafat was very clever. You couldn't catch him red-handed at anything.

Actually, from the moment he goes in, I often come to meetings with him in the Strip. The meetings take place at midnight. The prime minister's contact person was Yossi Ginossar, may he rest in peace. Avi Dichter was the head of district, and the three of us would meet him at his home. The meetings were always very nice. The heads of his defense administration would come, [Palestinian Authority intelligence chief] Amin al-Hindi and [Palestinian Preventive Security Force commander] Mohammed Dahlan and guys like that, and we'd sit there and chat. From the first moment, we had very firm demands, mostly because of the rise in Hamas activity.

Suicide Attacks and the Dilemma of the Ticking Bomb

"Without shaking, we wouldn't have achieved the results we achieved."

So says the head of the Shin Bet. The suicide bomber handler, Abed el-Nasser Issa, a student of "The Engineer" [Yahya Ayyash, chief bomb-maker for Hamas], was arrested two days before the attack in Jerusalem. He wasn't "shaken," and did not cooperate with his interrogators. Only after the attack did the director of the Shin

Bet authorize the use of special methods of interrogation, and then the terrorist revealed how he'd conveyed the explosive charge to the suicide bomber who blew up the bus in Jerusalem. He also admitted responsibility for the terrorist attack in Ramat Gan. Shin Bet Director: "If I hadn't authorized the shaking, the blood of the next victims would be on my hands."

(*Ma'ariv*, August 24, 1995)

Carmi Gillon: When I started my job, what greeted me was Hamas suicide attacks. I remember that the first bus I was on was Bus 5 in Tel Aviv on Dizengoff, on October 19, 1994. It was the first suicide attack within Tel Aviv. And I remember myself getting there on a motorcycle. All the roads were blocked, so an Operations motorcyclist took me there, and I won't forget that thing. It was the first time I felt I couldn't disengage from that vision . . . of the stench, of the burning bodies. I won't forget it. Then I got over it. Later I was on a lot of other buses, and I got over it.

And you actually think about it. You're here in the heart of Dizengoff, my daughter, my mother-in-law, my friend could have been on this bus. Here on Dizengoff, in the heart of Dizengoff. And I'm not from Tel Aviv; I'm from Jerusalem. These are the moments when you feel very, very alone. The weight of responsibility is immense. Really immense.

Yuval Diskin: In May 1993, the first suicide attack took place in Mechola. A terrorist with a car who wanted to explode on a bus full of soldiers. He had a work accident, and lucky for us, he was killed in the car, and nothing happened to the soldiers. Initially, we weren't convinced that it was a suicide attack. It took us time to understand that he'd just come to commit suicide there. This was the first time a suicide attack by a Sunni Muslim took place in Israeli territory. Till then the prevalent belief among us was that only Shiites in Lebanon carry out suicide attacks. That axiom shattered. It wasn't really based on facts, of course. If they had checked, the whole religious and ideological infrastructure was there in the Sunnah, too. You just needed someone to say it and someone to execute it.

Let's talk about [Baruch] Goldstein, the lone Jewish terrorist, who actually tries to take a gun and change or stop the process—how does the Service experience Goldstein's massacre?

Diskin: What Goldstein did was a very brutal terrorist attack. I wasn't working in the Jewish field at the time, but the feeling in the Service every time a terrorist attack that you couldn't prevent takes place is a very harsh feeling of failure, of disappointment. Definitely more so the larger the attack is. A very harsh feeling of disappointment. How come we didn't prevent that? And then there's always the story of the lone terrorist, which always raises the question to what extent he was really acting alone. To what extent is this a person who acted on some momentary or temporary impulse that motivated him without sharing it with anyone else. But on the timeline, the attack in Mechola we were talking about is actually the first suicide attack, then came Baruch Goldstein's massacre in the Cave of the Patriarchs, twenty-nine Palestinian worshippers murdered, and dozens injured. Everyone's looking for the chicken and the egg. It's not right to take the Goldstein massacre story and turn it into the egg for everything else. Baruch Goldstein further nourished the cycle of blood here. The religious connotation of massacring worshippers evoked, without a doubt, waves of a desire for vengeance, and that was very profitable for those who had already been carrying out attacks, and this way they had more legitimacy to carry out attacks which would be on the same scale as what Goldstein did. That way one thing feeds into another and a kind of *perpetuum mobile* is formed, which can't be stopped or is very hard to stop. I always tried to explain to Service people that their professionalism is crucial. Because sometimes the difference between preventing a terrorist attack and not preventing it can have strategic implications.

Carmi Gillon: One of the things characterizing Fatah was that they worked in large groups. There were collaborators. It was easier to crack them. Hamas, the minute it switched to suicide attacks, was working with incredible compartmentalization. [Hamas military chief] Mohammed Deif could determine, "You two abduct Nachshon Wachsman,* and you just bring the car, and you just bring the food." Everyone has a role, and the only one who knows the whole picture is Mohammed Deif. Same thing with Yahya Ayyash. He would

---

* Israeli soldier Nachshon Wachsman was abducted by Hamas and held hostage for six days. He was killed by his captors following a failed Israeli rescue attempt.

catch the suicide bomber, convince him, pair him up with an escort, and those connected to transporting the explosive charge and those connected to transporting the suicide terrorist to the destination, in Jerusalem or in Tel Aviv, no one knows who the others are. The second problem is that they're fanatical.

Yuval Diskin: We were already familiar with the characters working in the organizations. No aliens landed and changed the map. What changed was field conditions. In the past, we controlled the territory and prevented terrorist attacks by our very presence in the field and our ability to arrive at any given place at any given time. With Oslo, suicide attacks entered the picture, along with transferring the territory to the Palestinians, and your prevention ability was dramatically decreased. You were politically prohibited from entering the territory. How do you invent some trick that lets you thwart attacks even though you're no longer in charge of the area, and have no tools to do it? It took us time to get used to it, and to develop capabilities and doctrines which could effectively handle the topic. During that time, Hamas believed it could cause the process to collapse, and by the way, it was pretty successful.

Avi Dichter: All kinds of anecdotes came up in the interrogations, where sometimes you can't even understand how you can get to a suicide attack from a situation like that. There was a student from Birzeit University who was brought in for interrogation because he intended to carry out a suicide attack. He told his dispatcher, who I think was a Hamas activist, that he could commit suicide on Sunday or Monday and on Tuesday he couldn't. The dispatcher told this during the interrogation, since he was arrested before the suicide bomber. When we arrested the suicide bomber, the interrogators got a confession very quickly, but they were curious about this story of yes on Sunday-Monday, no on Tuesday. So he says, Sunday-Monday I'm free, Tuesday I had a test at the university. You're standing at an interrogation across from this person, and even the interrogators can't understand—is this serious? Is this a joke? But it's serious.

Another time, a suicide bomber in Gaza who arrived at the Erez Crossing [a pedestrian and cargo terminal on the Israeli Gaza Strip barrier], ran toward a group of Israelis, yelled, "*Allahu Akbar*" ["God is great"], operated the explosive charge, and, fortunately for us, the main charge wasn't activated. The only things that exploded were the detonator and the secondary explosive, and he lost consciousness. They brought him to Barzilai Hospital in Ashkelon. I was a head of district then. I sent the interrogator to question him the minute he opened his eyes. And then he opens his eyes, looks and sees the interrogator. The interrogator says to him, "Ah, Mahmoud, do you know where you are?" And he tells him, "In heaven." The interrogator says, "What heaven, you're in Barzilai Hospital." So he says, "No, in heaven." An argument starts, heaven, Barzilai. The interrogator understands you can't make progress like this. He says to him, "Okay, Mahmoud, and who am I?" He says to him, "You're a Jew." So he says, "Right. And are there Jews in heaven?" He says to him, "No. Ah, right. I'm really in Barzilai," and started talking.

Carmi Gillon: A person who's willing to sacrifice his life, whether he does it for the virgins in heaven or not, he's got nothing to lose. That's not an interrogee who really cares what happens to his family. He's already relinquished everything anyway. So they're very difficult interrogees. They have, of course, the bad habit of submerging themselves in prayer, and that way they actually barricade themselves and defend themselves. So interrogations of Hamas or Islamic Jihad people are a lot tougher than regular interrogations. They necessitate that the interrogator also be extremely knowledgeable about the Islamic religion, to create a conversation. You have to understand that in an interrogation facility, it's not questions-answers. You create an atmosphere. You converse. You try to create, as strange as it sounds, a relationship of trust.

Now, cases get more complicated when you have what's called a "ticking bomb." When you have a piece of information that a suicide attack or another attack might take place, and the way to get to the answer where and when is in the hands of your interrogee. It's called a "ticking bomb" because time is limited. It's not an attack that will take place in three months. It's something that could happen at any minute, and in that situation, the Landau Commission has authorized the use of what's called "moderate physical pressure." I want to make this clear immediately: we're talking about pressure, moderate pressure, but it doesn't involve torture, but rather all kinds of measures actually intended to decrease the interrogee's resistance. For example, sleep. We're all human beings who need sleep. I'm giving you the things that are already known. Or the matter of the head cover. What's the actual effect of covering the head? You lose your orientation. You're in total darkness and you don't know what's going on around you. Those are types of moderate physical pressure.

And shaking?

Gillon: Shaking happened. It doesn't anymore. What is shaking, really? Shaking comes to create a presence. It contains a threat. It's not torture. It doesn't hurt. If I grab you by the collar and shake you like that, it doesn't hurt you. It might threaten you. When an interrogator stands up and shakes you, you feel threatened. But what happened was that a man named Harizat, a Hamas member from Hebron, was short and he was shaken. And what happened was that due to the "shaken baby effect," it damaged his brain and as a result he died. Meaning if you apply shaking to a grown person, he doesn't give a damn. If you do it to a baby, you're shaking up his whole brain in the box, and that's what happened there.

Some very harsh arguments developed as a result between Michael Ben Yair, who was the attorney general, and me, whether it was permitted or prohibited to use moderate physical pressure. The means of interrogation were authorized at the time by a ministerial committee on interrogation matters, headed by Prime Minister Rabin. The members were Minister of Justice David Libai, Minister of Police Moshe Shahal, and Yossi Sarid. And in this committee, bitter arguments would take place between me and Ben Yair. The discussions were highly confidential, and would take place once every three months. And there they would authorize or not authorize, based on the Landau Commission's conclusions.

As the number of suicide attacks increased, so did the necessity of using moderate physical pressure. Michael Ben Yair thought it was immoral and shouldn't be used. On the other hand, I said that if we don't use it, if today we prevent ninety percent of suicide attacks, we'd only prevent seventy percent of suicide attacks. And the implication is dead Israelis. In between sat the prime minister, who had to decide, and Rabin was driven mad by these arguments. Once he even got really angry, got up all red and yelled at Ben Yair, "You keep telling me what I can't do, for once tell me what I can do!"

At some point, the argument reached the media following the story of a suicide attack in Ramat Eshkol. An interrogee we were holding had information about this planned attack. Because of interrogation procedures, we couldn't use moderate physical pressure on him, despite the fact that he was a "ticking bomb" in every sense of the word. But even if he's a ticking bomb, you still have to conduct a normal interrogation first, and only in the second phase can you switch to moderate physical pressure.

Are you actually saying that that limitation stopped you from preventing a terrorist attack?

Definitely.

And what happened after that attack? Did you shake him?

After that attack we shook him and arrested the whole cell; we got lots of information. And it's a good thing we shook him, because we prevented other terrorist attacks that were already in the pipeline. But the media caught wind of it. And like anything that the media gets hold of, it turned into a treacherous swamp, with mutual badmouthing between C., which is me, and Ben Yair, and all hell broke loose. Ultimately you can say that the discussion was never decided. It went on till 1999, when the Court of High Justice came and effectively erased the Landau Commission report, which I thought was very pragmatic. Landau himself was really a man of extraordinary scope, and he managed to grab the bull by the horns, to shake up the Service. He shook us up more than all of the shakers who were ever in the Service, and initiated a revolution in the Service and installed order. The Court of High Justice ruling also allowed moderate physical pressure, but it just weighed the Shin Bet down with additional conditions that didn't exist in the Landau Report. I also allow myself to think that the state attorney at the time, Dorit Beinisch, supported the Shin Bet's stance on the matter. She was consistently very on-point, and didn't succumb, for example, to her anger at the Service on the topic of Hassan or Mohammed.

What's actually the claim against shaking? The claim is that you can shake ten people—five of them actually had information, and with five of them you made a mistake, so you violated the individual's civil rights. I claim that the public's right to live has equal weight to civil rights, mainly if I don't leave him disabled and don't cause him irreversible damage. So I caused him inconvenience, maybe even ongoing inconvenience, but I didn't hurt his right to live. On the other hand, if in regard to that one person, there's a suspicion that he knows that ten students at the cafeteria of the Hebrew University of Jerusalem are going to die, then I come and place the right of every citizen in the State of Israel to personal security opposite his civil right—as long as I don't torture him like in Guantanamo and I really am applying moderate physical pressure. And this is the question of questions: civil rights opposite public rights. And that's the dilemma of a Service director.

I'll give you another example: how did we get to the house in which Nachshon Wachsman was held after he was abducted, in Bir Nabala? In the Jerusalem District, they started looking for a needle in a haystack. At the initiative of a desk person, and of course under the supervision of Gideon Ezra, they went for vehicle rentals in East Jerusalem, and uncovered a man named Jihad Yarmur, who was a Hamas member. They didn't know he was a terrorist, only that he was active in the Hamas organization, which is also a social organization. They found out he'd rented a vehicle in East Jerusalem, and we arrested Jihad Yarmur. And then Gideon Ezra calls me. It was, I remember, Thursday night. The next day, on Friday evening, the ultimatum expired—when they would kill Nachshon Wachsman. I'll remind you that we had a tape of him in captivity, and they conducted negotiations and demanded we release a great many terrorists, headed by Sheikh Ahmed Yassin.

And this Jihad Yarmur is under arrest. His entire sin, let's not forget, is that he's a Hamas member who rented a vehicle on a day matching the day Nachshon Wachsman was abducted. And he's taken to interrogation, and he doesn't know what they're talking to him about. And Gideon Ezra turns to me and requests permission to interrogate him using moderate physical pressure. What are the reasons? There are no reasons. The only reason is that in twenty-four hours, the ultimatum expires and Nachshon's life is in danger. On the other hand, you don't have intelligence information here. And I don't know what to do, it's a dilemma. Then I decide to authorize it. According to Landau, I'm not allowed to authorize it. I mean, I'm allowed to do anything, it's within my exclusive authority to approve it, I don't have to ask anyone, but in retrospect not only would I pay the price if I was wrong, but so would all my subordinates, primarily the interrogators.

So I try to protect the interrogators in advance. I call Dorit Beinisch, a very rational woman. She was state attorney then, and I tell her, "Dorit, here's the story. I'm authorizing this, but I'm out on a limb here. And I want you to know it, not so that you protect me.

You can't protect me. But if, God forbid, we're wrong and something happens, protect the interrogators. We have no other choice." And she says, "It's a deal." Of course it never occurred to me to call Ben Yair. And Jihad Yarmur is interrogated and admits to his involvement in the abduction. In the morning hours, our forces were already circling the house.

Sayeret Matkal conducted an operation in the evening, which unfortunately failed, and Nachshon was killed, and Nir Poraz, who commanded the force, was also killed. It was a very sad story, but intelligence-wise, it was a brilliant success story. The quality of intelligence we provided to Sayeret Matkal was extraordinary. We gave them a full, accurate description of every floor and where he was and how many stairs are there and in which direction the door opens and everything, and in the end, "for lack of a nail," right? A tiny mishap. They tried to bust the door in instead of pulling it out, and then the abductors shot through the door, killed Nir Poraz, who was commander of the force, and that was that.

I was there at the command post with Ehud Barak, who was chief of general staff, Amnon Lipkin Shachak was his second-in-command, Uri Sagi was head of Aman, Ilan Biran was chief of Central Command, Shaul Mofaz was commander of the operation. It was a very sad evening for all of us. That night, I saw what leadership was. The person who approved the operation was Rabin, as prime minister. We drove from there to Tel Aviv, gathered in his room. The media had already heard that something had happened, and hundreds of reporters from all over the world were huddled there. And the problem is they couldn't find Nir Poraz's mother; he was the son of Maoz Poraz, who was killed in the hijacked El Al plane [in July 1968]. And in IDF, until the families are informed, you don't come out with a statement to the media. On the other hand, everyone had already started to find out.

We sat in Rabin's room, a very bleak atmosphere, and finally Rabin makes a decision that although they still hadn't found the mother, he's going out to the reporters. And he went out with Ehud Barak. And that's where you saw the difference. Ehud Barak was squirming, answering in a very clever way, it's like this and like that. The kind of answers where, when the chief of general staff is speaking, even Ehud Barak doesn't understand what he's saying. And Rabin takes the microphone and says, "I authorized it, I take responsibility for the operation. That's what happened, and one time it works, in

Entebbe* it worked, here it didn't, and the responsibility is all mine. Now ask the chief of general staff whatever you want."

Avraham Shalom: Nachshon Wachsman, that was a tragic mistake. A mistaken consideration by two people who think all of Israel's wars are on their shoulders, and they won them all by themselves, those people being Rabin and Barak. You couldn't win in Wachsman's case, when two terrorists are standing with Wachsman in a fortified house that you couldn't enter, that was impenetrable, you could only blow it up along with its inhabitants, and then all three of them are dead. So if they thought they could take over this house, kill the terrorists, and leave Wachsman alive, they had their heads in the clouds. I asked myself then, where's the operational logic here? You could starve them, you could talk to them with loudspeakers, you could bring the big Imam from the mosque in Cairo to appeal to them, you can do all kinds of things, but to attack this reinforced concrete house, and to still think Wachsman would make it out alive? Why would he make it out alive? Those inside, when they see they have no chance of making it out alive, they'd kill him and die, too.

From what I understood, the explosive charge didn't blow down the door.

Shalom: Listen, the target was reinforced. When you're working with bombs, you can't get out of it alive. It could have happened that Wachsman died and both Arabs would have lived. It's really messed-up reasoning. It's a shame to say it, but it's really messed-up reasoning. There are some actions that the army commemorated as successful operations, but they didn't necessarily have to succeed. In the Entebbe liberation, there was no other choice. You had to go there, release them, and whoever gets killed gets killed, and whoever survives survives. In liberating the Sabena flight, it wasn't like that. They stormed a destination that was actually in your territory, and you were in control of every centimeter and of every interval,

* Operation Entebbe was a successful counterterrorist hostage-rescue mission carried out by IDF commandos on July 4, 1976, at Entebbe Airport in Uganda to release passengers from a plane hijacked by the Popular Front for the Liberation of Palestine. One hundred and two hostages were rescued.

every second of the operation. You could stop, start, go back, go forward, hide. There was a good chance of it both succeeding and failing. With the Wachsman thing, there was no chance of success.* No chance. And I don't understand how these people rely on operations like Beirut or Tunis in the attempt to rescue Wachsman. That's a military operational worldview which progresses like a tank. Instead of a spy, you go with a tank. It doesn't work. Today it's the same thing. We have an Israeli-Palestinian conflict, we proceed like a tank.

The Writing on the Wall

"Tens of thousands took part in right-wing demonstration; demonstrators attacked Fuad."

The marauders severely damaged the prime minister's limousine. 17 right-wing demonstrators were arrested following an attempt to break into the Knesset building. Two police officers and three demonstrators were mildly injured. A poster bearing an image of Rabin in an SS uniform has been distributed. The police estimate that about 30,000 people were present at the demonstration early in the evening.

(Itamar Eichner and Ilana Baum,
Yediot Ahronot, October 6, 1995)

Carmi Gillon: The days after Oslo were a very, very difficult period. On the one hand, you have Arafat, who's stuck in your throat, so you can't swallow him or spit him out, and then you've got the terrorist attacks. Brutal attacks, one after the other. And Rabin, as I said, is in the middle of all this. On the other hand you have the right-wingers, from the moderate, sane right to the extreme right, radically opposing the continuation of the Oslo process. Rabin is in political distress. Shas [an ultra-orthodox religious party] leaves the coalition, and he's required to take all kinds of political actions that

---

* Sabena Flight 571 from Vienna to Tel Aviv was hijacked by four terrorists from the Black September organization in May 1972 and landed at Lod (later renamed Ben Gurion) Airport in Israel. A team of sixteen Sayeret Matkal commandos, led by Ehud Barak and including Benjamin Netanyahu, managed to take control of the plane, saving all passengers, although several were wounded.

aren't exactly in accord with his character in order to pass decisions in the Knesset. It's a very tense, difficult period. I, as head of the Shin Bet, am a lot more focused on the Palestinian side, on terror and on diplomatic aspects, and a lot less focused on what's going on with the right, when a very basic question arises here: should the Shin Bet have noticed this?

That connects me to what Peres said a while ago about intelligence. This activity by the right in Israel was not covert. You didn't need a head of Shin Bet to translate into Hebrew what Bibi Netanyahu or Arik Sharon were saying on the balcony in Zion Square.* You didn't need a head of Shin Bet to explain to the Israeli public, and especially to the prime minister, what was the meaning of the coffin in the mock-funeral in Ra'anana. All of these things pose a very major question, and to this day I don't know where the answer is. Do I have to come and say to the prime minister: Sir, pay attention, there was such and such speech by political personages, and Bibi Netanyahu, head of the opposition, is not some Rabbi Kahane [founder of the extremist Jewish Defense League], who gives a speech in some town square in the middle of nowhere? And I think to this day that it's not my role or the role of the Shin Bet director. It's also not the police's role. It's written in the newspaper. People should assess reality.

Avraham Shalom: SS uniform? Who would dare to do that thirty years before the murder? Forty years? Who would put an SS cap on Ben Gurion? But the right-wing state of mind in Israel had escalated to a point where they thought everything was permitted in order to win the elections.

Carmi Gillon: The attempts at physical attacks led us to the conclusion that the prime minister had to be protected, not necessarily from murder, but also from violence, just someone who would come in the heat of an event, spit on him or beat him with a stick.

And then the idea of an armored car was raised. He didn't agree, of course. A Cadillac, God forbid? But unfortunately, an armored car, if it's not a Cadillac, nothing can bear its weight. Mercedes

---

* In this October 1995 demonstration, right-wing leaders called for a cancellation of the Oslo Accords and for Prime Minister Rabin to be deposed.

couldn't manufacture an engine that could carry the chassis of an armored car. And so we bring him a Cadillac, and Emmanuel Rosen from Channel 2 finds someone who leaks to him that the prime minister's car is coming, and we all see, on Channel 2, the car being lowered with a crane from the ship, and Rabin's driver getting into the vehicle, taking it from the port. And, of course, the story follows—what an extravagant, wasteful prime minister, why is he driving in a Cadillac, the Chevrolet isn't good enough for him? . . . And he's attacked from every direction. And what's the result? The prime minister is a political man, so he doesn't want to ride in that car. Unlike me, he can't say, "I don't give a damn," and he refuses to ride in that car.

And then matters heat up more and more. There was an assault attempt at the Wingate Institute. After Wingate I come and tell him, "Listen, Yitzhak, it doesn't work like that. They'll hurt you in the end. I don't know if they'll shoot you, but they could hurt you. I'm asking that you start wearing a bulletproof vest, and riding in the armored car, and we'll start increasing security around you, and mostly weeding out events. You don't have to show up to everything." And then he lets me have it: "I, the Palmach veteran, won't wear a bulletproof vest, and no one will hurt me. A Jew here wouldn't hurt me. I'm chief of general staff, after all!" He was very determined, and certainly wasn't willing to hear about not taking part in mass events.

I'm sorry to say this, but let's assume he was a different man, and would have agreed to have all the security measures that are in use today employed around him, before a prime minister in Israel was murdered. I assume you don't need me to explain what they would have done to a prime minister like that. They wouldn't have complained about the Shin Bet. They'd come primarily to him: why are you surrounding yourself with a squadron of security people, behaving like Ceausescu here, like some leader of an African country, a "banana republic." . . . And he wasn't willing to hear about any special security measures. He and I agreed to add one security person, and that was it.

Around July-August '95, about three months before the murder, I start feeling we have increasing potential here for the assassination of a prime minister. So I took a very unconventional step. I went to Rabin and asked his permission to meet with the political leadership, which was Bibi Netanyahu, Arik Sharon, Zevulun Hammer, RIP, from the Mafdal (National Religious Party), and maybe one other person. I conducted personal meetings with each of them in their offices at the Knesset, and I talked to them about it. I told each of them, "Listen, when you're talking from the balcony in Zion Square, I can't imagine that you have any idea what could happen, you're certainly not supporting it, but it could happen."

Do you use the word "murder"?

Gillon: Yes, definitely. The second thing I did was a meeting with carefully selected journalists. The most senior journalists were there, Ze'ev Schiff, may he rest in peace, Amnon Abramovich, Nahum Barnea, Ehud Ya'ari, Ronnie Daniel, really, the top members of the political and military media. And I talked to them about these scenarios. The decision was that it was an "off-the-record" meeting, and my intention was that they start integrating it into their stories and in what they were saying and reporting, in an attempt to stop the process of incitement and sedition. What happened, which is what happens when you bring the media in, is that, ultimately, I think the first one who leaked it was Nahum Barnea. He reported it in the main headline in *Yediot Ahronot* the following day. Ehud Ya'ari already reported it in the lead story in the news on TV that same evening. And the rest immediately followed.

They told about the meeting with the head of Shin Bet, and that the head of Shin Bet thinks so and so, and published it all in big bold letters. But then you don't see any sort of process where, for example, the newspaper editors weed out the hate speech they publish in the paper. By the way, that same Friday, Yoel Marcus, who wasn't invited to the meeting and apparently felt very slighted, wrote an editorial in *Ha'aretz* newspaper in which he mockingly asked, "What does the head of Shin Bet think, that we live in a banana republic, that a political murder is possible here?" I wonder what he thinks today.

Do you approach rabbis?

Yes, I meet with rabbis, with the members of the Yesha Council. We meet in one of the Service's secure apartments in Jerusalem. The head of the branch also responsible for Jewish topics invited the heads of the Yesha Council. Israel Harel, Uri Ariel, and others were there. We talk exactly about these things, about incitement and sedition.

What do they tell you?

Not from our quarters, and nothing we said, meaning not from here and not from there. No one agrees with me. Let's put it like this: no one can see, in the things he says, something that could lead to those consequences. I could say I was maybe the only one who had foresight, but I guess it wasn't enough. I didn't convince my conversational partners.

But all that is just half the problem. The other half is the Ministry of Justice. People are actually talking publicly, in full view. It's not something covert. You don't need the Shin Bet for this. If you're the attorney general and you get up in the morning and read about things like the coffin in Ra'anana* just as you'd initiate an investigation on the subject of fraud, for once initiate an investigation on the subject of incitement and sedition. The State of Israel has never handled incitement and sedition. There's only one case, of Rabbi Ido Alba, who, if I hadn't insisted, and hadn't recruited a subcommittee of the Foreign Affairs and Defense Committee to handle the matter, would not have been prosecuted. The state attorney's office kept saying, "We don't stand a chance, any judge will clear him of incitement and sedition."** And when I insisted that one time, and I really threw my weight around with Dorit Beinisch and her people, Ido Alba was prosecuted and sentenced to three years. And that was even before the murder. I came back then and said, "Take this case, start prosecuting rabbis. At least conduct warning talks, threatening talks." They didn't do anything.

Why?

Because they're dealing with the topic of civil rights, and you're violating his rights as a citizen.

Ya'akov Peri: The radicalization that occurred prior to Rabin's murder was expressed in a level of incitement that had been previously unknown in the State of Israel. The state attorney, law and order, the police, couldn't handle it, and it got completely out of control and

---

* Several weeks before the Rabin assassination, a protest procession took place in Ra'anana, with the participation of Benjamin Netanyahu, in which a coffin bearing the words "Rabin Is Killing Zionism" was carried.

** Alba was charged with incitement for racism and violence due to an article in a book published to commemorate Baruch Goldstein, the perpetrator of the Cave of the Patriarchs massacre.

lost all proportion. In my term there were outbursts against Rabin, but they were very focused. Not at the level of a popular movement, of a demonstration of thousands or tens of thousands in Zion Square in Jerusalem or in other places. At the end of my term, it started to be out there more and more. And in the ten months between my retirement and the murder itself, we're already talking about larger movements. Although the hard-core demonstrators, the ones protesting across from his house and organizing all the demonstrations, are limited to dozens and hundreds, and the Service knows who they are. But the Ministry of Defense, the state attorney and the Israeli legal system can't find answers to this.

Carmi Gillon: [Conservative journalist and provocateur] Avigdor Eskin performs a Pulsa diNura ceremony* against the prime minister. Sixteen- and seventeen-year-old kids look at him like he's God, and they don't care. And that's it. What actually happens after the murder? Nothing. The Israeli government doesn't discuss it, the Shamgar Commission** doesn't discuss it, everyone runs away from it. You know why? Because it's politics. It's unpleasant. What will the right say and what will the left say, and what will some righteous Gentile write in the *New York Times*, and what will some righteous Gentile write in an article translated in *Ha'aretz* tomorrow? No one in the State of Israel except yours truly thinks this should be dealt with. Even in the shadow of the murder, when Yigal Amir comes and says, "I was influenced by the rabbis and the public atmosphere and everything, and I felt I was pulling the trigger for the people of Israel . . ." even then it wasn't dealt with.

You're constantly calling out and warning, "It's going to happen, it's going to happen!" And what are you doing operationally?

Gillon: Operationally, obviously we have the branch, it still wasn't a division in my time, which deals with the extreme right, and we're constantly getting information on how they're talking in Hesder Yeshivas [a program that combines advanced Jewish religious studies with

* A ceremony in which the angels of destruction are invoked to block heavenly forgiveness of the subject's sins, causing all the curses named in the Bible to befall him, ultimately resulting in his death.

** The official commission set up to investigate Rabin's assassination.

IDF military service] and so on. The warnings keep getting worse and worse. They're not talking about murder, but they're saying an uprising is necessary, the State of Judea [a Jewish holy state in the West Bank advocated by Israeli settlers] needs to be established; all kinds of very grandiose things need to be done. We tried to increase security around the prime minister to the extent he agreed. We also create a direct flow of intelligence between the intelligence unit collecting the information and the VIP security branch. We appoint an intelligence person in VIP security who constantly receives information and warnings. I still want to point out that the security guy, despite all the briefings and the talks, including with me, envisions the potential attacker of the prime minister as a Hamas man, not a Jew.

Tell me the Shlomi Halevi story.

Why? I'm not a historian. You're talking about a Central Division Intelligence Corps sergeant, who comes of his own initiative, knocks on the door, and says he heard a conversation in the restroom of the Central Bus Station in Tel Aviv between two people. He was sitting in a stall when he heard people who were pissing outside talking about a possible murder of the prime minister, one of them a curly-headed Yemenite. I can tell you that in retrospect it's clear that he was lying to our faces—to the faces of the coordinators who handled him. In retrospect, we know what he meant to say. Gideon Ezra claimed after the murder that we should have taken him and shaken the crap out of him. In retrospect, he was right. We should have taken him and shaken the living hell out of him, but before the murder, an Intelligence Corps sergeant is sitting across from you, part of the system, part of the intelligence community, who comes and tells the story of his own free will, why wouldn't you believe him? Give me one reason not to believe a man like that. An intelligence agency is built of thousands of items of information like that that it receives every day. So we all know after the fact that Yigal Amir was both Yemenite and curly haired. . . . What can you do with this information before Yigal Amir? Before you know it's Yigal Amir? Do you arrest all the Yemenites or just the curly-headed Yemenites?

No, you shake Halevi.

You shake Halevi, that's for sure. Today. But back then, you didn't have a reason. It's all retroactive wisdom.

The Assassination of Rabin

"Rabin assassinated—Israel is hurt and weeping."

Yigal Amir, a law student from Bar Ilan University, shot three bullets at the prime minister following a rally in Kings of Israel Square. Rabin was fatally wounded and passed away a short while later in Ichilov Hospital. His wife, Leah: "I wish he'd shot me instead of Yitzhak." The assassin had previously tried twice to hurt Rabin.

(*Yediot Ahronot*, November 5, 1995)

Where were you when Rabin was murdered?

Avraham Shalom: By chance I was here in Israel, at home. A friend called and said, "Rabin was shot!" I turned on the TV, [military journalist] Eitan Haber was speaking, not yet the famous declaration, just that he was wounded. I called someone close who said the situation was very bad. I understood it was the end. I only asked if they'd caught the shooter. They told me they had. I didn't know if it was a Jew or an Arab, but I thought it was a Jew, because I'd seen what they were capable of ten years earlier, when they wanted to blow up the Temple Mount. I was amazed, because I thought he was well protected. I went to talk to them and understand how this happened, and I understood they weren't following their own instructions, the security force. With security, you need iron discipline. He shot all his bullets, and they didn't even kill him.

Where were you when Rabin was murdered?

Ya'akov Peri: In New York. I was president and CEO of Cellcom; we went to negotiate with Motorola, because of the famous issue with Cellcom,* to demand compensation from them, and we sat in the offices of Republic Bank in New York on Fifth Avenue. We negotiated all of Friday, and on Saturday morning we went shopping, Yigal Arnon, Shlomo Peuterkovsky, Dov Tadmor, and yours truly. We went back to the hotel. My rich friends wanted to save on hotel rooms, so they all came to my room. And with the mayhem of four or five of us being there in the morning, I didn't notice that the

* In the mid-90s, Cellcom cell-phone users suffered repeated disconnections and cell-phone service disruptions due to faulty software from Motorola.

message light was blinking. And then one of the people present in the room told me, “You have a message,” and I picked up the phone and heard my wife’s voice: “Something terrible happened, Yitzhak Rabin was wounded, call urgently.” And then we got on the Saturday evening flight—it was the four of us, and the whole American media, and we came here. I made it to the funeral, of course.

Where were you when Rabin was murdered?

Ami Ayalon: As Commander of the Navy, I was in Newport, Rhode Island, in a conference of Western navy commanders. I made it that evening to a flight from New York and attended the funeral.

Where were you when Rabin was murdered?

Avi Dichter: In preparation for the event in Kings of Israel Square, there was a warning about an intention by the Islamic Jihad to carry out a terrorist attack, so we were dealing with the question of how to handle it from that angle here in Gaza. I was at home that Saturday evening, and the first report was that Rabin had been shot and he’d been taken to the hospital; it still wasn’t clear that he was dead. The moment they informed me that Rabin had been shot and injured, still before they announced his death, I remember that all the drawers were shut and only the professional drawers opened. Nothing else was on my mind. Immediately I gathered the people in the district, and we sat down to listen to what people were thinking about what would happen in Gaza, as far as uprisings. This stage is completely professional, I don’t remember myself even dealing with the sentimental and personal aspects. It’s a trait that many who work in these fields are familiar with; you just disengage. You don’t let any emotional matter, any familial matter, any social matter, or any other matter filter in. Sometimes it’s even infuriating.

It opens later, when you finish everything and are left by yourself. We didn’t go home, I stayed by myself and later we drove to Tel Aviv. And on the way you start running the images and you tell yourself—hold on, what does this mean? What does that mean, “A prime minister in Israel was assassinated”? How did that happen to us? The organizational failure is horrible. And you also try to play back the images of Rabin the man. You see him across from you. You hear his voice. Rabin, you couldn’t visualize him without hearing him at the same time. And he always had very particular sentences, with this really booming, slow voice. And those are the images playing.

Where were you when Rabin was murdered?

Yuval Diskin: I'm coming back in the evening from visiting a really close friend from the army, from Nativ Hagdud moshav [agricultural cooperative] in the Jordan Valley. We're coming back taking the Trans-Samaria Highway, I'm with the family, close to Ariel, and I get a phone call where they update me. I was already a head of branch in the Service. We knew about the rally in Kings of Israel Square, and even had a warning at the time about a Palestinian intention to commit an attack. And the moment they said something had happened, I said, "It must be that warning about the Palestinians," and, "this is bad, we knew about this, how could it have happened?" The possibility that a Jew had hurt the prime minister didn't even cross my mind.

Where were you when Rabin was murdered?

Carmi Gillon: I'd gone to Paris two days earlier. The murder was on Saturday evening, as far as I can remember, I went on Wednesday or Thursday, for a mission forced on me by Rabin. There were terrorist attacks on the Metro in Paris, and the Mossad really wanted me to go for meetings with the heads of the French security organizations. It kept getting postponed again and again, and finally I went there that week. So I'm in Paris, and on Saturday evening, about 8 p.m. France time, I'm driving to Charles de Gaulle airport, from which the El Al flight I was supposed to board was departing. I was supposed to land in Israel at 5 a.m., so I'd be in time to attend the government meeting on Sunday. I wanted to see El Al's security procedures, so I came earlier. On the way I get a phone call from my bureau chief, who tells me Rabin was injured. When I got to Charles de Gaulle, you could already see images on TV, and I go into the El Al security officers' office and start to get reports. It's not like I had a lot to do at that moment. I was in shock, of course, but you're surrounded by people, so you have to function. That's it. And then I boarded the flight.

What's going through your head, the minute you hear Rabin was shot?

Nothing. In the first minute. In the first minute, let's say, on a personal level. I couldn't process it. You have to function. I remembered, for example, that in that meeting with the reporters, they asked me what was the profile for Rabin's assassin, and I told them, "I can't tell you what the profile is because you're probably thinking straight away of some bearded settler, and I'm actually thinking of some young guy from Kfar Saba, or Hertzelia. . . ." And now my bureau chief told me, "You won't believe it, the shooter's from Hertzelia!" Prophecy was given to fools, as you know, so there's no doubt I was a big fool.

Then I talked to the person who filled in for me in Israel, with the head of the Security branch, with the head of the VIP Security unit, trying to understand how it happened. Later, when I understood that five or six shots had been fired and none by us, I was in shock. It's something I wouldn't have believed would happen. Now you have to understand, the Service trains hundreds of security people every year, but its elite "Sayeret Matkal" is VIP security, and the "Sayeret Matkal of the Sayeret Matkal" is the prime minister's security detail. And the fact that none of them had fired a shot, that was an echoing slap in the face, as far as I was concerned.

On a personal level, in fact, until I was sitting in the darkened plane at night, on the flight to Tel Aviv, I think that was the first time what was in my brain permeated my heart. I was lucky I had that flight. That I had those four hours, maybe more, where you're with yourself. No one was bugging me, no one was asking me questions. They didn't ask me if I want to eat or drink; I just sat there in the dark and I had time to think and be with myself in order to land and be fully functional.

Where do you hear that Rabin had died? Still in the airport?

Yes.

That moment must be an electrical shock.

It probably sounds great to say I felt an electrical shock. I don't remember it that way. I remember myself sitting there in that room, with an open phone line, and my bureau chief keeps connecting me with different people and I start investigating the event for myself. And then in the middle of all that I also get the information that he died from his wounds, but I can't tell you that when they told me that, the receiver dropped from my hand. It didn't happen. I kept on working. Till I was on the plane. What happens to you on the plane is that you're nothing. You have no ability to function. It's not like today, when there are phones and satellites and things like that. We were primitive then, which isn't always bad. So I just sit there with myself. And I at least thank God for those four hours, because I got the opportunity to process the loss of a man who was really extraordinary, as far as I'm concerned. A man with whom I had intimate moments that no one shared with us.

For example, I underwent cardiac catheterization once. I underwent my first catheterization as Service director on the eve of the Jewish New Year. They catheterized me in Ichilov while the hospital was empty, literally on New Year's Eve. So God forbid, no one sees my face, you know, or that during the catheterization I'd start saying that I'm the Shin Bet director or something. . . . So I was completely isolated, and then he calls me at 9 p.m., from his holiday meal, to hear how the catheterization went. Before the catheterization he explained to me exactly what I was going to experience and how I was going to experience it, and how the tubes pass through.

On the other hand, I remember I was at a Bar Mitzvah with him once, and how he suffered. He told me, "That's it, we're going." And I dare say I was pretty similar to him in that we both disliked mass events, and always looked for some quiet corner on the side. And there, too, we found ourselves a quiet corner to chat about all kinds of things that were unrelated to work. That's it. On the one hand, I wasn't part of that group of people who were his personal friends. I never considered myself a personal friend of his. I had personal moments with him, and I think we got along great. I think he was pleased with me.

By the way, and this is a very interesting thing, throughout the whole period when he was alive, I had no connection with Leah, and after the murder, my relationship with her got a lot closer. I think Leah simply knew the whole truth. Leah knew the bulletproof vest story, Leah knew the car story. He shared a great many things with her. And she always told me, "Listen, you don't have to be mad at yourself, and you don't have to be defensive. You had an impossible client." Leah Rabin was a very good friend. Until the day she died, I had a very close connection to her.

And all these memories are going through your head on the flight to Israel?

The intimate moments, for sure. And that's it, I land in Israel, and the Service's senior people are waiting for me at the airport by the runway. I drive straight to Kings of Israel Square, and then start working. Start functioning. The entire Shin Bet, where the atmosphere is very grim, has to be managed. Everywhere I went, coordinators jumped up and told me, "Damn, if these security people screwed up, why are people saying, 'The Shin Bet screwed up'? The Shin Bet didn't screw up. Shin Bet security people screwed up." And I actually have to deal with this in every single place because I need people to work.

Simultaneously, of course, we start dealing with the actual murder investigation. I establish an inquiry committee consisting of three Service heads of branches, and ask for a report from them within three days. I report to the government that I've established the committee, and within three days they do indeed give me a report. By the way, what the Shamgar Commission did was more or less copy that report. But the point here is I laid it all out on the table.

What was the conclusion of the committee you appointed?

A stark failure of the security apparatus. A failure stemming from faulty planning, faulty execution, and mainly from an engagement that didn't exist.

An engagement?

Yes. Look, Yigal Amir was supposed to die. The second bullet was supposed to be fired by one of the security people. The prime minister went down there surrounded by five security people, a sixth one was by the car door. None of them fired. They were all a meter or two away from the killer. I'm not even talking about how the killer managed to position himself behind Rabin's back. I'm talking about the engagement stage. Let's say he did it, fired the first bullet. Three security people could each have put a bullet in his head. And in actuality, he fires five bullets and also wounds one of the security people.

He fires five bullets? I always thought it was three.

No, he fires five bullets total. One bullet hits Yoram's arm. And . . . you understand, and that killer, he's still among us, it's just . . . It's the thing I can't accept, and can't process. Now, immediately after the murder, of course people come and say, it's "blaming the last man on the totem pole" syndrome; totem, schmotem, whatever. . . . Ultimately, why do you put those security people there? It's your last line of defense. And if a killer can shoot the prime minister in the back with three bullets, and add another bullet for the bodyguard, and get out of it alive, it's unbelievable.

Avraham Shalom: I'd toss all of them out immediately, including Carmi Gillon. He didn't accomplish the mission. The security people weren't scared to death of him. Rabin's murder is war, and you have to treat it that way, almost like in the movies. There was no iron discipline. You warn that it's going to happen, and don't look into it. Ask him how many times a month he went to the security team's shooting ranges, commented on their performance and told them they're not okay even if they were okay. Kept them on a tight leash and was there as head of Service, so they understand how important it is.

Rabin's murder is primarily a purely professional failure. Lack of discipline. In Carmi's term, there was no discipline, which is a result of Peri's term, when he opened up the Service, which reduced the tension of discipline. Security which is undisciplined and doesn't do the work and doesn't operate by the letter of the law is not going to succeed. That's what happened to Rabin. They were screwing around there. Those are the basics. You fire the second shot. Here they didn't fire the fourth shot. The first bullet could kill the prime minister. But the terrorist can't win at the end! The terrorist wins when he gets out alive. I'm not even talking about him getting married in prison and having a kid and blowing smoke. . . . But the concept should be that the terrorist doesn't get out alive. Wasn't he shaking inside when he didn't shoot, the security guy? How could that even be? A security person in even the most primitive country—in Egypt, in Afghanistan, in Katmandu, I don't know where—throws himself into the fire. If he dies, he dies. Here they didn't think about it. They weren't ready to die.

Do you talk to the security people who were there?

Carmi Gillon: Of course, I talk to them, I try to encourage them because of course they felt responsible. But the media was on their side. The media doesn't like generals, the media likes peons. And they were the poor peons. But I, following the report, immediately suspended the head of the VIP security unit who was with the prime minister, within the team, and the team commander, and one more person.

What do they say to you?

They don't have a lot to say. A total eclipse. They have no explanations. Look, they won't be able to explain this to themselves until the day they die. This isn't something that can be explained away. When it happens to five, six people, I have no explanation. Yigal Amir was in the heart of the sterile zone. He didn't come with a counterfeit policeman ID. He came with nothing. And he gets there and easily manages to get into the sterile zone and sit there on a planter, and no one asks him, no cop, no one talks to him. He just sits there! The police probably thought he was a Shin Bet man, and the Shin Bet thought he was a cop, and that was that. And he was sitting there with the pistol hidden in his clothing, waiting. And he sees Peres come down, but he's not a worthy enough target in his eyes, and then he shoots the prime minister. A total eclipse. Nothing. I don't know what to tell you.

Everything you predicted—happened. As if you had profiled this thing in advance.

Yes, but I didn't imagine this thing would get through the immediate security circle. I mean, you're working with quite a few circles. The intelligence is an external circle, and you have the police, you have the sterile zones, and finally you also have the immediate team that is supposed to give up its life to protect the life of the secured person, in this case the prime minister, and they didn't do one thing out of all the things they'd learned and practiced for many years. And I don't have any explanation for that.

They're still in the Service. The team commander is still in the Service.

So I understand. I don't look into it anymore.

You go through a terrible time, don't you? After. What are you going through personally?

First of all, and after consulting my wife, I decide to claim ministerial responsibility and submit a resignation letter, and I did that immediately after the report from the three heads of branches. I explained to Peres that nothing would help him here. Peres told me, "What are you talking about? How can you compare where you, director of the Shin Bet, are, and where these security people are! I'm not willing to hear of it, and don't resign." The same thing with Moshe Shahal, who was minister of police. And I said that the pandemonium around the Service would stop only after I quit. Until then, they'd drink the

Service's blood, and we couldn't allow ourselves that. Not to mention that buses are still continuing to explode and all that.

So Peres tells me, "Okay, I understand your considerations, but in the meanwhile, keep going. First of all we have to get through this period." So on the one hand I have to continue functioning as head of the Service, to come to every political discussion, government meeting, go out on operations, make decisions, interrogations, shaking, no shaking, and on the other hand the story of the investigative commission, the Shamgar Commission, begins.

As legal counsel I took attorney Eli Zohar, who was already working for the Service as an external legal counsel, and I didn't exactly help him later. He was pretty frustrated about my whole attitude to this. I had one important speech to give the commission. I got help from my brother-in-law, who's a Mossad man and speaks perfect English, and he read the Warren Commission report for me, the report written about the Kennedy assassination. The question of who killed Kennedy remains open to this day. It's not over. In the United States, conspiracy theories persist. And I told the commission in the opening meeting, "You can't leave any stone unturned, because if you don't do it, and they don't believe you that you did it, the conspiracy theories won't die." In the meantime, Peres started to be accused of being behind Rabin's murder, and I was accused of being the murderer. I don't really look Yemenite, but that's not a big deal. All kinds of people wrote books, a real pandemonium.

Why would a citizen be convinced that there couldn't have been a conspiracy? The best of the best of our sons protected Rabin, "the Sayeret Matkal of Sayeret Matkal," and nothing happened to Yigal Amir. And what about the angles of the bullets, and all the findings that were waved around?

Look, the two previous occasions on which he had tried to kill Rabin are documented and known and exist. He managed to outsmart the cops there and find his spot, without a lot of effort. Why? Because cops are dumb and because everyone there was waiting for a Hamas man who would come and kill the prime minister, and they didn't imagine a Jew would come to kill the prime minister. No security person—and I checked this, one by one—conceived of the possibility that a Jew would try to assassinate the prime minister, even though in the operational orders it appears as a PMO—Possible Means of Operation.

That a Yemenite—

A Yemenite with curly hair. . . .

Would come and kill the prime minister.

Yes, but it didn't sink in, it's a whole network of cops and Shin Bet people who are convinced that only an Arab could try to kill the prime minister, and surely not a Jew. It just wouldn't compute in their heads. That's the first, important, central point. Later, when he got up and managed to wiggle in there, what happened there, in my humble opinion, is that the security team had gotten so used to his presence that they were already treating him like a detective or a cop or something like that, and it didn't bother them that he was actually getting into the range between them and the prime minister. I believe that's the story. The combination of all these things together makes me say—wait a minute, what is this? But there was no conspiracy here. Because Yigal Amir actually worked on this for years. He shared the idea with his brother, and he also had Dror Adani and Margalit Har-Shefi,* and the motives are known, everything is known.

Ya'akov Peri: For anyone who looks with professional eyes at what happened there, it's completely clear. Yitzhak Rabin finished singing and started going down the stairs after he said goodbye and traded kisses with some of those present there. And his security team were also overcome by this euphoria, by this general atmosphere of enthusiasm which ruled the Square. And instead of looking at the audience, which was on the stairs and included Yigal Amir, they look at Yitzhak Rabin.

Yigal Amir says in his testimony that if a bodyguard had caught his eye, he wouldn't have pulled out the gun. That tells you everything. The minute the Security Service is charged with securing a VIP, and that VIP is murdered, that's a clear, unequivocal and apparent failure by the Security Service. And you can't see Rabin's assassination in any other way. Not as a conspiracy, and not that there were four shots, and not all kinds of movies and other fantastic hallucinations.

---

* Adani and Har-Shefi were both convicted of conspiring with Amir to murder Rabin. Adani was senteneced to seven years, Har-Shefi to nine months.

Yuval Diskin: I was working at the time more on the Palestinian and Islamic terror side, but still, as a member of the Service HQ, you ask yourself how did this happen to us. A while later, I read the inquiry committee and investigative commission reports, and I also dug deeply into it again as Service director. New conspiracy theories are raised every time, and at a certain stage I said that we should investigate every one of these things and thoroughly disprove them, or if, God forbid, something true is uncovered, at least we won't whitewash it. I dug a lot into this story from every possible direction, including in recent years. It's a very harsh story as far as the organization is concerned, but I can say with certainty—there was no conspiracy here.

Carmi Gillon: The Shamgar Report didn't kill the conspiracy theories. It didn't manage to do it even though he explicitly writes in the report that there was no conspiracy, and he provides answers to all the questions, "blank, blank"* and all the rest of it. Even Dalia Rabin [the fallen leader's daughter and former Knesset member] to this day doesn't accept the Shamgar Commission's conclusions. At least in the interview she gave to the paper.

I, by the way, nominated Shamgar to head the investigative commission, and I regret it. There's no doubt that as far as public personalities go, Shamgar was first in line, but he made a big mess out of this whole investigative commission and left the same situation in his wake. He should have handled the whole issue with a much more system-oriented approach. He left the police out of the whole thing. Gabi Last was police district commander. He was present at the scene. They were there for the security, not for anything else. How come they just left them out of the picture?

Shamgar also retained this concept of "It was the Shin Bet's fault." Rabin's murder wasn't the Shin Bet's fault. Say it was the security unit, mention the Jewish intelligence unit. You can point at the guilty parties, but don't say, "It was the Shin Bet's fault." You're causing

* One of the conspiracy theories about Rabin's assassination claimed that after the shots were fired by Amir, someone in the audience yelled, "It's blanks, it's blanks," increasing the confusion at the scene.

immense damage not to the Shin Bet, but to the State of Israel, with this, if you demoralize the workforce.

They also decided, making a conscious decision, that they weren't examining the subject of incitement and sedition because the Israeli government, in the Commission's appointment letter, didn't state that they should look into incitement and sedition. Now, why didn't the Israeli government say that? The government was trying to go with an image of a united Israeli nation, and not create a chasm between the left and the right. This is a pretty left-leaning government, you have to remember. And then, what did Shamgar say? That because we didn't get a mandate, we didn't do it. I said at the time to Mr. Shamgar, so why did they appoint a super-cannon like you? You're a prominent personality, because you don't give a damn about the government, and if you think something here is improper and should be investigated, then you write about it without hesitation, like you did in your rulings: even though the government did not request us to do so, the commission decided to approach the government and ask for a correction in the writ of appointment, since we do want to look into the subject of incitement and sedition. But he chose the easy way, and that's why I'm disappointed with him. I'm not disappointed by politicians. That's why, ultimately, this commission is worthless and insignificant in my opinion. There have been other commissions since, Winograd [the commission that investigated the 2006 Lebanon military engagement] and others, and past commissions are always brought up again, but no one mentions the Shamgar Commission following the prime minister's assassination, which is possibly the most brutal event in the history of the State of Israel.

Did you ask him why he did it?

My relationship with Shamgar was strictly formal, as part of the testimony to the commission.

Did he say anything?

No, he's a judge. He doesn't speak to commoners.

Did you meet with Yigal Amir?

Not directly. I was behind the glass.

What did you see?

I wanted to hear the testimony, his explanations. But he was just talking to his interrogator, and, you know, sometimes you can't let another party into the room.

And what was he saying to the interrogator?

All these stories. How much he was influenced by the incitement, how much he felt like a representative who was pulling the trigger for the people of Israel. It's all in his testimony reports. Very few people are interested in what Yigal Amir said in his testimony, because who has the energy to read the crappy handwriting of the cop taking the testimony. . . . So people limit themselves to what was in the media or in the verdict. But it's very interesting. His ideological agenda is very clear.

First of all, he explains how much he was influenced by the incitement. He understood that he was representing the political system. He's representing the rabbis. He indicated a certain yeshiva as one that had greatly molded his worldview on this subject, that sometimes the individual needs to take action in order to save the Israeli people. He spoke about the incredible ease with which he infiltrated the inner sterile zone. He was surprised himself. And, finally, he was surprised to get out alive. When he said goodbye to his brother, he didn't tell anyone where he was going. He passed through the synagogue, offered his last prayer, as he thought, and went to kill himself.

A suicide terrorist.

Yes.

Where do you release what you're going through?

Sari, and my daughters. My elder daughters were already fifteen, sixteen years old, and the younger one was seven. They're very involved and engaged. Especially Sari. She was and remains my best friend.

What does she tell you?

She tries to keep me alive. It was a very hard period. The terrorist attacks didn't stop, and the Service continued to work hard, and this commission, and the media was horrific. Initially I attempted to protect the Service's people. I recruited "explainers," a kind of spokespeople who would speak on behalf of the Service, but those were shots in the dark. It was a kind of "no one will ever forgive you for this" situation, and I kept trying to correct that message, at least get them to stop talking about the entire Shin Bet that way. But to no avail. And of course, all kinds of people within the Service who just like to spit into the well they drank from and dance on the blood. They did it all the time. All together, it really eats at your heart. So it really did eat at my heart. I ended up with heart problems.

Ya'akov Peri: One of the worst things that can happen to someone who has a senior role in a sensitive system like the Security Service or other intelligence systems is that during his term, an acute failure occurs, which he'll carry for the rest of his life. Now Carmi is truly a man of values, a man who also wrote his thesis at the University of Haifa on this very subject, fluent in the material, very intelligent. And this is certainly a trauma that you bear for all of your life. And you can't treat it, it has no cure. There's no solution. There's no pill you can swallow to make it disappear.

You met with Carmi Gillon. What did you tell him?

Peri: There are different versions of that. I told Carmi I had no doubt whatsoever that responsibility needed to be claimed here. This is the kind of ministerial responsibility that we were reared on since the Agranat Commission [the national commission set up to investigate IDF failings in the prelude to the Yom Kippur War]. Although Carmi Gillon is not directly responsible for the horrible incident that happened, he is the head of the organization. And the person at the head of an organization sometimes has to bear the consequences for an individual soldier or individual soldiers who made a tragic mistake or violated procedures or didn't function as was expected of them. There's no alternative when it comes to these things. VIP Security is a unit at the very heart of the Security Service, and the moment there's a security failure, the failure is that of the Security Service. There's no doubt that the assassination of a prime minister for which the Service is responsible creates a crisis which might be even worse than Bus 300.

I think personal example is crucial. It's the main key to the rehabilitation of an organization after a trauma like that. And ultimately, the role of the head of an organization is to take responsibility upon himself, even if he has no direct bearing upon the event. In most cases you don't have a direct bearing. When does the head of the Service have a direct bearing on a failure like that? Come on, am I the one conducting the operation? Do I secure the prime minister by myself? But ultimately, I'm responsible for the procedures and for the proper operation of this organization.

I can tell you why Carmi was mad at me. I'll tell you that very honestly. At the time, Rafi Ginat was the host of *Behind the News* on Galei Tzahal [IDF's popular radio station], and he wanted me on the air. I said, "No problem." This was even before the funeral. At the end of the interview he asked me, "If you were Service director now, what would you do?" I told him, "I'd quit." Since then, the relationship between me and Carmi Gillon, to whom I was a teacher, a mentor, and who I recommended to be head of the Service, has become so shaky that we don't even talk. That's his full right, I don't deny it.

Carmi Gillon: During that period, there are all kinds of friends, Rafi Malka, Amos Manor, all "ex"es in the Service, who are very supportive and helpful. But ultimately you're alone, there's nothing you can do about it. I'd be riding with my driver, come home at 1 a.m., leave at five in the morning, and those four hours at home, when you have no work, are the most threatening thing you're dealing with.

[Military industrialist] Ilan Biran, after Rabin's murder, told me something very nice. At the end of one of the routine meetings he asked me how I was holding up, and I told him, "You can see. . . ." And he said, "Listen, it's amazing how you're functioning and all that, but I know that at night, when you're alone with your pillow, the tears flow and there you're as alone as you can be in the world." And it's true. That's how it is. Now it's true about other days as well, not just days of sadness.

What do you take with you from those events today, when you look back at it?

When Ami Ayalon replaced me as Service director, he said at the farewell event that my claiming of responsibility and resigning was a very uncommon action in these parts. And I was definitely the "right-hand outlier," but when I looked left, I won't find anyone else there. . . . It's a nice statement, isn't it? And he was right. I look at the screw-ups that have happened in this country. People are constantly telling me, "Stop saying you were the one who screwed up." But it's true, it was my screw-up as head of the Service. Two units subordinate to me should have done their work differently, and then this murder would have been prevented, and they didn't do it, and that's why I'm home. And I'm completely wholehearted about my resignation.

Ami Ayalon: Carmi did an extraordinary thing, this concept of taking responsibility, which is so rare in Israeli culture. I think Carmi is one of the only people in Israeli culture who did know to take responsibility for the fact that the murder had happened. I told him at the time, "I think you did something that's not only worthy, but worthy of imitation—claiming public responsibility in such a clear way. I wish upon us, Israeli society, that as a 'right-hand outlier,' you won't be left alone." Years later, I can say that he was indeed left alone.

Carmi Gillon: The interesting thing was that people who were involved in some difficult affairs, such as Tse'elim [when five Israeli soldiers died during a training exercise], worked very hard to convince me not to resign. Very hard. I got lots of messages like that, that, God forbid, we shouldn't set a new standard in this country. Then I think everyone calmed down. They realized that no new standard had been set in this country. The world continues in its regular course. I still think I did the right thing; I wouldn't change it in any way. Personally, I miss Rabin very much. And I'll say something which may not be modest, but Amos Manor, who was head of the Service for five years and molded the Service, said at the farewell event that the Service might have lost the best Service director it could have had.

Yigal Amir, on the other hand, succeeded. He changed history.

Gillon: Succeeded. Changed history. Succeeded big time.

To this day.

To this day. On the contrary, it just gets worse and worse. I think the moment the first political murder happened, it's just a prelude to the next political murder. I estimate that there will be another political murder here. That it will relate to the evacuation of the West Bank. I think the ability to assassinate a prime minister today is very low, due to security methods. So they'll hurt someone else. It will come from all directions, especially the rabbis. Because the rabbis, they have no reason to learn any kind of lesson. As far as the extreme rabbis are concerned, the system has proven itself. We've already said Yigal Amir succeeded in his actions, so the incitement and sedition will continue, and the legal system in Israel will continue its self-righteous pose. There's incitement here every day, and everyone has freedom of speech. And sometimes words kill just as much as bullets, you know.

Ya'akov Peri: Rabin's murder cut short the hope. It showed in the clearest way that a little pissant assassin, with a pistol that barely shoots, can cut short a whole hope, a whole process.

Yuval Diskin: I can't say whether, if Rabin hadn't been murdered, the Oslo process would have succeeded, but it's clear that without Rabin, its chances of success dramatically decreased.

Ultimately, Yigal Amir succeeded.

Unfortunately, he succeeded. Big time. It's sad to say, but this is one of the strategic terror attacks with the largest effect to which I can testify. And if I'm saying something about Rabin here, Rabin was a leader. There's no doubt. He was willing to make very weighty decisions, he made historical decisions. I think Rabin's problem was that he wasn't supported by a sufficiently dramatic and decisive majority, and when terrorism increased, it significantly shook up the public's faith in this process.

Ami Ayalon: In retrospect, I can say that the murder changed my whole world. The way I look at things. The way I see Israeli society. Suddenly I saw a different Israeli society. I suppose it happened over a process of years of which I wasn't aware. I wasn't aware of the power of the chasm and the hate. Of the gaps between us. How do we see our future? What's our common denominator? What did we even come to be here, in this place? Those are things that I seemingly took for granted, and everything collapsed. Today I suddenly see a torn, disintegrated Israeli society.

At the time I expressed myself on this matter in a way that didn't earn me a lot of sympathy, when I said that throwing Margalit Har-Shefi in jail was running away from the truth. Margalit Har-Shefi didn't know that Yigal Amir was going to kill the prime minister. Now you'll ask—how so? He had told her that he was going to kill. Well, I'm telling you that the State of Israel's problem at the time was that thousands of people, thousands, said, "We're going to kill the prime minister." When you come to court and say Har-Shefi never conceived it was possible, you have to establish an impossible reality in which thousands see it as a legitimate thing to say, "I'm going to kill a prime minister."

I dismissed a security person from the General Security Service, from the prime minister's security team, by the way, who started dancing when Rabin was murdered. He came to the unit years later. At the time, I asked him a simple question: "Say, did you dance?" He said, "Yes." He was a boy of sixteen or seventeen when Rabin was assassinated. I asked him, "How do you explain that?" He said, "Listen, it was a burst of joy; what could we do?" I asked him, "Tell me, today you're securing the prime minister; you're part of the security detail. If right now the prime minister comes and conducts negotiations to withdraw from the Golan Heights, what do you do?" He said, "I quit." I told him, "So take your stuff and go home."

He was an outstanding soldier, maybe an officer, I don't remember, and his parents are crying. They're saying, "What do you want from him? Everyone was dancing!" His mother's a teacher, his father's an important man. And they tell me, "Our whole community was dancing. Our whole community! The threat of withdrawing from the Golan Heights had been removed." I said, "Can you hear what you're saying? Say, do you listen to yourselves?"

What were you thinking when Rabin was murdered?

Avraham Shalom: Yasser Arafat asked me that question. . . .

Yasser Arafat asked you?

Shalom: Yes. I told him this is irreparable. So he thought for a minute, and said, "Listen, I think you're right." I think history would have taken a slightly different turn, not all that different.

I think it changed everything.

Everything? No. Rabin wasn't strong enough for everything. There would not have been peace. But there could have been almost peace. I don't think Arabs and Jews are very different in their character, in terms of believing each other.

In what context did Arafat ask you this? When did you meet?

At the time I went to see him in Gaza. I was told he wanted to see me. I asked if it was approved. They told me—approved. Everyone had met him. I was insignificant at that stage.

What did he want to ask you at the meeting?

He said it was a catastrophe that Rabin had been killed and understood that the murder effectively ended the game. He was very, very worried and wanted to know if the peace process would go on after Rabin's murder. He understood the depth of the misfortune, more than most people in Israel. I told him yes, but I didn't really know that. I told him it was irreversible. We've now entered a process where you can't retract all the progress we'd made. I believe to this day that it's true. Only peace won't be the result there. . . .

Why did he want to ask you specifically?

They'd told him that I, I have that opinion. Service director, what do I know? I don't know.

Was that the first time you met him?

Yes.

And what was your impression of him?

A pleasant man who knows how to market himself. A first-class manipulator. I got a better impression of him than of the Christians in Lebanon. Then he invited me to dinner.

You mean, during Peres's term, after the murder, he calls you to discuss with you whether the peace process would continue or not?

He doesn't "call me." Don't make this a Kennedy-Khrushchev meeting, or something like that. . . . He wanted to talk. There were two or three more people sitting there. Abu-Mazen was listening, listening, listening, listening, and he kept smiling and nodding his head. Later I took a drive with Mohammed Dahlan, and he took me on a tour of all the main streets of Gaza. And I was really impressed, because I remembered Israeli Gaza, and suddenly there's a Gaza with tall buildings, and kind of . . . definitely impressive, what they did. But he kept wanting me to tell him how to conduct surveillance on Hamas. He asked that I help him convince the Israelis to give them the equipment. Apparently they did give them equipment. I was out of it.

What influence has the murder had on Palestinian society? What do you see?

Avi Dichter: The truth is that there wasn't a dramatic change, at least not in Gaza. I think that deep within ourselves, we interpreted certain behaviors of theirs as if they slightly despised us for the fact that here, "welcome to the club," welcome to the club of countries whose people kill their prime minister or their king or their president. . . . It was a real sensation of shame in how it's happening to us. We believed a Jew wouldn't murder another

Jew, and suddenly it's happening to us in the most extreme way, in the heart of Tel Aviv, under the most shameful circumstances possible.

Getting Even: The Engineer's Last Cell Phone Call

"Hello? Yahya?"
"Yes?"
Explosion.

The irony of fate: the explosives expert who was responsible for the brutal deaths of 50 Israelis and for injuring 340 was himself killed by a sophisticated explosive charge. 50 grams of a powerful explosive hidden in a cell-phone battery took out Ayyash on Friday morning, in his apartment hideaway, only several hundred meters from the Erez Crossing. The dim explosion was barely heard on the street. The owner of the house in which Ayyash was hiding was injured in the explosion and detained for investigation. A manhunt is being conducted in Gaza for his son, who brought Ayyash the deadly cell phone. Palestinian sources: He escaped to Israel. Officials in the Gaza Strip embarrassedly admit: "It was brilliant execution."

(David Regev and Ronnie Shaked,
Yediot Ahronot, January 7, 1996)

"C. has resigned."
The Shin Bet director has decided to retire after becoming convinced the investigative commission would assign him responsibility for the failure leading to Rabin's assassination.

(*Yediot Ahronot*, two days later, January 9, 1996)

Carmi Gillon: Yahya Ayyash was the most senior terrorist to ever act against Israel. Definitely the most senior member of Hamas. The man was an engineer, a graduate in Chemical Engineering of Birzeit University, a resident of a small village in Shuafat in Samaria and a renaissance man, it turns out. First of all, he knew how to put together explosive charges out of improvised explosives, but with a very high chemical quality. These were the explosive belts that blew up in buses. In addition, he could get a suicide bomber to commit suicide. To come to a person and convince him that he should commit suicide. He had first-class operational ability, meaning constructing an operational plan in a very compartmentalized way. In every terrorist attack, he worked with different people. And the last thing is indescribable survival ability.

For years he was wanted, and we couldn't catch him. I got the authorization to kill Yahya Ayyash from Rabin, who would ask me every week what's happening with that, and later it passed on to Peres. Every soldier, every IDF officer passing through the West Bank, walked around with his photo. He was fugitive "Number One," without a doubt. And this man orchestrated a whole series of suicide attacks. He was responsible for fifty-six Israeli casualties. Counting carefully, you could say he's responsible for the deaths of eighty-two people. We conducted an intelligence operation, first-class operations, which you could make movies about. Sequels. The number of search hours invested in him—planes, submarines, what wasn't utilized against him—was immense, and all unsuccessfully. The man did not spend more than one hour in one place, I believe.

Until one day he got unlucky, and we managed to detect that he'd succeeded in escaping to the Gaza Strip. We knew he'd joined Mohammed Deif, who was providing him with cover. So we went to our friend Arafat, because now we have a friend in Gaza. I come to Arafat and I tell him, "Yahya Ayyash, The Engineer, is in your turf." "Really? I didn't know. I'll check." Three days later, I go to him and he tells me, "I've checked, he's in Sudan." Okay, so I tell Rabin, and Rabin loses it and goes to Arafat. They meet in Erez Crossing and he screams at Arafat and tells him, "I know you have him, and if you don't find him and don't extradite him to us, I'm dismantling this whole agreement, and I'm putting Gaza under siege!" And Arafat persists: "He's in Sudan, in Sudan, in Sudan." And we know he's in the Strip.

Now, obviously every man has his weakness. My weakness is my wife, my daughters, and my grandchildren. Yahya Ayyash's weakness was his wife and son. And after a long period when he was living alone in Gaza, he asks them to join him. Hamas members make contact with them and give them fake documentation, and we know about the whole story. And I decide to let them into Gaza. My consideration was that the minute they're in Gaza, he'll constantly want to see them, and maybe that way the mouse will step out of his hole. And that's what happened. He did step out, and he did meet them.

Avi Dichter: At a certain stage it was clear that the wife was pregnant. We estimated there was no chance she was pregnant by someone else. So we said, she's a "lead." And we started tracking her. We looked for gynecologists, through whom we could get to him. We weren't making a whole lot of progress. And then we started looking for a lead to him. And we started watching who was around, where he could get to. We started constructing innocuous platforms and seeing whether he would connect to them. We started observing which platform would ultimately enable us to hit him.

Carmi Gillon: And then we discovered the fact that he really missed his father. His father stayed in the West Bank. Ayyash never talked on the cell phone; others would make the calls for him. But after literally weeks of persuasion, he agreed to talk for a few minutes with his father on the phone. That's the stage where we decided we need to provide Yahya Ayyash with the option of talking to his father. And we succeed.

How do you know he wants to talk to his father on the phone?

Gillon: We hear.

From a human source?

The rumors reach us . . . on the wings of birds.

Avi Dichter: And the minute we started working on this topic, we gradually started to create the conditions which would enable our cell phone to get to his surroundings. We saw who his collaborators were, we approached one collaborator, we came to him with a cell phone, and we saw that Yahya Ayyash was using that collaborator's cell phone. Now, you say—okay, let's take that cell phone and think how to turn it into an implement that destroys Ayyash. And then we decided to start doing the auxiliary work and make sure that the innocent phone becomes a cell phone with explosives. Technology in the Service is really suffused with experts who can make little devices with a lot of power. Not so much broadcast power as explosive power. And they did manufacture this really extraordinary thing for us. It was also important to pass the device on to Yahya Ayyash in an authentic way, so he doesn't suspect it, God forbid.

Carmi Gillon: So we organize a good-quality cell phone for him. From Gaza. There's a difference between Israeli phones and Gaza phones. And we insert a minimal quantity of explosives in there, but of very good quality. And through a third party, a middleman, we transfer the phone—which is a safe phone, bought in Gaza completely at random, and which belongs to Hamas, and an Israeli eye and an Israeli hand have never seen it.

Where's the person who gave him the phone?

Today?

Yes.

You want an address and a phone number?

No.

You could sell it to Hamas for a lot of money. . . .

Not within Israel, I presume.

Somewhere. Today life takes place in the global village.

Avi Dichter: One Friday, all the conditions were ripe. Ayyash used the cell phone, we activated the explosive device in the phone, and nothing worked. Nothing happened! What can I tell you, it's a real experience watching people and seeing everything that had been built over eight months collapse in front of our eyes. I mean, it's all there. The HUMINT [human intelligence, based on agents and interrogations] people did their jobs faithfully, the SIGINT [signals intelligence from electronic surveillance] people did their job faithfully, technology, VISINT [visual intelligence] observations. Everything worked extraordinarily well. Finally you press the button so that the coffee comes out, and the coffee doesn't come out. Nothing happens. It was awful.

That was Friday. I think people's faces were funereal, in the full sense of the word. And then I said, "We're having a discussion. Guys, no one goes home without making a decision what we're doing about the operation. This is unacceptable. An operation against Yahya Ayyash can't remain without direction for one minute. That's not reasonable." And we actually sat there almost until the Sabbath came in, and we discussed what to do. Each of us gave his contribution, and on Saturday evening we had the cell phone back, which is an intelligence achievement by the HUMINT people that's really amazing in scope. And the technology people have to process a tool with explosives, which isn't a trivial matter. It's absolutely prohibited. And here, as an exception, they knew how to handle this matter without putting themselves at risk, and at worst some robot that costs a few million shekels is lost, but no one gets hurt. And that's what happened. They checked, and it turned out a technical malfunction had occurred because of the need to work fast, and the device wasn't working because of that malfunction. The malfunction was fixed and the phone was returned. And I'm describing everything in brief here, but you have to understand—this is a whole course of action that involves numerous people, and it all takes place within days. The gadget was back in its natural environment, we saw that nothing had happened as far as raising suspicion, and, in fact, two weeks later, the process repeats itself on Friday. The whole system assembled one more time, Carmi said he wasn't coming because he was a jinx. I told him, "It's got nothing to do with you." But Carmi, because of superstition, didn't want to come.

Carmi Gillon: And then, on Friday morning, as agreed, the father calls Yahya Ayyash, talks to him, and when the monitor identifies the voices of Yahya Ayyash and of the father, he calls it out and someone presses the button, and the cell phone explodes while it's pressed against the ear of Yahya Ayyash, who is killed on the spot. No one around him got hurt, and more than that, the people who were in the house on the ground floor didn't hear the explosion! It took a lot of time before Hamas even knew he was dead.

Now, we didn't know whether he was dead or not, because the phone had exploded. We assessed he was dead, that he couldn't be alive, but we didn't know anything. It was a very beautiful, very clean, elegant operation; I like operations like that, they're beautiful, they're clean. It took a lot of time until we got definite information that he had indeed been killed. We just didn't have a clue. Until they suddenly got wind of it and then it started getting out and spreading, and Mohammed Deif suddenly got hysterical and also broke all the rules, even started talking on the phone. And then I drive over to the Ministry of Defense; Peres is the prime minister and the minister of defense. I go into his room, the chief of general staff is sitting there with a few other people, and I tell them, "Yahya Ayyash is dead." And that's how they found out.

Avi Dichter: A few hours later, when they came to take the body, there were very good conditions in place to hit a very significant group within Hamas, an additional group. There was definite identification, definite incrimination, and definite ability to hit them, and, unfortunately, there was no authorization. Yahya Ayyash was taken out during a period that seemed relatively calm. January '96 was relatively quiet as far as terrorist attacks, and killing Ayyash created some noise in the system. Some people didn't like the whole Yahya Ayyash story. As far as they're concerned, he did what he did. There's no reason to get even with him now. You have to wait or do nothing.

Two months later, the whole country blows up.

Dichter: Listen, two months later, the wave of terrorist attacks by Hassan Salameh [Hamas military chief in the West Bank] began. But if you have no strategy to fight terror, you live from wave to wave. If you have a strategy, you know how to deal with it all along.

You don't see the connection between the hit and the terrorist attacks?

Dichter: Yes. We know for certain that after the hit on Yahya Ayyash, a squad escaped by illegally crossing the fence from Gaza to Hebron. It was Hassan Salameh and his group who came to Hebron and orchestrated the terrorist attacks in the West Bank area. I certainly see the context, but if we think that if we carry out a targeted prevention, they carry out terrorist attacks—"so let's not carry out targeted preventions and then they won't carry out terrorist attacks"—that complementary part simply doesn't exist.

For a terrorist organization, it doesn't matter if it's Hamas or another organization, its existential goal is terrorist attacks. It has no right to exist without manufacturing terror. The only thing it can offer the population is its ability to manufacture terror. I also saw it during the second Intifada. When we killed Raed Karmi [a senior official in the terrorist al-Aqsa Martyrs' Brigade] in Tulkarem. He's another despicable killer. All kinds of people said, "Listen, you awakened a wave of terror. You recruited Fatah to enter the wave of terror." Sometimes there's a feeling of quiet, and you say, "Now we actually ruined the quiet. . . ." That was the case with Yahya Ayyash.

And if there really is a calm, say, like in the Yahya Ayyash story, you, as head of the Shin Bet, have to take into consideration that perhaps as a result of this preventive action, an explosion occurs where innocent Israeli citizens are killed, which is indeed what happened.

But that's exactly the difference. When you, as head of the Shin Bet, come to the prime minister with recommendations, the prime minister can say no, can say yes, it's not that the Shin Bet is the only factor; the Shin Bet comes, the army comes, then comes the Ministry of Defense, and the prime minister. If they want to, they bring it before the Cabinet. There are enough people debating whether to do it or not. The thing is that if you make the political consideration yourself, what's left for the political echelon to do? You can't come contaminated with political considerations.

I'll make it tougher: when we hit Yahya Ayyash, the result is that the terrorist attacks of March '96 start just before the election, which directly results in a change of the regime in Israel—Bibi Netanyahu becomes prime minister.

I don't even want to analyze it like that, because that's not a consideration that a Shin Bet director or the head of a district in the Shin Bet makes, and I hope that's also the case in the future. If you, as head of Shin Bet, are constructing a political strategy, you should resign from your job just before you do. Don't be a Shin Bet director with a political agenda. Be a Shin Bet director with a strategy for fighting terror.

Many have said that the whole series of brutal terrorist attacks in March 1996 was the result of Hamas's wish to avenge Ayyash's death.

Carmi Gillon: No way. Do you know how long Hamas works on an attack like that? A few months. These terrorist attacks are in the pipeline, they're just waiting for an operational opportunity. And all these operations will be launched, with Ayyash and without Ayyash.

When you described the hit on Yahya Ayyash, you said, "My job was to bring the cell phone to the ear." Seven years later, when authorization is granted, the State of Israel drops a one-ton missile and can, say, take out a whole neighborhood and fourteen

uninvolved casualties, all to kill one person. Who determines the scale in these things?

Gillon: If you're talking about hits, the authority to approve hits, targeted preventions, whatever you want to call it, belongs to the prime minister, and sometimes he's assisted by additional people. There was a period of the Prime Minister's Forum, and so on. And then he makes the determination. I, at least, can tell you one case of a scale issue, where the political echelon decided we're not going to act. Mohammed Deif, in the Gaza Strip, as far as I can remember, has been wanted since '89. Dichter would throw darts at his photo when he was a coordinator. And this Mohammed Deif, who's responsible for the abduction and murder of soldiers, including Nachshon Wachsman, has not been caught to this day. In '96, we had a golden opportunity to take him out with a helicopter. He was riding in a vehicle, we were tracking the vehicle, we knew exactly where he was, the vehicle was on a street in Khan Yunis, and a helicopter could have dropped a missile on him and ended his story. The price: a) you leave a fingerprint, and the whole world knows you shot a missile from an Israeli helicopter, and b) that there would be collateral damage, you're in the middle of a busy street. And Shimon Peres, who was prime minister, didn't give me authorization to do it. Not that I recommended otherwise; I admit I was very troubled by the fingerprint, and also by the fact that it was clear there would be additional casualties. But I still raised that possibility with the prime minister, and, by the way, there was complete agreement in the room, by the chief of general staff, the deputy chief of general staff, the head of the Mossad who happened to come by, that it shouldn't be done.

Why did anyone think someone other than Israel had killed Yahya Ayyash?

You could hide. Look, it's like the settlements. You could hide behind a wink. . . . The question of questions is always whether these targeted preventions are generating more terror or not. In my humble opinion, they're great deterrence, meaning if, for example, Mohammed Deif's activity profile is almost non-existent, I think that stems primarily from the hit on Yahya Ayyash, which we know just greatly depressed him. He lost all his self confidence. And this is a man who's been behaving like a fugitive for twenty years now, sleeping in orange groves. Life as a fugitive is a very hard life. The fear of being taken out. Take [Hassan] Nasrallah [Hezbollah secretary general], for example. Think how many years that man's been living in a bunker. He manages to function publicly, but I assume his personal life is completely messed up. He's dying of boredom. How long can you watch [cable/satellite TV service] Hot or Yes? The same thing with the heads of Hamas in the Gaza Strip. So you're creating an effective deterrence balance here. It won't solve the problem. The problem will be solved through dialogue, through negotiation, but it creates a balance of deterrence.

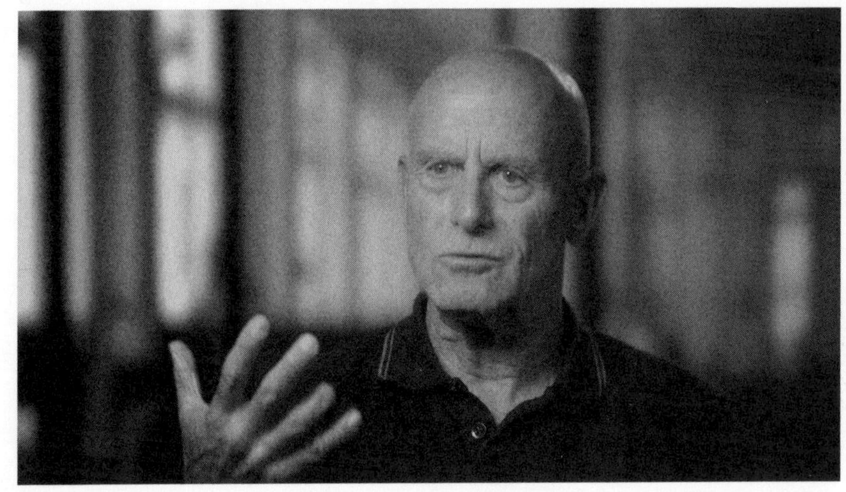

Ami Ayalon

Ami Ayalon (1996–2000)

I had a happy childhood. I was born in Hatser Kinneret, and after the War of Independence, my parents moved with me to Kibbutz Ma'agan. My mother returned from the Scottish Hospital in Tiberias, and the most natural thing for her was to put me in the communal nursery on plywood planks, because the theory at the time was that it was healthier than on mattresses. After one of the girls almost froze to death, they understood there that maybe that theory was good, but it was a little dangerous. But ultimately, I have wonderful childhood experiences of sharing. I grew up in a communal children's house, like children grew up in all the kibbutzim at the time, and we grew up with communal sleeping arrangements. I went to a school which to me is a great school to this day, in the Cooperative Education House in Degania. I had wonderful teachers both in elementary school and in high school, some of whom later became university professors.

Dad was a public figure and Mom was by necessity the stable island in the kibbutz. [After World War II], when I was a year old, Dad left for Hungary for two and a half years, until '48, to coordinate Aliyah Bet [a group that worked to facilitate illegal Jewish immigration to Palestine, in violation of British restrictions during the Mandate]. He came back to the kibbutz for the War of Independence and fought in the kibbutz, and in kibbutz Gesher. When I was three, a few months after he came back, we were evacuated to Haifa for a few months because the Syrians had invaded and gotten as far as

Degania A. Dad, along with the other members, of course, stayed to protect the front line in the Jordan Valley. Those were the experiences of the War of Independence.

Is that the source of your connection to the sea? From Ma'agan?

Ami Ayalon: That was the source of my connection to the sea, although when I got to the Navy, to Shayetet 13, they asked me, "What are you doing here?" So I said, "What do you mean? The sea and I are one." So they laughed their heads off, because there's a concept called "*marinero de agua dulce*," which means "sweet-water mariners." We who were born on the shores of the Sea of Galilee didn't understand to what extent it wasn't a sea. But up to the age of eighteen, I really saw it as a sea in every sense of the word. Even though some of it was still controlled by the Syrians, for us it was a whole world.

At the end of the fifties, I left with my parents for South America. Dad left as an envoy for Zionist youth movements, to bring new immigrants to Israel. We were in Buenos Aires for a year and a half, and then a little over half a year in Montevideo, because Dad was declared "persona non grata" by the Argentinians, after Eichmann's abduction. We had to cross the Rio de la Plata within forty-eight hours. Dad wasn't a direct collaborator in Eichmann's capture, although here and there he had connections with the prime minister's office, and he might have been involved in indirect support. He was involved in organizing a defense system for the synagogues and the Jewish communities.

In Buenos Aires, and especially in Montevideo, I first encountered anti-Semitism. The first time I got beat up thanks to being Jewish was in Buenos Aires, when we were leaving a youth movement meeting. I was thirteen. We had to escort the girls, and we walked into a fight with boys who would throw stones and curse and harass us. As an Israeli coming to a place like that, in the beginning it seemed very strange to me. Especially since in South America, the Argentinians would make a distinction: "Oh, you're Israeli—you're okay. We hate the Jews. . . ." So I ran into anti-Semitism in a physical way, which was not at all ambiguous. They explained to me that I was a Jew, and ever since then, they don't have to explain that to me anymore.

I don't remember political discussions in my childhood home, but the experience of the conflict was very immediate. The Syrians sat above us, and every time our parents went out to plow the fields of contention, east of Tel Katzir, it was clear to us we'd be in shelters for hours or days, as needed. Here and there kibbutz members were injured, and in the neighboring kibbutz, Tel Katzir, also killed. So the conflict experience was an everyday experience, not an experience of discussions and ideology. My parents' Zionism was a Zionism of settlement and security. A Zionism that stated that the borders of the State of Israel would pass in every place in the Land of Israel in which we build a settlement, know how to work the land, and know how to protect ourselves or to fight for our place. That was true in the Tower and Stockade period* in the '30s, and it was true for the Zionism of my parents, at least in '67, '68, '69. Also after the Six Day War. My friends from the Valley or from the kibbutz settled in both Jordan Valley and the Golan Heights, because it was clear that was the Land of Israel. What happened later happened later.

Somewhere in my teens, I knew I'd be in Shayetet 13, the naval commando.

Benny Shalit, who was the psychologist for Shayetet 13 and for the Navy, was the first person who asked me, "Why did you come here?" and I didn't really know what answer to give him. I don't even remember what I told him. I think I knew it was dangerous, I knew it was the sea, and I knew that there were good guys there. That was enough for me. I wasn't thinking about saving the State of Israel. I wasn't thinking in the terms in which my parents' generation thought, of doing it for someone else. I did it because it really seemed to me like the most dangerous place that was also wet, so that's already a double advantage.

And what do you discover when you join the flotilla?

I discover that there are wonderful guys there, I discover that it's wet, I discover that it's hard. And later it became dangerous.

Explain "hard."

Ayalon: Look, I'm 1.66 meters, 1.67 meters on a good day [about 5'4" or 5'5"]. . . . With me in the course is Uri, a good friend. I have nothing to say against him except that he's about 1.90 meters [6'3"] or 1.95 meters [6'4"], and they put 20 or 30 kilos [44 or 66 pounds]

---

* In 1936–39, the Tower and Stockade method was used by Zionist settlers for the rapid establishment of Jewish settlements in Mandatory Palestine, despite the British prohibition on establishing such settlements. By law, even an illegal building could not be demolished once its roof had been completed.

on each of us. Now, I weigh 60 kilo [132 pounds] or 57 kilo [126 pounds], something like that. Does that seem fair to you? Going into the sea in the winter in January or in February, when it's not raining but hailing, and the waves are between 3 and 5 meters high [about 10 to 16 feet], and it's really freezing cold, without the improved rubber suits we got years later; going on treks with 30 to 35 kilo [66 to 77 pounds] on your back, where we get to Haifa Port and then dive there and do these or other exercises, or marching from Tel Aviv to Atlit.

It's a physical challenge that very quickly becomes a mental test. A test of willpower and endurance, and you find out things about yourself that you didn't know. First of all I discovered that I was capable of it. That's more or less the big discovery of my first two years in Shayetet 13.

And then we get to the Six Day War, and for Israel, the Six Day War is an experience of success, victory, and for some factions of Israeli society, maybe even a messianic phenomenon. For us, for the Navy in general and for Shayetet 13 in particular, it's an abject failure. We left behind six divers in Alexandria with the Egyptians as prisoners of war without having carried out their mission, wonderful guys infiltrate the Port Said port and don't carry out their mission. Operations in the north don't even get to a point where they're diving to attack. And I'm in the south, chasing the Egyptians and chasing after the war, and not getting there. We didn't get to operational activity—not because it wasn't possible and not because it wasn't necessary, but due to a series of factors: low proficiency, and unacceptable standards relating to perseverance and determination, things we grew up on. An abject failure.

What I take away from there is the sense of failure, and the sense that "this isn't going to happen to me anymore." In any place that I get to. Not as a fighter, not as a young officer, not as the commander of Shayetet 13, and not as commander of the Navy. Before the Six Day War, I was approached about becoming an officer, and I vehemently refused. I thought only those people who had nothing to do in life stuck around to be officers. After the Six Day War, everything changed. Then I understand a few things: a) that I'm going to be in the military for a few years, as long as the military wants me, and b) that I'm going to train to be an officer. Among other things, I decide to switch from being a raiding diver to the

"Pig" unit, which I thought at the time would be the future battle queen of Shayetet 13.

These Pigs are mechanized underwater vessels. A raiding fighter is a fighter who knows how to get underwater by diving, but takes everything he needs with him. Whether it's planting a mine on a ship, or whether it's his entire land gear, which is a Kalashnikov and grenades and a combat belt and so on, to get to the shore, take off his diving equipment and fins, and become an infantry soldier in every sense. It's a method of warfare that to a large extent was invented and improved upon during those years, and that's what we were doing during the War of Attrition [the ongoing fighting between Israel and Egypt from 1967 to 1970]. Fighting in face-to-face warfare literally in range zero from the enemy. That's what we did on Green Island.

The Battle over Green Island

"Dozens of Egyptian casualties during IDF incursion into Green Island."

The fortified island, in the entrance to the Suez Canal, served as an Egyptian base for anti-aircraft cannons; our forces controlled the area for an hour, sabotaged all the cannons and machine guns, and blew up structures; 6 IDF soldiers were killed and 9 were wounded.

(Eitan Haber, *Yediot Ahronot*, July 20, 1969)

Ami Ayalon: At the time I was a young officer, deputy commander of the rear half of a small kayak team. I more or less commanded myself and two other people, and I thought I was a big commander. By the way, relative to the twenty people total who stormed the island, I did command a large force. Green Island was a milestone in the flotilla's warfare. It's a special story, a sad story. First of all because, as stated, six fighters died there. Three of them were very good friends. I recruited them, I trained them, and they fought by my side on the island. One of them was Haim Sturman, on whose shoulders I climbed to begin my fighting on the roof. He was the son of Moshe Sturman, who died in Jezreel Valley, and the grandson of Haim Sturman, who was killed in Beit Shean Valley, and for whom he was named.

Green Island is located in the northern part of the Suez Bay. The British established, on some reef or natural coral island, a kind of fortress of anti-aircraft cannons, intended to protect the southern entrance to the Suez Canal. When we stormed it, it was protected by a hundred Egyptian soldiers. Seventy or eighty of them were commando soldiers, and the rest were the anti-aircraft force manning the cannons. We knew we needed to conquer the island, as part of the War of Attrition. It was in retaliation for a very complex and difficult operation the Egyptians had conducted at a post in Port Tawfiq in the southern part of the canal, where they infiltrated the post and killed Israeli Armored Corps soldiers, some of them in their tanks.

That was actually the first time we poked our heads out of the water and began the land assault phase. I'm not familiar with a precedent in world naval history where an operation like that was carried out. It required that we achieve perfection in everything related to the transition from an underwater fighter to a land fighter. We knew that if we didn't do it within seconds, we might be butchered by the Egyptians who were up on the roof, and if we couldn't manage to open fire from the moment we poked our head out of the water, then we didn't stand a chance. For months, we constructed a battle plan, which actually turned into an operational solution for Green Island. After every drill, we sat and asked questions with a kind of openness I'm not familiar with in other IDF units, and with which I was previously unfamiliar in Shayetet 13. With that proficiency, we actually got to a state in which, when the order comes down and we have a few days, we arrive prepared like I don't think we've ever arrived before.

In the last briefing, we present the operation to Chief of General Staff Lieutenant General Haim Bar-Lev, and I don't want to insult anyone, God forbid, but the chief of general staff arrived in dress uniform and with a cigar to the last briefing. And I remember saying to myself at the time, "Just a minute, what's going on here?" And in retrospect, I can tell you, when I was commander of the flotilla and I was commander of the Navy, I knew that even if I ever started smoking cigars, I wouldn't bring cigars to the last briefing of people who are going out to battle, which for some of them would be their last battle.

We conveyed to the chief of general staff, in a very clear way, that there would be intense fighting on Green Island. The Egyptians had nowhere to retreat to. And we know we have nowhere to retreat to, because we're leaving our diving equipment underwater. And then the chief of general staff says to us, "Guys, not at any price. If you see that there's fierce resistance, if people start getting wounded, retreat." And I say to myself—just a second, what's he talking about? Maybe he doesn't understand what he's authorizing? Anyway, I erased all that. I gathered the large force I was in charge of, those three fighters who were under my command, and I told them, "Guys, everything the chief of general staff said was very nice. We're clear on the fact that there's nothing true about it. We're going to fight. There's no option of retreat. There's nowhere to go. I want this matter to be clear and unequivocal." And with that, we leave for the island.

The dive itself was very tough. We ran into currents after each of us had loaded himself down with an amount of magazines that was a lot beyond what we'd taken on during training. I found myself at certain times at depths of fifteen to twenty meters [fifty to sixty-five feet] instead of seven meters [twenty-three feet] as planned. Which was dangerous in itself. There was a crucial moment where Dov Barr, the commander of the force that took us to the island, took us out and said, "Gentlemen, if any of you expects not to get there and fight as a result of the delay in the timetable, I have news for him. That option doesn't exist." He said it in language that was a lot less genteel, including words that don't get included in the dictionary. And, in short, explained to us in a very clear manner that we had only one direction to go in.

By the way, I, personally, was very glad we arrived about an hour late, because it enabled us to arrive at a much higher tide, and actually get a lot closer to under the wall, or under the little bridge. The original plan said that we should arrive early in order to retreat in darkness. I wasn't worrying about retreating at all. I was worrying about opening fire at the best moment, which was the highest tide.

From that moment onward, I don't remember feelings. Before that there were fears or doubts, would we come back or wouldn't we, but from the moment the firing started, under our initiative, the only thing that bothered me was getting to the roof as early as possible. From that moment on, the experiences are very simple. I did all my fighting on the island barefoot. When I got to the hospital, the doctors understood the bullet that had entered here, and the shrapnel that had entered there, but they didn't understand the cuts on my feet.

I remember climbing on Haim Sturman's shoulders, and he was an extraordinarily strong fellow. The roof was covered with Egyptian fire, so I tried to throw grenades, but all the grenades had gotten wet. I threw about three grenades before I understood there wasn't a chance. I stormed the first post with Zelly, a guy from Afikim, who stormed right after me into the post. We had to kill the first two Egyptians at the post so we'd have a place to hide. While we were shooting, Zelly tells me, "Ami, I'm injured." I looked and saw two of his fingers were cut. I said, "Can you operate the Kalashnikov?" He said, "I can." Okay, it was completely clear that we were proceeding.

We opened fire to enable the other pair behind us to storm the right side of the roof. And the fighting continued. By the stage where the guys from Sayeret Matkal were supposed to arrive, we had to conquer the outskirts of the destination, and they were supposed to pass through us and continue into the destination. At that stage we'd all understood that they weren't coming and that there was a delay with the boats, so we had to continue fighting. Almost the entire force eventually found itself coming up to the roof, and joining the ongoing fighting. When we got to the third post, the second heavy anti-aircraft post, and we were beginning to run out of ammunition. In retrospect, I know we shot like crazy for no good reason. It might have been part of our lack of professionalism at ground warfare during those years. I went through twelve magazines within a very short span of time. The grenades, as stated earlier, didn't work because they'd gotten wet. And that's where I got wounded for the second time.

The first time, I got hurt by shrapnel when I climbed on the roof. The second time, a bullet entered me and passed by the major artery in my neck. I remember sort of losing my consciousness for a few seconds, and I can still see Ehud Ram, the commander of the Shayetet 13 force, getting briefed by Gadi Col next to me—and being killed on the spot. Then, just for a few minutes, I lost consciousness, nothing serious, but the Sayeret Matkal guys arrived, and I started to evacuate myself. That's more or less my story about Green Island.

Do you remember the moment the bullet entered you?

Ayalon: I remember something else. I remember waking up, apparently after a few seconds, and hearing my breath rattling. A few weeks earlier, we'd invaded a destination in Arabia, not far from there, and there was face-to-face fighting there, too. I remember shooting at Egyptian soldiers. And I remember them rattling a moment before they died. And I hear myself rattle. And I say in my heart, hold on, this might be your last moment. So you better think. Think hard.

I also remember being evacuated with the rubber rafts. Dr. Slavin, who was our doctor, was in the raft with me. They evacuated me along with a few other wounded people and two guys who were no longer alive. I was already on morphine so I suffered a little less pain, but I was pretty groggy, I couldn't understand why he was tending to me and not to them.

That night, Neil Armstrong landed on the moon. We're fighting on the island and he lands on the moon. And really, I often ask myself, maybe we really need to watch ourselves from a different planet to get some perspective and even reassess all our fighting here in the Middle East. I say that because the recovery room, the next night, was apparently the only place where they had a TV and they were broadcasting the landing. Apparently there was no live broadcast in Israel. And all the nurses from the hospital came to me in the recovery room. I don't think it was me. Apparently I wasn't very impressive with all the bandages, but I'm ashamed to say, they're sitting on my bed and they're moving my mattress, and I'm in excruciating pain and I couldn't care less about Neil Armstrong. All I want is for them to leave me alone already and let me sleep. And that's more or less my personal experience of Neil Armstrong's moon landing, and the small step for man and the giant leap for mankind.

Ultimately, twenty Shayetet fighters were injured in the first wave. I think that except for three people who participated in the raid, most of us wound up at the hospital. I was diagnosed as moderately wounded. Others were very severely wounded. Israel Assaf was, as well as Yedidiah Yeari, who would later be commander of the Navy. The flotilla emerged very bruised from Green Island. It was a heroic operation, but it exacted a very high price. All of Shayetet 13 at the time was around thirty fighters, part of whom were not raider fighters,

It was the first time, as far as I was concerned, where it wasn't a personal adventure anymore. I'd enlisted because I was looking for risk and challenge, and suddenly we all found ourselves in a situation where, if we could, we really wouldn't do it, but we didn't see an option of not doing it. Throughout my childhood, "the decree of the collective" and "the call of duty" were empty words for me, and suddenly I find myself connecting with those grandiose words, which we really didn't appreciate, that belonged to my parents' generation, and I also preach it to my fighters, and the amazing thing is they take it seriously.

Ultimately, it was an incredibly heroic battle, which wasn't really successful.

The question is what you define as successful. We conquered the island, destroyed the anti-aircraft artillery, and retreated. I don't know how to measure success, certainly not in terms of forty or fifty years back. I think that in terms of warfare, it was a very ambitious and very successful operation. You're asking me whether it would be plausible, in today's reality, in our ongoing battle with terrorist organizations, to carry out an operation where six warriors are killed? I don't think so. On the other hand, in our fighting against Egypt there was an important element of attrition and awareness. That was the first time IDF reached a state where victory wasn't defined as conquering territory, but as endurance. That's a whole other kind of victory, which to this day we haven't really wholly defined in the Israeli perception of security. Was it appropriate to storm the island, after they'd killed the Armored Corps soldiers in Port Tawfiq? To kill dozens of Egyptian commando fighters, to conquer the island and set up some kind of milestone in the fighting opposite the Egyptians, maybe even enable the Air Force to take part and attack better the following day? It's very hard to conduct that analysis.

But it's mainly a battle of perception.

The War of Attrition was also perception-based warfare. To a very large extent. I think that's also the reality today.

For your part in the battle over Green Island, you received the Medal of Valor. That's the highest commendation that the State of Israel bestows on its warriors. How does that affect you?

Look, these are already very elevated words. Green Island wasn't actually personal combat. Green Island was fighting by many people. I think every one of the fighters arrived amazingly prepared, so I really thought that was appropriate commendation for the operation. It's an operation worthy of commendation.

When I get out of the hospital and get to Kay House for rehabilitation, I get wind of a new operation that's brewing, of sinking torpedo boats, to enable IDF to carry out an enforced landing with tank carriers on the other side of the Gulf of Suez. It was an amazing operation carried out by the Navy and the Armored Corps, and which I believe even influenced the balance between the Egyptian and Israeli armies. The claim is that it caused [Egyptian President Gamal Abdel] Nasser's mental breakdown, when he suddenly discovered Israeli armored forces moving from post to post on the Egyptian side of the Gulf of Suez. But to enable that operation, two torpedo boats which were preventing the Navy from landing the Armored Corps had to be sunk.

That was supposed to be a Shayetet 13 operation, and after the Green Island operation, there was no one left to do it. So I escape from the hospital, go to Ze'ev Almog, and ask to take part in this operation. Ze'ev, as commander of the flotilla, is of course very worried about me and doesn't let me do it, even though I know and he knows he doesn't have a lot of options. The fact is he brought in two fighters on reserve duty to man the crew. You need eight fighters in all. Four fighters who know how to exit the vessel and affix the mine, and four more to operate the two vessels, the Pigs. Almog said to me, "Only with authorization from the flotilla doctor." The flotilla doctor, a wonderful man, an athlete through and through, of course gives me authorization, and I arrive for the operation after three weeks in the hospital.

The operation itself is less familiar in Israeli awareness because it didn't involve shooting, only a long dive of many hours. It was the longest dive carried out until that operation. The Gulf of Suez had extraordinary long detection ranges for radar, so we had no choice but to switch the Pigs from floating to diving mode at a much earlier stage than we'd planned. That also made the operation very complex from a professional, technical standpoint. We dove one time, for many hours, we got there and discovered the torpedo boats were in motion, while shooting. I don't know if they were alerted, or they just maintained a very high alert level. Anyway, the conditions didn't enable us to carry out the operation. The next day, the torpedo boats moored. We got there again after having being forced to turn back, to debrief about the operation that hadn't been carried out, to take care of the vessels and charge the chargers. Eventually, we carry out the operation in very rough conditions, and affix the mines to the two boats.

On the way back, as a result of a malfunction, a self-destruct explosive charge which exists on every vessel in case we're taken prisoner blows up. Three fighters are killed, and one is severely wounded, not in my vessel but in the other vessel. I remember that on the way back, we didn't even understand that the explosion we heard was the explosion from their vessel. We thought the explosion was the torpedo boats exploding, even though it was a little early. But when we rose and emerged from the water for minimal floating, we tried to talk to them on the comm system and report we'd affixed the mines, and we found out they'd actually been delayed and didn't arrive after we did.

We started looking for them with helicopters, while getting very close to the area of Egyptian anti-aircraft artillery. With me in the helicopter was Gadi Col, who was on the boats as the security force. I finished the dive exhausted, but I didn't think I had any other choice except to board the helicopter and take part in the search. When we found the bodies, I didn't have the strength to go down with the cable and bring them up, so Gadi brought all three of them up, one after the other, every time we found one of them. And that was the end of the operation. A very important operation that actually enabled the armored landing, but a very sad operation. Some of the casualties had time to convey a will to Arye Yitzhak, who survived. He was very severely wounded, swam for hours. Since the operation he was never really rehabilitated. He lives in the Port of Jaffa on some kind of fishing boat.

The Yom Kippur War, Leading the Commando

Ami Ayalon: A few weeks before the Yom Kippur War, I finished my role as commander of the Dabur-class patrol boat company in Sharm el-Sheikh, and enrolled in the Command and Staff College [an educational institute serving senior IDF officers]. On the Thursday before fighting broke out, I heard from the head of Aman's research division that there was no chance of a war, and on Saturday at 2 p.m., they recruit me as part of the Navy's reserve force. The active Navy force wasn't really surprised. The head of the Naval Intelligence Division came to the Navy commander in chief and told him, "Listen, I'm certain there's going to be a war." He interpreted the escape of the Soviet advisors from Syria through the Port of Tartus as a certain indicator that the Syrians were going to war. As a result, the Navy commander came to the chief of general staff, but IDF didn't accept his position. Either way, the Navy was prepared.

The Yom Kippur War was one of the biggest military success stories in the naval history of the modern world. First of all, it was the first time that missile boats meet each other at sea and conduct missile battles. In this case, the Syrian Navy on the north and the Egyptian Navy in the west, opposite the Israeli Navy's missile boat companies. Those two navies were beaten and didn't leave their ports after the second week of the war.

I joined the war the following day, and underwent three very tough weeks of combat as commander of the Dabur-class squad. One of my soldiers was killed, many of my soldiers were wounded in battles in the Gulf of Suez. It's the first time I'm exposed to phenomena of combat shock among warriors on the Dabur boats. I'm exposed to a reality in which I don't know if I'll have a port to return to.

I received Shayetet 13 in a very difficult crisis status. I was called in to serve as deputy commander of the flotilla, but Raful dismissed the flotilla commander through no fault of his own. An officer was killed during an exercise in Tiran Island. The exercise file wasn't properly organized, and Raful decided to dismiss the unit commander because he wasn't willing to tolerate operational accidents in IDF. During that period, Raful had no faith in the operational abilities of Shayetet 13, and I think this dismissal was the straw that broke the camel's back. So I experienced the challenge of rehabilitating a unit from a state of crisis.

As flotilla commander, you led twenty-two operations in two years, which is extraordinary in terms of workload.

Twenty-two violent operations. Endless covert operations of gathering intelligence and so on, but twenty-two operations which involve contact with the enemy. In those years, terrorist bases and their infrastructure in Lebanon were the main threat facing Israel. Navy Commander in Chief Ze'ev Almog, who in the past had been the commander of Shayetet 13, did everything possible to include the Navy in general and Shayetet 13 in particular in operational activity. I, as commander of Shayetet 13, was willing to do anything to accomplish that. I'm saying that because there were periods in which the flotilla didn't like the activity in Lebanon or in the Territories. In later periods, the flotilla didn't understand that it had to be in every location in which IDF was fighting.

Moshe Dayan once said, "I'd rather stop galloping horses than thump at lazy cattle." I really think commanders at the level of special unit commanders, regiment commanders, brigade commanders, should be those who push for action, while the one looking at the whole picture is the one to stop it. A culture of storming doesn't develop in a reality where there is no storming. There's a limit to how much you can encourage a culture like that through simulators. So on the one hand, we can't manufacture a war to create that culture for ourselves. But on the other hand, a unit commander can't expect his fighters to storm a target if he didn't let them experience storming targets everywhere that IDF is present. He should do anything to get there.

Part of the operations in Lebanon were hits.

You insist on using the word "hit," and I insist on the word "prevention." There was one operation where we had to kill the head of Fatah's military wing in southern Lebanon. Information about him had arrived both through the Shin Bet and through Aman. We knew he was sitting at a café in the port. We could identify him based on his build, and he was also limping. We also knew more or less at what table he would be sitting. We were supposed to arrive by diving, then swimming, to the breakwater, climb the breakwater, and using two snipers, hit him and get out. The truth is, although it was a commando operation in every sense, it's a prevention operation. This terrorist was creating terror activity, and when we take him out, we prevent a whole lot of terror activity that he generates. Therefore, what you call a "hit," I call "prevention."

Do you ask yourself what the reason is when you're told to do it, or don't you?

Did I ask myself then? I didn't ask. But it was clear. At the time I didn't debate about dilemmas which I did debate later, when I was head of Shin Bet, and when I was in fact responsible for developing or enhancing the concept which today we call "targeted prevention." But concerning this action, I had a very intense argument with Raful, the chief of general staff at the time, who instructed us, after we hit him, to shoot with machine guns, MAGs, at the rest of the people around him, some of whom might have been terrorists and some of whom weren't, and to leave explosive charges on the pier, on the breakwater. And all based on Raful's operational thinking, which states, "You have to secure the retreat. If you don't shoot, they might hit you while you're still swimming away." I argued with the chief of general staff in what was an operational debate but also had a moral aspect. First of all, we came to kill one person who generates terror. We didn't come to kill the public on the breakwater or in the port café. Second, I also had an operational reason—if we fire two shots, the chance of them knowing where the shots originate from was very low. On the other hand, if we initiate an exchange of fire there, then we mark exactly where we are. Beyond that, I know the people finding the explosive charges aren't necessarily fighters. They could be fishermen who arrive the next day, or kids walking around on the breakwater, and I have a problem with causing the deaths of people who have nothing to do with the fighting. There was a big argument, not very pleasant, which continued into the last briefing, and finally a "Mapai"-style compromise was reached: we'll take everything with us and decide in real time whether we open fire or not, based on the level of resistance we expect or our ability to retreat safely. To the best of my memory, we didn't have to open fire, but I don't really remember.

Raful was a fighter from head to toe. He wasn't a man who would arrive with a cigar to a final briefing. He's really the warriors' commander. I had tremendous esteem for him as a fighter and as a commander. I didn't accept his moral standards. I didn't accept his form of expression later, when he described the Palestinians as "drugged cockroaches in a bottle," I really didn't. I accepted from Raful what I considered it right to accept, and didn't accept from him what was improper to accept, or at least I saw it as my right and duty to argue about it. To his credit I can say that at least in cases concerning me, he exhibited a lot of forbearance and a lot of patience.

Submarines, Second Strike, To Be or Not to Be

"The chief of general staff's wife launched a new submarine."

The launching ceremony was conducted in northern Germany. The submarine "Liviatan" [whale] is the second of three submarines which Germany promised Israel after the Gulf War.

(Eran Tiefenbrunn, *Yediot Ahronot*, May 28, 1997)

Ami Ayalon: When I started my role as Navy commander, in the summer of '92, the situation was exactly opposite to what it had been when I started commanding Shayetet 13. In my personal, subjective view, the Navy was in a deep crisis, but the Navy didn't feel it was in a state of crisis. How can you create change in an organization that doesn't feel it's in crisis? How do you get a very broad group of people on board, people who were a part of all the previous action, and come and tell them, "Gentlemen, we're wrong, let's change things. . . ."?

The major dilemma at the time was the balance between surface vessels and submarines. The Navy in those years granted an unequivocal preference to surface vessels. I thought that in the twenty-first century, in a reality where all kinds of countries are developing weapons of mass destruction, the State of Israel must have submarines. But we got the German submarines after the State of Israel, in a decision by Defense Minister Moshe Arens, gave up on submarines, and I, as deputy commander of the Navy, see us giving up something that as far as I was concerned was "to be or not to be." If it weren't for the Gulf War—then we encountered a situation where Germany was pleading to help us, based on the feelings of guilt which have accompanied it since World War II and the Holocaust, and up to the aid they provided the Iraqis in the whole complex of Iraq's chemical and unconventional warfare—it's possible that the Navy still wouldn't have had submarines.

Based on foreign publications, those submarines enable Israel's second strike capability.

I'm not getting into that discussion. I think that's not a discussion that should take place in the media. I think the perception of Israeli security should be part of a public discussion in the State of Israel, but the whole topic of second strike should not be part of that discussion. On that matter, we have no choice.

Ultimately, the State of Israel received two submarines, and my dilemma as Navy commander was, do we need a third one? Now, you need a third submarine so that the submarines can begin to enable an era where they give the Israeli people what the Israeli people need. You need an active submarine at all times. Ehud Barak was chief of general staff and I was Navy commander. We had a very serious disagreement on this matter, and eventually we approached

Prime Minister and Minister of Defense Rabin. It was the only topic over which I was willing to resign. After countless debates and two letters of resignation which I ultimately still have in the safe, Rabin agrees that the State of Israel, the Navy, will have submarines. Rabin understood the strategic mantle we were striving toward. I think that unlike the chief of general staff and unlike many others, he saw the importance of, on the one hand, having submarines that will secure the State of Israel's future, and on the other hand, having peace agreements and diplomatic agreements to secure the same future.

A New Middle East?

"Shaking."

When they shook hands, the distance between them was as long as Yitzhak Rabin's outstretched arm: on one side the prime minister of Israel, a man who doesn't like touching, who was forced into this ceremony and especially into this gesture. In the middle was the president of the United States, who was pulling Rabin's hand almost by force. And on the other side the head of the PLO, Yasser Arafat: the wrong uniform in an event which is so right.

(Nahum Barnea, *Yediot Ahronot*, September 14, 1993, the day following the signing of the Oslo Accords on the White House lawn)

Ami Ayalon: When we received the tidings of Oslo, it wasn't a natural thing. On the contrary. It was contrary to everything we'd done for decades and to everything we'd assessed would happen. I think days, maybe a few weeks before Oslo, Elyakim Rubinstein, who was then legal counsel for the Ministry of Defense, and was involved in all the negotiations in Madrid, arrived at the General Staff. We talked about the diplomatic subject, and he explained to us, through signs and wonders, why it wasn't conceivable that we would speak to Arafat. And we accepted his statements as if they were the word of God. And a few weeks later they come to us and tell us about the negotiations. . . . Now you also have to understand, every one of us, myself . . . how far I'd gone to chase terrorists in general and Arafat in particular—Tunisia, the Adriatic Sea, the west Mediterranean—where haven't we gone in out battle against terror, when Arafat was really the personification of terror as a whole. So it wasn't a natural thing for us. But I think we all understood it was the need of the hour.

As someone who generally knows the Palestinians from chasing after them, do you feel the change occurring in the General Staff forum, yesterday's enemies suddenly turning into partners?

Look, I think it didn't happen to all of us simultaneously. The discussions are very difficult ones. I recall that at the time, I commented on the army's role in this process. I thought, and I still think, that the Army made a mistake in the extent in which it took part in the process. It was very convenient for Rabin to bring in the Deputy Chief of General Staff, Amnon Lipkin-Shahak, to coordinate the defense negotiations, and I think that was a mistake. When Uzi Dayan, who was head of the IDF Planning Division, joined Amnon, he came and declared, both in the media and in the General Staff: We went to try and reach an arrangement, and we found friends. So I said in the General Staff, listen, Uzi, the Israeli people didn't send you there so you'd find friends. The Israeli people sent you so you'd ensure the security of the State of Israel.

You also said later, "I object to the level of certainty in which people are saying that the Middle East is striding toward peace. The Middle East is striding toward an era of uncertainty; there's a wonderful chance of peace, but also many dangers." In a way you almost predicted. . . .

I don't know if I predicted. I think we should have participated in that process, but not all of us participated in it with a proper understanding the depth of the problem. The public discussion of the Oslo process was initially accompanied by a level of naiveté that really troubled me. This whole realm of concepts of "a new Middle East." On the other hand, I find it hard to complain, because at the end of the eighties and the beginning of the nineties, it's true that we experienced an Intifada, but the world experienced the fall of the Berlin Wall, the unification of Europe; [political economist Francis] Fukuyama wrote about what's called "the end of history." The feeling was that we really are in some other, better era, in which the whole concept of a nation state, born 150 to 200 years ago, ceased to be relevant. And in general, we're advancing not toward international borders but towards borders of currency and culture. So I can't say that history isn't going there, and maybe it will get there in another fifty, one hundred, or two hundred years, but the road to salvation has ups and downs. And for us in the Middle East, that perception was a naïve one.

I also think we made a lot of mistakes and didn't really take advantage of the opportunity formed during that period. That's also true for the Palestinian side, of course. I mean, the responsibility and the blame don't all lie on one side only. So that on the one hand I was troubled, and on the other hand I think that in retrospect, we missed an opportunity.

In an interview I conducted with Ehud Barak, he told me he came to Rabin and told him, "Listen, you're paying with all your assets, with your reputation, with your good name in matters of security, and in actuality, what you're getting from Arafat is words that may not be backed by anything." How does Rabin cope with something like that?

He replies in simple words. He explains why it has to be done. He's aware of the difficulty. Rabin is a security man from head to toe. He's not someone who needs explanations. When we come and tell him, "We don't have the tools to provide security," he understands it very well. On the other hand, he explains why we have to do it. Rabin, in his second term, came to the conclusion that in order to provide security for the State of Israel, he has to change his positions very radically. In contrast to the promise that he wouldn't withdraw from the Golan Heights, he led a policy that stated that for the State of Israel, a diplomatic agreement with Syria was better than settling the Golan Heights. And Rabin lived in that dilemma. Listen, I saw his face; you can see he understands the intensity of the problem. You can see he's torn. He made a decision. You have to understand that parallel to this, there's also the divide within Israeli society. Some think the Israeli government has no authority to give away the territory of the Land of Israel. Some think it's an unworthy security gamble. There's an opposition that's gradually growing stronger. I think Rabin understood the security problem better than anyone—better than the chief of general staff, better than all his cabinet members—but he also understood the political opportunity. And I think what he was trying to do was bridge that divide. Ultimately he was murdered over that divide to a certain extent.

From the Navy to Heading the Shin Bet

"Major General Ayalon agrees to head the Shin Bet."

Ami Ayalon (51), until 10 days ago commander of the Navy, consented to the urging of the prime minister and President Weizman. His appointment still requires government approval.

(Alex Fishman, *Yediot Ahronot*, January 10, 1996)

Ami Ayalon: In fact, Rabin's assassination brought me to the General Security Service. A year earlier, I refused Rabin when he asked me to be head of the Shin Bet, and less than two months later, when Shimon Peres offered me the position, because Carmi Gillon had resigned, I didn't even have the option of declining. As a member of the General Staff, I knew the Service less well than almost all the other major generals in the General Staff, because in the Navy you see less of them. It was clear to me that the Service was in a very severe state of crisis. And it was clear to me that its people knew it.

Avi Dichter: When Ami Ayalon's candidacy was being considered, Ami was quite wary of accepting, so he sent Itzik Eitan, his neighbor from Kerem Maharal, for an exploratory launch. Itzik Eitan was Gaza Division commander, then head of IDF Central Command, and we're good friends. Of course, without saying what his role was, Itzik came and started asking questions. Since we make our living off these things, I understood after the second sentence exactly what his goal was, and I told him, "Listen, tell Ami not to worry about it. He can come to the Service, and as Service director he'll get all the help and all the support, for one simple reason—there's currently no candidate for head of Shin Bet in the General Security Service that's really ready for it." Because when Carmi was appointed deputy Service director, a group of six division heads retired from Service leadership, and we were actually left without a command leadership. I was at the rank of division head at the time—the most senior among the pertinent divisions to apply for the position of Service director, and I'd only been division head for three years in my first position. Supposedly, the person with the highest aspirations to become Service director is me. And if I'm telling him he can calm down—believe me, he can calm down.

Yuval Diskin: There was a feeling that everything in the Service had collapsed. Security had collapsed, intelligence for the Jewish department couldn't provide the warning that could have prevented Rabin's murder, the districts' ability in the area of preventing suicide attacks wasn't delivering the goods. All this is happening simultaneously to the Oslo process. All these things together brought the organization down to a level where everything you touched didn't actually work.

A month after Ami Ayalon arrived, the terror attack wave of February-March '96 began, and actually he came in during the roughest, lowest period when you could join the organization. Ami brought some very significant things with him, which I think changed the face of the organization, even though some people complained more or less, because no one liked the idea of an outsider being forced on us. But I think he was the most appropriate person for the job.

Ami Ayalon: My feeling was that the strength of the blow was so intense that the Service was really in a state where it was aware of the depth of the crisis, and had the willingness to examine everything. That's actually the beginning of any managerial opportunity. On the other hand, I understood that I didn't know and I wasn't familiar, and I couldn't be the one coming and telling the Service what to do.

When I came to the first Service HQ discussion, I hardly knew anyone from the senior command by sight, except one or two I'd met during activities. I had to give them my credo, and I estimate I said a lot of things they didn't see as relevant. But they understood there was no choice, and really laid out the red carpet for me, and didn't snicker in many cases when I said things that professionally, of course, were a mistake. But I said, almost in the first sentence, "Look, gentlemen, I don't know the Service, I don't know how to gather intelligence, I don't know how to recruit agents, I don't know how to thwart terror, I know how to ask questions. And that's what I'm going to do. Now, the only answer I'm not willing to hear is 'that's the way we've always done it.' The fact is that, indeed, that's the way we've always done it, but we've gotten to a place where we don't want to be. So we'll examine everything, we'll examine the method of collection, the method of recruitment, the method of prevention, everything. Maybe we'll examine things and come to the conclusion that what we've always done is excellent, so there's no reason to change it, but we'll get there only after we question all the conventions and all the axioms."

And that's actually what I did over more than four years in the General Security Service.

Yuval Diskin: Ami brought with him the value of inquiry. He installed many management approaches that didn't exist in the organization. He installed planning that didn't exist in the organization. In those years, the Shin Bet was between a tactical and a micro-tactical organization. An organization that reacts, collects information, thwarts a terrorist attack—but it wouldn't really try to plan for the middle and the long term, much less compose a work plan, recruit people for new roles. Ami installed all these things in the organization in a long, systematic process, which I believe has left its impression on the Service to this day. And I don't know to what extent he became a Shin Bet man. I don't think he was a Shin Bet man even when he was done. He may have a different opinion. I believe that's not where I give him the excellent grade, but rather on the aspect of values, management, leadership, inquiry—in my opinion that was a lot more important at the time.

What did you discover in this inquiry?

Diskin: We understood that something is apparently deeply wrong with the organization. We discovered we're an organization with lots of muscle, but an underdeveloped brain. That's my interpretation. One of the upheavals we made was to determine that from now on the brain would control the muscles, rather than the muscles controlling the brain. Easy to say, hard to do, because organizational culture is something very hard to change. It's important to understand that the organization was led, including even today, by people who had grown up in the field, led by muscle. And those were the very people who had to lead a course of action that transfers the weight from the organizations in the field to the thinking people sitting in rooms under neon lights, in front of computer screens.

Rabin's assassination is a clear security failure. Why do you actually find a Service that's shaken up at every level? The security division was actually the one that should have been shaken up.

Ami Ayalon: Rabin's murder wasn't just a failure by the security apparatus. It's equally an intelligence failure. The General Security Service was very close, intelligence-wise, to Yigal Amir. The Service handled agents who had met Yigal Amir. It had received information about "the little Yemenite who said in the restroom that he would murder Rabin." That means that the general intelligence service failed in regard to the intelligence aspect no less than in regard to the security aspect.

I also disagree with the conclusions of the Shamgar Commission on the subject of intelligence. They were right about the main conclusion they came to, which was that the Service made a mistake in handling Avishai Raviv,* and didn't understand the boundaries of what's permitted in handling agents in violent targets, because the General Security Service set up Avishai Raviv as "number one" in an organization. Now, you can't set up "number ones" in an organization, because that's the stage where you're transitioning from a state where you have to act as an intelligence agency to get intelligence, to a state where you have to manufacture the reality against which you're actually fighting. So we never set up a "number one" in an organization, no matter how non-substantial that organization is.

So it's true, the General Security Service made a mistake in handling Avishai Raviv, but I think that's just a small part of the intelligence failure. Beyond that, we have to be honest with ourselves. What did the first Shamgar Commission, established following the massacre in the Cave of the Patriarchs, say about the General Security Service? You weren't aggressive enough about obtaining intelligence. You should be more aggressive about the way in which you recruit and act within these violent groups of the extreme right in Israel. Then the second Shamgar Commission comes and says to the General Security Service, "You employed agents in a too-aggressive, inappropriate way." So the Shamgar Commission was right both the first time and the second time, but the General Security Service was left with the dilemma.

---

* A Shin Bet agent who participated in many violent events, established two fictitious underground organizations, and, according to the attorney general, acted as an agent provocateur.

But I don't want it to seem as if, as Service director, I arrive and start conducting academic debates and deliberating. Ultimately, it's completely clear to me that I came to the Service to provide security for Israeli citizens. The first thing I dealt with, at least within the first week, was really the crisis in the security apparatus. The head of division was replaced, the head of VIP Security was replaced, and I was troubled by the question—did we really learn the right lessons? My impression was that we hadn't. I asked a very simple question: what was actually the problem? And from the answers I received, I couldn't say why the chances of it happening again were now lower.

The VIP Security apparatus was born as a plane and airport security apparatus, where the ultimate emphasis was on training the fighter. The central measure was the time passing between the moment he discovers the threat and the moment he fires the first bullet. According to that perception, in the case of Yigal Amir, there was no chance of the Service security team firing the first bullet. You can't screen every area in such an absolute way. So the question is, what do you do to cope with the assassin's first bullet? The approach characterizing the setup today is actually to surround the prime minister, not with two people or three people but, if necessary, with five or six people. When he enters an unfiltered zone, there's a human belt around him that makes getting to him almost impossible. It stands as a barrier between a bullet and him. The intention is to absorb the first bullet and not necessarily kill the aggressor, because you assume in advance that you probably won't fire the first bullet. That means you actually need to start changing training courses, instruction, the whole team structure, and ultimately the whole apparatus.

Simultaneously to dealing with the security apparatus, already in the first days of my service as head of the General Security Service, the Arabic terror prevention apparatus actually collapsed. The terrorist attacks in which we lost 57 citizens of the State of Israel, and 214 were injured in less than two weeks, at the end of February and the beginning of March, without a doubt signal the collapse of a system whose purpose is to thwart terror.

The whole system of recruiting agents needed to be re-examined. Pulling out of the territory following the Oslo Accords created a situation where the ability to collect human-based information gradually decreased. Beyond that, the organizations had changed, too. The Fatah of the mid-nineties was less and less an organization manufacturing terror. And on the other hand, Hamas was on the rise, and that consisted of completely different populations. So many areas of activity had to be diverted and updated in accordance with a portrait of reality that's in flux, and is changing at impossible rates during that period.

When you enter the Service, we're actually not in control of that territory. How do you cope with that to provide the information which can prevent terrorist attacks?

The statement "you can't recruit agents" is never acceptable. The reasons why a person provides information are very diverse. Some of them really see terror as a threat to them, as well, and do it out of ideological considerations. Not joining Zionism, but a willingness to fight terror. Some of them do it due to these or other reasons concerning making a living, or any other reason which is actually a means by which the General Security Service recruits agents. These reasons always exist. In every situation. And we have to see how a General Security Service continues to recruit agents in a different reality, as well. Beyond that, I won't say one word to you about recruiting agents. I think the collection methods of a General Security Service shouldn't be exposed to public discussion. I can tell you we should have made much smarter use of the information technology which developed in the nineties.

If you ask me, the big revolution of the General Security Service in the second half of the nineties was the information revolution. I estimate that's the thing that contributed, at least at the end of my term, more than any other single factor, to the General Security Service's prevention ability. As intelligence people, we always want more and more information. And then I start hearing more and more in inquiries, which we conduct in the Service in cases in which we fail, a kind of statement saying, it was all in the files. What does that mean, "It was all in the files"? It means there was information in the intelligence files that, had it been at our disposal in real time, would have enabled us to prevent a terrorist attack that we didn't manage to prevent. That statement brought on a revolution in the General Security Service. It brought us to change the center of gravity from collection—which still continues, of course—to making the most of the information. Meaning, how do I take the endless collection of information existing in the files or in the collective memory or in the individual memory of one of the Service's people, and turn it into something pertinent in the decision-making process.

Yuval Diskin: During those years, we made very far-reaching decisions, and decided to dedicate the majority of our budget to developing our information technology within the organization. We actually put almost all of our money into that, at the expense of other things. When you invest in technology, you don't get results within a week or two. It takes months and sometimes two or three years till you start to see any yield from those things. But that focus raised the organization and placed it on the launchpad and got it off the floorboards to a large extent.

Ami Ayalon: In 1995, when I was commander of the Navy, I could sit in the Navy "pit," the place where the Navy commander makes his decisions when he sends ships to Syria, to Libya, to Tunisia, or to the western Mediterranean, and I could see on graphics monitors exactly where each of my ships was located, where each enemy ship was located. My ships in blue, and their ships in red, and neutral ships in green, all to simplify it as much as possible for me. And if I had fighters on the shore, I could, once every five minutes, see exactly where each one of my teams of Shayetet 13 fighters was located on the Libyan shore, thousands of kilometers away from Israel. To see it in a graphic image. The General Security Service didn't have information systems like that. And then you say to yourself, hold on a minute, today's information world lets you do anything. It lets you translate every speck of information into something that becomes a factor in the decision-making process, and they'll present it for you in any way you want it presented. Do you want them to draw it in a particular color? As a particular character? The graphics are possible. The technology exists. That's the revolution.

Yuval Diskin: What the Service actually did is take all the systems that enable us to cope with the quantities of information and intelligence we know how to produce, and make the most of them and turn them into something that is ultimately useable in an operational way. We revolutionized things and reached what I believe is also a high level in relation to peer organizations I know in Israel and in the world. Some of them later came to learn quite a few things from the approaches and capabilities we managed to develop here. There's an area called data mining, and I won't expand any further on this topic, but I believe we're on a world-class level.

Expand on that.

No. I can say these aren't just information systems, but operational information systems. And the bottom line is they saved many lives in the State of Israel in real time.

Avi Dichter: Every person also manufactures a great amount of information. Think about it, any one of us, how much did you talk on the phone twenty years ago, and how much do you talk today? It's at scales that are not even comparable. So the key is to constantly keep up with technological developments. And people make mistakes, definitely terrorists who are in distress. The volume of information people produce is immense, and in the past there was no chance of retrieving it, because you had to start going over the files, paper files which we started working with years ago. Today, by running a computer, you can get characteristics instantly. If they tell you that in Jenin, we're dealing with a redhead, you can extract all the redheads in Jenin, and already, instead of dealing with an abstract redhead, you're dealing with ten people whose names are known. Or different characteristics which you can cross-reference: the short man, the thin man, the tall man. Even based on clothing. Listen, those are major capabilities on any scale.

There's a saying that computer people have saved the lives of a whole lot of people. Explain it to me.

Yuval Diskin: I'll try to make it as vivid as possible. If we get intelligence or certain signals in real time, and these signals tell us that a suicide bomber has just left from Nablus to Jerusalem or to Netanya, and he intends to blow himself up, to understand that the signals are saying these things, you need very high capabilities. Technological ones, and the capabilities of intelligence people, mostly our desk people, who are the ones reading this operative information and who have to understand that when you put this signal together with that signal, the conclusion is that a suicide bomber has now started moving, armed with a belt of explosives, to this or that place, and that dictates a series of operational steps with which we've reached a very high level in cooperation with the army and the police. If we hadn't taken those steps, we would actually have arrived at the Second Intifada without many of the capabilities we had, even if some of them were still only budding capabilities. I believe the Israeli people would have paid interest for that. Even so, we paid a very heavy, painful price, but it could have been a lot heavier and a lot more painful.

Ami Ayalon: In the rehabilitation process of the prevention apparatus, we also had to influence the cabinet and the prime minister. I really appreciated Rabin for his determination, but on the other hand, from a historical perspective, I think there was a problem with the policy the State of Israel adopted under his leadership, which actually stated, "We'll fight terror as if there was no political process, and conduct a political process as if there was no terror." If that's the situation, then think of it from Arafat's perspective—why should he fight terror? If he doesn't pay a price for not fighting terror, he has no reason to fight it. Understand, fighting terror for him means entering into an inter-Palestinian conflict where people have to be in prison, and some of them will be killed on the way. He has to go to his *Altalena*. That's not something a leader like Arafat does if he has a choice. He has no incentive.

That policy was changed by Prime Minister Shimon Peres after the February-March attacks. He was supposed to hand over Hebron in March-April, and he didn't hand over Hebron. He told Arafat, "We're not continuing. If you want a political process, you have to create security." That equation was phrased by Shimon Peres and of course became Benjamin Netanyahu's central policy when he was prime minister. That made it perfectly clear to the Palestinians that they actually had to start thwarting terror, and in certain periods created exceptional cooperation with the Service.

So long as the Palestinian perception was that they were really going toward a political process that would grant them a state alongside the State of Israel, they had full willingness to act in order to thwart terror. They had additional reasons as well, of course. After the January-February 1996 attacks, when we actually posed this as a condition, and they started acting against Hamas's terror infrastructure in the Gaza Strip, they discovered a very deep infrastructure of which they weren't aware. What especially troubled them was the covert arm of Hamas led by Dr. Ibrahim al-Makadmeh, whose role was to fight Palestinian security mechanisms and the Palestinian political leadership. When they discovered that, at least for Dahlan and Jibril Rajoub, they got the memo. They understood they had to [do] their [own] *Altalena,* and in certain periods, they definitely did that.

There's a lot of controversy about whether they made it to their *Altalena* or didn't make it to their *Altalena*.

There may be controversy, but it looks very clear to me.

Was it an *Altalena*?

Unequivocally.

Avi Dichter: They understood, following a near-ultimatum by then–prime minister Shimon Peres, that if they didn't put an end to it, we would put an end to it in some way, including by going into the territory. And then they really made arrests on a scale of close to four hundred people. The immediate impact was very significant, especially in Gaza. I'm not talking about the beard shaving*, that was already an act of abuse that, internally for them, bears a different significance, but, unfortunately, it wasn't a thwarting measure. It was a preventive measure. Something like administrative arrest—hold them for a certain time period, and afterwards "we'll see what happens." They arrested them just to calm things down. Unfortunately, it just wasn't enough.

Ami Ayalon: I sat with [Palestinian security chiefs] Jibril Rajoub and Mohammed Dhalan and with [Palestinian intelligence boss] Amin al-Hindi and told them, "Gentlemen, we won't make peace. Make no mistake. The leaders will make peace. But we're the necessary condition. Without us providing security, without us creating a bridge on which they can meet and sit and discuss how the Middle East will look from the political, social, and financial aspects, nothing will

---

* Arafat instructed his security forces to shave the beards of Hamas and other Islamist movement arrestees in order to humiliate them.

happen. And so your role and my role is to thwart terror, and I'm telling you, we'll do anything to thwart terror." And there were periods when we did it, but ultimately that process is a process that starts with the statesmen.

The Era of Netanyahu

"The day in which the Shin Bet Director almost resigned."

Ami Ayalon told his inner circle that he decided to stay so as not to cause an additional shake-up in the organization. Later, he read to a subcommittee of the Knesset's Foreign Affairs and Defense Committee a compromise letter which he had phrased together with Netanyahu. Sources within the Prime Minister's Office: "It's doubtful if Netanyahu and Ayalon can work together in the resulting atmosphere."

(Alex Fishman, Nahum Barnea and Shimon Schiffer, *Yediot Ahronot*, December 17, 1996)

Let's go back to '96. Netanyahu replaces Peres as prime minister. With you acting as Service director, does anything change?

Ami Ayalon: On the surface, nothing changes. I didn't try to analyze Netanyahu's statements from previous years, that he was opposed to the process and opposed to a two-state solution. It didn't really interest me. So in terms of working relations between a head of Service and a prime minister, nothing changed initially. Over time, there were two incidents of very serious internal conflicts for me, as a citizen and as Service director.

Once, after a brutal terrorist attack in the Binyamin Region, Prime Minister Benjamin Netanyahu received a recommendation—as what's called "an appropriate Zionist response"—to build a settlement. And the chief of Central Command at the time, Uzi Dayan, suggests that he actually transform a military base into a settlement, or establish the settlement within the military base, all kinds of methods of various types. And at that stage I say, "Mr. Prime Minister, I want to make it clear that I don't deal with 'an appropriate Zionist response.' I need to provide security. If you want to have this discussion in the context of how to increase security along the roads in the West Bank, which means more patrols, more lighting, more roads, anything you want, that's legitimate, I'm part of the discussion. If you're demanding that I present to you how I'll gather more information, that's all legitimate. If you're going to steer the discussion toward how to build the settlement and where to build it, I'm out. I'm not participating in a discussion like that. As far as I'm concerned that's not a defense discussion. That's a political discussion." That's exactly the distinction I made, and the chief of Central Command didn't make. My opinions on the subject of settlements don't matter in this context. They're not a part of the discussion on what security in the State of Israel means. There were other incidents, but this is really a very distinct case in which I found it appropriate to come out and say which discussion I would not participate in.

But it is part of your interface. If Bibi Netanyahu goes and establishes a settlement, you can anticipate that it could cause a blow-up with the Palestinians.

No, I'm sorry, but that's exactly it. The blow-up with the Palestinians is a whole other discussion space. I can tell you, for example, that we were wrong in certain cases when we estimated there would be or wouldn't be blow-ups, for example, the settlement in Jerusalem. Irving Moskowitz* built a neighborhood east of the Temple Mount. We assessed it would cause a great uproar. Ultimately, they decided not to adopt our stance and built the neighborhood. Except for ten Israeli members of the left and fifteen Palestinians, no one went there to protest. I was interested in finding out where we'd gone wrong. I went out there and met a police officer. The police had claimed in advance that there wouldn't be a blow-up there. I asked him, "So tell me, where did we go wrong? How do you explain this?" So he told me, "Ami, you know what? You weren't in touch with the local reality." I can tell you that in cases where the local population doesn't feel it's been harmed as a result of it being relatively unpopulated territory, and they're promised construction of parks and nursery schools, an improvement to their quality of life, the local population isn't necessarily violent. Not everything we do necessarily brings on violence. Since my job is to provide security, I can't start making

---

* A Jewish American businessman and philanthropist, who has dedicated significant funds toward creating a Jewish majority in Arab neighborhoods of East Jerusalem by purchasing Arab homes for Jewish settlement.

unsubstantiated assessments just because of my political views. That's just inconceivable.

In the other incident, I had a very harsh argument with Bibi Netanyahu on the topic of the Western Wall tunnels. I supported opening the tunnels. It came up during Rabin's term and came up during Peres's term; they all supported it, but they always said, "The time isn't right." And I said, "Look, in Jerusalem, the time is never right. We've been waiting three thousand years, and the time isn't right. The question is a different one: can we create conditions that will make the time right?" And then we conducted an analysis that said that in order for violence to break out in Jerusalem, three conditions must exist: Arafat must have a motive to create violence, or no motive to suppress it; the local population must have a motive to create violence; and religious factors in Jerusalem, primarily the Waqf, also promote violence. At least two of these conditions have to exist in order for violence to ultimately break out.

So I came to Netanyahu and told him, "In our estimate, if Arafat has no motive, if the Waqf has no motive, and/or if the local population has no motive, it makes sense to assume things can be done in Jerusalem." Then he asks me, "What do you recommend?" And I told him, "Look, Arafat's motivation is political. He has to know that he gets something he wants in the diplomatic process. The second thing is the Waqf [the Temple Mount's Muslim security guards]. The Waqf needs to know what the borders of the excavation are going to be. You have to understand, the Waqf has real concerns. We see it as a surreal joke, but they really believe we mean to dig and get under the Holy of Holies and dig under the Mosque of Omar! As far as they're concerned, they have to make sure it's not going to happen. The third thing is to take care of the local population, and explain to them why opening the tunnel would mean financial well-being from their perspective."

Ultimately, when the tunnel opened, those conditions weren't fulfilled. The Service was entirely not involved—not with talking to the Waqf and not with talking to Arafat—and suddenly you hear at midnight that they're going to open the tunnel in a few more hours. Supposedly, opening the tunnel is a political decision, but even if the political echelon wants to open the tunnel, I have to be the one who says, do conditions enable it without undermining the security of Israeli citizens, and my personal opinion is irrelevant at the moment.

You're sitting with Bibi Netanyahu a month before the tunnel opens, and you tell him what you're telling me now?

Yes.

What does he say?

He's very accepting. The mistake he made was one of management. He misread Arafat so badly that he sent his emissary to him and they agreed on something positive or negative about Hebron, and he thought that as a result of that, Arafat now has no motive for violence. He apparently also instructed the police to talk to the Waqf; I don't know if the police did or didn't talk to the Waqf. That's improper management. He received the status assessment, he received the recommendation, but he had no apparatus that really knows how to carry these things out. To ask whether, from what you understand of Arafat, of his internal discussions, he's really in the state of mind we want him to be in if we're opening the tunnel. All these things don't take place. In retrospect, I understand there was some kind of activity that was completely different from what I assessed should take place. But that's the way the Israeli government made decisions. I say that regretfully. To the best of my knowledge, by the way, there was also no cabinet discussion.

Seventeen soldiers killed. Injuries. Casualties on the Palestinian side.

True. True, it's a tragedy, but that's the truth. I'm not going to prettify it. The moment the tunnel is opened, Bibi Netanyahu travels abroad. Ehud Olmert, Mayor of Jerusalem, stands there with some big American donors, and they conduct a celebration in honor of the tunnel opening. No one instructs the security apparatus, the General Security Service, the police, in advance, to prepare in case anything happens. We see that there's a general strike and some beginnings of an uproar, and there's no one to talk to! The minister of defense says, "Jerusalem isn't my problem. The prime minister's abroad and he doesn't think he needs to return." The minister of finance, who had some security background, doesn't think it's the time to return, and he's in the midst of financial discussions, and the minister of tourism, former president of Israel Moshe Katsav, is filling in for the prime minister. He's the one who has to run the country. He's the one who has to run the military battle. In short, total chaos for forty-eight hours.

Afterwards, when things end in a very problematic way, we're summoned to a press conference where we have to explain what happened. I think that's not right, but the prime minister issues an instruction, so we go to a press conference, and then I say, "I recommended opening the tunnel, but under completely different conditions." The prime minister sees what I'm saying as betrayal. And it's really a world of deaf-mutes. I'm telling my truth, and he apparently sees a completely different reality in front of his eyes, and a very problematic media debacle between the prime minister and the head of the General Security Service begins, where I'm, of course, prohibited from being interviewed.

We later had a very honest and direct conversation where I made things very clear and laid out my worldview. The prime minister leaked an actual transcript from our private meeting, according to which I recommended opening the tunnel. He just didn't leak the part where I conditioned it on those terms which must be created. A very, very difficult situation.

Did you consider resigning?

A), in some statement on the Knesset stairs, they asked me, "How do you not resign?" I said, "There's a song by an extraordinary songwriter [Ehud Manor], saying, 'I have no other country, even if my land is on fire.' Which is true. In the end, that brings us to a state where we're not so quick to resign. . . ." And b), I didn't think I'd have a problem continuing to work with the prime minister, because I had no preconception that a relationship between the head of a general security service and a prime minister should be a relationship of mutual trust. The relationship between a prime minister and a head of Shin Bet is not a bedroom-type relationship. On the contrary. I think that in periods when this relationship was built on trust and closeness, the heads of Shin Bet didn't always know how to tell the prime minister, "This far and no more." So I don't think you need to fight with the prime minister in order to create an appropriate relationship, but I didn't think at the time that I was in a relationship which would not enable work.

Did he raise the subject of your resignation?

No. I think he also understood that ultimately, it was neither in his best interest nor in my best interest.

Who ultimately restores calm to the burning ground? Is it really the Palestinians or is it IDF?

When you don't see fire, it's not always because someone restored calm to the area; sometimes there's just no energy to start the fire. At this stage, Arafat still believed that he could set the diplomatic process in motion. By the way, the fact is that he succeeded. That's one of the things about which I argued with Netanyahu later. After seventeen Israeli soldiers were killed, I told him, "Now is the time to stop the Oslo process. If you want, now you can come and say, "Gentlemen, from this moment on I want to discuss the permanent settlement. I'm not in a position to provide more any more territories and ultimately discover, after I've given away more than ninety percent of the territory, that that's when I start dealing with the core issues." The prime minister didn't accept my recommendation.

I also told him the only way to convince the US president and Arafat that we have to start with the core issues now, without transferring additional territories, is to completely freeze the settlements. You have to stop the time lock-in. Because the time lock-in is the strangest factor in the equation between us and the Palestinians. Both sides think time is working against them. If you ask the average Israeli, he'll say, "Listen, because of demographics, time is working against us." If you ask the average Palestinian, he'll tell you, "What are you talking about, look at them, they're building more and more settlements, and will create a situation where the process is irreversible and there's no Palestinian state." Meaning, both sides see time as a negative element. And I said to Bibi, "If you freeze time and say 'no settlements' for six months, one year, two years, for as long as you can, and then only later will we decide where to build and where not to build, if you can do that, then after you've provided them with weapons and they killed seventeen of our soldiers, you can drum up international legitimacy for us changing the characteristics of the process and starting the process by discussing core topics." That was actually the best course of action.

He didn't do it. He traveled to the United States, gave away Hebron, signed the Wye River Memorandum,* and brought the Americans

---

* Signed in October 1998, this agreement between Israel and the PLO was meant to specify the steps and timetable to carry out the Oslo Accords, including a three-stage process according to which Israel would hand over Gaza and the West Bank. The agreement was ultimately only partially consummated.

into the equation. Three weeks after the events of the Western Wall tunnel end, he handed over Hebron.

What did Arafat conclude from that?

Arafat concludes from that that we only understand force. Arafat understands one simple thing. When he tried to continue the process after Bibi rose to power, he couldn't create anything. And then he employs violence, kills seventeen Israeli soldiers, and he understands—hold on, fellows, right after I killed seventeen Israeli soldiers, I met Bibi in the United States, we shook hands, Clinton, this and that, and I got Hebron. What can he understand from that? Exactly what the Palestinians understood when we unilaterally retreated from Lebanon, and when we unilaterally retreated from Gaza, with no diplomatic context. All we've been doing in recent years is explaining to them that we only understand the language of force.

Why does Netanyahu hand over Hebron? It contradicts his very essence.

Listen, psychology is my wife's area of expertise in the family. I'm not worthy of examining his internal workings. I estimate he thinks or estimates or is afraid that the United States is not receptive to changing the process. That's my assessment. I can't say. I personally thought it was a mistake, I stated my opinion, I wrote my opinion. I wrote a letter to the prime minister about it, and he didn't accept my opinion and handed over Hebron. But that's his decision. I don't think it's right for a head of Shin Bet to start grading the behavior of a prime minister making political decisions. That's his right, his authority, he was elected and he's the one who's accountable.

You told me that after a terrorist attack, there was a discussion in the prime minister's office, in which the prime minister wanted to establish a settlement as an appropriate Zionist response, and you said, "That's enough, this is a political discussion. I don't think it's my place to sit in on this. I don't deal with appropriate Zionist responses." And yet after the events of the Western Wall tunnel, you come to the prime minister and tell him, "You can withdraw from the political process. Stop it." How do those things fit together?

On the contrary. In my view, they actually complement each other. In the case of the tunnel events, I put my personal opinion aside. I personally believed that if the process was carried out in good faith—then there's a real chance to reach an agreement. But when I came to the prime minister, I put my personal belief aside. I didn't tell him we have to continue the process at any price—I did the opposite. I know his stance. My personal stance is irrelevant. If he wants to carry out his stance, now, from a defense standpoint, I can tell him that based on my analysis of the international system, you can change the process. I'm not stating my opinion, whether it should or shouldn't be done. I'm in charge of fighting terror, and I'm in charge of the assessment regarding all the implications of the diplomatic process, because I'm one of the instruments of assessment for the cabinet and the prime minister.

To the same extent, after a terrorist attack, there's what I call "an appropriate security response," which is everything the General Security Service does, or what IDF does. You, as prime minister, want to build a settlement? Do it; I'm not a part of it. I am a part of those discussions dealing directly with security. I even remarked that on the topic of those settlements we establish as an appropriate Zionist response, I don't know how to measure the long term. I can say it would cause a loss of trust in the diplomatic process and to a large extent would cause lots of groups and individuals to join the cycle of terror and the opposition to the diplomatic process within the Palestinian public.

Where do you set the borders of your mandate as head of Service, between politics and security? It's actually in the gray zone.

The borderline is very much in the gray zone. Even in retrospect, it's hard to tell whether the place where I drew the line is the right place.

As head of the Service, were you a part of the decision-making process in the failed hit attempt on Khaled Mashal?

Khaled Mashal is a sad tale in the defense history of the State of Israel. Following some terror attacks, I don't even remember which ones, Prime Minister Netanyahu decides to react. That's his right, his authority. He calls me, as Shin Bet director, and wants me to present possible operations to him. And I explain to him that it would take me a few more days, at least a week or two, to gather the intelligence and present an operation for someone who needs to be hit. With the goal being to thwart terror, not to start taking revenge against Palestinian civilians. In retrospect I know that Danny Yatom, who was then head of the Mossad, was also summoned to see Netanyahu, and actually set the Khaled Mahsal process in motion.

What do you mean, "in retrospect"?

In retrospect, because I wasn't a part of the decisions at the time. Khaled Mashal was a topic of discussion as part of the SDC—Service Directors Committee—and in fact, his role in the Palestinian terror chain of command justified targeting him. But there was no discussion about the decision to target him. At least, I didn't take part in such a discussion. The next thing that happens is that the prime minister is at the General Security Service, as part of a routine visit, and receives information about the fact that an operation took place, and the operation failed, and Mossad fighters have been captured by the Jordanians.

I want to understand the process for a second. There's a discussion at the Service Directors Commission, in which the name Khaled Mashal is raised, and the next time you hear about it as head of the General Security Service is when the prime minister is informed, during a tour in the Security Service, that such an operation had failed? Meaning, they embark on an operation like that, which might also have implications on what happens in the Territories, and the head of the Security Service is not aware of this?

Correct.

What do you think of that?

I think it's wrong. You're asking me if that's the way to plan an operation? The answer is no. I hope we've learned our lesson. Time will tell. By the way, later Mossad Director Danny Yatom claimed that he did call me. I, of course, claim that he didn't call, so there's a difference of opinion between us, since neither of us had to take a polygraph test. His claim, at least in the investigative commission, was that he phoned me and asked if I was opposed to an operation against Khaled Mashal. He claims I told him I wasn't opposed to it. I really don't remember a phone call like that. That's more or less where the matter ends.

Avi Dichter: I don't know how to state it gently; it was just a strategic mistake by the political echelon, to go for an operation to hit Khaled Mashal in Jordan, three years after the peace treaty with Jordan. It's . . . I admit I couldn't put together what I understand with what happened there. Not that Khaled Mashal deserved to live, but he could have croaked in any other country. In Jordan, three years after the peace treaty, which is the "number one" strategic asset in that regard for the State of Israel, after Egypt? But I suppose distress, and possibly a lack of attention by the person dealing with it, from the defense side, simply pushed us into carrying out an operational action in Jordan. By the way, even if it had succeeded and Khaled Mashal had died and all the fighters had returned safely to their base, what would the Jordanians have thought? That the Thai did it? . . . I don't know what King Hussein's reaction would have been, but this is a classic example of "look before you leap."

And what do you say to the prime minister when you hear something like that, that the hit attempt failed?

Ami Ayalon: The prime minister more or less informs me of the information he's received, and goes off to the Mossad. The next time I'm involved in the matter is when they ask me over the phone do I support or oppose Sheikh Yassin's release. I really don't like Sheikh Yassin's release, but a decision to free him is made. By the way, discussions on Sheikh Yassin rise and fall over the years. I remember that Ya'akov Amidror, who was the minister of defense's diplomatic secretary, thought at the time that Sheikh Yassin should be released. I thought throughout that period that Sheikh Yassin's release is very problematic, both from the aspect of strengthening Hamas and weakening Arafat, and due to the ideology preached by Sheikh Yassin. I think we didn't understand the extent of his influence because we didn't understand how such a disabled person, who really wouldn't have been elected, not on American television and not on Israeli television, to any significant public role, to what extent he represents, for many Palestinians, Palestinian suffering, and to what extent he's linked to the same ideology he preaches, which ultimately is Jihad and terror, and opposition to the whole process which Arafat tried to head in Palestinian society.

Are you even consulted regarding this release? Does a discussion take place?

The head of Aman, Bogie Ya'alon [Israel's current defense minister], called me, and said the prime minister intends to release Sheikh Yassin in order to return the Mossad fighters home. Usually I'm a great proponent of release, including of people with blood on their hands, in return for our soldiers who were abducted or taken prisoner. In this case, I really don't understand the urgency. Mossad fighters were trained their whole lives to be imprisoned. If there is a prison about which I believe you can take your time, it's Jordanian prison. This isn't Hamas prison, this isn't prison in an African country. I have a very close relationship with the head of Jordan's General Intelligence Directorate, General Batichi. I really don't understand what all the fuss is about, and why it has to be done without discussion, without understanding the implications.

So I say, "Guys, I really don't know what to tell you, I don't think he should be released, but if the prime minister wants to, I won't prevent it." No discussion. That's all. Not even in the General Security Service. This is not a situation where they tell me, "Listen, take an hour, come back with a stance on the matter." A short phone call: "What's your stance?" I said, "Guys, I don't know what to say, I think Sheikh Yassin is the establisher of Hamas, and a dangerous man. From what we understood based on his behavior and statements in prison, he really doesn't herald peace. He's very problematic."

Avi Dichter: Sheikh Yassin was sentenced to two life sentences, for [abducting and] murdering the soldiers Avi Sasportas and Ilan Sa'adon [in 1989]. He returned to Gaza as a hero. That's the kind of price you pay; you know some element of deterrence has been damaged. Sheikh Yassin's contribution to initiating Hamas terror attacks against Israel, to harming those suspected of collaboration in Gaza, and to building the military cadre in Gaza, is a very significant contribution. To his credit, Sheikh Yassin clearly understood that the Hamas can't be built as an alternative to the Palestinian Authority in Gaza, in a reality in which only the terror apparatus, [the] Izz al-Din al-Qassam [Brigades], exists. You have to build an army. So they established what's called "The People's Army." He reached a very significant strategic decision, that for any weapons smuggled for the Hamas into Gaza, half of them would go to the People's Army, and only half of them would go to Izz al-Din al-Qassam, and later he expanded the army's share, and that's how the army was built.

How do the Palestinians react to the release?

Dichter: Look, Arafat is certain there's a conspiracy here, which we and the Jordanians concocted to weaken his leadership over the Territories. Sheikh Yassin may be the most extreme opponent to the whole stance Arafat has been leading since 1988, which basically states, "Two states for two nations." This greatly intensifies the battle between Hamas and Fatah. But the question is, how does the State of Israel reach a decision? Was it done in an appropriate manner or not? And the answer is unequivocal—in an inappropriate manner.

When Arafat Orders to Cease Terrorist Activity

"The Awadallah brothers were killed while they were eating dinner."

Palestinian factors: IDF knew the brothers' location in advance, and killed them in cold blood. IDF commander in the West Bank: "This was a random-encounter engagement."

The time was 4:35 on a Thursday afternoon. Fighters from Yamam—Israel Police's special forces anti-terror unit—took rapid, quiet steps toward an isolated structure located 7 km [about 4.5 miles] west of Hebron. A few of the fighters silently approached the open door, stopped for a moment, and suddenly burst into the room while directing sustained fire toward the two brothers Adel and Imad Awadallah. The fire lasted several seconds, and when it ended, the bodies of the two brothers were laid out on the floor of the room. . . .

The Shin Bet did not trust censors to prevent publication of the hit on the Awadallah brothers, and in an unusual step, requested a suppression order regarding all details related to the affair. The military court in Adoraim granted the request and issued a suppression order on Thursday night.

(Alex Fishman and Amir Rapaport,
Yediot Ahronot, September 13, 1998)

Ami Ayalon: Adel Awadallah was head of military Hamas in the West Bank in 1998. The main instigator of terror. He constituted a direct, immediate, and main threat to us. The Palestinian Authority also tried to pursue him, unsuccessfully. His brother Imad was sent to Palestinian prison and underwent a very intense interrogation process in Jibril Rajoub's interrogation facilities. They tried getting to Adel through him, and apparently as a result of the fact that

Palestinian prison is not a particularly secure place, he managed to escape and reunite with his brother. And we received intelligence, never mind the source, that actually enabled us to start constructing an operation to catch them.

After we understand that they're *the* legitimate target, I of course present it to the prime minister. Netanyahu had some intense doubts, and rightly so. He was very troubled by the response, especially after the wave of terror attacks in February-March '96, which we knew was to a large extent in continuation with the killing of Yahya Ayyash. But I made it clear, unequivocally, that it's inconceivable that we manage to manufacture an operational opportunity to target him and we don't do it. We have to take the risk. I, of course, promised to also handle the implications of Palestinian violence as a result of targeting him.

After a harsh argument, mainly between me and the prime minister, a decision was reached that we have to target him. By the way, targeting him still doesn't mean killing him, because we conducted the operation in order to capture him. That was also debated, because we knew that if he was sitting in an Israeli prison, there would be abduction attempts to bring about his release. My claim was that we had to bring him to an Israeli prison, first because he needs to exit the orbit of the military leadership which he's leading at the moment, and second because we need all the information he has. He's a trove of knowledge about the existing infrastructure in the West Bank.

Ultimately, even though we're planning to arrest them, the minute the Awadallah brothers pick up weapons, the Yamam fighters do exactly what they're supposed to do, and shoot to kill. The operation ends with the deaths of Adel Awadallah and his brother. But he had the whole archive with him, and all the information we thought we'd get from him through interrogation fell into our hands in an unplanned way. He gave us the whole layout and Hamas's whole intelligence-operational infrastructure in the West Bank in 1998, and enabled us, through meticulous collection, analysis, research, and assessment work, dozens of intelligence operations, and operational activity, to continue to thwart terror. And I believe that's actually the most important operation, which dramatically affected the level of security throughout the rest of '98, '99, and 2000. The whole infrastructure we meant to reach by interrogating Adel Awadallah ultimately fell into our hands, because he walked around with all the information on his back. A terrible mistake, by the way, which is basic for an intelligence man, and definitely a guerrilla fighter, but we got lucky and he made that mistake.

When the Awadallah brothers are killed, in contrast to the plan, there's very heavy pressure both in the prime minister's office and in the ministry of defense. There are very problematic discussions there around the question why they were killed, with me explaining the very simple thing that every fighter knows, that if you go into a house, and the person confronting you is armed, and he shoots—you have to shoot to kill. This simple truth is apparently not universally understood in the places where I was at that time. Anyway, on that night, close to morning, I arrive at the prime minister's house and explain the situation to him, and actually move on to Stage 2, which is ensuring the Palestinians now do everything to suppress Hamas's and other organizations' counter-response. And I inform Arafat that I'm traveling to him in Ramallah.

It's 2 or 3 a.m.; for him, those are the hours when he works. Usually he sleeps through the day, so there's no need to wake him. I just ask that he bring Jibril and Dahlan to him. I get to the office in Ramallah, and I tell him, "Adel Awadallah was killed." He doesn't play the game that Bogie Ya'alon describes, where he asks, "Yahya who?" as if he doesn't know who Yahya Ayyash is. . . . Arafat is fluent to a very high degree, and in this case the situation is completely clear to him. I tell him, "We killed them, and now we expect you to do everything along with us to ensure the survival of the political process, which is in your best interest as well as in ours. Because it should be clear to you that if a series of terror attacks occurs now, there's no political agreement, no political process."

He asked, "How much time do I have? I want two days to get set up." And I told him, "Listen, I think you have between three and four hours, because I know that in the morning the media will come out with it, and I don't think we can stop publication through censorship or any other means." He asked what to do, and I said, "Ask Jibril and Dahlan." He looks at them, and Jibril says to him, "What we need from you is just to tell us what to do." He tells them, "Do everything necessary." So they just go out there and do what's necessary—starting with mosques, through the whole Palestinian action network. When they want to do it, they're capable of doing it. And this operation, which I believe might be the most operationally significant in our war against Hamas since the First Intifada, goes through without a Hamas Palestinian counter-reaction of the kind we've grown accustomed to in the past. And I, of course, take all these insights with me in regard to what needs to be done to provide security for the citizens of Israel.

That means that by the end of 2000, you'd actually succeeded in eliminating Hamas's infrastructure in the West Bank.

Ayalon: Some people would tell you that this was the operation that ultimately brought about the elimination of that infrastructure. My claim is that it was an important, central element, but by no means The Element, with a capital "T." I think the reality of those years was created through the Shin Bet's activity as well, but to the same extent, as I said, also as a result of our cooperation with the Palestinian security apparatus.

There were periods in which the Palestinian prison held a lot more Hamas terrorists than the Israeli prison. I don't want to commend them. There are a lot of things that they never did. I also don't want to get into the whole subject of the revolving door. But ultimately, to a great extent, the security graph goes up from 1996 till the year 2000, and in a dramatic way. In 1996, within less than two weeks, we lost 57 citizens and 214 were injured as a result of suicide attacks. In the year 2000, in the twelve months before the Intifada, one Israeli citizen was killed as a result of terrorist activity. I think the Israeli public forgets how dramatic that graph was. Every year we thwarted more. Every year we attained more security. It happened to a great extent because of the things we did in the Service, but the truth must be told—the more significant achievement was the cooperation between us and the Palestinians.

Did you share the information you had gotten from Adel Awadallah with them?

We decided each time, on a per-case basis, what to share and what not to share. We didn't give them the intelligence, and we didn't share the research with them. But there were a lot of shared operations. There were operations in which a Shin Bet man in Bethlehem or in Ramallah and Gaza received information, and led them all the way to the doorstep. That was the level of project-specific cooperation that existed during those years.

Yuval Diskin: If we hadn't killed the Awadallah brothers, captured the archive, exposed the military arm of Hamas, arrested the people we arrested, and passed on the intelligence and applied pressure along with the Americans, the Palestinians wouldn't have handled what they handled even then. They didn't become proactive. Here I can give you an example, because I have a basis for comparison. Today's Palestinian Authority, the one after 2007, has understood that Hamas doesn't only kill Israelis, but also endangers them to a dramatic extent, and they decided to be proactive against Hamas. They developed intelligence capabilities, they started dealing with Hamas without being pressured, and they attained amazing results we haven't seen since '94. If the Palestinian Authority had acted in '94–'95 the way it's been acting from 2007 onwards, I think things would look a lot better than they did, on a major scale.

Because they understood it threatened them?

Diskin: Without a doubt. Not because they suddenly fell in love with us. They just understood it threatened the future of Fatah. If the Palestinians had adopted not a line of terrorist attacks but a line of nonviolent resistance, it would have created much larger problems for us than the attacks. The suicide attacks weakened the legitimacy of the battle. So I totally reject Ami's analysis. I think that's not what actually happened. Eighty percent of the prevention that happened was us! Twenty percent is the Palestinians, and even that is with our contribution. The Palestinian security apparatuses weren't delivering the goods. To phrase it simply: and not because they couldn't. First of all, they didn't want to do it enough, and second, they weren't getting enough support from Arafat during those years. If they had wanted to, they could have obtained intelligence a lot more simply and easily than we could. When they're working within their population, it's not perceived as betrayal to cooperate with them.

Avi Dichter: Dahlan and Jibril said, "If we're not here, the Hamas will come." We told them, "Guys, we're not your bulletproof vest, where we get killed and you build yourself up. . . . You won't build the Palestinian Authority or the Palestinian Authority's security apparatus on the back of the State of Israel. You can forget about that."

It was clear that instead of progressing in a productive direction, they were going in a direction of strengthening the security apparatuses instead of strengthening security. Every apparatus there was an entity in itself, and looked at the other apparatus in terms of saving face opposite it; the head of each apparatus took care to maintain proper leading status. Each of them worked directly opposite Yasser Arafat. And as long as they didn't have to act against terrorists, they didn't act against terrorists.

In the twelve months preceding the Second Intifada, one Israeli citizen was killed. Ami Ayalon says this is largely thanks to the Shin Bet, but that it's also to a large extent due to the cooperation with the Palestinians.

Dichter: You always have to ask whether the quiet is a result of lack of motivation or of effective activity by security agencies. Because if it's effective action by security agencies, then these agencies will also be effective when motivation increases. And, unfortunately, I don't remember effective activity by Palestinian security apparatuses. At the time when they were really required to be security apparatuses—and we're talking about a scale of thirty thousand people, that's a huge mass—they just disappeared. In their most significant test, the Second Intifada, they disappeared in the best case, or joined the Intifada in the worst case.

Ami Ayalon: I would meet Jibril Rajoub, Mohammed Dahlan, Amin al-Hindi, all those people, once a month to coordinate intelligence activity. They kept telling me, "We're not your agents. We don't put Hamas members in prison for you. We're only doing it because our public believes that at the end of the line, at the end of the day, we'll have a state alongside the State of Israel. The minute we don't believe that, forget about us." That was the reason cooperation was so tight. We got to a state where a Shin Bet coordinator would go with a group of "Palestine Security" people, and he gives them the intelligence, and they carry out shared anti-terror activity. Why? Because it was clear that terror is a common threat to all of us.

And if you ask me, that's why it was so clear to us at the end of 1999 and the beginning of 2000 that we were heading toward another Intifada. It was written on every wall. The minute the Palestinian public, and we saw it in surveys, started losing faith in the diplomatic process, it was clear to us, even if there were no signs of it in the field, that eventually, within a few months, we're heading toward another round of violence.

Understanding the Enemy

Do you think that empathy or understanding what's happening on the other side is important to us in conducting the battle?

Ami Ayalon: Unequivocally yes. I don't think we can beat a phenomenon if we don't understand it. And to understand it, we have to get into the other side's head, understand reality as he sees it.

One of the most brutal terrorist attacks, if not the most brutal, was the killing of the Hatuel family during the disengagement process. A mother and her daughters were not only murdered, but the terrorists also verified the kills from zero range, shot little girls in the head. And that's really animalistic, cruel, there are no words to describe that degree of cruelty. The following day an argument developed, and I was asked to address the issue. The speaker before me was an academic, a philosopher. The interviewer asks him, "How do you explain the animalistic, inhuman behavior of those terrorists?" And he tells him, "I don't intend to explain it, and we shouldn't explain it, because if we understand, we might forgive." I, of course, thought he was wrong. I said there's no doubt we shouldn't forgive, but if we don't understand, we can't win. I don't expect public discussion to bring us to the realm of understanding, because there, empathy might really turn into sympathy or justification. But I think professionals have to understand the phenomenon, and to understand a phenomenon, you have to see it through the other side's eyes. Otherwise we can't change things, otherwise we can't explain and we definitely can't fight. That's true in regard to the Palestinians, and it's true, despite the clear distinction, in regard to the extreme right.

And you also apply that in the Service?

In my term, yes. The major question is whether the change I created will continue to exist even when I'm not there. I know that during my term, the very fact that I met with rabbis, with Palestinian scholars or members of the media, gave it legitimacy. And legitimacy by a Service director ultimately has a dramatic influence. So I can say that not only did I meet them, but the heads of branches met them. For example, I met with rabbis who, to our understanding, were dealing in a very problematic way with the topic of "Pursuer's

Law." But I thought it was right to meet with them. I didn't think it was my role to judge them. From the minute the state attorney didn't deal with it, I decided I had to understand the phenomenon.

And did you manage to understand it?

I think so. I'm talking about the more militant, violent, extreme groups. There's a religious, theological belief there that really, really, not due to political reasons, no one has the authority to give away territories, the territories of the Land of Israel. Some of them view anyone who gives away territories, parts of the land of Israel as a "Pursuer," and the "Pursuer's Law" applies to him. So, to many, the person who killed the prime minister saved the Israeli people. These aren't fringe elements. This is a belief that thousands, many thousands accepted then, and also accept today. And if we repress that, if we don't understand that, we don't understand the society in which we live. And if we don't understand the society in which we live, we certainly won't be able to fight these phenomena and we certainly won't beat them.

The ability to understand the other side is actually a tool for the Shin Bet director who has to combat terror, as well as for the statesman trying to bridge those gaps and produce some kind of diplomatic process. It's an instrument. I'm not a poet. I'm not going to write poetry for you. My relationship with Jibril Rajoub, with Mohammed Dahlan, with Amin al-Hindi, is also a very pragmatic relationship. I met with them on a regular basis to get information and to cooperate in order to fight terror. It was one of the central factors that brought about such a dramatic decrease in the level of terrorism during those years. But I didn't meet with the Palestinians in order to seek friendship or recognition. Both when I was in the IDF General Staff and when I was Shin Bet director, I met with the Palestinians in order to provide security for the State of Israel and for Israeli citizens. If there was friendship, if there was something beyond the instrumental level, it came years later, by the way, with Palestinians who had nothing to do with terror, such as Professor Sari Nusseibeh [president of Al-Quds University in Jerusalem and the former representative of the Palestinian Authority in Jerusalem], whom I think very highly of, and am to a very large extent friendly with. But that definitely wasn't during that period.

Does this empathy not lead to a weakening of our conviction in the rightness of our path?

Definitely not. In the place where I live, until '48, lived three thousand Palestinians. The village was called Ijzim, and if you ask me, I have no compunctions and no regrets. In my view, the year 1948 was the constituting event for which my parents illegally immigrated to Israel, and only as a result of that were they not annihilated or murdered during the Holocaust. I'm completely wholehearted about the reality, about the truth and the justice of the Zionist movement or idea. I have no regrets or compunctions. There's a difference between self-flagellation and understanding of and empathy for the opposite side. Both in order to be able to fight the phenomenon and in order to create a bridge.

Where do you use this as a professional tool?

In the fifty-year anniversary of Israel's independence, 1998, I suddenly notice that the more we, the Israeli public, the Israeli government, start to construct the Golden Jubilee celebration, on the other side, really as a counter-measure, the myth of the "Nakba"* is gradually built up, and for me, as Service director, that's very worrying. I see that the connection between Israeli Arabs and Palestinians is growing stronger, and is already not just at a level of communication and of politicians, but of commemorating the Nakba in '48.

As Service director I'm very worried by this, and I try to create a situation where the Israeli cabinet constructs a policy regarding Israeli Arabs, and I can't do it. The last time there was a real discussion on the subject how Israeli Arabs can be integrated into Israeli society was during Rabin's term. He was the last prime minister that gave them the feeling that he's really talking to them at eye level.

And this worry about a radicalization of Israeli Arabs is what led me to recommend to the prime minister to go to Kafr Qasim in October to commemorate the Kafr Qasim massacre. I recommend to Netanyahu to go to the assembly in Kafr Qasim and to come and say it was murder, that it won't happen any more in the State of Israel, that we're the only army in the world that actually educates its soldiers in light of the approach that there's a limit to obedience, that there's a point where a soldier should not obey when the command

---

* Meaning "disaster" or "catastrophe" in Arabic, the term refers to mass displacement of more than seven hundred thousand Palestinian Arabs from their homes following the 1948 Israeli War of Independence.

is "blatantly illegal," and this whole approach was born in that tragic event in Kafr Qasim. I told him, "By your very arrival, you'll create what no prime minister before you has created—willingness to listen and willingness to discuss a shared future. How do we do it together? First of all by me telling you—what happened here in 1956 won't recur."

What did he say?

Never mind what he said. He sent me straight to Minister of Education Zevulun Hammer, who of course didn't show up. I think that's a lack of understanding of the complexity of Israeli Arabs and their feeling of belonging or not belonging and the ability to make them feel that they're a part of or belong to this society.

Is that why, as head of Shin Bet, you approach Aharon Barak and ask him to appoint an Arab judge?

First of all, I don't ask. I recommend. The person who initiated the discussion was, as far as I can remember, Supreme Court President Aharon Barak. I, of course, was a strong supporter, but an Arab judge in the Supreme Court, that's not my doing. I think that ultimately the feeling of partnership can't exist if we compartmentalize and exclude populations from participating in decision making. I do everything to include non-Jewish populations in the General Security Service. Without much success, by the way, also without much success when I was Navy commander. I didn't succeed in bringing some of them to Shayetet 13, even though I defined it as part of my policy.

Who blocks it?

No single individual. I think every system has its mechanisms of resistance. These are long processes.

You don't think suggesting to Bibi Netanyahu that he go to Kafr Qasim and state what you requested him to state is surreal?

I completely don't think it's surreal, because that's my professional stance in view of the profound processes I see in Israeli Arab society. I think that if I hadn't done that, I wouldn't have been doing my job properly, and it doesn't matter that I can assess in advance what his answer will be, and it doesn't matter that I also understand that he may have these or other political limitations. I don't care about that at all. I reach a professional conclusion that processes within Arab society in Israel are worrisome processes. I see it in statements, I see it in patterns of participation in elections, I see it in surveys, I see it in the level of violence encountered when coming to expropriate lands for Highway 6 [the trans-Israel highway] or for these or other army training areas. I have all the warning mechanisms. The writing's on the wall. In Arabic, in English, in Hebrew, in Aramaic, in every language we can read, and we refuse to read it. And I come to the prime minister almost pleading and tell him, "You have to initiate a discussion on the subject of the Israeli government's policy among minorities." It's my professional duty to come to the prime minister and make recommendations to him, which I believe are some of the components that might enable creating some inhibiting processes.

By the way, eventually the minister of education does go. During Barak's term, Minister of Education Yossi Sarid goes to Kafr Qasim, as far as I can remember. He also accepts my recommendation to include this event in the educational curriculum as the place where the "blatantly illegal command" was born. I recommend that in every school, in every classroom, on the same day, one hour be dedicated to what happened in Kafr Qasim, and that a discussion be conducted about the limits of obedience and democracy and security. As far as I know, that does happen.

With our leaders, those opposite whom you worked, did you sense a real attempt to understand their narrative in conjunction with our narrative?

No. I didn't sense that. I think most discussions in which I took part were a lot more about concepts of justice and blame than about terms of understanding the other side and claiming responsibility. We, by the way, are always right. Even when we suffer more than a thousand casualties in the Intifada, and even when we kill more than three thousand to four thousand in the same Intifada. If we only conduct the discussion in terms of justice and blame, Yehuda Amichai has already said,

> From the place where we are right
> no flowers will ever
> grow in the spring.*

So apparently we'll keep spilling lots of blood and no flowers will grow. . . .

---

* From the poem "The Place Where We Are Right," by Yehuda Amichai.

When Dichter assumed the job after you, he said, "I want to look at, say, Balata refugee camp from puddle height. I want to bring operational intelligence; that's what interests me at the moment."

That's the coordinator's job. The coordinator has to be within the swamp of terrorism and Palestinian society. If the head of Shin Bet stays in the swamp, he certainly won't emerge from there healthy, but the Israeli people aren't going to benefit from it, either. There's inherent tension in acting as a leader. And I deliberately say leader, because the head of the General Security Service needs to see himself as someone heading the organization, and lead it. On the one hand, you expect a leader to look and see the vision and the long-term implications of everything he does, and that, of course, takes him in the direction of being almost a philosopher. On the other hand, he needs to have his feet on the ground. If my head's in the sky, my feet are disconnected. If my feet are on the ground, I don't see the ranges I really need to see.

My everyday dilemma is what tools we're developing to create that dual image. This is already related to the way you manage the organization, to levels of openness. For me, it was very important that every discussion, starting with immediate prevention and up to our recommendations to the political echelon, also include people who think the opposite of what I do. I encouraged disagreement. I brought in people who I knew in advance thought the opposite of everyone else. The opposite of me. Otherwise, we might take off with the philosophy and talk about the second and third derivative and not thwart today's terrorism, or, on the other hand, we could try to dry the ocean with a little bucket. And the ocean won't be dried if we try to dry it from inside the swamp.

The Era of Ehud Barak—Dawn of a New Day

"We won't let Hamas ruin it."

"We want to erase and forget the three and a half years of Netanyahu's regime, and renew the relationship with Ehud Barak from the point where it was stopped due to Rabin's murder," Mohammed Dahlan, head of the Palestinian Security Service in Gaza, tells *Yediot Ahronot*.

(Ronnie Shaked, *Yediot Ahronot*, May 25, 1999, a week after Ehud Barak is elected as prime minister of Israel)

When Ehud Barak was elected, there was great hope. The dawning of a new day. I was there in Kings of Israel Square.

Ami Ayalon: I was there, too; I had to provide security for him.

You were there at the square?

I wanted to ensure the elected prime minister would stay alive. . . . I was with Benjamin Netanyahu at his victory celebration, and I was with Ehud Barak at his victory celebration. That's a Shin Bet director's job.

Were you afraid something would happen to Barak there?

Without a doubt. Don't forget that I'm a head of Shin Bet who joined the Shin Bet as a result of the assassination of a prime minister.

And you hear the "dawning of a new day"?

I don't remember. I wasn't really listening to the speech.

And where did it go wrong during the next year and eight months?

I think things went wrong in an ongoing process. The seed of failure already existed in the way the Oslo process was actually initiated. I didn't understand it in the beginning. I admit I understood some of these things mainly when I was in the General Security Service, and definitely afterwards. I think the Oslo process was built on creating trust. The first documents actually said almost nothing about how the permanent treaty would look. On purpose. We decided to postpone discussing the core issues—Jerusalem, security, settlements, settlers, right of return, refugees, water—till the last stage. All we did in the first two to three years was postpone the whole discussion on sensitive topics, not touch the aching nerves of the conflict, when it was perfectly clear we'd have to address them later, in order to enable a process of building trust.

The main parameter through which you see how painful that failure is is that the level of trust, according to any measure, including surveys, at the beginning of the process, in '94, was a lot higher than the level of trust in its last years, and definitely higher than in the year 2000, when the process collapsed. Meaning that a process which was supposed to establish and build trust to enable discussion of those sensitive and painful subjects actually did the opposite. And ultimately, we find ourselves arriving to discuss core topics with the level of trust a lot lower than in the beginning of the process.

We talked a lot about steps to establish trust, and we talked about the economy, and we talked about education, and we talked about everything, but there's a legal term called "good faith." I claim that the whole diplomatic process, both on our side and on the Palestinian side, through fifteen years, was not conducted in good faith. That's the main problem. There was no good faith, not on the Palestinian side and not on the Israeli side. Even though the Oslo process was a process that the majority of the Israeli public supported and the majority of the Palestinian public supported. Both sides actually arrived at the process as a last resort, and in order for it to succeed, both of them had to deal with fringe groups which opposed the process.

The Palestinians should have handled the opposition, a terrorist opposition in every sense of the word, in a completely different way, and they never did it the way they should have done it. We wanted security, and the process decreased our security. On the other hand, we never seriously dealt with the settlement rate. When we embarked on the Oslo process at the end of '93 and the beginning of '94, there were 100,000 settlers in Gaza and the West Bank, not counting the neighborhoods in Jerusalem. In the summer of 2000, when the process collapses, there are more than 220,000 settlers. By the way, today there are more than 300,000, and if you include the neighborhoods in Jerusalem, the number is around 500,000. Now we want security and get terrorism. They want a state and see more settlements.

The problem doesn't start with Ehud Barak. Ehud Barak came to the process without believing in the process. From the beginning, when he was still chief of general staff, he thought it was Swiss cheese with more holes than cheese. . . . And all along he opposed a process that ultimately leads to a discussion of the core issues when we have no assets, in cases like this meaning land. Territories. Because the process was built in a way that eventually, when you come to discuss core issues, we're holding less than ten percent of the territory. So he actually tried to change the process without harming its goal.

But the background to Barak's arrival was already very, very saturated, after the Palestinians had lost their trust, so they see conspiracies everywhere. He already arrives after Rabin, may he rest in peace, is murdered as a response to the process, which raised hard questions among the Palestinians regarding whether a prime minister could ever come to an agreement with them and actually pay its price, even if he wanted to. He arrives after Shimon Peres, after

Benjamin Netanyahu, after three prime ministers, four ministers of defense.

And he doesn't like the process, and he doesn't want to give them what Netanyahu promised them—thirteen percent of the territory at the Wye conference, because he really wants to discuss the core issues first and change the process, without them understanding why and without them necessarily agreeing. By the way, when Ehud Barak was elected, the Palestinians really believed that Rabin, may he rest in peace, had returned, and that the process would begin where it had stopped on November 4, 1995.

Barak tries to change the process and convince Arafat to delay everything Bibi promised to give him in Wye, and in return to enter very intense discussions, and by February 2000, to sign a framework agreement from which we'd proceed for another six months, and around September, the permanent agreement would be signed. That was actually the plan. And then, as far as the Palestinians are concerned, a few strange things happen. Arafat appoints a delegation, which includes two ministers. Meaning a delegation which was appointed in advance to discuss the core issues. That was the whole issue, after all. Now Ehud Barak tries to appoint a delegation head. He tried to appoint Gilead Sher, his close associate, and Elyakim Rubinstein, the attorney general, refuses because Gilead Sher is not a state employee. Ehud Barak argues with Elyakim Rubinstein and with the legal system, but in the meantime there's no delegation and Arafat doesn't understand. In talks with me, which are intended to ensure he's instructing the heads of the security apparatuses to continue with the policy of thwarting terrorism, these questions come up and I don't have any unequivocal answers. He asks why things are delayed. I can't give him answers, because that's not the realm I'm responsible for. Straight away I divert the matter to the way they're thwarting, or usually not sufficiently thwarting, terror infrastructures and fighting Hamas.

Eventually, a worthy, extraordinary person is appointed, Oded Eran, but as far as Arafat is concerned, opposite a delegation with two Palestinian ministers, there's Oded Eran, who wasn't even an ambassador in a major country, but ambassador in Jordan. Not only is he not in the same seniority level, which is very insulting to the Palestinian side, but in the first discussion he comes out and says, "Gentlemen, I don't have the authority to discuss the core topics,

I'm here to tie up any loose ends regarding safe transit subjects and these or those arrangements." There are many things on the agenda, that's true, but they're not why the Palestinians essentially relinquished the transfer of territories that was promised to them still by Bibi Netanyahu. And slowly, trust begins to erode. Arafat essentially asks—hold on, is the person standing opposite me really Rabin, may he rest in peace, or is there someone here who doesn't mean what he says? . . . And just like we lose faith in Arafat, Arafat loses faith in the Israeli side.

We do listen not only to what Arafat is telling us in his shaky English, but also to what he's saying in Arabic; but to the same extent, he listens to what we, and especially the prime minister, say in Hebrew. Ehud Barak is very proud of the fact that he's built more settlements than Bibi Netanyahu and than any other prime minister before him. Now Arafat hears this. He says—one minute, I don't understand, we're heading toward a diplomatic agreement and he tells us one thing and says something else in Hebrew? He and all the people around him start to lose faith.

Yuval Diskin: Through Palestinian eyes, the question of the settlements is a dramatic one. Their perception that it actually eliminates the whole peace process is very clear. When you drive around in the West Bank and on every hilltop and on every tree, as they say—and it doesn't matter if it's three houses, five houses, or twenty houses—you see the Israeli presence, then of course, as far as the Palestinians are concerned, they get the feeling they're being strangled.

Ami Ayalon: And then we enter negotiations with Syria. Now Ehud Barak apparently means to conduct negotiations in both channels, but as far as Arafat is concerned, this is betrayal. We have to understand that when Arafat moved from Madrid to Oslo, from the Syrian viewpoint, he betrayed them. The whole Syrian approach in Madrid was that no one would do to us anymore what the Egyptians did to us when they negotiated a diplomatic treaty with the Israelis by themselves. Our whole advantage here is that we're in it together, all the Arab countries. That's what Arafat betrays when he says, "Guys, forget Madrid. . . . I don't trust you. I'm going to sign a diplomatic treaty with Israel, and the Syrians can take care of themselves." [Syrian defense minister] Mustafa Tlass calls Arafat "the whore of the Middle East" from every stage. So every time Rabin goes to Syria, when Bibi goes to the Syrians, when Shimon Peres goes to the Syrians, as far as Arafat is concerned this is stabbing him in the back. He completely loses faith that we actually mean it.

When you meet with Arafat, do you feel this shift in him?

Ayalon: Arafat's insecurity is evident in every meeting. I can't see into his heart and I'm not a psychologist or a psychiatrist, but the fact that his sense of security is dwindling is actually apparent in his body language, and also in a lot of information, part of it public and overt and part of it intelligence information, regarding the essence of discussions on the Palestinian side.

[Israeli military official] Amos Gilad claimed you fell under the spell of Arafat, and that the Shin Bet was compromised because of its close connections with Palestinian security elements.

That must be poetic language. I never heard Amos say that, but whoever says anyone, and definitely me, fell under the spell of Arafat apparently never stood next to Arafat.

I imagine he meant the security cooperation.

I didn't hear Amos, so I'm very reserved, but anyone who says something like that doesn't understand the political-military reality of the late '90s. In a reality in which the leadership decides on a diplomatic process, brings the Palestinian leadership back from Tunisia, and manufactures a process that grants them municipal authority—in that kind of reality, in order to provide security and thwart terror and collect intelligence, you have to meet with Palestinians and you have to cooperate. Whoever says we fell under that spell doesn't know what the General Security Service was doing simultaneously. And my concern is that the Israeli public and political debate was influenced by these things.

I'm sitting in the defense cabinet as head of Shin Bet, and Arik Sharon, as minister of infrastructures, complains that Shin Bet personnel are "sitting in a Jacuzzi and eating decadent meals with the Palestinians' preventive security people. . . ." That drives me insane! Because I don't really sit in Jacuzzis, and I don't smoke cigars, and I don't eat decadent meals. And he sends me a note: "Listen, Ami, I really respect you, you understand that that's not addressed to you and the Service, this is to obtain political goals." And later on you have to return to the Service people who read and hear these things, and this is really in their hearts' blood. If there's one thing you can't say about them, it's that they're hedonists, that they do it to have fun or to make some kind of personal or private profit.

I think some of these statements enabled the public discussion to go in directions that made it very difficult for the General Security Service, but we succeeded in spite of it all. We decreased the level of terrorist attacks from a level where, in less than two weeks, 57 Israeli citizens were killed and about 214 were injured in March 1996, to a state where, in a way that was not gradual but dramatic, every year there were less terrorist attacks and less losses and less injuries and less casualties, and on to a state where, in 1999–2000, it was actually possible to conduct negotiations correctly or in an inept manner.

You said that from one article by Amira Hass [who covers the West Bank and Gaza for *Ha'aretz* newspaper], you learn more about Palestinian society than from all the secret intelligence gathered. Can you explain that?

Ayalon: First of all, saying I learn more than from all the intelligence, that's a little excessive. An article by Amira Hass paints a very precise, authentic portrait of the state of Palestinian society through its eyes, through the eyes of Palestinian society. Since I've said I have to take into account what they think and how they act as well, as part of defining or understanding reality, then one article by Amira Hass gives me a much better portrait than a report by an agent trying to deal with the same question. So that seems like an accurate thing to me, definitely.

I've said more than that. When we're dealing with the phenomenon we call Intifada, the Intifada is not a focused terrorist attack. In order to prevent a planned terrorist attack, I need HUMINT and SIGINT intelligence. That's the kind of thing that Shin Bet agents and Shin Bet technical sources can cover. But if I come and tell you that the Intifada is not planned. If I come and tell you that there are lots of attacks that no one planned. No organization. No planning, no weapons. There's a tractor driver in Jerusalem who decides in a moment of anger, in a moment of madness resulting from humiliation, from loss of hope, to kill Israeli citizens. How do you deal with that phenomenon? My claim is that an intelligence organization has no tools to foresee that phenomenon in real time.

To foresee this phenomenon, you have to actually expand your collection spectrum. You have to go to those places where hate, loss of purpose, frustration, humiliation are created, since those are the factors causing the violence you encounter in the street. Now, we'll never be able to tell you when it's going to happen. But if we're doing our job, if we're reading the surveys and reading the articles in the press and reading Amira Hass, and reading Palestinian poetry and dealing with the school curriculum, if we're meeting the people Arafat puts in jail because they opposed him due to Arafat's corruption, if we collect all that information, then we see the writing is starting to appear on the wall.

We know we won't know the date when it will erupt. In the very best case, we'll know what the conditions are under which it will erupt. That's why we could say in 1999–2000 that the potential for violence existed, and that that violence would erupt in the context of the holy sites or in the context of settlements, or in the context of land or road expropriation, things like that. These are the three things that can be the spark. But that's only the spark. The spark itself, if there's no energy, is meaningless. If Arafat does everything to suppress it, it doesn't even matter. But if the reality is that Arafat doesn't have the power, doesn't have the ability, doesn't have the will, and the energy exists and the spark exists and there's fire on the Temple Mount—then everything explodes.

Now, from the end of 1999 and the beginning of 2000, the gravest thing happens, and this is already beyond Arafat and beyond Ehud Barak. Arafat is no longer leading Palestinian society, and Ehud Barak is no longer leading Israeli society. As we go into the year 2000, I believe Ehud Barak has already taken on the role of five, six, or seven ministers. He's left without a government. The Israeli Knesset members, and his cabinet members, have started to lose faith in him. And this is just as true for Arafat. At this stage, we believe Arafat lost the Palestinian public a long time ago, because he really built a corrupt regime.

At this stage, I had an argument with the CIA people and with the American representatives, both Dennis Ross and Martin Indyk, who really thought we should go with Syria. I told them, "We already don't have time with the Palestinians. If nothing happens in the next six months to a year, we're heading toward another round of violence." And then they said, "No way, we talked to Arafat!" I said, "Guys, Arafat doesn't represent anything anymore. No one in the Palestinian public sees Arafat as a leader anymore." By the way, you don't need to read intelligence. You need to read the Palestinian press, you need to read Palestinian literature, you need to read [Palestinian political scientist] Khalil Shikaki's surveys. Arafat is no longer a leader except of some irrelevant group that sits in Ramallah and doesn't even represent the elites at the universities or the business elite, and definitely not Palestinian society.

So for Camp David, we get two weak leaders who don't have the leadership capabilities of the leaders of the first Camp David. Ehud Barak has no real ability to make the concessions required to reach an agreement. And Arafat doesn't have the legitimacy and not the presence of mind to make the decisions really required to reach an agreement.

I talk to Barak at the end of 1999, beginning of 2000, and he explains the logic of the framework accord to me. I don't accept that process. I tell him I believe that the perception that states, "I'll make Arafat an offer he can't refuse" actually assumes that it's all intimidation and agenda. And I tell him—it's not going to work. You can't intimidate someone who, in his subjective view, has nothing to lose. Arafat is reaching the stage where he's willing to go back to Tunisia and start all over again. He won't be the one who caused the failure of the Palestinian revolution and signs an agreement which, in his view, he can't sign. To this day I believe that the whole perception of creating some process that brings on a moment of truth, of "all or nothing," is mistaken. The reality between leaders and their public, both on the Israeli and on the Palestinian side, is not the reality of Begin and Sadat.

But Barak doesn't accept my position. Someone who believes it's all a matter of agenda sees a person like me, who think a certain chemistry needs to form between leaders, that trust has to be established in order to eventually enable the process, as a naïve man. So he doesn't accept my position. Not him, and not the American regime. And when I come and tell the Americans, like I did the Israelis, "We're heading toward a round of violence toward the end of the year 2000," I'm perceived as not grounded. "What's he talking about?" Look, there has never been security here like there was at the end of 1999 or 2000, and I know that's virtual reality. I know the writing's on the wall. I know how to explain what needs to be done to prevent it, but my position is not accepted, nor is my forecast, and of course not my recommendations, either.

Did you get a chance to talk to Barak after he fell from power and Sharon replaced him regarding this matter, your forecast which came true?

Not like the investigations we used to conduct in the special units, when the need arose. We're adults now. We've matured beyond the innocence, the naïveté and the honesty we all possessed during the period when we were in the places where we were. As statesmen, as political men, I didn't conduct that discussion with Ehud. But I conducted that discussion in every public debate in which I participated. It was also expressed in the political campaign which I conducted against him in the race for chairman of the Labor Party.

Ultimately, this discussion between us was held in a very open and public way. I think the whole campaign, despite Ehud's silence and despite the amount of my verbiage, revolved around the big questions—how to bring about a reality in which the State of Israel is Jewish, democratic, and safe? The things I'm saying now I said under every shady tree and from every political and public pulpit given to me. And ultimately, the Labor Party chose Ehud Barak, and the policy of Israeli governments is more or less in the same worldview characterizing Ehud's policy, which ultimately was also Ehud Olmert's policy and Bibi Netanyahu's policy, and definitely Arik Sharon's policy. Unilaterality.

In the Gaza Strip, I believe we could have pulled out from fewer territories, because in the north Strip, it was possible to start the dialogue regarding exchanging territories. It was completely unnecessary to evacuate Eley Sinai and Nissanit, with the dozens of families and hundreds of settlers we evacuated from there, because according to the territory exchange approach based on demographics, security and territorial continuity, there's no logic in getting out of there. But that's what you do if you arrive with good faith. You say—guys, let's really talk about territorial exchange and let's conduct a "pilot" here so that we can see what happens in the future in the West Bank. Remember, we left Lebanon in the same way, without a partner. With no agreement. To a very great extent, we ran away from Lebanon. I don't know if I'm convincing you. I didn't convince the Israeli people.

I'm interested in your personal aspect, not the national one. You return home as Shin Bet director and tell yourself this whole cart is toppling toward an abyss, which ultimately did result, after the Second Intifada broke out, in more than one thousand casualties on

the Israeli side and more than three thousand on the Palestinian side, not to mention many more people injured and families destroyed. You see that it's heading in that direction. Why don't you . . .

Ayalon: Why don't I knock over tables? First of all, by my terms, I did knock over tables. No one could mistake my stance. I'm not a person who's misunderstood. The bad thing, as far as I'm concerned, is that my stance is not accepted. I'm perceived as someone who's really making mountains out of molehills. And that bothers me. My assessment of the situation is not accepted, and in that context, and also because I've already completed four years, I actually approach Ehud Barak and recommend replacing me. He tries to convince me to stay till after September, because then we'll sign the permanent treaty and it would really be a lot more easy and relaxed to replace the head of the General Security Service. But I tell him unequivocally that in my assessment, we're definitely not going to be signing a peace treaty, or any kind of diplomatic agreement, in September. On the contrary, I think the head of the Service should be replaced as early as possible, so that when September, or any other date, comes around, he'll already be ready. He shouldn't be new to his position at the time. That's it. And we essentially agree on my resignation. I leave the position right after Israeli Independence Day. In May 2000. And that's regarding the personal aspect.

No. You didn't actually give me anything personal. I want to understand what's going through your mind. You drive home, in the evening after you've ended your work day, and you see this truck going where it's going, what do you tell yourself during those drives and those moments? Do you share it with someone? Do you talk to anyone? Do you talk to your wife? I'm trying to understand someone containing information like that within himself, who knows what's about to happen. . . .

I don't talk about it with my wife. I don't talk about it with friends. It's not the type of thing I share with friends. We do talk about it in status assessments in the General Security Service. The fact is, these things are in writing. But I don't have any people with whom I share the emotional aspects of my experience. I don't really need to. And I also need to qualify things. There's a professional status assessment, which I remember sometimes even reaches harsh notes, but it's not that I see any sort of apocalyptic vision. I don't see thousands of casualties on the streets. I don't take the images of horror from the terrorist attacks, multiply them in my imagination, and go to bed with that at night. That's not the situation.

But that's what happened in the end. That's what it means when you tell the prime minister there's going to be another round of violence.

I estimate that if a poet had undergone that experience, he'd go home very upset, couldn't fall asleep, and would write poems in his heart's blood. I'm not a poet. I was head of the General Security Service, and before than Navy commander, and before that a flotilla commander. The fact that I enjoy fine literature or that I read poetry doesn't mean I'm a poet. I don't walk around at night. I sleep well at night. Why? Because my head's on the pillow and I'm not troubled. I sleep well at night. That's it.

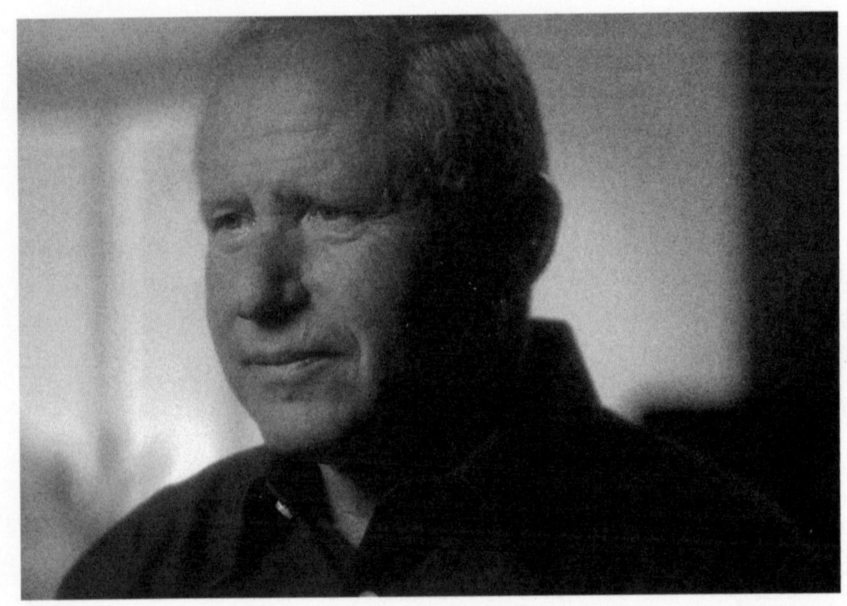

Avi Dichter

Avi Dichter (2000–05)

I was born in Majdal, which became a proper city in Israel—Ashkelon. I called it Migdal when I was an Ashkenazi and Majdal when I learned Arabic. I was actually born at home, because my mother didn't make it to the hospital. My first memory is that I took a group of kids with me, and we ran away through the nursery school window to my house. The teacher, an Ashkelonian I still meet from time to time, can't forget that event.

I remember living with another family in one house. Our family, my parents, my sister, and me, and another family who had emigrated from Romania. That was the arrangement at the time. I remember a shared bathroom, a shared kitchen. When I told my kids and took them to see it, they of course thought that I was joking with them. Two families living in one house, and Poles and Romanians, no less? That's a lethal combination. . . . By the way, I'm in touch with the Romanian family to this day. They live in Ashkelon, too.

Both my parents are Holocaust survivors, from a small village called Rozhist, which was in eastern Poland, and today is in western Ukraine, in the Volhynia district. My father actually lost his whole family in the Holocaust. He, by the way, never said anything about the Holocaust. I tried endlessly to get him to talk about it, and after all, getting people to talk was my profession, but with Dad I just failed. I know he faked his age by two years and then they let him enlist in the Polish Army at age sixteen, and he was a horseman in World War II. Think about it, German tanks and horseman Shayke Dichter. Even as a cartoon, I have a hard time imagining that working.

When he came back after the war with the Russian army, they crossed the river and reached his village, and he took a friend and went into town to see what had happened. He had no idea whatsoever what happened beyond stories and rumors. And he got to their street, and the street was by and large still intact, including their house, which was definitely handsome. And he saw there were Gentile Poles living in his house. And then he saw children on the street walking around in his brothers' clothes, and understood he wouldn't be going back there.

Until he passed away, seventeen years ago, he wasn't even willing to think in terms of going back there. My mother, eighty-seven years old now, is already starting to weaken a bit, and I believe we'll go there for a visit. Just recently, a book was published about my parents' town, and my mother was even interviewed for the book, and I learned about her part in the Holocaust from that book more than I learned throughout my years with her. There are brutal sentences in there from which I can maybe understand what she actually went through. How many traumas she retains within her to this day, after almost seventy years.

I was the son of Holocaust survivors, with everything that implies. It starts with eating everything that's on your plate. There's no such thing as leaving food on your plate. It immediately invites a statement, usually from my mother—"Eat, there's not always food. . . ." And I, as a child, ate it all. There wasn't a crumb left on the plate. Not just because I was hungry, but because I knew that if I didn't, a very long talk would then ensue.

Or combing my hair. I was a kid with his hair parted and combed in one direction, and never in the other direction. And you know, as a child you want to rebel a little, and comb it in the other direction, and they wouldn't let me. Later, I understood. Hitler combed his hair in one direction, and no Jewish child would comb his in that direction, certainly not if he was the son of Holocaust survivors.

And from time to time, there were memorial events for those originating from my parents' town. A tiny town, where the Germans didn't even bother to put them on trains and transport them to the death camps. The town was too small. It was more convenient for them to take all the people and just shoot them at the outskirts of town into pits. They just slaughtered fifty-seven thousand people, and in that way effectively buried my whole history.

Does the land of Israel become a beloved place because of what happened in Europe? Or, as Arik Sharon would say, "the only place where a Jew can protect himself by his own means"?

For me, that insight started to sink in at slightly later ages. I had the privilege of being in the army during the Yom Kippur War. In the war I was really in the last third of my mandatory service, and there were a few events where the distance between me and getting hurt or killed was almost non-existent. There were cases where someone else got hurt, someone who sat where I was supposed to be sitting at that moment. My jeep was hit by an RPG. I was the driver, but I'd gotten out to perform some bomb disposal mission in Fayid Airport, and Amitai Nachmani, who was a commander in the unit, took my jeep with Amiram Levin and went for a tour in Fayid. I was very angry that they'd taken my jeep, but I stayed to clear the explosive charges that the Egyptians left on the runways, and when I was done, I entered the control tower. The jeep returned to the control tower at the end of the tour, was hit by an RPG, and the driver was killed. My guys, who were on the east side of the Suez Canal, got a report that the Pole's jeep was hit by an RPG, and the driver was killed. They'd already divided my equipment between them, and then they're crossing the Canal to the west, and suddenly they meet me—and then you hear the most banal question you could hear in situations like this: "Hey, Dichter, aren't you dead?" Something that makes you laugh initially, and gives you a lot of food for thought later.

So, when I was done with the war, I kind of stopped myself for a minute and made my first strategic decision: that I was getting out of the army and not going to study, but getting married, starting a family, and establishing myself in a place of employment. Period. When I told my parents I wasn't going to attend university, it was a crisis for them.

They told me, "What do you mean, you're not going to study medicine?"

"No."

"Okay. Engineering is also important."

"No. I'm going to learn a new language."

" . . . English is also very important in life."

"It'll be Arabic."

They looked at each other, and my mother told my father in Yiddish, "We have to take him to the doctor."

But the main reason was I couldn't see myself leaving the family without lineage. I couldn't even think in terms of, God forbid, something happens to me, and my parents, after the whole Holocaust, after everything they did and went through, are left without a future generation. In the war, my brother-in-law's brother was killed. He was an artillery man, and we enlisted together, Avraham Dagan. He was killed in the Canal, and was missing for a while. So I understood what it does to a family, and definitely a family of Holocaust survivors, and therefore that was my decision. And I decided to "get it out of my system" after the army. I went to an aircraft security course.

Before that, you decide to enlist in Sayeret Matkal. The unit was then comprised of those coming from kibbutzim and moshavim, graduates of prestigious schools in Jerusalem. What does a guy from Ashkelon have to do with a unit like that?

I didn't decide to enlist in Sayeret Matkal. We arrived at the induction base, and we didn't really know where to go. . . . We got to the induction base, and they informed us we were going to some unit—I don't remember what it was anymore—and I said I didn't like it. We were three Ashkelonians. Someone with a little bit of knowledge said, "We have to volunteer, and if we volunteer, we have a good chance of going to the unit we volunteered for and not to the unit to which we were assigned." So we went to volunteer for all the units.

At a certain stage, one of those three said, "There's Sayeret Matkal. They say it's something intense, but you can't use the actual name, you have to say 'Rakefet' (the cyclamen flower) to the sorting officer." Okay. They told me, "Avi, you go in first." I went in, and I was so flustered, I forgot the code. I forgot to say "Rakefet." He asked me where I needed to go, I saw I couldn't remember, and said, "Sayeret Matkal." He wrote it down. Nothing happened. The earth didn't stop spinning. I went out, signaled to them that everything was okay. I said "Sayeret Matkal" and we got through it. The three of us went to screening tests, and I made it through. By the way, I was on "stand-by," because I wasn't good enough. It took a few more days till I got to basic training, and that's how I got to Sayeret Matkal. No decision and no nothing.

I always say that "I went through three births." My biological birth, almost fifty-seven years ago, the second time in Sayeret Matkal, and the third time when I started working in Arabic in the Shin Bet. Sayeret Matkal molded me as a person with insights, and I think abilities as well, that I didn't have previously. They'd always ask me, "So, tell me, Avi, is it true that in Sayeret Matkal they conduct operations like in the movies?" I said, "Guys, I wish the movies could reach the ankles of what they do in Sayeret Matkal. Steven Spielberg, he's got a lot to learn to get to Sayeret Matkal. . . ." But those insights, getting down to details, the way of learning, the way of thinking, friendship, love of country, love for the land, all that and a lot beyond that is what you receive in heaping portions in Sayeret Matkal, and it's a part of you for life.

In the book *Team Itamar* by Avner Shor, you're described as someone with irresistible willpower. Someone whose physical fitness wasn't great, always arrives looking pale, but no one can withstand his willpower.

I don't know about the pale face, I can tell you what I felt on the inside. I felt like an engine where all the oil had come off and now the cylinders were seized. There's nothing, the engine just can't work. I had no serious preparation for Sayeret Matkal, and apparently my physical fitness wasn't exactly sky-high, and I just arrived at situations where I was running on the steam of willpower.

Ehud Barak always tells me some story I wasn't aware of, about some team exercise where he was with Yoni Netanyahu [Benjamin's brother, commander of Sayeret Matkal and the only Israeli soldier killed during Operation Entebbe in Uganda], and they decided they were [simulate] wounding—within the exercise—Itamar Sela [commander of a team within Sayeret Matkal] and wanted to see how the team conducts itself. At a certain stage in the exercise, they "wounded" two or three soldiers, and then informed Itamar Sela that he was wounded, in the middle of an assault. I was actually a MAG machine gun bearer, and they were waiting to see which of the fighters in the assault assumes control and leads the force in charging. And then, Ehud tells me, suddenly they hear someone yelling from the back, "Come on, Itamar was wounded, come on, charge!" And they see a MAG bearer along with a bazooka bearer and one more guy running toward the target, conquering it and beating the enemy. And he says, "So, suddenly we saw it was you with the MAG, and we more or less fell in love with you." I'm glad that that's really the trait they recognized in me at the time, because based on physical fitness, I probably wouldn't have stayed in Sayeret Matkal. . . .

But you improved your physical fitness later?

Yes. I improved it. I maintain it. I'm prepped and ready to be recruited to Sayeret Matkal at any time. In the unit, you really have to scrape the limits of your personal capability, the limits of your courage, and the limits of your friendship. You really sometimes arrive at situations where you have to finish something within a given time schedule. And you know you don't have one minute beyond that. Or that you have to do the last meter or the last kilometer, and if you don't do it, you just make your way back home in daylight, and you might be exposed. You could be taken prisoner, or shot, or just expose the whole force and cause injuries, not to mention the mission and so on. Every time I thought I'd discovered the last drawer of human capability, and yet I always found out I have another drawer and another drawer above that. Really, in the most simple language, it just reveals you anew to yourself.

The actual goal of the unit is intelligence. Does that prepare you for things to come, in the Shin Bet, or is it actually unrelated?

No. It's not the kind of information collection I dealt with later in the Shin Bet. If in Sayeret Matkal you're more an "execution contractor" for people who understand what information collection is, in the Shin Bet you're the "company owner" or the "company man," and you collect the information with your own two hands. I started out as an "agent handler," and in the period when I started, most of the information came from live sources or interrogees, and less from "SIGINT," from surveillance, and that's a whole other method of collection.

Why do you decide to join the Shin Bet?

The beginning wasn't exactly classic Shin Bet. I was discharged on April 30, '74, and on May 8, I was in the aircraft security course. I worked in aircraft security for a year. I wanted to see the world a bit, and that was the first time I'd actually been abroad with a passport. For me, at the age of twenty-one-and-a-half, to fly to New York and Johannesburg and Paris and London and Teheran is suddenly a big "wow," to discover that the world isn't just between the Mediterranean and Lebanon, Syria, Jordan, and Egypt—those were the countries we'd more or less visited throughout my military service, but always at night, without a passport.

After I finished the security chapter, I decided I wanted to do something comprehensive in the Service. My background made me more suited for operations, because I came from Sayeret Matkal. I heard about work in the Arab sector, and I decided to learn Arabic in a language lab for a whole year. And like I said, that was my third birth. You just feel yourself suddenly becoming a fish in water and capable within a moment of swimming with all the fish and breathing through gills.

In high school, I'd learned English, I'd learned French. You might live the language, but you don't live the people. Here you live the people. I'd sit every day, all day, with Arabs and talk to them in their language. And you start to talk with nuance and with jokes and stories and fables. Now, with us, who grew up in Gaza, it's immediately easy to recognize our Gaza Arabic that way. In one of the interviews for Al Jazeera, I was interviewed live. I always interview live there and in Arabic, because I'm not willing to be edited or translated, because then they misstate things. I talked in Arabic, at eye level, and a Palestinian I know calls and tells me, "Damn, Avi, I heard you, you were talking like a Palestinian guido!" I didn't know if that was a compliment or not.

Do you like Arab culture, Arab mentality, this thing you're studying? Does it appeal to you?

Yes. Look, it's a world I didn't know. I'd never been opposite that sector. Not the Palestinians and not Arabs in general. Remember that as a soldier in the unit, you cross borders so as not to meet with Arabs, not in order to meet them. And if, God forbid, you did meet them, then you're supposed to shoot them. Suddenly you enter a niche of getting to know the Arab world. Talking to it. Convincing it. Working with it. Pulling one over on it. Manipulating it without it being aware.

When I entered the field after the language lab, my Arabic still wasn't great. I happened to step into the shoes of Shimon Romach, currently the head fire commissioner, who was an outstanding Arabist with perfect Arabic. I remember I went to overlap with him, and we went in to see the collaborators, and I told myself—my God, how can you even step into Shimon Romach's shoes? They called him Abu-Samir. It takes time and it goes slowly, but eventually, they start seeing you as a serious personality out in the field. They say, listen, that's Abu-Nabil, a serious person, he can be helpful. Ultimately, no one collaborates for free.

To Be or Not to Be: Complications across the Border

Avi Dichter: At the end of the '70s, while I was still in the Service, I went back to Sayeret Matkal for operational activity. Every year I'd go out on an operation, in coordination with the head of the Service, because I was already a coordinator. Happily for me, the head of the Service and the head of Aman or the chief of general staff always understood the importance, and I tried to do the work simultaneously, except for the interval when I already had to commence combat training.

In '84, I was a student at Bar Ilan University, and then I told the unit, "Look, we can do more now, because in the future, I won't be able to continue." During that time there was a terrible shortage of people in the unit, and I was considered a good professional in my field. And I did end up going out on an operation for three months during the course of my studies. I finished it, we got home safely, but three weeks later I get a call from Omer Bar-Lev, who was commander of the unit, and Ehud Barak, who was head of Aman, and they tell me, "We've got a problem. You have to replace someone in the operation."

I was in a very problematic situation. I had exams at the university, and my wife was pregnant with our little daughter, and she fell and broke her arm, and underwent a series of X-rays, after which the doctor said she'd been exposed to too much radiation, and he recommended she have an abortion; she already had an appointment with the abortion committee, and I was involved in consultations about that, so as not to have an abortion if we didn't have to. And right in the middle of that boiling cauldron that phone call catches me, and I tell Omer, "Okay, give me just a day or two to see what's happening with the abortion." So he tells me, "Avi, listen, we can't. The operation is in five days, and tomorrow there's an interrogation by the chief of general staff."

I tell him, "Listen, this is a little problematic. . . ." There's no such thing in the unit, that five days before an operation, someone arrives for a significant role. And then I ask, "Who's in the team?" And he tells me, "It's Yoram's team." And I say, "Wait a minute, is Toby Shor on the team?" And he says, "Yes."

Now, you have to understand. Toby is the brother of Avner, who's my teammate. Their third brother, Avida, was killed in the "Aviv Neurim"* operation in 1973. If, God forbid, something happens to Toby in the operation, I couldn't look Avner and the family in the eyes anymore. And everything flips just like that. And I tell my wife Ilana, "Listen, there's some story, I might have to go on reserve duty." And she tells me, "You haven't asked my permission till now, so don't start making things complicated for me at this stage. . . ." And then I tell Omer, "Okay, I'll come. But under one condition, that Toby Shor is in the force with me."

Musa Tsabari, who's the closest thing I have to a biological brother, and with whom I've done quite a few operations previously, was the squadron commander, and he was supposed to go with me on this operation. I went into very quick combat training lasting five days, and I went on the operation with a team whose fighters I barely knew, which is very rare. Unfortunately, there were complications during the operation, and we found ourselves with one casualty and eight people injured deep in enemy territory, having to get home safely. At least one of them was severely wounded. And that's where we had to give the force time to get organized in order to make our way back.

That was the stage where I learned more about people than I'd learned throughout my life. Sometimes we think that when an operation encounters complications, everyone's at peak alertness and at peak attention. Life is a lot more complicated. There are quite a few people who enter a state of nirvana, and you have to be very sharp so that no one on the force makes a mistake that the whole force ends up paying for. And paying for it here means anything from being taken prisoner to death or injury, nothing simple. And here, because of the location, I think each one of us understood that no one would

---

* Aviv Neurim ("The Spring of Youth") was an IDF operation which took place on April 9, 1973, involving several elite units, including Sayeret Matkal and Shayetet 13, against Fatah and the Popular Front for the Liberation of Palestine targets in Beirut and Sidon.

come rescue us with helicopters. We either get to a point from which we can go home, or we apparently ascend to some other state.

It took a pretty long time for us to get organized again. You really had to hold on to time with your teeth. With your teeth and your tongue. You have to give the force, which has to get organized and get back home, time to do its job, to take care of the wounded in a place that's close to people who, the minute they know there are Israelis there, it'll end like the Convoy of 35* in the worst case, or with being taken prisoner in the best case. You understand that the lives of a whole lot of people simply rest on your shoulders. If, God forbid, there's an exchange of fire, you might acquire more wounded, you might acquire more casualties, making the situation a lot more complicated. So you make an effort to finish everything quietly. To give everyone in the surrounding area the feeling that nothing serious has happened. Just a local event. And that's how we get organized to get back home.

What's going through your mind while it's happening?

The truth is my mind is completely blank. It's completely focused on the next threat. And the threat, you don't know exactly where it's coming from. Because of the fact that everyone's busy taking care of the wounded, you can't ask for other people's attention. You understand what a "solo assignment" is. In Sayeret Matkal, you do lots of solo assignments, but that was the most prominent time. And you have to make sure the whole time not to be surprised. And when someone local comes to you, you have to identify him early enough, so he doesn't come too close and recognize he's dealing with Israelis.

It's actually about conducting everything in the most quiet, calm way, and initiating. Constantly initiating. Not to find yourself in a situation where you have to provide answers. You have to be first all the time. So you have to be very alert. You don't think about anything. You don't think about home, and you don't think about family, unlike what you'd imagine, where your life is playing like a movie. No movie and no nothing. . . . You just think only about your stuff.

---

* A convoy of Haganah men who were ambushed and killed by Arabs during an attempt to resupply the blockaded kibbutzim of Gush Etzion in January 1948, during the Israeli War of Independence.

I remember there was a soldier, a fighter, there, whose injury had apparently affected his orientation a bit, and we had to quickly find someone to take him and keep an eye on him, so he wouldn't disappear on us suddenly just as a result of his injury. And really, all the time, you're just like a nursery school teacher, but at the wrong nursery school.

Was Toby close to you?

Toby, after a certain stage, was already close to me. And here I had what's called a secondary mission, to constantly keep an eye on him, because to get to the place from which we returned home was a very long way, very problematic, with quite a few encounters with the enemy, and the distance between opening fire and getting through it quietly was non-existent. And the minute you open fire, you're already maybe at a momentary advantage over the one you opened fire on, but at a terrible disadvantage regarding what comes next.

You also encountered the army there, right?

I don't really want to go into details, because it's still a very sensitive operation, but there's no better exercise than that for what came next.

How deep inside were you?

Very deep. Too deep.

And what's happening in Israel at the same time?

Moshe Levi, who was chief of general staff at the time, really highly praised the fact that this story ended without opening fire. Because every exchange of fire would bring on complications that would require bringing in the Air Force and possibly ground forces. To make a long story short, to tumble from there into war is a pretty simple scenario. I think that was the first time I felt like a stage actor. You imagine yourself on the stage and you have to play that role till the very last minute. There's no possibility here of faking it. And there's no possibility of a "take two." It's "to be or not to be." You can't say—like kids do when they're playing—"do-over," and start again. And you have to watch your game. And you have to remember there are fighters who aren't in that theater. They don't even understand what's going on there. They just don't understand what's going on.

Musa [Tsabari]understood me, I understood him, but that's where it ended. None of the other soldiers had any idea whether we were in a more or less complicated situation. They're aware of the complications. They're not aware of the severity of the threat they're under because they really don't know whether when you clap someone local on the back, that's a friendly clap or whether in a minute, you're about to chop his head off.

How do you manage them? What do you say to the soldiers?

The goal is to constantly make sure they're not seen. Or not seen from too close. And the fact that we did manage to make our whole way quietly until the point from which we got home, it was really a sublime sensation, of returning children home. Of returning home a lot of people when you know the distance between getting them home and receiving them as prisoners of war or, God forbid, as casualties, is nothing. And look, I was already a big boy. Anyway, I was already a father to two and a half kids.

Hamas, Jihad, a Different Culture

Avi Dichter: Until 1987, I celebrated my birthday every year on December 14 by myself. In December '87, I got a very unwanted partner. Hamas Day was actually declared on that same day. Hamas and the Islamic Jihad began to flourish during that period. Those were the two organizations that, as far as the Palestinians were concerned in the beginning of the First Intifada, were a great venue to join, because there's religious affiliation there. In Gaza, where I served, there's no such thing as "a non-believer." Even if you take people from the Popular Front, with a seemingly communist orientation, you'll find them in mosques. But when you get to people from Hamas, it's different. These are people for whom religion is borderline fanatical, and there are characteristics of terror there, with definitely heavier damage as far as we're concerned. And then soldier abductions started in the West Bank, and the business went up a grade as far as daring is concerned. Suddenly Fatah had stiff competition, and that already brings on other characteristics, a different culture. And when all that happens together, you can't put the brakes on it.

In the First Intifada, from '87 to '92, six hundred people were murdered due to suspicion of collaboration, of whom maybe three percent had some sort of connection. Ninety-seven percent were completely innocent. Ninety-seven percent! And you tell yourself—one minute, for heaven's sakes, how do you get to a state like that? That's a different culture.

In Khan Yunis, one man came to us in the middle of winter, with a wool cap on his head, and asked to see the coordinator. We didn't understand why, what happened, and we said, "Take your cap off." Eventually he takes his cap off, and we see a man whose ears had been cut off. We ask him what happened, and he tells how people from his neighborhood chopped his ears off. A while later we arrested those people because they were linked to the terror infrastructure. We thought they'd done that to him because he was suspected of collaboration, even though he had no connection to us. And then the head of the terrorist gang told us the story. He says, "That guy was selling drugs to people. We told him, 'Stop selling drugs!' He got beat up, apparently went back to selling drugs. We took off his ears because he wasn't using them anyway. . . . He didn't hear what we were telling him." And he tells this story in an interrogation, believe me, less dramatically than I'm telling it to you.

Another story: a father in Bureij whose daughter had gone out with the herd and was two hours late coming back. In the end he met her by Wadi Gaza and asked her, "Where have you been?" She gave him this look and told him: "I've betrayed your honor." He took her by the hand, walked all of Wadi Gaza with her, crossed the fence, entered a herding pasture and murdered her, his daughter! She was fifteen, sixteen. Her only crime was that she had a suitor who was another Bedouin, and they'd had an affair of hand gestures and signaling to each other from afar. Nothing beyond that. But she'd been delayed because of this courting. And her father murdered her. By the way, he murdered her in Israel and was sentenced to life in prison. If he'd murdered her in Gaza, he wouldn't have gotten two years.

Now, murder over what they call "family honor" is not one case, two or three. They sit down, they have a family council, and they decide that a female family member who has dishonored the family or is suspected of dishonoring the family will be murdered, and the person who will murder her is usually the bachelor, the young guy. They elect him to carry out the murder. They tell him—tomorrow. By tomorrow, everyone leaves. One goes to Ramallah, one goes abroad, one leaves for Egypt, to create an alibi. And that's the end of the story.

Another story: they took a woman who was supposed to carry out a terrorist attack in Soroka Hospital in Be'er Sheva. She was recruited. They knew she had a permit because she was being treated with radiation in Be'er Sheva. They told her, "You leave for Be'er Sheva—the explosive charge is on you; you'll go through Erez Crossing and carry out the suicide attack in Be'er Sheva. If you're discovered at Erez Crossing, during the crossing, you activate the belt on the spot." And she [asks], "It won't be discovered in the magnetometer?" They said, "No, there are no nails." That's what happened in the attack at Mike's Place,* they got the explosive belts through Erez Crossing without being discovered. The belts didn't have any nails, so during the inspection, they weren't discovered. And then the woman says to them, "Wait a second, a few months ago I broke my arm, and I have platinum in my arm. It might beep." They told her, "Of course it will beep!" They took her, they operated on her in some clinic, took the platinum out, closed it up, and sent her to carry out the attack. Lucky for her or lucky for us, we had prior information, and she was discovered and didn't manage to execute the attack.

I gave you three stories. Believe me, I've got thirty, three hundred, and three thousand stories, and the Palestinians will add more. We come from different cultures. The lynching in Ramallah is another tier. It was actually carried out in a police station. Not in the terrorists' private residence. It was a lynching carried out in a police station to which two [Israeli] soldiers who had lost their way were led. They were brought there in order to be interrogated and, I presume, to be taken back. And when the mob came to the police, the situation there wasn't two camps—the police camp protecting the soldiers and the marauder camp which came to lynch them. No. The lynching was carried out by everyone together. Security forces are already terrorists. Not all of them, but starting to come from among them.

I coined the phrase "soul preventions." We called it soul preventions because we couldn't find a more touching phrase. Soul preventions are certain terrorist attacks which really had an unusual dimension. It was the murder of Shalhevet Pas, the baby in Hebron, or the lynching in Ramallah. The guys knew that what had been defined as a soul prevention receives priority, by the way, not always

* A 2003 suicide attack which took place in a Tel Aviv nightclub, in which three people were killed and more than fifty injured.

because of multiple casualties or injuries. We determined that anyone involved in the lynching in Ramallah would end up in prison or in the grave—never mind which. But I said, "The man with blood on both his hands,* we're focusing on him. He'll get to prison and will be photographed with both his hands and handcuffs between them." I don't remember myself making that decision in other cases. This was really a case where we wanted to create a different level of deterrence. And slowly, we started to round up everyone who had participated in the lynching. I think upwards of twenty people. And the man with the two bloody hands was indeed eventually arrested, after more than one or two years. And in prison, after he confessed, a photographer working for us took a photo of him with both hands in the air and handcuffs between them. And there was harsh criticism against me by a few members of the media, how come the Shin Bet was staging pictures. I said, "Guys, that's what happens to a person who violated soldiers' honor."

You're not going to change their culture. You're not going to put them through a workshop to change their values. You hope that they, as a developing civilization, will also acquire more and more values which are Western values, or more civilized values—not necessarily Western, but more reasonable—of less violence amongst themselves. I hope we'll also reach that solution one day. But to analyze why they do it, and try to understand?

How can you try and understand the murder of a girl on the background of dishonoring the family? How can you understand that? Try as an Israeli, as a person who lives within Western culture, try for one minute to imagine yourself taking a step like that. Look, we have one case of the child Rose,** which we haven't recovered from for years. With them, if you kill a girl in the context of family honor, you're a hero. You, the father, are a hero. As they say, your shame has been absolved. I know it's very hard for us to process that.

I saw a movie once about the murder of the athletes in Munich. Not Spielberg's *Munich*, the previous one. They screened it in Gaza,

---

* During the course of the lynching of the two Israeli soldiers in Ramallah, one of the perpetrators, Aziz Tsalaha, leaned out of the police station window, displaying two blood-soaked hands while the mob cheered.

** Four-year-old Rose Pizem was murdered by her grandfather in 2008, while other family members, including the child's mother, colluded in hiding the murder.

in some theater. I happened to be sitting in the theater. To watch the movie. They, of course, didn't know Avi Dichter was there. I was a coordinator then. Maybe a district coordinator. Someone told me, "Avi, you have to see this movie—in Gaza." I asked why and he said, "Listen, it's just amazing to see the audience."

I went to see the audience. There's a part where the athletes, in helicopters, land in the airport to transfer to the plane. With the terrorists. And then the charge starts and the terrorists shoot and murder the athletes who were with them. And the whole audience applauds. In the theater, applause. And you know what, as an armed Israeli, instinctively the first thing you want to do is open fire there. You see a phenomenon you can't believe you're seeing. An audience of people, not animals, God forbid. And what's happening in the movie? There are no soldiers there. Just athletes. And they know it's athletes. The whole movie describes this thing.

Later, when I was Shin Bet director, I saw people's reactions to suicide attacks. By the way, not people from the last house in the row in a refugee camp, but people in the regime, security apparatus people. Not in front of us, among themselves. In front of us, of course, they clucked their tongues and expressed sorrow and so on. I saw their statements and their behavior among themselves. I don't know what strength of character you need to sit after a brutal attack in a security coordination meeting with people who, a moment before, were very cheerful in the context of the terrorist attack that happened. In the context of casualties. Look what happened with us when the Goldstein story happened. How the country stormed over the Purim party with Hanan Porat. The amount of upheaval in the country. That's a crucial difference between the cultures.

So I don't want to start going easy on them because their psychological state, their mentality, is such that I'm supposed to understand that if a terrorist attack takes place, I'm supposed to accept their reaction. I don't want to sit down now and say, "He's in a difficult psychological state, don't be hard on him." I'm not willing.

What's happening to them, to the Palestinians? On their side? Try to explain it.

The Americans kept asking me, like you're asking me, "Avi, what do we need to give them? More weapons? More means of breaking up riots? What do we have to give them so they do the job better? More intelligence?" I told them, "Guys, just one thing. Give them balls." They don't have the guts to cope with them, with their terrorists, with their rioting elements. That's what they pay the price for every time, and they'll pay more, until they understand. And I've told them this lots of times: "If you don't act against your terrorists who harm us, these attacks will eventually turn around and harm you." That was almost a self-fulfilling prophecy. Until June 2007, even Mahmoud Abbas didn't understand that. In June 2007, when he lost Gaza, that's the first time they came to their senses.

There were attempts to recruit the Palestinian Authority into dealing with terror through their own means. All in all, there were very serious guys there, who we thought would do the work. There was Mohammed Dahlan, head of the equivalent general security service, and there was a whole series of other people who we had good reason to believe would get the job done. For them, not just for us. But the Palestinian security apparatuses failed colossally, in scales that I would call shameful, humiliating. For them, not for us.

Take Tawfiq Tirawi, head of general intelligence in the West Bank. That man took his apparatus and simply turned it into a terrorist organization. He would sit with us in coordination meetings, go back home, and give instructions to carry out terror attacks. I personally went in Hanukkah 2000, at the prime minister's request, to Jordan to meet Yasser Arafat to tell him our understanding regarding Tawfiq Tirawi, and that if he doesn't cease terrorist activity, he'd be handled by us as the last of the fugitives.

We were standing opposite security apparatuses whose command wasn't brave enough to take actual steps against terror targeted against Israelis. They didn't understand their obligation was to thwart terror, as Rabin explained to them in the beginning. It came up in a lot of meetings. Here and there there were very, very few bright spots. There were cases where they understood that no one believed them at all anymore, so they'd stage all kinds of displays of handing over explosives. It became a joke. We had to collect intelligence on their staged preventions. Listen, it doesn't work that way. The State of Israel works with quite a few security agencies. There's Egypt and Jordan with whom we have peace treaties, and you know exactly how much they invest in thwarting terror there. By the way, even when they fail and an attack happens, you don't come to them with complaints. But when there's nothing, zilch, no beginning of work or law enforcement chain of command, you understand it's hopeless.

A year before the Intifada broke out, Ami Ayalon says, there was only one Israeli casualty, and part of that was due to the work with the security apparatuses. What changes there?

You want to learn about the Palestinian security apparatuses? Fast-forward to 2004. Yasser Arafat's funeral. The helicopter with the coffin flies in from Cairo after a very impressive, very dignified ceremony. And then the helicopter flies to Ramallah and is supposed to land in the Mukataa [district in Ramallah, where the Palestinian Authority is headquartered]. A security force of three thousand was supposed to ensure that there would be a dignified ceremony in Ramallah. Three thousand security personnel! Believe me, that's a number above and beyond what's necessary.

I remember that Omar Suleiman, the Egyptian intelligence minister, was supposed to arrive in the helicopter to the ceremony in Ramallah. I told him, "Don't come with the helicopter." He says, "There are a lot of security people." I told him, "Omar, believe me, the helicopter will land, and before the rotor stops spinning, it'll be surrounded by people." He says, "Three thousand security people!" I said, "It'll collapse like a house of cards. Let it go, it's sugar. Water will melt it in a second." He tells me, "No, listen, the Palestinians. . . ." In short, we all remember the photos. The helicopter landed, three thousand security people disappeared. By the way, disappeared is the best case. Some broke in, ran toward the coffin. The people who organized the funeral told me they were supposed to take the coffin, lead it to the Mukataa, where Mahmoud Abbas was supposed to conduct a ceremony with all the dignitaries, and then take it to the burial plot. At some stage, actually using good instincts, they understood there was no chance, so they gave the order, "Toss him in the grave." Just like that. They put the coffin on the car roof, drove to the plot, took it down, covered it with dirt, and that was the end of the story.

So the Second Intifada and Arafat's funeral are two events from which you can understand they have no inclination to place the welfare of the country or the Palestinian Authority before their private interests and their own security. That's why they paid the price in Gaza, and they're only now starting to recoup in the West Bank.

And why? Is it in their DNA?

I don't know. Look, I'm telling you, it's a matter of command. Like anything else. The spirit of the commanders. It's not the spirit of one commander, it's the spirit of the commanders. Listen, when they decided to deal with Hamas in Gaza, they established a "death unit." The idea was to establish a quality unit. Like, to make a very clear distinction, our "Unit 101" [a special forces IDF unit tasked with carrying out retribution operations across Israeli borders]. So who did they put at the head of it? The Palestinian Al Capone, the criminal Nabil Tamuz, a name which would cause any Palestinian in Gaza to tell you, "Listen, that guy's a criminal." Take the biggest outlaws leading the crime gangs here, and now imagine the Shin Bet takes one of those guys to head a special unit to deal with terror. And I said, "Listen, out of the whole professional cadre, that's what you've got?" They said, "He's the only one who understands their language." They picked him so the confrontation would be a confrontation of criminals—the crime gang he heads against Hamas. These will be killed and those will be killed. Of course, ultimately there wasn't any chance of success.

In quite a few meetings, including with then–Secretary of State Colin Powell, and later with Condoleezza Rice, who replaced him, I always told them, "We're not willing to put up with the Palestinian culture of *ya'ani* anymore." And then they asked me, "What's *ya'ani* culture?" I told them, "*Ya'ani* is a key word in Arabic." And I'll demonstrate it to you through a true story. There was a terrorist in Bethlehem, a master terrorist, named Ataf Abayat. Imagine—the president of the United States demanded that Yasser Arafat put Ataf Abayat in prison, and Yasser Arafat committed to arresting Ataf Abayat and putting him in prison. Because Israel threatened that if it didn't happen, it would go into Bethlehem to get him.

After that, Minister of Foreign Affairs Shimon Peres summons me to a meeting in Jerusalem with Abu Alaa [Palestinian political leader Ahmed Qurei], who was chairman of their legislative council, with Jibril Rajoub, who was head of the Palestinian security service in the West Bank, and with Saeib Erekat, who was Yasser Arafat's assistant. So I go into the room, and the three of them are sitting across from Shimon Peres, and Shimon Peres tells me, "Avi, they're saying that Ataf Abayat is in prison." I knew it was bullshit, because he was just in some operation we were working on at the time. So I say, "Listen, Mr. Minister of Foreign Affairs, I hope you're not accepting this stuff." So he says to Abu Alaa, "Abu Alaa, please tell him." And we switched to Arabic, because in English it's very hard to thwart terror. And then Abu Alaa says to me, "Avi,

I'm telling you, the man's under arrest, the man's in prison." I tell him, "Abu Alaa, I'm sorry, the man is not in prison." And then very quickly you could tell he wasn't fluent in their version. He looks to Saeib Erekat and tells him, "Saeib, *mish hek*? (Isn't that so?)" Saeib Erekat, believe me, has no idea who Ataf Abayat is, has no idea what's even happening on this topic, but he immediately improvises and says (in English)—"Definitely"—of course he's in prison.

And then they both look at Jibril Rajoub and tell him, "Jibril, he's in prison, right?" Now, Jibril knows that if anyone can arrest Ataf Abayat, it's only him. And he's in a bind. Because Jibril knows the man is not in prison. Beyond that, he knows I know the man's not in prison, and worst of all, he knows I know he knows the man's not in prison. . . . So they apply pressure, and tell him, "Jibril, isn't that so? He's in prison, right?" And then he says, "*Ya'ani*. . . ." Now, "*ya'ani*" is he's in prison, "*ya'ani*" is he's not in prison, and "*ya'ani*" is wherever you want it to be. . . .

One day I had a delegation from the United States over, and I told them the story. In the end, I asked them, "Did you understand the meaning of the word?" So they looked at each other, and one of them says, "*Ya'ani*. . . ." I said, "So, you got it."

Ya'ani culture is the source of all that's evil in our relationship with the Palestinians at the time. It was obvious we couldn't continue with *ya'ani* any more. *Ya'ani* under arrest, *ya'ani* we did it, *ya'ani* we transferred it, *ya'ani* we prevented it. It's insufferable. By the way, just to finish the story, two days after the meeting with Peres and the Palestinian senior officials, Ataf Abayat exploded with a car in Bethlehem, and it wasn't a police car transferring him from one prison to another prison.

The Cake Isn't Baked Yet—Why the Camp David Summit Failed

"The Palestinians are pessimistic: the Camp David summit is destined to fail."

"Members of the Palestinian delegation take care to lower the level of expectations and assess: no chance of resolving the conflict."

"While the Americans and the Israelis try to convey optimism regarding the Camp David summit's chances of success, extreme pessimism reins among the Palestinians. "The summit is destined to fail," said Abu-Alaa, head of the discussion team regarding permanent status and a member of the delegation to Camp David, yesterday. "I don't believe the necessary preparations were made. Negotiations should have been conducted at lower echelons, but President Clinton succumbed to Ehud Barak's pressure and his request to convene the summit. I don't think there's a chance of resolving the big problems like Jerusalem." In an interview to Palestinian newspaper *Al-Ayyam*, Abu-Alaa said that Barak applied immense pressure on Yasser Arafat to consent to participate in the summit.

(Ronnie Shaked, *Yediot Ahronot*, July 7, 2000)

Avi Dichter: I took on the role as Service director in the middle of May 2000. A week later, we exited Lebanon, and suddenly I found myself dealing with six thousand members of the Lebanese Armed Forces (LAF) and their families, who had left southern Lebanon. In your first month on the job, you suddenly find yourself dealing with something that's at the bottom of the organization's priority list. I admit that in all my mental preparations for assuming this position, that was not on the agenda. But you have to quickly adjust to changes, because simultaneously, in July, the Camp David summit with Prime Minister Barak, Palestinian Authority Chairman Yasser Arafat, and, of course, President Clinton was held.

I admit that my feeling was that we're leaving for Camp David without sufficiently serious or detailed preparation. When Camp David actually ended with nothing, it was a real anti-climax, both for us and for the Palestinians. The buildup of expectations was so high, that the scale of the disappointment equaled the scale of the expectations.

I'm trying to understand. You're actually the agency that's supposed to know the Palestinians best. The prime minister leaves for negotiations in which he's actually trying to resolve the Israeli-Palestinian conflict without consulting with you? Without making use of you?

I don't know if it was only Israel. The impression was that Yasser Arafat also wasn't really overjoyed about Camp David, and it was more that he was drawn to Camp David under American pressure.

We didn't see any massive preparations for Camp David, with very orderly items regarding what they're going to say, on the Palestinian side, either. There was a clear lack of maturation here. Not lack of maturation in the sense where you might say, ninety-eight percent is baked and we're unsure about the other two percent. It was unbaked on a very significant level. It was clear there was no chance. The egg whites for the cake hadn't even been whipped yet.

There was no enthusiasm on the Palestinian side, and I think on some level, we, as intelligence agencies, need to learn to identify not just information, but also atmosphere. And maybe that should teach us a lesson. You know, when you come to a wedding, it's not enough to bring the Ketubah (the marriage certificate) and bring the engagement rings, you also have to come with enthusiasm. And that's not what we saw in Camp David.

I think the most significant signal that the summit was destined to fail was the fact that during the two weeks it lasted, there was not one encounter of coordinating expectations, of exhibiting enthusiasm, of creating chemistry, between the prime minister and the Authority chairman. There'll be no situation of a summit or of something heading toward a summit without it being preceded by a one-on-one meeting between the two leading personalities in the State of Israel and in the Palestinian Authority. Just like it was with Sadat, just like it was with King Hussein. With these things, in the end there's the chemistry between two people who have to assume personal risk on themselves, and that risk is substantial. I heard a few stories about what Yitzhak Rabin was going through during the whole Oslo process, and how hard it was for him to even get to the situation of the handshake on the White House lawn on September 13, '93. But in the end there's the part where you have to secrete a bit of those chemical substances that create that glue which completes all the other agreements. Without that, it apparently doesn't work.

There's no situation where one head of state pushes who they perceive as another head of state. I think that when Clinton was hugging Rabin and Yasser Arafat, that's a reasonable picture. I don't think we would gladly accept a situation where Clinton was pushing an Israeli prime minister. There's even something, I would say, a little humiliating about it. And I presume that's also what the Palestinians saw,* even though I believe Ehud Barak did it out of an earnest and real wish to create closeness. But in terms of body language, it didn't look good to the Palestinians, and I also heard quite a few statements from them about it.

Do you sit with Ehud Barak before the summit, and analyze what the implications would be for the Palestinians, if it fails or succeeds?

No. I don't remember actual meetings about scenarios and reactions. I also don't remember that as Shin Bet director, I was very involved with the preparations for Camp David. They were conducted more in the forum of the Prime Minister's Office, the bureau. Danny Yatom, I believe, was coordinating things then. I wasn't privy to the question of what red lines were going to be drawn, if there even were red lines. Even though in retrospect I understood that they wanted to draw the Palestinians to the edge, in order to show that the Palestinians didn't really intend to reach a peace agreement, I have a hard time saying that was our goal and that was our target. I think that's more of an explanation for the failure than a pre-constructed plan.

I think the feeling around the prime minister, perhaps including by the prime minister himself, was that with the Americans' help, in this specific situation of Yasser Arafat in July 2000, things could somehow be turned around in order to arrive at some kind of agreement, which turned out to be simply incorrect. Because I believe Yasser Arafat had a very serious problem with making real strategic, super-significant decisions. Oslo was a strategic decision in which his gains were so large and so clear that it was almost obvious he'd grant his agreement. Everything that happened afterwards was already problematic, because in Camp David it was clear to Yasser Arafat that he was also obligated to give a few things.

Ami Ayalon: It's not that we had a partner. We didn't have a partner. But the question isn't whether we do or don't have a partner. Both sides are conducting a discussion among the deaf. Both sides blame each other. Ehud Barak lost Arafat as a partner months earlier, and

---

* In famous photos from the 2000 Camp David summit, Israeli Prime Minister Barak is seen pushing Palestinian Authority Chairman Arafat through a doorway.

Arafat lost Ehud Barak as a partner months earlier. Neither of them did what he had to do to gain a partner. Arafat didn't take care of security like he should have done, and Ehud Barak didn't stop the settlements in good faith like he should have done. And so the question isn't whether there's a partner. Arafat has no partner, and Ehud Barak has no partner. The question is what both sides do to create one, and this discussion is missing from the Israeli narrative.

The army didn't actually believe in the first place that peace might happen in Camp David. It's building itself up for a confrontation. Zvika Fogel, who is the chief of Southern Command's chief of staff, says two months before Camp David, "I'm creating all the necessary conditions so that I can apply force. I know this thing's going to fail." The army prepares itself in the best way possible for a confrontation. More than that, it's saying, "I apply pressure on the Palestinians because I see them as hostile, so I thrust them into a kind of corner where they have no choice but to do what I expect them to do, and then I react with the force I've been preparing."

Avi Dichter: I suggest being cautious about strident statements being made, whether it's by military factors or others, according to which there's no chance of peace and it's a waste of time and we should only prepare ourselves for war. The army's role is to prepare itself for the Intifada, whether it breaks out or it doesn't. When Sadat landed in Israel, the army was also preparing for war. I remind you that the chief of general staff at the time, Mota Gur, declared that it was the biggest deceptive maneuver in history. That was the statement, and that's what IDF was preparing for, and rightly so. If the army thinks it's the biggest deception, its duty is to prepare for that. If the Army thinks Intifadas or upheavals are about to break out, no matter on what scale, it needs to prepare for that, obviously. But beyond the reality existing at the time, I'm not aware of indications in the intelligence materials that implied we were heading toward an Intifada. The Palestinians didn't know that an Intifada was about to erupt, either.

Yuval Diskin: The atmosphere within the Palestinian public, and to a large extent within the Israeli public as well, was that we're heading toward an inevitable confrontation. I don't know if you remember the media at the time. Everyone was preparing for an Intifada, forecasting it, and the prophecy fulfilled itself. We were scarred from the events of the Western Wall tunnel and the Nakba days* which occurred later, in which Palestinian cops turned their weapons toward Israelis. There were also the events in Joseph's Tomb**, and this time IDF decided to prepare itself for an outbreak. No one thought we'd be entering into five, six, seven years of suicide attacks, and such a large cycle of violence.

What happened here, according to my understanding, is a state of great frustration on the Palestinian side, on several levels. First, internal frustration. The younger generation in Fatah, headed by [Marwan] Barghouti, is very unhappy with the corruption of Arafat and the Tunisia contingency, and with the fact that they didn't manage to fit in within the Palestinian regime or win any truly influential role. In fact, the people who came from the outside were those enjoying life's pleasures, clipping the money and the coupons, while those who bore the burden of the first Intifada, and paid the price, were tossed aside. That created immense frustration. On the eve of the Second Intifada, there were elections for Fatah in the West Bank, and Barghouti won. Arafat flipped the election results, because as far as he was concerned Barghouti was part of the opposition, and gave the keys to his rival. Barghouti remained frustrated here as well, so it's not a coincidence that he, rather than Arafat, led the events of the Second Intifada.

Then another thing happened. We were very well prepared for the Intifada. The army was extraordinarily well prepared, and they couldn't surprise us this time. It came excellently prepared, and the ratio of people injured during the first period of the Intifada was approximately fifteen to one. Meaning, for every Israeli, fifteen Palestinians were killed. But blood doesn't turn into water, and the

---

* Nakba Day, commemorating Palestinian displacement during the Israeli War of Independence, is generally commemorated on May 15. On Nakba Day 2011, Palestinians and other Arabs in neighboring states marched towards their respective borders, or ceasefire lines and checkpoints in Israeli-occupied territories. At least twelve Palestinians and supporters were killed and hundreds wounded in the resulting clash with IDF. Further clashes occurred during the 2012 commemoration.

** In April 2011, Palestinian Authority police officers opened fire on three cars of Israeli worshippers after they finished praying at Joseph's Tomb, killing one and wounding three.

cycle of vengeance begins. In the first one or two years, Fatah was more dominant than Hamas. Hamas woke up slowly, but when Hamas wakes up, it really wakes up, and becomes a dominant factor in suicide attacks. Actually, a snowball starts forming here, or a blood-ball, and it takes a pretty long time to stop it.

But in contrast to what the big experts say, Arafat didn't set the Intifada in motion. He rode the wave at a later stage. Fatah's younger generation started the riots, and Arafat was surprised in the first stages by what was going on in the streets. He even tried—not as hard as he could, but tried—to stop the events in the first two or three weeks. At some stage he decided to join them, and rode the wave in a very skillful way. As far as he was concerned, he thought that now he'd back us into a corner, while simultaneously we were conducting talks with him.

Avi Dichter: There was an argument between us and Aman that lasted until Operation Defensive Shield in 2002 [the large-scale IDF offensive during the Second Intifada culminating in the siege of Arafat in his Ramallah compound and incursions into six West Bank cities]. Aman's research division claimed that the Intifada was an intentional initiative by Fatah factors in the West Bank, maybe in Gaza as well, and we claimed there was no intelligence support for that, it's all speculation. In Defensive Shield, all the supposed initiators of the Intifada were arrested, and sat there during interrogations and told us how the Intifada began, how they found themselves surprised, how they saw themselves led into the Intifada, how they grabbed the bull by the horns to earn assets, just like Marwan Barghouti had done.

Barghouti had actually made the exact same maneuver that all the others had made. He lost the elections for Fatah Central Committee in the West Bank, didn't pass the torch to Ahsan a-Shaikh, who won. The Intifada broke out on September 29, and he very quickly understood, like the others, that there's an opportunity here, and turned from a man of peace into a man of terror. He actually built a hive of terrorism around himself, started to spin terrorist attacks, and was suddenly riding this wave called the Intifada. In Defensive Shield, when we interrogated people, they actually described how they were dragged in. How they started putting together names and terms. I remember there was someone very senior in Aman's research division who said, "It's a good thing the Shin Bet is interrogating, it can direct its interrogations so they support its thesis. . . ." That was a wretched statement, and it certainly doesn't bring credit to a man I respect very much.

Ami Ayalon: We were directing the wrong round of violence. Everything we did was not only wrong and misguided, but brought on an escalation of the cycle of violence. Meaning, if what you actually see in front of your eyes was what Ehud Barak apparently estimated, and IDF definitely estimated, to be a planned initiative by Arafat as a result of failure of the talks in Camp David, then the army's response was apparently an appropriate response. Shooting more than a million bullets, I don't know, at a rate which has no equivalent in any of Israel's wars. . . .

But if the Intifada is a different phenomenon, if the Intifada isn't Arafat's initiative, if I tell you Arafat was surprised by the Intifada no less than Ehud Barak was, if I tell you the Intifada is really a reaction, an outburst, a mass rage directed against Arafat as well as against the Israeli occupation and the Israeli government. That the Intifada was aimed against Arafat because he was corrupt and because he lost his leadership long before Camp David. Because even the little he promised, which was a diplomatic process and Palestinian independence and less occupation and less roadblocks, he couldn't provide; if I tell you that that was actually the source of the Palestinian violence—then IDF's reaction was not just ineffective, but it's also what escalated the Intifada, which in the beginning, by the way, did not include any guns. It also didn't include any beards, and no green flags by Hamas and the Islamic Palestinian Jihad. These were young people disappointed with the political process. Most of the flags were Palestine flags. Most of those who took to the streets at first were students.

If I tell you that that was the Intifada, then IDF's response is a mistaken response. So, until we analyze the phenomenon which I believe we're still arguing about to this day, the Shin Bet's stance is my stance, and IDF's stance is ultimately IDF's stance; Israeli public discourse has, to this day, not come up with an answer for what happened in October 2000.

When Bogie Ya'alon, Ami Ayalon, and [veteran military leader] Shaul Mofaz, as well as Ehud Barak, say "Yasser Arafat is running

this thing," and they say it at the beginning of the Intifada in October, it's in contrast to everything you think and know. Why isn't your voice heard at the beginning? Almost everyone conforms to the theory that states that Yasser Arafat is controlling this thing, is running it and is the source of all that's profane.

Avi Dichter: Look, factually, that wasn't true. We at the Shin Bet knew it then, and when the Intifada initiators were brought in, they said it publicly in their interrogations. But what can you do—the army is a big agency, the Shin Bet is a little agency. The number of reporters on military affairs is very large. The number of reporters on Shin Bet matters is zero. The Shin Bet makes its voice heard in the pertinent discussions, and that's what's important. If you're saying Arafat is the supreme commander of the Intifada—hurt him, arrest him, kill him. I think we could say, intelligence-wise, in a pretty good way in the beginning, and in a very conclusive way following the interrogations, that there was no prime initiator for the Intifada.

Ami Ayalon: I met Khalil Shikaki a few weeks after the Intifada broke out, and he told me then, "This is a popular uprising, but if Arafat doesn't join it in the next few weeks, the physical violence itself will be turned against him." And Arafat understood that, and he joined, and of course gave it legitimacy and played the game as if he were actually controlling it. Now, he's far from being a martyr, but we have to analyze the phenomenon professionally and not emotionally in terms of "right and wrong."

Avi Dichter: Yasser Arafat, his contribution to the Intifada was by failure, not by deed. That was the main problem. Arafat understood this Intifada was rolling along very badly. The person who told him was Mahmoud Abbas, Abu-Mazen, who told him—during the first week of the Intifada, "Abu-Amar, if you don't stop this Intifada now, it'll blow up in our face." And Yasser Arafat avoided dealing with it. Later, the deeper the Intifada got, the stronger Hamas got, the more appeals Yasser Arafat received to stop Hamas and let the authorities—the intelligence agencies, the army, the green [border] police, the blue [regular] police, intelligence apparatuses—act more resolutely against Hamas, and Arafat just didn't make that strategic decision. By the way, Abu-Mazen, too, until the Hamas coup in Gaza in

June 2007, didn't reach any decision to really fight the Hamas effectively. This is a case where, if you don't deal with it correctly, you set another road sign on the way to disaster.

That's clear, but I'm not asking about that. The testimony I heard about the beginning of the Second Intifada is severe testimony about our side—about an army conducting a completely different policy than the political echelon's policy. The political echelon issues commands to the army, and the army doesn't obey them. It came from [Prime Minister Barak's chief of staff] Gilead Sher, [security minister] Shlomo Ben Ami, [transportation minister] Efraim Sneh—they all admit unequivocally that because the army had an agenda that stated, "We're heading for a confrontation," and because of Shaul Mofaz, who didn't believe in the chance of a resolution—the army pushed the Palestinians into going wild.

Dichter: I know all the army commanders, both the senior ones and the more junior ones. Listen, they're people that, during role playing, it was very easy to switch our roles with theirs, in the Shin Bet, in the police, in the army. It's the same group of people. They don't see the official state view differently than me or than others, so it's hard for me to say it's a trend. "The political echelon, pardon me, can go take a hike, we'll do what we want." That's not the reality I know.

I know of quite a few cases where the political echelon decided to remove roadblocks, and it was clear that from a security standpoint, it was a very problematic risk, and nevertheless, it was decided to remove roadblocks so as to create a more comfortable environment. In some cases, we had to return the roadblocks because terrorist stacks forced us to do it, but the political echelon is the one ultimately taking the risks. Because who is the political echelon? Ehud Barak and Danny Yatom and later Fuad Ben Eliezer and Mofaz and Sharon. Listen, these are all people who came from the army, and they're not exactly the types you could fool by disobeying orders, Yitzhak Rabin also knew how to ask questions, believe me.

And what about the proportionality of IDF's response when the Intifada broke out?

I don't know exactly what "proportionality" means. You can't say—let's wait. How long? Two casualties? Four casualties? Ten casualties? When does this proportionality go into effect? When do you go up the scale of proportionality? A country can't conduct a struggle against terror or against an Intifada with tools of "fair play."

They're at a level of knives, so we're at a level of clubs. It doesn't work that way. I think it took us time to understand you can't disperse demonstrations just with the Border Police, because this Intifada, its prominent characteristic was that it started with live fire.

And what about the wisdom of approving Sharon's visit at the Temple Mount?

I can't say, intelligence-wise and practically, that Sharon's visit in the Temple Mount on September 28, 2000, caused the Intifada. As far as I'm concerned, the Second Intifada started on Friday morning, September 29, 7:30 a.m. The joined patrol in Qalqilya is about to start, the Palestinian cop approaches an Israeli Border Police jeep from behind, shoots and kills a Border Police officer. That's the beginning of the Intifada for me. Even before the casualties on the Temple Mount.

Sharon's visit was on Thursday, and the events that took place on the Temple Mount on Friday, mainly the casualties, caused it all to flare up.* It's a lesson that today we understand a lot better than we did then. The Temple Mount is not another front, it's not just another site, it's not just another place where every event is like another event somewhere else. The Temple Mount is a totally different issue. It's already a nuclear bomb. An event in the Temple Mount, a casualty in the Temple Mount, is something completely different. We understand that well after September 2000.

What's your conclusion from what happened in Camp David and to this day? Can you gather insights from it and use them in the future?

Look, in the first seven years after Oslo, we tried a system which isn't simple, because we made concessions way beyond those specified in the items of the Oslo Accords. The guideline from above was to make concessions and, if necessary, ignore certain things, let them be, let this baby chick stand on its feet. And for that we paid a price that was not simple. The events of the Western Wall tunnel are just one example. In the nine years from the Intifada to this day, you can see a situation where we gradually understood that that reality was bad. So if in the first year—from 2001 and up to Defensive

---

* Four Palestinians were killed, and 250 people were injured in the riots ensuing following Sharon's visit on September 28, 2000.

Shield—there were still attempt at communication, to reach local agreements, we saw that it was hopeless. I think we sobered up, justifiably so, I'm glad to say, and we went for it under our own flag. Defensive Shield was a classic example, the West Bank Barrier was a classic example. It hurt the texture of life opposite them, but it saved lives. It was obvious they'd also sober up one day as a result of their own reality. June 2007 is a date of crisis for them. They lost Gaza, and after that, they're now starting to wake up. When will they have a law enforcement chain of command that will really enable them to stand up on their own two feet, and then we can look them in the eye and say, "Let's take some risks"? I don't know yet.

What actually happened to us during those years? We said, "Let's take less and less risks." And less and less risks means more roadblocks, more barriers, more arrests, more preventive actions. Those are military methods; you don't produce peace with military methods. You ultimately have to build peace on a system of trust, after military actions or without them. I claim, as someone who knows the Palestinians well, that there shouldn't be a problem in creating a real relationship of trust with them.

We, on our side, didn't really build trust, either. If when Oslo started there were about one hundred thousand settlers, today we're at about five hundred thousand settlers. We say one thing, and meanwhile the settlements make progress and develop.

Here we're entering the political niche. That's my biggest disappointment with the Netanyahu government—how it managed to bring us to a situation where the central concern in the peace process between us and the Palestinians is the settlements. In the disengagement plan, the State of Israel made a move in Gaza and in the West Bank, and evacuated twenty-two settlements. Not illegal outposts—actual settlements. Destroyed houses. Not caravans and huts—houses, villas, synagogues, removed bodies from graves and transferred them to Israel. Ten thousand people, civic settlers, out, ousted, uprooted—everyone has their own terminology. So, do we need to teach what "evicting settlers" means? The State of Israel has done it. Twice. Once following the peace treaty with Egypt, and once following its own strategic decision. So when we need it, Israel will know how to do it one more time. Difficult, complicated, chasm, all true. But we know how to do it.

So, as I said, I was a little disappointed, and I also told Bibi, "How did it happen to us that the main topic on the agenda is settlements?" The problem is that when you don't put anything else on the agenda, something gets put on the agenda for you. And what we got was settlements, because there's a consensus about that. Moreover, Jerusalem was presented as a kind of settlement, and some of the riots in Jerusalem are a result of the fact that today the Palestinians understand that they've got support in the United States, in Europe, not to mention in the Arab countries, that Jerusalem is also in the game as an illegal settlement.

I think that when the Palestinians have leadership and command that understand their obligations as a state, it will serve Israeli interests, but primarily their own interests. Until that happens, unfortunately, we'll have to do things alone.

A Riddle Named Yasser Arafat

"To be displaced."

"The cabinet's decision to displace Arafat does not have immediate implications because it has yet to be determined when, how and to where. Sharon, who formulated the decision, preferred to leave it vague and without determination: banishment or elimination. The decision was received with the support of all cabinet ministers except for Minister of the Interior Poraz, who objected."

Shin Bet Director Avi Dichter: "Arafat currently rules all the security apparatuses, and has in fact reassembled the power he possessed in '94. It's better if he stays here under our watchful eye than that he be exiled into the world at large, where we won't know how he's harming us."

(Itamar Eichner, *Yediot Ahronot*, September 12, 2003)

You said you'd spent a lot of hours with Arafat, you knew him well since he came in. Try to explain the riddle named Yasser Arafat to me.

Avi Dichter: First of all, unlike the image a lot of people have, he's a very warm person. You'll never sit next to him and have to peel an apple all by yourself. He'll serve you the apple, he'll peel your cucumber, he'll slice the meat for you, as is the custom in Arab culture. He's also very humble. He doesn't lead a life of luxury. All in all, when you talk to him and meet him, he's a very nice man. And sometimes you wonder, such a charismatic character to the Palestinians, really their symbol, how can it be that he doesn't understand what's so clear to any one of us? What's his strategy?

I'm an Israeli, I was head of the Shin Bet, maybe I think differently. But the Palestinians, including the senior ones, also gave up. They just didn't understand his strategy. I'm talking about very senior people, including the heads of the Palestinian security apparatuses, but not only them, who raised an eyebrow and said, "We can't understand how he doesn't stop this flood of the events of the Intifada." Saeb Erekat said to me, "He can't. This tiger has broken free and he understands he can't stop it. So he preferred not to appear impotent but as someone who's supposedly running this thing."

He didn't understand that his role as a leader is to dive or swim against the current and do what many expected him to do. To stem the tide of the Intifada. Because with that, he really would have won the world over as a leader. I think he missed an immense opportunity, and I deal a lot with the subject of leadership. The truth is I was very surprised and very disappointed by the fact that what was clear to all of us, Israelis and Palestinians, was not clear to Arafat, or that he had a hidden agenda that I really don't know how to analyze. But there's no doubt that Yasser Arafat missed an immense opportunity to really be the creator of the Palestinian state.

We once sat in a meeting with the Palestinians. The Americans were also there, and one of the senior Palestinians says, during some small talk between the discussions, that "Yasser Arafat was the Palestinians' Ben Gurion. . . ." We didn't have time to answer, and immediately another Palestinian, very senior, jumps up and tells him in Arabic, "I wish he was our Ben Gurion. . . ." Why does he wish that? Because they could analyze exactly where Yasser Arafat didn't make the required decisions—not required by Avi Dichter, required by them—in order to really start building the infrastructure for a Palestinian state.

The ultimate leader we had in the State of Israel was without a doubt David Ben Gurion, and you take a look at the most significant event in the history of the State of Israel, meaning the declaration of independence on Iyar 5 [May 14, 1948]. And I've actually studied thoroughly what preceded that event. Look, the battle over

Gush Etzion took place on Tuesday, Wednesday, Thursday, before the Friday on which independence was declared. That was the most brutal defeat of the emerging state in the War of Independence. There were 520 warriors in Gush Etzion. And on Thursday night, Gush Etzion fell. Half of the fighters were killed, including twenty women, and the other half were taken prisoner, including eighty women. Can you try to imagine what was going through David Ben Gurion's mind on Thursday night, when they inform him that Gush Etzion had fallen, and more than two hundred people had been taken prisoner, including eighty women? Look what happened to us in Israel because of one soldier who was taken prisoner. We were in a state of upheaval for five years! And David Ben Gurion declares the establishment of the State of Israel on Friday. That's leadership! That's what Yasser Arafat missed. And I think if they'd let him do everything over today, he'd make a completely different move.

Do you believe he'd fight the Intifada?

He would enforce the Palestinian Authority regime on Hamas and on the Islamic Jihad as well. And if he had decided that an Intifada by the Authority needs to take place, he'd conduct what's called an Authority Intifada. What happened to him was that he was dragged into an Intifada that was already in motion, and later Hamas jumped on board as well. Notice that during the first month of both Intifadas, Hamas waited on the sidelines. Only when it saw where the front was going did it join. Both in the Intifada of '87 and in the Second Intifada.

What happens after September 11 and after the *Karine A* [a Palestinian freigther loaded with fifty tons of weapons that was seized by the Israeli Navy in 2002]? What crosses out Arafat as far as the Americans are concerned, too?

After the September 11 attacks, they wanted Arafat to make some kind of gesture toward the Americans. They told him, "Give blood." He said, "I can't give blood, I'm not allowed." So they told him, "So pretend. *Ya'ani*. . . ." So they put the blood donation bag next to him, and he lay down and they photographed him as if he was donating blood, and that's what they sold to the Americans. So, really, are the Americans dummies? Do they not understand that it was all a show, from A to Z? You, as Chairman of the Palestinian Authority, fake a blood donation? I'm providing that as an example. If they did a blooper show on Yasser Arafat. . . . Smuggling out the wanted man in '94, the fictitious blood donation, the lack of really dealing with events, and ultimately he didn't decide to stop the Intifada. If he had decided to stop the Intifada, either in 2000 or in 2001 and also in 2002 and also in 2003, he still could have. The Palestinian Authority and security elements there and the Fatah movement at the time were strong enough. What was lacking was direction. Everyone expected Yasser Arafat to provide direction, including Marwan Barghouti, who drifted into terrorism. But instead, he was dragged into all kinds of corners where they said, "Let's exploit this to do the *Karine A*. The Iranians made a donation of weapons, so let's take it." That was deplorable on every possible scale.

Is that why Arik Sharon, after Defensive Shield, says, "Ramallah first?" Is that why he decides to leave Arafat in the Mukataa, and actually end his life there?

I think that was Arik Sharon's greatness, that he knew how to combine leadership, military strategy, and an understanding of fighting terrorism. There were different recommendations on where to start Defensive Shield, and Arik Sharon determined that Ramallah was the main front. It had a very significant influence on the other areas as well. Ultimately, I think Ramallah was the easier front from a military standpoint compared to other places, because Ramallah is run differently, but from the moment they entered it, all the other places started rolling along more easily.

Why do they decide not to kill Arafat at that stage? I know Sharon wanted it very much.

Look, I don't think it's a continuum of arresting or hitting the heads of terrorist organizations, with the next stage being a head of state, or head of authority. A head of authority is already something completely different. It's not a trivial matter. Deciding to harm a head of authority is a very serious quandary. The dilemma was whether to deport him or not. There were also statements about harming, eliminating. Some "hard-liners" said, "Sheikh Yassin and Arafat are the same thing." I don't think it's the same at all. Yasser Arafat is a head of state, or the head of a recognized authority. He won a Nobel Peace Prize, rightfully or not. He's a personality known around the world on a very significant scale. I think it would have been a fatal mistake if they'd accepted the recommendation to harm him.

And I think it also would have been a very serious mistake if they had accepted the recommendations to deport him. All the years after Defensive Shield were very paltry years. He didn't count anymore, people almost never came to him. He was there, enclosed by himself in his little room. He was a pretty pathetic figure. The West Bank became the arena where Defensive Shield was conducted, thousands were put in jail, the curve of terror decreased, and I'd say that in the Palestinian Authority, there was almost satisfaction about this. Somehow life was being conducted more and more normally, and they understood that Yasser Arafat was an anti-climax.

The Suicide Attack Period

"Three years of murder and bereavement."

"867 casualties; 5,878 wounded; 18,876 terrorist attacks; 306 suicide bombers; a loss of 75 billion NIS."

(*Yediot Ahronot*, September 29, 2003, a summary of three years of Intifada)

Avi Dichter: In the beginning of Sharon's era, the main problem was how to decrease the scale of terror attacks, which were landing in very problematic quantities. By the end of 2003, we had 900 casualties as a result of terrorist attacks. In meetings with the Americans, I'd try to explain to them what we were dealing with. I said, "Imagine that in the proportions of Israel versus the United States, 45,000 Americans, most of them civilians, are killed in terror attacks within three years. You conquered Afghanistan over the 2,700 Americans killed on September 11. And I'm not even talking about those wounded. We had over 7,000 people wounded in this story." No one believed that Israeli society would be able to hold on so tightly during three years of terror. We haven't had a period like that since the state was established. And I'm not even talking about the difficult financial reality created, among other things, as a result of this wave of terrorist attacks.

The problem was you suffer an attack, and you have no direction in which to hit back. So you can hit Palestinian Authority sites, which are relatively defined places, but you know the Palestinian Authority didn't issue the attack. You act against the Authority because it didn't prevent the attack, but it was clear that that wouldn't prevent attacks. There were days in which there was more than one attack, and the feeling was that the intelligence response, even if it was precise, wasn't successfully converted to an IDF Operations Directorate solution which would prevent the attack. There were sometimes cases where you knew a terrorist attack was on its way, but they didn't have time to roll out the forces before it actually took place.

The hardest thing about intelligence is when there's information and there's no operational ability to convert it into prevention. Or the time is too short and you don't manage to grab hold of the attack, or you succeed in preventing six attacks in one day, and the seventh kills twenty people. It's like a machine lobbing tennis balls at you; you can return ninety percent of the balls, but just one ball, or ten percent, causes casualties. And you see the victims. You see the attack at the Matza restaurant [a March 2002 suicide attack killing sixteen people], later there was also an attack at the Maksim restaurant—I mention both of those because they were brutal attacks not just in terms of the large number of casualties. Because within all the data you receive, you also try to look a bit at things that also touch you more personally, and not just professionally. I remember that one of the senior managers in the Service, a very serious man I appreciate very much, came to me and told me, "Avi, listen, three generations—children, parents, and grandparents killed in the same event—we haven't had that since the Holocaust." A difficult statement.

Suddenly, instead of the date of a terrorist attack, you start to hear characteristics: "the soldier bus," you know they're talking about Megido [a June 2002 car bomb that killed thirteen IDF soldiers]; "the youth attack"—the Dolphinarium [a June 2001 suicide attack at a Tel Aviv dance club that killed twenty-one young people]; "the Matza restaurant attack"—the family attack; and then comes the Park Hotel attack on the night of the Passover Seder, March 27, 2002, which was the most brutal attack that occurred during the Intifada, thirty casualties, more than 120 injured. Also, its timing during the Passover Seder, within an event hall where a Seder was conducted, on people who came to celebrate the Seder; it was a very brutal attack.

A year after the attack at the Park Hotel, a day before the Passover Seder, I held a meeting of Shin Bet staff at the Park Hotel, in the event hall where the attack occurred. The hotel manager, whose relative was killed in the attack, arrived, and he described to the staff members how the attack happened. And then one of our people got up; we'd brought him to describe the attack from a professional, intelligence perspective—how it developed, where the terrorists originated, what the target of the attack was. It wasn't even the Park Hotel! It was a mall in Netanya, and they didn't know it was Passover Eve and it was closed, and then they continued on to a mall in Herzliya, and saw that it was closed too, and they went back, canceled the attack, they were on their way back to Tulkarm, and then the suicide bomber, who was dressed up as a woman, said, "Let's go through Netanya; I used to work at the Park Hotel there, let's see if there's anyone there, and if there isn't, we'll go back to Tulkarm." And that's how they got to the hotel, saw the line of people going into the Passover Seder, and this suicide bomber got out and carried out the attack.

And the manager of the hotel listens to the description of the attack from the man who conducted the investigation, and he gives his description, and you see a forum of professionals who unfortunately have experienced quite a few terrorist attacks, real old-timers, sitting in the hall where the attack happened, and it was a formative experience. It was difficult, but sometimes as the head of an organization, you have to do something to make people understand that it's not just technical-operational aspects. You have to look around a little, otherwise you get into this routine of thwarting an attack or being frustrated by the fact that you didn't manage to thwart an attack.

Listen, there were people sitting in the team dealing with receiving intelligence or locating intelligence or pointing out irregular indicators. Sometimes it's students, or women soldiers. It's not people above thirty; we're talking about eighteen-, twenty-, and twenty-two-year-olds. And you see these young people handling an attack rolling toward Netanya, and summoning the forces and summoning the police and the Yamam, and there's a chase, and bam, you get the report—an explosion in the market in Netanya, I think two casualties or three. And you know it's an attack that slipped between your fingers because we couldn't close up the ring fast enough, and you go up to the place where they're receiving the information, look at the people, see an eighteen-year-old girl who has to keep working and looking at the next item of intelligence, and she knows one terrorist attack was carried out and there's another one in the pipeline.

She looks, and she knows she missed a terrorist attack an hour ago—or didn't sound the alarm quickly enough, or sounded the alarm and the forces in the field couldn't get organized quickly enough—and now the next terrorist attack is already in motion and she has to work on that attack, the attack that occurred previously is no longer relevant. Listen, how can I say this, you really need nerves of steel. And we didn't educate them to grow nerves of steel. We also didn't recruit them on that basis, of having nerves of steel. As they say, crying and working.

Yuval Diskin: I got to see people in the organization, for example, people doing surveillance who would, say, hear a conversation in which a suicide bomber is talking to the person who had launched him, and they sound the alarm, but we're lacking information and we don't succeed, and in the end you're informed that a terrorist attack just took place in Netanya, and you understand that was the conversation you heard. And I'm telling you, I visited those units quite a lot at the beginning of the Intifada, and people there would just sit and cry. You see people sitting and crying, in pieces because of this thing. And it didn't happen once, it happened a few times. It creates an immense mental burden on people, because they identified with this need to prevent the attack and understood the meaning of what happened when we didn't succeed, even if we had this or that contact with this thing. You can't describe that feeling. It's a horrible feeling.

Avi Dichter: In the beginning, we weren't even aware of what people going out every time to the attack, to the site itself, to investigate, were going through. It took us time until we started to understand we have to take care of them with the help of social workers. Service employees were walking around at a site where victims were present and had to talk to people, interrogate them, collect information.

People always use the phrase "shielded with his body" and don't understand what it means. It's a dilemma, and these are people who do it again and again. In Gaza we knew with certainty that there was a suicide bomber on his way to Gush Katif, and forces were spread out on a roadblock on the road which enters Gush Katif from Kissufim, in order to try and locate the suicide bomber. No one knew if he was wearing the explosive belt or whether he had to pick up the explosives elsewhere, but your assumption is that he could be wearing the explosive charge. And they took the vehicles, and one by one, they take out the people to be interrogated. And in the end the coordinator takes the suspicious guy, goes with him to a room where he has to search him, and during that part of the way, the guy blows himself up, and Oded Sharon, our coordinator, is killed. Uri Ben Amo, from Nesher, was also standing at a roadblock based on a report regarding a suicide bomber. The suicide bomber arrived, blew himself up, and killed Uri Ben Amo. Two Border Police guys in the French Hill who saw an Arab woman approach a hitchhiking station went over to her in order to inspect her, and she blew herself up on them. They were killed, of course.

A ticking bomb is in your head, and you know you could pay with your life. You can't say with certainty what the circumstances are: is he wearing the explosive belt, will he activate it, won't he activate it, where is it. Remember that we're all security personnel. We were educated that you open fire based on two conditions—you recognize a means and you recognize intent. You see a gun, a weapon, or a grenade and you recognize intent that he wants to shoot someone. With a suicide bomber, there's no recognition. Not of means and not of intent. You don't see the belt of explosives, you can't recognize intent. All those people who tell you, "I could see murder in his eyes"—there's no such thing. You don't open fire based on the fact that "you saw murder in his eyes." In suicide attacks, you have to be very careful, very quick, very determined, very precise in your intelligence, and be lucky.

I know a guy from our operations unit who was chasing after a vehicle that came to carry out a terror attack in Tel Aviv. The explosive charge didn't work, the suicide bomber took the belt and they drove to fix it back in Jenin. We knew they were on their way to Ummal-Fahm; they put up a roadblock on Wadi Ara road, and when they stopped the vehicle, he went up to identify the man and get him out. The minute he poked his head in the Transit, he saw the guy in the back; the guy blew up the belt while sitting in a vehicle in which there were Arab passengers. They were killed, and the operations guy was injured. That's the reality of dealing with ticking bombs.

How do you deal with that on a personal level? It's the worst period for the State of Israel. Your role as head of the organization is to thwart this thing, and you guys can't do it. Like you

said—there are seven attacks where you succeed and two get away from you. How do you deal with that personally?

Dichter: Look, the truth is you're so immersed in it that you understand that when you get home, you just have to sleep well. And I sleep well. You keep asking, hold on, how do you take care of the organization, an organization that's living with a very harsh feeling. At Service HQ there was a little flag, a regular one, which was affixed to the building wall. At a certain point I brought the head of the logistics staff and told him, "Listen, I want you to move it to the other side of the road, so that anyone who goes into the Service will see it, and make it the biggest flag possible." He looks at me and says, "Mr. Service Director, why?" I said, "The harder the situation is, the bigger the flag has to be."

The head of Service doesn't have the privilege of taking care of himself and asking himself how he feels. If I feel it's a little hard, I go swimming and try to improve the feeling a little and then you dive and . . . back to work. You've got no time to wallow in yourself. Family, in the nature of things, gets tossed aside. There's almost no real ability to conduct yourself within a family in an orderly way.

The biggest difficulty is a result of the fact that you think you know what you have to do. You try to recruit the other agencies into it and convince the political echelon that these are things that have to be done. I remember there was an aversion to going into refugee camps during operations. The army initially didn't want to enter a refugee camp, because the characteristics of warfare within a refugee camp are familiar to us. Later it became clear that there was no other way. You have to create deterrence and make them feel they're not safe in a refugee camp, as well. The whole idea was to take terrorists and, from a state of mind where they can deal ninety percent of the time with manufacturing terrorist attacks and ten percent of the time with survival, to turn it around. Keep them busy with survival ninety percent of the time, and with manufacturing attacks only ten percent of the time. . . . And you have to go into refugee camps so they understand they're not immune in those places. Nur Shams was the first camp. Afterwards there was an operation in Balata by the paratroopers, who developed a system. They went in through the walls, so as not to go through booby traps, and were extraordinarily successful.

The Balata tiger became a kitten?

I think this statement, beyond its colorful nature, has a lot of truth to it. Because I think that we, too, especially those who have to do the work, were quite averse to doing it. It was a very problematic step, but there was no choice. You have to understand that if nothing changes the face of the battle against terror, we'll continue counting the dead.

The Barrier* was the next element. Today there are more supporters of the Barrier than holes in the Barrier, but as someone who dealt with it from the end of 2000, the beginning of 2001, almost everyone in the Army was completely opposed to the Barrier, due to the complexities, the costs, routine security, and so forth. The political echelon didn't want to hear about it, and I remember very long conversations. Finally there was a long conversation with Prime Minister Arik Sharon at his ranch. We had a tradition where, when there were problems we couldn't agree on in general discussions, he'd say to me, "Avi, let's sit at the ranch." On the subject of the Barrier, I remember we sat in the ranch, and I explained to him that the roadblocks and the IDF ambushes had exhausted themselves. Their numbers could not be dramatically increased, and there was no chance that if we did increase them, they'd result in sealing the border.

He asked me for examples, and I told him, "Look, Arik, I'll give you the most tangible example. They army has actually said it can't block the terrorists. We handle sources, and sources manage to come to meetings in Kfar Saba and Netanya, from Nablus and Jenin. I'm not telling you from Tulkarm and Qalqilya. I'm telling you—from Nablus and from Jenin. From that you can understand that if sources make it, apparently the general Palestinian populace also makes it. And there's nothing you can do. If the lines are open, and he manages to make it to Qalqilya or Tulkarm, within ten minutes, he's inside Israel, and the rest is history." It took time, but gradually, both the political echelon and the army understood that there's no way around it.

---

* The Israeli West Bank Barrier was constructed by Israel in the West Bank and along the 1949 Armistice Line ("Green Line") in order to prevent terrorist attacks and unauthorized crossing of Palestinian residents into Israel.

When the building of the Barrier began, Sharon was in the United States. The Barrier was launched in Salem, the ministry of defense came, they had an initiation ceremony for what's called "the Barrier stone," and a week later I drove there to see how the Barrier was coming along. Nothing. Absolutely nothing. There was a tractor or two there. And I knew, this was a project we had handed over to the ministry of defense, the ministry of defense didn't believe in the Barrier, so it was taking its time. I called the United States, I talked to Arik, he asked me what was going on, I told him, "I'm really asking that when you return from the United States, block out some time to visit the Barrier being built."

He told me, "Mr. Shin Bet Director, usually the Shin Bet director prohibits me from touring along the front line, and your recommendation now makes me wonder. What's going on? What's changed?"

I told him, "Listen, this barrier after the 'cornerstone,' nothing's going on there, just a tractor or two. . . ."

In short, he came back, gave me a call after a week and said, "Mr. Shin Bet Director, I don't believe a head of Shin Bet would give a prime minister a false report."

I said, "Arik, I hope you're wrong."

He said, "If I'm not mistaken, you said there was a tractor or two on the line there. My understanding was that there were no tractors there at all. . . ."

When he got mad, things started moving along.

When the Barrier was completed, its first part, from Salem to the Alfei Menashe area, you started seeing an immediate change in the terrorists' methods of operation. You saw that crossing over was no longer simple as far as they were concerned. They're looking for roundabout ways. We started receiving it in intelligence, and understood that we were in the right direction. And really, that was the beginning of a decrease that became a drastic one. Sometimes, pursuing fugitives, when you have no direction and you have no solution, you shake things up. You see people come out of their holes, look for other holes, and it gives you an advantage. That's what the Barrier did, among other things.

In intelligence, there's an iron-clad rule that says, 1 + 1 equals 11, not 2. It's not that if you tell the secret to your best friend, then both of you know. He also has a close friend, and that guy has his close friend, so it spreads very quickly. That's why the barrier was important.

Because from Jenin to Afula is a ten-minute drive. But when there's a barrier, and you want to get out of Jenin to Israel, you have to go down all the way or to the Jordan Valley or go up to Jerusalem, and then you have to make use of a series of collaborators along the way, and that already significantly increases the chance of detection and that the information will leak, and that significantly raised prevention abilities.

You saw that the political echelon, Sharon, of course, didn't want it. And, in fact, you, as head of Shin Bet, enforce on the political echelon a solution which is a security solution but has very clear political significance. Sharon suddenly has to sit down and draw borders.

Dichter: That's true. Anyway, for a government headed by the Likud, that's a lot tougher than for a government headed by the Labor party, but the reality was so tough that in the end there's no other answer. I think the political echelon also understood that the sanctity of life is apparently more important.

He Who Rises to Kill You: The Era of Targeted Prevention

"Two missiles eliminated the senior Tanzim member."

Yesterday before noon, the Tanzim operations officer in the Bethlehem area, Hussein Abiyat, headed a team which was about to open machine-gun fire aimed at IDF base Shdema. Two IDF combat helicopters were tracking him from afar. After they had positively identified Abiyat, who had been under intelligence surveillance for weeks, the helicopter launched missiles at his car. Two female bystanders were killed. IDF: "We couldn't hold fire—Abiyat was causing losses and was responsible for the shooting on Gilo [a Jerusalem neighborhood repeatedly subjected to machine-gun fire from the adjacent Palenstinian neighborhoods during the Second Intifada]."

(Ronnie Shaked, Amir Rapaport and Rami Hazut, *Yediot Ahronot*, November 10, 2000)

When does targeted prevention actually become our main means of deterrence?

Avi Dichter: I think the first event of targeted prevention in this format was in November 2000, in Bethlehem. I don't remember the family, but there helicopters really did hit them, because we couldn't enter the territory by surprise with a small force that would carry out the job and get out safely. In order to ensure the chances of success, we had to work with the element of surprise. And how do you surprise a terrorist? From the air, from afar. But to send the missile from a large distance, you need very accurate intelligence, and not for one second but throughout the operation, and it took time to build up that system.

In the beginning, the main problem was between the Shin Bet and the Air Force. Shin Bet and Air Force is like soldering stone to plastic. A connection between a coordinator in the field and an F-16 pilot is more complicated than peace with the Palestinians, and yet you see this thing carried out, and information is relayed in real time. I remember operations where you pass the verified identification on to the Air Force, and tell them that the fugitive is now riding in the right rear seat of a specific vehicle. That lets them really aim the missile at a specific part of the car, because you want missiles to hit spot-on, and not destroy the whole vehicle and also cause collateral damage to other vehicles. And then the vehicle is driving and suddenly it enters some alley, and by the time you hone in on it, it exits somewhere else, and you don't know if the same passengers are on the vehicle or not. You stop the Air Force, and understand, the pilot already has his finger on the trigger. And then you have to run the identification again, and you can keep going like that again and again and again.

And it's all carried out from a control room, what's called a war room, which is a really fascinating story. It was built during the Second Intifada, because you need all the factors dealing with intelligence collection and all the factors dealing with executing the mission together. Meaning, you need Shin Bet collection elements, representing all agencies; you need the representatives from the special unit, if there is a special unit. It could be Yamam, Shaldag [the Israeli Air Force's elite commando unit], Matkal, the Flotilla, and so on; you need a representative from the command who wants to be there; an Air Force representative if they're involved in the topic; Unit 8200 [the Military Intelligence Directorate's surveillance and electronic monitoring unit] if they're involved in the topic. Everyone sits there, and each agency streams its information into that room.

The original room was a small, crowded room, which was just awful. And I remember, the Americans came after the invasion of

Iraq to learn how this miracle, as they called it, works. How does this Israeli miracle where the Shin Bet talks to the Air Force work. Apparently in the United States it's more complex. They came to this room, a general with "stars" from here to eternity came in, and they conducted an introductory presentation for him, and he's sitting in the little room and asking, "You do all the work from here?" The guy who was giving him the explanations there didn't really know what to say. He said, "No, this is just the drill room. But later on, we'll really build a model room, with very impressive human engineering." And ultimately this whole armada is conducted by a manager, and not an especially senior one. It can be a head of branch, it could be a deputy department manager, and he's in charge of the subject. The head of the Service and the chief of general staff and the minister of defense might attend, and they stand in the back. The person commanding the mission is that manager, and he can also give commands to a brigadier-general, to the Air Force commander, to the head of a Shin Bet district. He's in charge of the operation.

You see all the information streaming in from the information collection agencies. It requires transparency, which was a very significant test we had to pass. It's bringing to this place people who will take in all the information, and with part of this information, you can also deduce which sources it came from. It's deciding that the best interest of the Israeli people requires exposing one agency's sources to another agency. This was an obstacle it took time to get over. But once we got over it, I think it really opened new horizons. Not that there are no problems, not that there aren't status games, but it was really a breakthrough. Many Palestinians highly regret that breakthrough. Regret from above, as they say, or, like we say, "When the helicopter is out and about, Mohammed's freaking out."

When does the rate of preventive actions start to rise?

The most significant increase in the number of operations was a direct result of a strategic decision by Mofaz and me, Mofaz as chief of general staff and me as Shin Bet director. We saw that the fact that we, each of us in our own organization, have to approve the objectives and the mission plan created a bottleneck, because, anyway, as Service director you're a lot busier, and then we both determined in a shared meeting that he would appoint his deputy, who was Bogie Ya'alon, and I would appoint my deputy, who was Yuval Diskin, and the moment we delegated it to the deputies, the whole business opened in an extraordinary way. This tradition that the deputies, deputy chief of general staff and deputy Shin Bet director, are the factors leading the whole operation, enabled increasing the number of operations dramatically.

I think this increasing sophistication which happened over years throughout the Intifada, both between the various units within the Service and between the Service and other agencies—you can't even estimate how many lives were saved thanks to it. I don't dare think what we would look like if the curve of people injured in 2002 had continued. It was the most difficult year, I remember. 451 casualties, in one year. 451 casualties! In a period of so many terrorist attacks, inside this entire maelstrom, you also want in some way to provide the sense that there's a response, that there's an ability to deal with it.

Ami Ayalon: The targeted prevention was originally intended to provide security for Israeli citizens. If there's a person who we know on a high intelligence level is going to manufacture a terrorist attack and we have no other way of stopping him, we hit him, injure him, or even kill him. That's targeted prevention. Now, I believe it's morally justified, operatively justified and justified, in any context. The saying, "He who rises to kill you, kill him first" was true thousands of years ago and is also true today. My life takes precedent over another's life. The life of an Israeli citizen whom I'm responsible for takes precedence over the lives of those who rise to kill us.

Avi Dichter: Targeted prevention is a work technique opposite terror-generating saboteurs. Mass-murderers or master terrorists or people with special capabilities such as a bomb manufacturer, a missile manufacturer, and so on. You go for them the first opportunity you get. He doesn't have to be on his way to a terrorist attack for you to hit him. He could carry out the attack tomorrow or in a week, but you know he's one of the terror generators. That's the condition for being included in the category of an object for targeted prevention. It's not something that needs to happen now. If he's planning the Twin Towers attack for a year from now and you have no other way to hit him, then he fits the criterion of a "ticking bomb." But you need to have something concrete, not a general intention.

What was Arik Sharon's attitude toward this tool?

Dichter: Arik Sharon came from fighting terror in the sixties, the early seventies, in Gaza. The style of fighting terror at the time was different, the creativity was different, the possibilities were different. At the time, you couldn't blow up a cell phone next to a terrorist's ear because there was no cell phone. And Sharon, you couldn't mistake the light in his face when he'd see the creativity. And I'm telling you, in the Service, there are people that really, each of them is worthy of Nobel prizes and Oscars together—with such creative thinking, and such smart technology. Yahya Ayyash is just one example, believe me, not even the most exciting. It's a good, elegant example, it reaches the finals, but I'm not sure it takes first place. There are examples with juicy stories that unfortunately we can't tell.

The truth is that in targeted preventions, there's mostly a lot of mischievous thinking by the handlers. HUMINT handlers who are really supposed to read the way these murderous terrorists think, and get a grasp on it in order to get to them. These HUMINT guys, the handlers, sometimes they have a very cheeky approach to these things. They really build beautiful scripts, really. So Sharon really loved these things. He'd come to the Service every time, or they'd come to him to authorize plans, but it was really to give him the entire narrative. Arik, he had extraordinary cynical capabilities. He'd ask questions which could be understood from an operational aspect: "How can you ensure he doesn't open it in the presence of his wife and children?" So they'd tell him, "Look, this is an intimate item sent to him by his lady friend, and it's not likely that he would open it in the presence of his wife. . . ." So he'd say, "All right, so how do you ensure that the children won't be hurt?" And you saw he wanted to get to know the whole story. There was one time when he was skeptical. He said, "There's no chance that this thing is going to work!" And by the way, two days later it worked beautifully. So there'd always be a phone call from him: "Yes, Avi, I see the guy was really hot and bothered about opening the package. . . ."

There were operations of really extraordinary creativity. Once they asked for a new technology in order to carry out a terrorist attack. So they got it. I think there were six dead terrorists there. It was a really nice operation because you have to build a long platform, until you establish trust, until you succeed. You have to work to create the extent of the trust, and see that they believe that the person who sent this to them is a reliable man. A successful operation like that can take six months or a year.

Arik Sharon understood how smart and how creative an operation can be—and how quiet. Suddenly, a key person in some organization disappears. And they start to wonder how he was killed. And something like this explodes here and something like that explodes there. Even the Palestinians would say, "That one killed there, *min Allah* and *min Abdullah*." *Min Allah* is what's called death from natural causes, and *min Abdullah* is when they knew it was from the Shin Bet. . . .

It's a business that causes extraordinary deterrence. A week after Yahya Ayyash blew up with the cell phone, one of the Palestinian leaders who were sitting in a meeting with us took the cell phone of the man next to him, which was in Regular mode, took advantage of an opportunity where that guy wasn't paying attention, switched it to Vibrate mode, and returned it to the table. Then that man put the cell phone in his pocket—and everyone's sitting down, the Americans and the Palestinians and the Israelis—and the other guy dialed him, and suddenly this man feels the cell phone vibrating in his pocket, and he jumps up as if a snake had just bitten him. No one understood what was happening, and we all knew what it was, and started laughing. That's deterrence.

Ya'akov Peri: I don't think there's a prime minister who likes hits. I think Arik Sharon believed that targeted hits on those planning terrorist attacks or who had carried out terrorist attacks would serve to deter those who came after them. He did it in the Gaza Strip when he was chief of Southern Command, and he did it as prime minister. The Service has to come and tell him whether it thinks this system is effective, and if it will really bring about the same results. The Service can't be a supplier of a bank of targets to satisfy the prime minister and fill up his belly, which was already full of schnitzels and other delicacies, with more Arabs who are being killed morning and night; and I also had arguments about this with Avi Dichter.

Avi Dichter: I remember there was a master terrorist in Tulkarm, Raed Karmi, who initiated quite a lot of terrorist attacks against us, and we uncovered the fact he has a female companion whom he visits regularly. And we actually built the whole operation plan on this axis. In photos from the observation plane or from the observation post, you could see him walking, full of energy, to the house, leaving the house exhausted and hardly walking, and then of course getting to the package waiting for him and exploding with it. And we were actually rid of a very serious mass-murderer who caused us awful problems. I always remember the photo of him walking full of energy to the meeting and returning almost on all fours and ending up on all sixes.

Did you take into account that maybe as a result of this prevention, which came at a relatively calm period, there would be an explosion where innocent Israeli citizens would be killed?

Avi Dichter: First of all, when you're Shin Bet director, you come to the prime minister with recommendations. The prime minister can say no, or he can say yes. It's not that the Shin Bet is the only factor. There are enough people deliberating—to do it or not to do it. If you make the political considerations, what's left for the political echelon to do? You can't come contaminated with political considerations. Beyond that, Raed Karmi, we knew about his involvement in terrorist attacks literally three days before he was eliminated. His people went toward Ramallah and carried out a terrorist attack there. Miraculously, a West Bank resident was "just" injured. The doctors declared him dead, and to our relief he stayed alive. Now, it's not a secret that there are Israelis who, when the terrorist attack happens within the areas of the West Bank, take it a bit less hard than if it were an attack within Tel Aviv. . . . So when they talked about a quiet period, they meant a quiet period in Tel Aviv. No one "counted" the terrorist attack that occurred three days earlier in the Territories. They were referring to what was going on within Israel.

Ya'akov Peri: After the targeted prevention involving Raed Karmi, Ami Ayalon approached me, Avrum, and Carmi. The concern he expressed wasn't only specific to this incident. He said he was concerned, or that he had some indicators, that Avi Dichter should be a lot more determined and independent opposite Arik Sharon. Personally, Ami thought the targeted prevention with Raed Karmi was not right and was not well timed, and he asked whether we were willing to come and talk to Avi, to listen to him and also to speak out. And that's what we did. Each one of us spoke, and Avi sat and explained. My feeling, and here I can speak only for myself, was that the meeting didn't attain its goal. Because we didn't want to come and make comments to the head of Service about a specific targeted prevention. That's not our role, and we also weren't fluent in the details. We came to express some kind of concern, or to try and supply some direction or guidance, how we saw the role of the head of the Service in his operations opposite the prime minister. How independent he should be, how determined he should be, to what extent he should not be led.

And what did the concern stem from?

Peri: From Arik Sharon's dominance and from the fact that the head of the Service has to maintain independence in reporting. Not to tell the prime minister what his ear wants to hear. All those things we're always worried about when there's a dominant prime minister with a very hard, determined line.

Were you afraid that Arik Sharon may be leading Dichter to excessive use of targeted preventions?

I think you're phrasing it a little too extremely, but generally speaking—yes.

Ami Ayalon: When we get to Avi Dichter, I'm very concerned by the fact that targeted prevention had turned from a discrete and focused operative tool to a policy by a country fighting terror. The numbers bother me, and I'm troubled by the loss of control the minute it becomes a phenomenon. It's targeted prevention if you hurt the one who rises to kill us, but if he wanted to kill us a year ago, or he wants to kill us a year from now, but now he doesn't, do we hurt him then, too?

I think that within terrorist apparatuses, even an apparatus like Hamas, there are also nuances and processes. And the hit on Raed Karmi takes place exactly during the period when the whole Palestinian system decides to give the diplomatic process a chance. It's not because they joined the Zionist movement. . . . There's an operative consideration here. Arafat understands that the world is less tolerant, and America is less tolerant, of everything he's leading, and instructs to stop the terrorist attacks. By the way, we know he and his people want to initiate terrorist attacks, but he says, "Gentlemen, right now we're not initiating terrorist attacks, I received an instruction." And then we carry out the hit. That troubles me a lot. I go to Minister of Defense Fuad Ben Eliezer, and leave him with a very uneasy feeling, and then I get to Avi Dichter, waiting to hear some answers from him, and I leave more troubled than I came in.

Because what do you feel is going on with Avi Dichter? Does he not understand what you understand?

Ayalon: He doesn't accept my position. Period. There's no issue of understanding. He understands and thinks differently. He thinks differently about the Shin Bet's role opposite the political echelon. He thinks differently about how to deal with terror. He thinks differently about the relationship between the short term and the long term. He thinks differently about this very focused point—do we kill a terrorist even when he decides that at the moment, he's not carrying out terrorist activity, and this might turn out to be a kind of milestone that brings him, along with his entire group in Tulkarm, to a more moderate stance?

Avi Dichter: There's no basis in reality to the claim that Fatah started fighting terror; quite the opposite. Raed Karmi is considered a highly dominant factor in manufacturing terror. If he took a month off now and will return in a month, and you can hit him in that month, is that fair play? I constantly claimed, "There is no fair play when it comes to terrorism." You don't shoot with an M-16 when he's shooting at you, and throw a grenade at him when he throws one at you. You use a tank even if he's shooting caps, or with a BB gun. You use a one-ton bomb even if he sends a suicide bomber with five kilo (eleven pounds). Why? Because you're a state. A state makes use of stately tools. There's no point even thinking in terms of fair play. And if you strategically decide to fight terror, fight it with all your might.

Terror is a barrel which has a bottom, but you can get to the bottom of it only if you have a clear strategy. And you don't live off all kinds of whims and all kinds of statements about quiet periods. What's a quiet period? Is last year a quiet period? Who manufactures the quiet period for you? If they're now getting ready for a new phase of terrorism, do you interrupt it, chop it down, or do you let it develop?

Carmi Gillon: The point was that it was a pretty long period of relative quiet. The Israeli people were exhausted from a lot of suicide attacks. Raed Karmi, it was definitely necessary to get rid of him at some stage, but the timing didn't look right to us because it reawakened the whole Intifada and the suicide attacks.

Was your meeting with Avi Dichter actually a highly irregular step?

An irregular step, very rare. It's the only case I remember. But look, every Service director has people he consults. Service director might be the loneliest role, except for prime minister. You're ultimately alone with the decisions. And in such a hierarchical agency such as the Service, it's the Shin Bet director who decides. So you have to consult with people. I think that up to Avi Dichter's period there still existed what was called the Service Directors forum. Once a month, all the ex-Service directors would meet at the Service director's in a closed forum. Eat sandwiches, shoot the breeze, and talk about all kinds of topics. Dichter used it less. And Yuval Diskin made no use at all of the previous Service directors. I suppose he may have had other people he consulted with. What the previous Service directors have and the current Service director doesn't is that they bring, I think, a very unique viewpoint and a sensitivity to many subtleties when they leave for the civilian world, and they hear and pick up on a great many things that the Service director doesn't. But everyone has their own style.

Yuval Diskin: I'm thoroughly acquainted with the intense arguments about the Raed Karmi affair, especially between the Service and the Army. At that period, there was a willingness by the Fatah to conduct a sort of temporary ceasefire. Raed Karmi was a Fatah operative. IDF at the time, to the best of my knowledge, based on the discussions I was party and witness to, did not want to proceed to Defensive Shield. The Shin Bet was very actively pushing toward Defensive Shield. And that's why IDF was seeking any path to a ceasefire. Every Palestinian statement was perceived as an opportunity. We had less faith in it. And ultimately the political echelon authorized us to carry out the Raed Karmi prevention operation. IDF claimed it ruined the possible ceasefire. We claimed there was no real chance for that ceasefire anyway. It's an argument that can't be resolved, but looking at it eight years later, everyone understands that if we hadn't conducted Defensive Shield, the Second Intifada wouldn't have ended and we wouldn't have overcome terrorism, so I attribute a much smaller volume to the Raed Karmi affair. It has no historical significance. Some people, because of its controversial elements, attribute to it much more volume than it deserves. But it's always good for a head of organization to have some external mirrors. Because the moment you're in the swamp, you only see the frogs around you. And it's good to have external mirrors, even if it's previous heads of Service who will come and tell you you made a mistake, and even if you don't accept it. I don't know what Dichter was going through when four former Service directors came to him and told him he'd made a mistake with the Raed Karmi prevention, and that he was getting carried away because of Sharon. It's possible that even after he didn't accept their opinion, it raised some thoughts in him regarding certain issues. Our initial reaction doesn't always convey the heart of the matter. Happily, people aren't robots. You listen, you may react in this or that manner, but afterwards you think, sometimes you internalize and tell yourself: maybe there's something to what they said. . . .

Avi Dichter: I don't remember it as some dramatic event. There were meetings. I don't remember people familiar with the front having a problem. It's just that people who aren't really familiar with the front, are a little disconnected from reality, examine the intervals for short periods of time, and don't "zoom out" a little and take a look at the whole range, to understand where we are. You can't wait for a time where you have an opportunity to hit and then deliberate. You have to build that opportunity and activate it the minute you can. On this issue, you have to develop a long-term strategy and not panic.

And what does that strategy say?

Dichter: That strategy says: military infrastructures of terror in Gaza—grind them to a pulp, either through military means or through diplomatic means, such as a bloc of Arab countries which will help the Palestinian Authority dismantle the infrastructures in Gaza. If that doesn't happen, Israel will have to go into Gaza, for a military action of dismantling the military infrastructures of terror in Gaza, and listen to me, that's a step that will take years. Gaza is a classic model of what's happening in Afghanistan. For those who don't understand, Afghanistan is here, ten kilometers (six miles) from here.

And regarding the targeted prevention, what you're saying is, "No matter when he appears in my crosshairs, I take him down"?

Look, targeted prevention is a combination of opportunity, atmosphere, and capability. And if those three components come together, you're on your way. The problem is that sometimes you have capability, you have opportunity, and the atmosphere isn't right. And then you have to decide what's more important: is it better to postpone it, or is it better to expedite it, even if it stirs something up? And there's no choice, sometimes you decide to postpone because the prime minister's meeting with the president of the United States or, on a different note, with Abu-Mazen, is more important to you. And sometimes you decide not to postpone. By the way, a decision like that is made only by the prime minister, it's not a decision by the executive branch.

Ami Ayalon: And there's another question—where do we break the chain? Okay, we harm, if necessary, even kill the one who rises to kill us. The one who, in the immediate range of time, takes up the means, an explosive belt, a weapon, or any other means of killing, and is about to kill me. But what happens with the circles around him? What happens with those who prepare the explosives and those who transport them and those who plan and those who gather intelligence, and those who only preach the idea? They're not killing, but they're promoting an ideology which ultimately creates jihad and causes the killing of Israeli citizens. That's the real discussion. And when you make the transition from a "ticking terrorist" to a "ticking infrastructure," when you transition from an operative tool used by a general security service to a policy applied by an entire state when it encounters terror, then we lose sight of the line between what's permitted and what's prohibited. There's a concept called "the banality of evil" . . . when you actually start to do it en masse, when two hundred to three hundred people end up dead through this phrasing of "targeted prevention," then suddenly it's already a conveyor belt.

If you kill the one who rises up to kill you, the main parameter is the level of threat—if I don't kill him, he'll kill me. But if you also kill the one creating the ideology which enables him to kill, then the main parameter is already not the threat level, but the intensity of the malice. But you can't kill an idea. You can't kill an ideology by eliminating those who preach it. I can prove to you that Hamas didn't become more moderate when Sheikh Yassin was eliminated. I can prove to you that when we killed Abbas al-Musawi [co-founder and secretary general of Hezbollah, killed by the IDF in 1992] and got [Hezbollah leader Hassan] Nasrallah [also assassinated by the IDF in 1992], Israel's defense status didn't really improve. So when we deal not with the one who is currently rising to kill us, but with the one who preaches, we're going to a place that international law doesn't permit, and where basic justice raises some very major question marks regarding the moral aspect; but I'm talking to you as a head of Shin Bet—it's not effective.

How many targeted preventions were there?

Avi Dichter: I don't know. Hundreds. But the test is not how many targeted preventions there were, but how many targeted preventions were on the person we planned to hit. Here the challenge is immense. Zero false identifications, which is a very significant test.

Who decides whether a person is worthy of prevention or not worthy of prevention?

Dichter: The Shin Bet provides the information, in most cases. The Army, of course, is familiar with the information. There's full transparency. It's approved by the head of Service on the one hand, by the chief of general staff on the other, and is moved up for approval by the minister of defense and the prime minister.

Are there criteria?

Yes. He needs to be a terrorist with deep involvement in issuing terrorist attacks, preparing explosive charges, building missiles, something that gives him some prominence. There's no targeted prevention on a Hamas recruit. By the way, this subject is covered by the Foreign Affairs and Defense Committee, by the ministerial committee on Shin Bet affairs, and in meetings with the attorney general and the state attorney's people. We don't authorize the objects there, but they receive the reports later. The executive branch is the Shin Bet, the Army, and of course the minister of defense and the prime minister. The control channel deals only with what has happened, not with what's going to happen. The control agency later receives a profile of the deceased, and then they know or can judge whether he was actually worthy or unworthy. But that's already a post-mortem.

Were there cases when he was unworthy?

Look, it's very hard to get to a situation where you define someone as an object of targeted prevention and he doesn't meet the criteria. He has to float very quickly. The problem is generally with those who might be worthy, and you don't include them, and then you find out you were wrong. You find out you that when you could have hit him, he didn't meet the criteria, and when he did meet the criteria, there was no ability to hit him anymore.

When do you include the political echelon, such as Rantisi and Yassin, for example, in the lists?*

That's one of the most severe mistakes people make, including, unfortunately, the political echelon, mostly abroad, when they try to portray Hamas or the Islamic Jihad as an institution which has a political branch and a military branch. There's no such thing. Sheikh Yassin was the Hamas chief of general staff and prime minister. There's no division there. He's involved in everything. Ramadan Shalah [leader of the Palestinian Islamic Jihad] or [senior Hamas official] Khaled Mashal are not political officials. They're deeply involved in the military aspect. I had very intense arguments with the Americans, who said—"look, in Northern Ireland there was the IRA and there was the Sinn Féin, the military part and the political part." I said, "Listen, that doesn't exist, not in Hamas and not in the Islamic Jihad. There's no difference."

The truth is that Sheikh Yassin was just a menace. That man is, to me, one of the most misleading people I've met in my life. When you first see him, you think he's the most pathetic person on the face of the earth. In a wheelchair, contorted, emaciated, hardly talks, problems breathing, Mother Theresa looks like a gladiator next to him. And this man is responsible for the death of so many Israelis. And more than that, he's responsible for the death of innocent Palestinians murdered due to suspicion of collaboration, whose execution he authorized. And always in code, of course. Not "Kill him," God forbid, but he'd always say, "Treat him according to religion . . ." and everyone understood Sheikh Yassin's terminology.

---

* Both Hamas leaders, Ahmed Yassin and Abdel Aziz al-Rantisi, were killed in back-to-back incidents in 2004 when they were targeted by Israeli Air Force missile strikes.

Always in lectures, when the Americans would say, "The late Yassin," I'd say, "The too late."

I gathered that one time you missed an opportunity with him.

Yes, listen, September 6, 2003, was, as far as I was concerned, my most difficult day as Shin Bet director. The most frustrating day. It was the day the State of Israel had a chance to get rid of the largest terror group we could have gotten rid of in one fell swoop, and it was a real missed opportunity. Sheikh Yassin was one of the people there. I'll call them the dream team.

The story of this missed opportunity begins with the story of Salah Shehade, who was really the number-one operative figure, even more than Sheikh Yassin himself. He was the spring setting in motion the terror process of Hamas in Gaza. I know Salah Shehade almost from my first day in Beit Hanoun. He was a social worker in the civil administration. I remember him walking with this clerical-type bag. It was our first meeting, before he was even a Hamas man. From a religious standpoint, he was more authoritative than Sheikh Yassin. Sheikh Yassin wasn't really a certified sheikh. He wasn't really considered a religious authority. Salah Shehade was. Beyond that, Salah Shehade was the one who really forged the connection between the Hamas and Iran, and with that, he caused immense damage.

One of the Shin Bet interrogators, Micha Kobi, said in a newspaper article that even Salah Shehade, when he was being interrogated, actually gave the Service almost the entire Hamas inventory list.

Ultimately, when they get to the interrogation, and it doesn't matter if it's Salah Shehade or Sheikh Ahmed Yassin, there are other rules, and some of them open up. Sometimes they even tell these things because they're bragging, and not defensively. Meaning, he's not in distress when he tells you about the attack where they murdered here, they killed there, they blew up that. He knows he's done for anyway, so he doesn't mind talking, out of pride. And sometimes he knows the information's already been exposed to us, and sometimes we give him the feeling that that's what happened. But I don't think Salah Shehade spilled everything. Very far from it.

Shehade was a very careful fugitive, and the search for him was a very difficult one, with lots of investment in intelligence tools. At some stage, after lots of "almosts," it was clear he was at home, that his daughter wasn't home, and that only his wife was at home with him. Under those conditions, we reached an agreement by phone, between the chief of general staff, me, the minister of defense, and the prime minister, and then we green-lighted the Air Force. The Air Force dropped a one-ton bomb on the house. Shehade was killed, but unfortunately our intelligence wasn't accurate enough, so there were collateral casualties. No one knows the final number, between nine and fourteen. We didn't know the final number. If we had known with certainty that that was going to be the number of collateral casualties, I don't suppose that bomb would have fallen with that timing.

I understand that Yuval Diskin was opposed to that prevention operation.

Look, with such an array of operations, there were always those who supported and opposed, and there are those who were opposed and later changed their stance. Ultimately, there are operations where you, as head of the organization, have to decide what the organization's stance is. Independently of that, the deputy can object and the head of district can support and the head of operations can oppose, or some other cocktail. Sometimes there are differences of opinion in the Army as well, and ultimately the chief of general staff is the one who determines it.

Yuval Diskin: I'm not sure the Shehade affair is an affair I want to talk about, mostly since an investigation committee was established which examined the affair in retrospect. I have a lot to say about that affair, but I was a main agent in it, I took part in that operation, and there were deep disagreements, both during the operation and after it. So, at the moment, I don't want to talk about it.

You have to agree with me that when you drop a one-ton bomb on an occupied residential area like in the Shehade story, it's entirely clear that people who are not involved are going to get hurt.

Avi Dichter: No, because you gather information. You check where people live, how many live there, who the people are, what the chances are. All these considerations were taken into account in the case of Salah Shehade, but certain houses were occupied, unlike what we'd concluded from the intelligence. But that's the risk of intelligence. If we'd only go for an operation at a 100 percent certainty level, we'd have no operations. Or very few.

So let's talk in light of the results. Children were killed there, innocent people were killed there. You're aware of what happened there. In light of the results, I'm trying to understand what's the mechanism that says you should go for it. Couldn't we wait and get to a place where it was certain he'd be there alone? With Yahya Ayyash, which you were also responsible for, you took him down with a cell phone. Even his family didn't know.

Dichter: Look, first of all, if you can detain the man, that's ideal. The success of Defensive Shield is primarily in the number of interrogees you could detain and interrogate. That's the classic option. But unfortunately, that's not always possible, and in Gaza it's almost always impossible, and then you're already talking in terms of "to hit or not to hit," and then you build the arsenal of names of those who are "hit-worthy." Now, if, in the case of Salah Shehade, there were the conditions to give him a cell phone, then he would have gotten a cell phone. If it had been possible to kill him with a hundred grams (a quarter-pound) of explosives on the head, we'd do it with a hundred grams.

Since Defensive Shield, we haven't dropped a one-ton bomb, or a quarter-ton bomb, in the West Bank area, because every place is fairly easily accessible to us. Gaza is a completely different reality. You have to adjust your tools. If you can end it with an 0.22 bullet, end it with an 0.22 bullet. There are those to whom we bid farewell with an 0.22 bullet, and there are those you can only bid farewell to with a one-ton bomb. Why? Because they were on the bottom floor, which you can only access with a one-ton bomb. A state has the ability to use a one-ton bomb. There's no reason why we shouldn't use it.

The problem is that you've got an ultimate need on the one hand and a limited ability on the other hand. You have to ask yourself when you should enlarge the bomb because the intelligence is too small. It doesn't matter if you throw a one-kilo brick or one-ton bomb at him; in the end you have to verify that the deceased is dead at the other end. Ultimately the deliberation is between killing him with certainty with a ton and between not conducting the operation. Now, you also check the collateral conditions. If you can, for example, with a quarter-ton, ensure you hit him, but there are ten kids in the room next door, then you won't drop the quarter-ton, or a hundred-kilo (220-pound) bomb. The attack on Salah Shehade would not have been carried out in the format in which it was carried out if we had known, from an intelligence standpoint, that that was going to be the number of people injured. Without a doubt. I'm telling you, the operation wasn't carried out when we knew his daughter was home. So, do you think we'd have gone for an operation like that had we known that his neighbors might be injured on such a scale?

What do you mean, "known, from an intelligence standpoint"? Is this your people, sources?

"From an intelligence standpoint" is Shin Bet intelligence, which includes everything. A whole set of collection tools—HUMINT and SIGINT and VISINT, what's called photographic input. A very serious investment.

And all of those tell you there are no uninvolved bystanders in Salah Shehade's area?

From all of those you analyze what's in the area. The Air Force states what the damage from the bomb is expected to be, you analyze, and come to a conclusion. You have to take risks.

Ultimately, does the prime minister make the decision?

Yes, not just based on our recommendations. By the way, that Israeli model is the exception throughout the world. There's no other state where every targeted prevention is authorized by the prime minister and the minister of defense.

Avraham Shalom: This one-ton bomb, which is overkill, that's defense stupidity, military stupidity, I don't know how to call it, but it's unacceptable that to kill the most important man in the Strip, you have to drop a one-ton bomb on a house where families with children live everywhere. That can't be ethical. It's not efficient from a military point of view, and it's definitely not humane. Justified? Not that, either.

What was your personal opinion about the elimination of Salah Shehade with a one-ton bomb?

Carmi Gillon: I think it was mistaken. Definitely when tested by the results.

Why?

Gillon: I don't think he was worth the damage caused to us later. Including the fact that the people who were holding official positions at the time are wanted to this day in Spain, in England, in all kinds of places. And the delegitimization Israel underwent. We can't be brutal. We can be cruel as well if necessary, but you have to employ proportionality and carry out a very, very deep accounting on whether to do it or not to do it. It's absolutely wrong that an operation like that, involving immense collateral damage, would end with a statement by the Air Force commander at the time, and later the chief of staff, about a slight impact to the wing.* That just turns us into neighborhood thugs.

The person who actually changed the policy was Ehud Barak during the Second Intifada. As soon as it broke out, he authorized carrying out targeted preventions via IDF means openly, in broad daylight. I don't suppose he meant to create a trigger-happy atmosphere. But as the Intifada intensified, and of course I understand the motivation and what happened there, we used that measure more and more, and it started to lose effectiveness to some extent. Sometimes the fear of the slap hurts more than the slap itself. And we started to use it a little too much. If, for example, I look at using the phone, eleven grams of explosives, for eliminating Yahya Ayyash, compared with a ton of explosives, then that's surgery. Throwing a one-ton bomb is saying, okay, there's a plague, let's kill them all. It doesn't work.

Ami Ayalon: We didn't look into what happens if, when we kill him, we've stopped terror, but if we kill ten children around him, we might increase terror. It's a parameter. You have to take it into account. In the Service we deliberated, for example, whether we should do it discreetly or at high noon. All these considerations need to go into the targeted prevention equation.

Targeted prevention is intended to handle the topic of the ticking bomb. Explain to me how the preventions concerning Yassin and Rantisi fit into this definition. They're not prime examples of ticking bombs.

---

* Following a reporter's question about the extent of responsibility and sensitivity a pilot should exhibit, Danny Halutz, Air Force commander at the time of the Shehade operation, replied, "If you still really want to know what I feel when I release a bomb, I'll tell you: I feel a slight impact on the plane, as a result of the bomb release. It's gone a second later, and that's all. That's what I feel."

Yuval Diskin: The question of what a "ticking bomb" is a very complex one.

Avi Dichter: The Salah Shehade effect created a reality where, in my opinion, we started getting a little confused. Criticism began about how you throw a bomb on a house in the middle of Gaza. I remember in the United States, someone asked me about it, and I said, "Listen, we know about your methods in Afghanistan; you threw a bomb at a wedding, killing seventy people, and no one knows if the fugitive himself was killed. There's no doubt our hit was successful, but this is a failed operation in terms of innocents, and the influence of that was very strong."

More than a year later, in that weekend of September 6, 2003, we had very credible, precise information that Hamas leadership was going to conduct the meeting they'd never had and I believed they never would. They felt they weren't managing to come up with the goods, that Hamas was starting to decrease in its terror manufacturing capabilities, and they decided to have a leadership meeting, a summit, which is a classic mistake for a terror organization. But we, the Shin Bet, actually live off mistakes like that. And on Friday we saw the operation start rolling. Intelligence started streaming in, we started to focus capabilities. And then, among the alternatives of places where the conference was supposed to take place, we saw in the end that it was leaning toward a very convenient house. Not an apartment building, where it's more complicated to make a move like that, but a two-story house.

And indeed, on Saturday morning, we gradually saw each of the leaders, Hamas commanders, we tracked them from, as they say, the bed and the mosque and other places, and slowly led them, under intelligence surveillance, of course, to the same place. And we saw all of them start to assemble inside that house. Sheikh Yassin was, of course, the most significant clue that the meeting was really going to take place there. So we waited to see when the Sheikh would arrive. When the Sheikh arrived, it was clear to us that our dream team was all there. The Sheikh and Abdel Aziz al-Rantisi and Adnan al-Ghoul (developer of the Qassam rocket, D.M.) and Mohammad Deif. I believe they were all there. Ten or twelve people, but the cream of the crop, the crème de la crème, the crap de la crap. They were all there.

And after such an effort of almost twenty-four hours, you finally feel the state of Israel can also get rid of a collection of murderers, but mainly prevent in advance a whole set of terrorist attacks. This group was responsible for all of Hamas's terror. And then suddenly I'm informed, "Listen, there's IDF opposition, because of the fear of collateral damage. The Air Force gave its analysis, and a one-ton bomb would cause collateral damage."

Listen, there's no country in the world that would deliberate under those circumstances, opposite a terrorist group like that, between a ton and less than a ton. Not the Swedes and not the Norwegians and not all those that teach us manners and decorum today. I was amazed, but the Shin Bet doesn't have its own bombs, and the prime minister ultimately has to make the determination. And a very strident debate began. Ultimately, after a few hours, while the meeting was going on, the prime minister was convinced not to carry out the attack.

I returned to the phone to talk to the prime minister. To convince him it just wasn't reasonable. It was a very long conversation. Afterwards I talked to the then–Minister of Defense Mofaz, and another set of conversations took place over another hour, and ultimately they said the Army wasn't willing to drop a ton, and not half a ton, for fear of collateral damage. The compromise was a quarter-ton, which was a matter of probability. The house had two stories. If they were on the second floor, the quarter-ton would kill whoever was on the second floor. And if they were on the first floor, the quarter-ton won't kill those on the first floor. We didn't know if they were on the first or on the second floor.

This discussion is already in progress for six or seven hours after the meeting started. This whole Hamas dream team must have really had a very strong Zionist agenda, to wait until we'd finished our discussions. Let it be said to their credit that they waited patiently. Then the bomb was dropped, hit the target spot-on, the second floor was destroyed, and the whole dream team ran from the house on foot. Some insist they saw Sheikh Yassin running away on foot as well. Listen, we made a mistake there. We just made a mistake by denying ourselves. Due to what happened with Salah Shehade, we paid the price with this dream team.

The dream team really was a one-time opportunity; there are no two chances like that in a hundred years, to very significantly damage

Hamas capabilities in terms of "He who rises to kill you." That's an opportunity where you have to take a slightly more generous chance, even if there is collateral damage. And it took a very long time to reach some of those who were there, like Sheikh Yassin, like others. God knows how much damage they caused us until we managed to shoot down those who were shot down. And some of those who were there were not shot down and remain active to this day. I didn't calculate how many Israelis were hurt as a result of the fact that the terrorist team was not destroyed that day. Who can make the calculation whether twenty people were killed afterwards? Two hundred people afterwards? Where would we change the decision in retrospect?

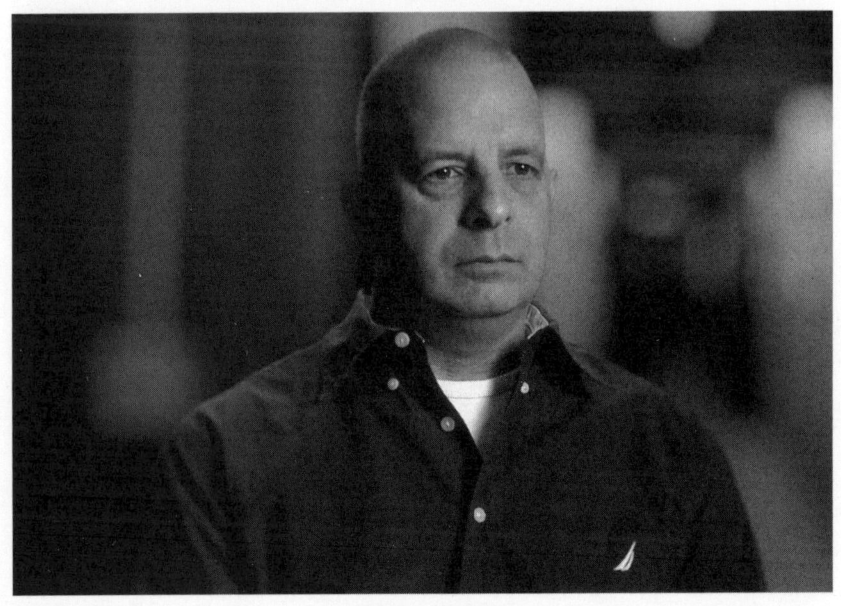

Yuval Diskin

Yuval Diskin (2005–2011)

I was born in 1956 in Tel Aviv. When I was five, we moved to Givataim, which at the time still had farms, even dairy farms. Even on the street where we lived, not far from Ort Technicom School, on Sde Boker Street, where the fire department was. That's where I actually grew up, until my army service. I attended Katzenelson School, then high school. All in all an okay childhood, you could say.

I'm the son of parents who arrived in Israel at a very young age. Mother was a nursery school teacher and piano instructor. Father was in the British army, and was severely wounded in World War II, in an Italian bombing attack in the Western Desert. He was left with a very large scar on his back, and as a child I'd gaze with wonder at that scar. It would always make me curious. I heard from him about the injury, about the war, about the British army, lots of experiences, and also about the period in the hospital. You know how a child looks at his father at that age.

My parents are very liberal people, to this day. Very open minded. I didn't absorb anything at all at home, from either the right or the left. Happily, I was not brainwashed in either direction, and I think that's something that has greatly influenced me to this day. It's very important to me to have the ability to think independently about things, and not through slogans. And it's also very important to me to have the ability to express my opinion—from professional subjects to ideological subjects. That's something I take great care with. But the education at home was Zionist. Lots of love for the people.

Lots of trips with Dad, who worked in Israeli water planning. He roamed everywhere in the country, all kinds of godforsaken places, and the greatest fun was always to drive with him in the jeep or the pickup.

In '67 [during the Six Day War], I was almost twelve. And I still remember it well, mostly in the context of getting ready and preparing the sand bags we placed in the entrances to the houses. We didn't have a bomb shelter at home, so they secured the staircase and a little space under the house we lived in, and you can say I remember that experience to this day. From the war, I mainly have memories of the alarms, and the kind of thoughts a child has about what war is. It's hard to say I really understood, but I do remember there was this feeling of fear. Our situation was really difficult. The Arab countries are besieging us from all directions, and we're in deep distress. And my brother, I knew, was tossed out somewhere in the Negev, and waiting out such a long alert period before the war. All kinds of flashes of memory from that period. And afterward the big victory and the great exaltation that prevailed in the country.

But more than anything, I actually remember after the war, there was some book, I don't even remember who wrote it, but I read it many times, and it was called *If Israel Lost the War*. It described a very nasty scenario there of what would have happened if we had lost the war and the Arabs had conquered the State of Israel. What the reality would have been like. I remember it really seared my memory and thought. It's a subject I thought about a lot as a kid.

I have one big brother, Doron, who to a large extent was my childhood hero. He was born in '48, the age difference between us is almost eight years, and my brother was always a role model to me. He was and still is a very Zionist guy. He's a man of machines and engineering, and when he went to the army, his dream was to get to the Armored Corps, even though he could have trained as a pilot. He was in [Shmuel Gonen] Gorodish's mythical 7th Armored Brigade in the Six Day War. It was a different army. I remember the closing ceremony of my brother's officer training course. You don't see soldiers like that today, dressed like that, polished like that. And from the moment he was recruited, he was already participating in wars. You could say he was born with the state and grew with all the state's wars, from the Samua operation* in 1966, through the Six Day War, the Battle of Karameh, the War of Attrition, and up to the Yom Kippur War.

The Yom Kippur War is also a very intense memory for me. I had less than a year left before my army service then, and I experienced a terrible feeling of missing out. Wow, how can it be that I'm not in the army, and not fighting! At that stage I was already obsessed with the army and elite units and volunteering and all kinds of things like that. In Yom Kippur, I volunteered along with my girlfriend, who later became my wife, in Tel Hashomer Hospital. We worked there mainly in transporting the wounded who arrived in helicopters, and that was the first time in my life I'd encountered scenes like that, wounded people, sometimes very severely wounded, burned. And despite the fact that you're still a boy, an adolescent, you somehow deal with it. It passes by you, so long as it's not really someone you know or someone close to you.

And then, after four days, I remember we received notice that my brother was injured. He was hospitalized in Poriya Hospital, close to Tiberias. And I remember we drove to see him. Even after the injury, he made sure that we wouldn't be informed of anything, because he didn't want to worry my parents. He was injured in a lot of places, but his serious injury was in the jaw. His jaws were wired together, so he couldn't talk. And I remember we got to the hospital. I remember I got to Poriya and I saw my brother from a distance. He was a curly-haired guy, and because of the triage in the hospital all his hair was still full of dried blood and his whole face was swollen from the injury. And I remember I saw him and froze in my place. I actually felt that I couldn't lift my feet and go to him. I had about a minute of being actually frozen. Then he walked over to me and dissolved the tension, but that's still an event I remember intensely.

In '74, I joined the army. I ended up in Sayeret Shaked, the Southern Command reconnaissance unit. I was already enlisted into

---

* A November 1966 IDF assault on the Jordanian-controlled West Bank village Samua, in response to a Fatah land mine incident two days earlier near the border. It was the largest Israeli military operation since the 1956 Suez Crisis and among the factors leading to the Six Day War.

the era of IDF after the shock of the Yom Kippur War. As a young rookie soldier in Sanur, I remember they took us in the summer of '74 to stop the first settlers in Sebastia. Not that I had a political opinion of it at the time, but I remember I didn't like the way we were standing there, rows of soldiers, holding hands. I believe they even took our weapons, and we pretty much took a beating from the good fellows there who were furiously eager to settle. It was a formative experience that really infuriated me. We didn't really understand what exactly we were supposed to do there.

After basic training, you could say I spent the majority of my military service in Sinai. I really loved Sinai. I love it to this day. Between '74 and my discharge, it was a relatively quiet period. There were no wars. Somewhere in that time we did have Operation Entebbe, but I didn't take part in it. Today everyone says they were at Entebbe. I wasn't. And that's it—I was discharged from the army in January '78, after a short period in the standing army.

I actually rolled into the Service with a very good friend who was in the army with me, Zvika Fogel, may he rest in peace. We both left the army still with "bubbles in our blood," with a feeling we still want to do something more. We weren't so interested in studying or university. And we were looking into all kinds of directions and ideas. And then I remember one day when Zvika comes and tells me, "Let's go to the Service." Now, the Service was not known to people at the time. We didn't know anything. The only thing I remembered was some encounter I had as an officer in Sayeret Shaked, in some operation in the High Mountain Region in Sinai, where we worked with guys from the Service. I remember the thing that most impressed me was the jeeps they came in.

Zvika told me, "Listen, let's go to the Service's operations unit." I asked, "What's that?" And he said, "I don't exactly know, but I was told that it's very interesting." Even coming in for an initial interview was a whole covert operation. There was no address, there was definitely no Internet site, and there were no ads, except for maybe a few mysterious ads in the papers, where you couldn't even know which organization you were joining.

They took us to some apartment in northern Tel Aviv, and we took all kinds of tests there. I made it to the last interview, and Rafi Malka, who interviewed me, told me, "Listen, you have good qualifications, you only have one little problem: you're color-blind, and in the operations units, that could hamper you a little." I told him, "Okay, I knew that, that's not news to me." And he said, "We'll send you for another checkup in Zamenhoff, anyway." They sent me to some old doctor, they gave me a book where you have to read numbers in all kinds of pictures. Bottom line, apparently I didn't read well enough, and they told me, "Listen, we're sorry, but you can't be in the operations unit." I said, "Too bad." Zvika continued on, I went back home, and a few days later they invited me back and told me, "We have something else to offer you. What do you think of going to Arabic language lab?" I asked, "What's Arabic language lab?" And they said, "It's a language lab where you learn Arabic." I said, "Okay, and then what?" They said, "It's an interesting position. Afterwards you'll be independent, you'll have a vehicle, your own work in the field, operations, and all kinds of things. But we can't tell you too much at the moment." I thought about it for a day or two, and told them, "I'm ready."

In the Arabic language lab I was the youngest trainee. I started at age twenty-two, a very long and interesting course, with a great bunch of people, and only then did I start to understand I was in the Shin Bet. First of all I find out I don't know Arabic. That's the first thing. In the language lab you actually meet Arab culture, you meet this world. Customs. Tradition. Language. It's a whole new world.

And then, after the course, there's a period where you spend some time in the field, in all kinds of places, and find out that you've been equipped with a lot of tools, but you still don't really understand it. You need more time, and mainly lots of experience, in order to understand that world. It's a different world. You come from a Jewish, Israeli, culture, and this is a different culture. I'm talking about 1979, many years ago. There wasn't a lot of modernization then. I really liked the scene of the villages and villagers and the agriculture and the view and the olives, and the different cultural codes, the hospitality. A lot of things that kind of fit in with all kinds of stories and a more exotic kind of worldview. But gradually, when you continue to go deeper, you actually say—hold on, I'm actually not a spectator here. I didn't come here to take a photo and go. I'm actually an active participant in this picture. What am I actually doing in this place? And then you understand you're actually an actor—minor? Major? Each according to his own worldview—but you're playing a role in the game of the conflict between the two peoples. And you, as a coordinator in the Shin Bet, have a role in that conflict.

Initially, you mostly live your security role. That's the side it's always easier to be on. I'm here to prevent terror attacks. For that purpose, I have to recruit agents, I have to provide intelligence, I have to conduct operations, and through that I save lives. It sounds good and it's also true. But the more you attain seniority, on the job and in age, you understand that life is a lot more complex. You see the reality from gutter height, not from university studies and not from newspapers, and not from scholarly articles. You see the most unpleasant things with your own eyes. You're part of those things. You understand the meanings of this conflict. The very great complexity of this conflict. Its very deep problems. More and more, you understand that it's a conflict over land, it's a conflict between nationalities, it's also a conflict between religions. A historical conflict with lots of pre-existing depth, where many truths and myths and perceptions are solidified, and become a new reality. And you understand that it's also going to be very difficult to resolve it. That an extraordinary leadership in this area will be required on both sides. That's apparently what makes it difficult. It's not enough that there's a leader on one side, apparently very strong leadership is required on both sides in order to change the course of history. Only leaders can really change the course of history.

I started as a coordinator in the area of the southeast villages of the Nablus district. It was a very beautiful area, full of olives and all of the outlying areas descending toward Jordan Rift Valley. In 1980, Moshe Golan, Musa Golan, who was a coordinator in our district, was murdered by an agent he handled, and they basically transferred me to his area. Musa was coordinator for all the refugee camps in Nablus, and you could say that after the exotic encounter with the olives and the view and the farmers and all that, I'm suddenly working in the heart of the Palestinian problem. In the refugee camps. Balata is the biggest refugee camp in the West Bank, and suddenly you see what refugees are. You see that there are people there, and as a coordinator, you study the population in a very thorough way. Residence in the refugee camp was divided according to areas of origin: those who fled from Lod, those who fled from Ramla, those who fled from other villages. You learn to know the last names according to the settlements, and then you start to search for what the villages of origin are, where they were located, what's there today. You can say I studied the Jewish-Israeli-Palestinian problem thoroughly through my feet.

So the first encounter starts to evoke some thoughts in me. But I'm still young. I don't think I had the ability to deal with this whole story yet. I still have the "bubbles in the blood" of the "army combat fighter" who comes to the Shin Bet and looks for the tension, the interest, the operations. And you really do a lot of fascinating things.

In that period, you have to understand, the Service has almost no technology. Most intelligence collection and most operations are based on HUMINT, intelligence you get from people in two ways—either from agents, or from detainees in interrogations. The relationship between a coordinator or a handler and an agent is a very interesting relationship. At the time they didn't really teach us psychology, but I think you become, as they say, a psychologist without certification. By the way, a lot of times when we tried to insert formal psychology into the world of handling, many psychologists failed there. There were sometimes big gaps between their recommendations and their forecasts and what actually happened there. I also saw other cases, but in the great majority of times, at least in my experience, there wasn't a whole lot of success there.

In handling, and in general in the coordinator role, you see people at possibly their ultimate low point. And you find out that ultimately, with people, the very basest instincts come into play: jealousy, revenge, money, greed, romanticism. Ego, of course. These base instincts motivate people a lot more than the more philosophical things. Ultimately, when you take a person apart, even someone who's the salt of the earth, flesh of our flesh, and try to explain why he did this thing or that thing, some horrendous thing that you can't even believe, you find out that it goes to the most primal place, the most base place, the lowest place possible. And that's how people are, to a large extent. Of course, people are a lot more than that, but that's the basic infrastructure. Sometimes we don't really like to admit that about ourselves, but I think that's really what we are.

When I got to the Nablus district, I was the youngest coordinator in the history of the Shin Bet. One day the Service director at the time, Avraham Ahituv, came for a visit. He was the kind of figure that inspires respect, he looked so mature to me, and very serious and strict in an extraordinary way. A very smart man. And I remember him sitting in a district meeting, and then he asks us, one by one, "What's your name?" and "Who are you?" So I told him, "I'm Yuval."

"And what's your job here?"

"I'm a coordinator."

"You're a coordinator?"

"Yes."

"But you look very young to me."

"I really am young."

And then he asked, "It doesn't bother you in your interactions with the population? Maybe you should grow a mustache?"

I answered, "I'll consider it."

The truth is that, surprisingly, even though I was very young, my biggest successes were actually with guys who were older than me by many years. Ultimately, it really depends on what you convey and how you're perceived.

I have to say that up to some stage in the first Lebanon war, I wasn't afraid of anything. But that's out of stupidity, not out of bravery. I still had this feeling that I hadn't done enough and haven't seen enough and what's the worst that could happen. I married young. My first son was born, I still didn't understand that I was a father, and I wasn't afraid. In the beginning, I'd roam around a lot. As a coordinator, I'd roam around even more than other coordinators. I really loved to not just drive around in a car; I'd pick up my feet and walk around the area on foot, refugee camp, alleys, godforsaken places, come in, knock on house doors, sit with people, sit in cafés, talk. I really liked that interaction with the population. The population was also very surprised that I don't just drive around in a car, open the window, and talk to people, but that I walk around, in daytime, in nighttime. I didn't think in terms of fear then. But again, it's not because I was that brave. I was just very stupid.

On the one hand, you feel that there's awe. But you're still an authority figure, you represent a country, you represent an organization they fear and respect on the ground. It gives you some sense of power as a young person, and anyone who says it doesn't affect them—it does. But with time, that noise slowly recedes, and you start to understand the broader situation.

In '82 I get to the First Lebanon War, as a relatively young coordinator. I joined the force headed by Gideon Ezra, which acted in the Beirut area before IDF surged into the western city, and we actually learned everything that was happening within western Beirut until the decision was made to go in. I joined more or less at the stage of surging in and conquering. The fighting was over relatively quickly, and I remember that one day the cease-fire began, and immediately, all the Lebanese are sitting in cafés as if nothing had happened the day before. It was just amazing. People sitting as if nothing had happened, you think you're not in Beirut but maybe in Paris, and in the middle of all that we're driving around in jeeps. That's some vitality.

And then came the story of the massacre in the Palestinian refugee camps Sabra and Shatila,* in the heart of Beirut. We didn't know what was going on. I only remember that that night, a lot of flares were fired. We could see it even from the base we were in, somewhere on the Beirut-Damascus road. We saw flares, but we didn't know what the story was. A day or two later, I don't exactly remember, I was asked to conduct a patrol in the southern area of Beirut, because until then IDF had not entered the Sabra and Shatila refugee camps, and we knew some of the senior members of terrorist organizations whom we were looking for at the time were hiding there. I was asked to study the area around the camps and see what could be done from an intelligence aspect.

Then we drove to that area, me and a few more friends, colleagues. And we approached the sports stadium area, at the actual border of the refugee camp, and recognized a horrifying scene. Initially we didn't understand what we were seeing, but we saw an endless line of people standing there. We approached them very slowly in the cars. We saw a really endless line of people, and the closer we got, it became clear that it's people in a state of shock. From their faces you could see these were people who had undergone a difficult experience, but don't understand it yet. I'm talking about a line that looks like the photos you and I saw of the Holocaust. And you understand

* In September 1982, between 762 and 3,500 civilians, mostly Palestinians and Lebanese Shiites, were massacred by a militia close to the Kataeb [or Phalange] Party, a right-wing Christian Lebanese party. In 1983, a commission chaired by UN official Sean McBride concluded that Israel, as the camp's occupying authority, bore responsibility for the massacre, which the commission called a form of genocide. The same year, the Israeli Kahan Commission also found the Israeli military culpable, stating that Defense Minister Ariel Sharon was guilty of "ignoring the danger of bloodshed and revenge," forcing his resignation.

something happened here, but you don't even grasp what. And then we started asking the people—what was it, what happened, what are you doing here. And they told us they're from Sabra and Shatila, and the Phalanges carried out a massacre there, and then they led them out of the refugee camps in the direction of the Beirut Stadium. In that period of wartime, the stadium became a very large PLO arsenal. Under the bleachers were big stores of weapons, and trenches were dug into the soccer field itself, which served as a training field for the organizations there. The whole area around the stadium was planted with mines, and then they led the people in front of them. The people there stepped on mines, got stuck, and then the Phalanges ran away and left them. We arrived there in the midst of this situation, and you could say I was in the first group of people who found out what happened in Sabra and Shatila. By the way, the investigative committee established later didn't get to us.

And then of course we contacted the Army. Sappers came and evacuated the people from the mined area. There were wounded people there who were bleeding. One of the worst experiences I remember was that some refugee who had run away from the camp took me with him, and we went into the stadium. The whole stadium had been previously bombed by the Air Force. All the bleachers were perforated by the bombs. He took me to the east side, I believe, of the bleachers, and on the way he tells me, "Watch out for all kinds of weapon parts that are scattered around there." And we stand, he and I, on the bleacher and look down, not far away, on Sabra and Shatila. And he tells me what happened there, and I can't grasp it. I don't believe him. He tells about an actual massacre, on a scale I hadn't heard of, certainly at that time. And slowly, you hear the people more and more, and you understand it happened.

Suddenly I started to understand and internalize that war is not this heroic thing, where you go and fight army against army. There are people who pay a very heavy price in that situation. I suddenly started to understand how better off we are, apparently, without it. But we're already there.

And gradually, the story was over. Actually, after everyone cleared out of Beirut, I was the last coordinator left there. I was still going into Beirut in the period afterwards. We had a very nasty incident there where we were almost taken prisoner by the

Lebanese Army. After IDF had retreated, a Shiite brigade of the Lebanese Army went in. During one of the patrols, we passed some kind of roadblock, one of our vehicles got stuck, and they detained us all. We were "half prisoners" for a few hours, in various interrogations. I was the only Arabic speaker there, so they thought I was the commander of that patrol. I was also, for once, on the interrogee side. But after a few hours they rescued us and we were out of that story.

A few of my friends who were in Beirut with me left before me, were discharged to go back home, got home, and, unfortunately for them, were immediately summoned back to Tyre. Some of them were in the building that collapsed there. I, exactly because I was left in Beirut, was spared their fate in Tyre. Among those killed there, as I said, was Zvika Fogel, may he rest in peace, my close friend, with whom I joined the Service.

In '83, I was summoned to Lebanon again, this time to the Sidon area, and once again I was a coordinator of refugee camps and a few more neighborhoods in Sidon. There was a combination there of Palestinians along with a few organizations that were unique to Lebanon and that we hadn't encountered before. Ain al-Hilweh is a giant refugee camp, on a scope we weren't familiar with. Very violent. There was very brutal fighting there, and when I arrive, it's already in stages where the camp is trying to recoup from the fighting. But then starts the period of violent terrorist attacks. Until then, I wasn't afraid. After a few incidents, I discovered that I was also afraid. We're practiced and experienced, and we were educated and trained, and we know how to carry out the operations very well, but suddenly you find there are thoughts in your head that weren't there before. I was already married and a father, with my first son, he was about two years old, and suddenly my friends and I went through a few events that were, as they say, very near misses. Roadside explosive charges, shooting incidents, all kinds of things that ended well but could also have ended differently. This was after the explosion in the first building in Tyre, and suddenly you really understand that it's possible that you won't make it back home. And what bothered me very much was what would happen with my son, with the kid. I hadn't had a chance to see him yet or anything, and it's possible I wouldn't return from here.

And then you start—I don't know whether to call it being scared—but suddenly you become more measured in what you do. It's a process that deepens gradually through the years. I don't remember anything I ever didn't do, if it was something I had to do, but suddenly there are thoughts that didn't accompany me before.

In Lebanon I started writing poems. My mother claims I started writing at a young age, but at some stage I grew ashamed of it. To this day she hides some notebook I wrote somewhere. But in Lebanon I started writing. It was a stage where I was apparently looking for a place to let out some of those tensions. Later I destroyed most things. I don't know, I was a bit ashamed. It didn't fit in with my "macho" image during those years. Stupid, but you learn over time. There were some things that I surprisingly found after a few years. There are these boxes that follow you from job to job, and sometimes you toss them in some corner and don't even look. And I found one of the only poems that survived from that period in Sidon. And that's one of the things I gave my oldest son, when he was approaching his army service.

What do you write about there? Why did you give him that specific poem?

I don't know. It was important to me to pass it on to him, even though I think there are ages when it's very hard to deal with those questions, that the military and war aren't really like they seem. That it's a lot more complex and complicated. And I thought what I had there was something that could express it a little, my experience of this thing.

The Assassination Doctrine, or Lunch with Chirac

"Rantisi is like Bin Laden."

Rantisi had already been added to IDF's "target bank" a few months ago. The Hamas spokesperson—intelligence reports stated—was in fact head of the military division, launched suicide bombers and planned to execute a mega-terrorism attack. Sharon's office: "Rantisi threatened to topple Abu-Mazen and to sabotage the renewal of the peace process." Political and defense personnel: "No Hamas leaders will be immune from now on, including Ahmed Yassin."

(*Yediot Ahronot*, June 11, 2003, the day following the failed assassination attempt on Hamas senior official Abdel Aziz al-Rantisi)

Yuval Diskin: In 2002, Prime Minister Arik Sharon traveled for a visit in Germany and France. By chance, I had flown previously as deputy Service director to inspect our security in those same countries, and Sharon talked to Dichter and heard that I was in Paris. He was still in Germany, and asked that I come meet him in the airport and join his meeting with French president Jacques Chirac. It came out of the blue for me. In the airport he took me with him and told me, "Listen, I want you to explain to Chirac what's happening here on the ground." I asked, "What do you want me to talk about?" And he said, "Anything you want."

And then we get to the Élysée Palace. First time in my life that I'm there, but there's a protocol, and according to the protocol, they didn't plan on Sharon adding another person to the meeting, and they didn't want to let me into the palace. Our VIP security unit, which specializes in situations like that, managed to finagle me into the palace, and then Sharon stepped aside for a one-on-one conversation with President Chirac, and I'm sitting there waiting until this protocol incident is over and they decide what to do with me. Half an hour goes by, forty-five minutes, and then they tell me, "Okay, matters have been worked out, and you'll sit at the dining room table around which the two delegations will be sitting." We walked into an amazing room with a big table on which, in accordance with the best of French tradition, all kinds of delicacies were displayed—all kosher, by the way—and I even found out they'd already prepared a place setting with my name. I sat there in some corner, Sharon sat across from Chirac, and they, of course, talked with translators between them.

In the meantime, they served the food, which was indeed very tasty, but Sharon couldn't eat because while everyone was eating, he had to talk to Chirac. And then at some stage I see Sharon look up and start to squint in my direction. I was sitting relatively far away, and the table was large, and he tells me, "Deputy Shin Bet Director, start talking already." So I tell him, "Mr. Prime Minister, I can't interrupt you." And he says, "Talk already, I want to eat. . . ." And then he adds, "President Chirac, sir, by chance we have Mr. Yuval Diskin, deputy director of the Shin Bet, here, and I want him to tell you some things about the situation." And then Chirac sort of raises his head, looks, searches to see who the deputy director of the Shin Bet is, and sees me there at the end of the table.

Chirac, by the way, even when he'd speak, would never look at his companion. He'd have his eyes stuck in the table and would speak as if talking to the table. I didn't even know how much time I had to talk, and I said, "Mr. President Chirac, I want to share with you a topic I know has been subject to a lot of criticism lately, here in Europe and in France as well. It's an attack we carried out against Hamas terrorists in the Jenin area who were planning a terror attack. A month earlier, during the night, we'd attacked a vehicle in which two very senior Hamas fugitives were driving, people who had carried out very brutal attacks and were planning more. It was a successful attack, and both were killed." And I told Chirac the whole story, and meanwhile Sharon is trying to make good use of the time and compensate himself for all the time the conversation had been going on earlier while everyone was dining. I told Chirac how four or five times, we'd relayed information to the Palestinians about those fugitives and they didn't do anything, and ultimately we received intelligence that enabled us to attack them, so we attacked them. There was no collateral damage or anything; they were the only ones killed. And I told him, "President Chirac, sir, I wonder what you'd do if a story like that happened here in France. Would you let them get to their destination?" And then Chirac said something that, as far as Sharon was concerned, made the whole visit worthwhile. He said, "Indeed, I have to say that from a distance of four thousand miles, things look a lot more simple than what you've described here. . . ."

And that was actually the end of my mission at that event. So beyond the joke about Sharon's appetite, I think a lot of times it was difficult to explain things in depth, including all the actions we took, and why that was really the last and only way in which we could prevent terror attacks.

Unfortunately, targeted prevention took on a volume that was larger than what it really deserved. Because targeted prevention came about to resolve for us, during the years of the Second Intifada, the almost impossible situation where, up to Defensive Shield in

March 2002, we're really not in control of all the "A Areas."* We respected Palestinian sovereignty despite the incessant waves of terror that originated from there, and, in fact, in those cities of refuge reside suicide bombers, their launchers, explosives labs, and all they're doing is preparing the next attack and launching it at you. You know that at any given moment, someone is currently being launched from Point A to Point B, or that in this or that structure someone is currently sitting in a sabotage lab where they manufacture the explosive charges. You have to actually act proactively. And that's essentially the whole idea of the targeted prevention. It's a tool that isn't intended to defeat terror. It's a tool intended to prevent emergency situations and brutal attacks that can't be handled any other way.

When we constructed this doctrine, we examined ourselves thoroughly, including with legal experts, in order to make sure that we were doing things that were in accordance with Israeli law and with international law. And as evidence, Justice Aharon Barak, former president of the Supreme Court, in his last ruling, which was the "Targeted Prevention High Court of Justice Ruling," analyzed in depth the do's and don'ts of what he defined [as] "preventive hits." Of course, you can't determine precise standards in a court ruling, but it turned out there wasn't a large gap between the principles that guided us and Justice Barak's ruling.

When you look at the intensity with which we acted, at the inconceivable number of threats we had to deal with during those specific years, at the number of citizens killed in Israel during those years, we acted in a proportional, balanced way, and used this measure only in cases where there was really no other way. And even then it was only after very comprehensive discussions—within the Service, between the Service and the Army, and opposite the political echelon. We dealt in depth with the implications, with questions of collateral damage and scale. I don't know any other countries where the levels of deliberation, restraint, and proportionality that we exhibited exist.

---

* In a classification adopted following the Oslo Accords, "A Areas" are territories under the civil and security control of the Palestinian authorities, consisting of about 20 percent of the territory of the West Bank.

Explain to me how the Yassin and Rantisi preventions fit into this thing. They weren't actually "ticking bombs" in the immediate, obvious sense.

The question of what a "ticking bomb" is is a very complex question. In Justice Barak's ruling in the Court of High Justice Authorization Ruling, which others called the Court of High Justice Torture Ruling, there's a very interesting discussion on this question. Is a "ticking bomb" only someone who is at this minute driving to the university and is about to explode there, or is it a threat that can last several weeks, even if it's not immediate, but the plan is real?

As head of the Jerusalem and West Bank District at the time, I addressed the Court of High Justice and gave my opinion. I said it was relatively easy for the court to deal with a detained terrorist, who I know with certainty placed an explosive charge in a bus station in Jerusalem, but he doesn't want to reveal which station. Obviously that's a very easy situation, and the court won't exact a price from you for the actions you took in order to obtain that information. But the situations we deal with are a lot more complex.

Let's say I don't know at the moment about the terrorist who placed the explosive charge or that he's currently on his way to the destination, but I do know that in Nablus or in Ramallah or in Hebron, I currently have a team of military Hamas activists who have already launched suicide bombers in the recent past, and in effect their entire approach and ideology and the instructions they receive are to launch the next terrorist now. I don't know about the next terrorist, but I know they're constantly dealing with preparations for it. They have a sabotage lab where they manufacture explosives, and I just don't know, at this stage, the name of the next terrorist and at what time or on what day he's leaving. To me, that's also a "ticking bomb," because that's an infrastructure that has only one role—not to make peace with me, not to conduct negotiations with me, not to discuss solving the problems in this or that neighborhood in Hebron, but solely to launch terrorists who will kill people in Israel.

We can't only look at the "pure and easy" ticking bomb, because that may be good in court, but life is a lot more complicated. In life there are also ticking infrastructures. The only way we had of dealing with this lethal bunch was solely through precise intelligence and all kinds of methods of sophisticated targeted preventions, not necessarily just the ones you're familiar with. Usually, with targeted preventions, people think it's a plane or a helicopter bombing a house or shooting at a car. We also did things that were a lot more sophisticated and focused and "sterile" in terms of collateral damage. Meaning, they hit only the person who was supposed to be hit, and no one around them. I can prove that we saved a great many citizens in the State of Israel as a result of this activity.

So let's suppose there's a ticking infrastructure. Where do you draw the line? Ahmed Yassin, for example, you can't say he came and placed explosive charges. He preached. He broadcasted ideology that encourages these things. Where do you draw the line?

Regarding senior Hamas members in the Gaza Strip, like Ahmed Yassin and Rantisi, there were very intense discussions. There were also differences of opinion within the defense system whether these are worthy targets. These discussions also reached the Israeli legal system—the state attorney and the attorney general—before the action was carried out. And the defense system ultimately did act, at least to the best of my knowledge, after it understood that it was in accordance with the law. Now, I'm not just hiding behind the law, because I'm among those who believe that even if the law permits it, you shouldn't always do it. I have to say that I'm ambivalent about the effectiveness of this. Some claim that hitting Hamas seniors in the Strip harmed Hamas to an extent that it wasn't functioning for a while. I believe the interval during which we enjoyed the effect of hitting those people was short. After hitting those senior officials, at the end of 2003, the beginning of 2004 was one of the roughest years in terms of terror in the Gaza Strip. I believe hitting those senior activists didn't achieve the hoped-for effect and didn't topple Hamas during that period.

Really, anyone who thinks you can thwart terror from a distance and win a war against terror organizations is making a serious mistake. I don't know a trick like that. There's no way to just stay put and shoot at them with planes, or with other means, and by hitting X people dismantle a terror organization or annihilate its abilities and decrease its motivation and cause the roots of terror to stop growing. It doesn't work. The only way I know, and that, too, is only partly effective, so long as it's not accompanied by a diplomatic course that completes it, is the way we dealt with terror in the West Bank after Defensive Shield. We reconquered the A Areas, we reached all the nests of terror, all the fugitives, the explosives labs, in a series of very complex operations and over a very long period. It's just amazing to see the dramatic decrease since Defensive Shield. You can see the data, but the decrease in the amount of injuries and terror attacks comes to about fifty percent every year. And that, to me, is a very significant achievement.

I was told that in the organization, you're considered the originator of the "combined prevention." Can you explain to me what that is?

I didn't develop the "combined prevention" doctrine. I helped it develop and I aimed it in certain directions and I had a lot of influence on it, but it's something that developed over a very long period in the organization. It started developing to a large extent when I was head of the Jerusalem and West Bank District, through an approach that managers in the organization and I led, when we understood we should already start to combine abilities at the employee level—I call it the "organization manufacturing floor"—not at the executive level. Meaning the workers at the end, who ultimately hold the "stick" in their hand, would cooperate, and we'd combine all the disciplines we have in the organization—collection from live sources, collection from the media, our interrogations, our operations desk, and our interface with external organizations. If we know how to approach all these capabilities per each individual mission and per work plan, and everyone is contributing their relative advantages in order to, for example, arrest a fugitive in Hebron, then those handling sources, those who know how to conduct surveillance, those who know how to process the information, and those who know how to conduct operations will sit together and think how they can succeed in this mission. And then each of them would understand that if he can utilize the other's relative advantage, then maybe a breakthrough can be made more efficiently than with each worker acting alone. It's the old cliché about the whole being more than the sum of its parts.

We managed to do it in a very neat process that started, by my assessment, twelve to thirteen years ago, and intensified greatly during the years of the Second Intifada. We constructed work processes, tools, and methods that in effect elevated the combined prevention into an art form. People leave their egos outside the door, which is the hardest part, and understand they're now being assessed by how they manage to get to a fugitive who we didn't manage to get to, by cooperating, without each of them trying to win the war alone. We took this thing and later applied it to our interfaces with other organizations—with the Army and the police and all kinds of other organizations. And here, too, we discovered that not only people but organizations as well have an ego. And we learned, mostly in the difficult days when there's a lot of pressure, a lot of terror attacks, to leave our ego outside the door. And you discover it's better that way.

Give me an example.

Look, I can say that almost every one of our war rooms is a classic example of the combined prevention doctrine. The minute information starts to come in, say, about a terror attack in progress, representatives of all our disciplines arrive, sit down in the same war room, and say, "Okay, that's the terror attack, what can we do in response?" And then the source handler says, "Listen, I can call an agent now, send him to stand at a particular spot, and see if the terrorist who we suspect is going to carry out the attack is passing through there." The SIGINT guy will say, "Listen, if you think that's the terrorist, I suggest looking into all those we know are his friends, checking to see if they have this or that connection." And the third one will say, "There's a taxi driver in his family. Maybe if he wants to get there by car, he'll use that taxi driver. Let's check where he is, and whether they're together." You see how this group sits together, and each of them throws out an idea, and there's a manager who synchronizes everything. Sometimes, if we don't have enough intelligence, we build intelligence hypotheses, and we verify and input them at very high speeds until we get to what we want, and then we start to incorporate the other agencies. Usually in a war room like that we have a contact person—a "matchmaker," we call it—from the military division in the same area, and he's already tuned in to the intelligence picture. We decide with him where to place the roadblocks in order to contain the suicide bomber within a certain sector. Simultaneously, a lot of times there's already a police officer who's in contact with us. Because if the terrorist crosses the Green Line,*

* The borders of the Green Line are based on the demarcation lines set out in the 1949 Armistice Agreements between the armies of Israel and the neighboring Arab states. Territories beyond the Green Line include East Jerusalem, the West Bank, and the Gaza Strip.

we can quickly "pass the torch" from the Army to the police, within Israeli territory, and the police can wait with roadblocks in a certain sector and handle the story. And for that you call in the operations unit team. This team has been called in many times. That's the team that deals mainly with suicide bombers who are already in motion. And you already call in the team so it can shorten distances to the presumed area where we think the terrorist is, so we can stop him before he crosses the Green Line.

There's actually a process here that works today without me or other senior managers having to step in. People see the information, summon the war room, all the disciplines converge there, and start to connect everyone almost immediately. It's an amazing process. I presented this approach, this idea, to some of my colleagues in friendly intelligence services in all kinds of places in the world. They were very interested, and often the question would arise: could it work only for us, or in other places as well? So, theoretically, I think it could work anywhere, but I think there's something about Israeli mentality that helps it work better. I call it "the Israeli chumminess," where there's no formality, especially not in the Shin Bet—even though it's a very formal organization, and to me it's the most disciplined within the intelligence community and the defense system.

I can tell you something I'm really proud of, that in the years 2000 to 2001 up to, let's say, 2006 to 2007, I won't be exaggerating if I say we managed to stop at least 120 suicide bombers, who were already armed with explosive belts or explosive bags, and were already on their way to their targets in the State of Israel. Some of them were arrested, some of them preferred to commit suicide at the arrest stage, and therefore these are operations at very high risk levels. But we didn't let them get to their destinations. Take 120 terror attacks like that and multiply it by the average amount of people hurt. Think how many more people would have been killed in Israel as a result of those attacks! I think it's a very great achievement by the defense system, in which the Service played a key role. And that's also something that many countries in the world today have come and still come to learn from us. Of course, we don't share everything.

I still want a specific story.

I'll give you a specific story. The Sha'alavim story. In March 2006, a suicide bomber leaves the Jenin area, and starts moving, crossing the whole West Bank, gets to what we call the "Jerusalem Wraparound,"* crosses the Jerusalem Wraparound, and starts moving toward the Check Point junction in Haifa's northern exit, and that's where he's actually supposed to commit suicide. We get this information in dribs and drabs, and start to understand first of all that someone with very bad intentions left the Jenin area, and that he's starting to move south within the Bank. Why south? Because at that time the Barrier is up, the enclosure area doesn't let him leave the Jenin area to the Check Post junction using the short route, and the area that was more permeable then was the Jerusalem Wraparound area.

He moves in the direction of the Jerusalem Wraparound. There are all kinds of ways to circumvent the roadblocks using illegal residents, transporters. We understand that someone like that is in motion, but since we'd just gone through a period of relative quiet in regard to these attacks, we were a little "rusty," and there was a gap between our intelligence insight and our operational action. And the terrorist had already made it to the Jerusalem Wraparound and started moving down Highway 1. He descends toward the Sha'alavim area. A bit earlier, we'd alerted our operations unit, along with a Yamam team. We actually act like one unit, and together they've already handled many dozens of cases like this in the past. We're essentially trying to locate the vehicle in which the suicide bomber is currently moving. As far as we're concerned, it's a guided missile that's currently progressing toward its destination, and we have to shoot it down. If you like, the Arrow missile that has to shoot it down is that team of the operations unit with the Yamam. Eventually, we get to Sha'alavim, we construct some kind of roadblock there, and we start to inspect the cars there.

Avi Dichter: Now, you have to pass between the cars to identify him. And understand, the person among the fighters who does this, and it doesn't matter whether it's Shin Bet fighters or Yamam fighters or cops, knows that when he gets to the terrorist, the terrorist will blow himself up. He's already on his way to a suicide bombing, what does he care whether he blows himself up in the middle of the traffic

---

* A section of the barrier fence separating the Jewish population from the Palestinian population.

congestion instead of at the destination? If there's slightly more accurate information, you start to receive it. They tell you, "Listen, he's got a red shirt on." Suddenly you know to look for something more specific. You try to look for a vehicle where you know in advance the passengers are Arabs. And finally you get to the vehicle. You know he's in this vehicle. What do you do now? You see people trying to momentarily disconnect what they know is about to happen to them from what would happen if they didn't approach that vehicle. What goes through the mind of a fighter like that?

This reality of dealing with "ticking bombs," listen, you're running into an event, you know it's a "ticking bomb," and you know you might pay with your life. Sometimes it's chilling, obviously. You don't know with certainty what the circumstances are. Is he wearing a belt on him, will he activate it, won't he activate it.

I'm trying to enter the mind of people in the operations unit who pursue a person like that, and know that if they stop him, he'll commit suicide next to them. How do they function?

Yuval Diskin: Look, the guys in that unit are very high-quality people, and I also think that during the operation, you don't have a lot of time to think, to even be scared. You're scared between operations. When you're inside the operation, I believe you don't have too much time to think.

And we've had more than one case like that. For example, the story of the terrorist from the Jenin area who had a Jewish Russian girlfriend, and they put the explosive charge in a kiosk on [Tel Aviv's] Allenby Street. We pursued him, understood he was returning from Tel Aviv to the Jenin area through Wadi Ara, and we're chasing after him, and in the end succeed in isolating a few vehicles, and the people in our operations unit conducted a chase there that I think even thrillers haven't featured a lot of chases like that, in terms of the risks they took along the way, until they managed to go around the suicide bomber and block him, and then the guys came over and started to search the cars. Understand, you're searching a car that has a suicide bomber in it, and it's very probable that you open the door and he presses the switch at that moment and goes up, and you're gone along with him. And then one of our guys, one of our commanders there, arrived and poked his head into the vehicle, and the terrorist took a gun he had and shot the charge to activate it and blew up the explosives. Our man, luckily, was not killed, because he only poked his head in and didn't go into the vehicle with his whole body. He was injured, but relatively lightly. That's really putting your head into the maw of the lion.

Later, we enhanced the tools and the methods in order to minimize the risks to the force. You can write thrillers based on these things. Also very brutal stories based on these things.

Do you talk to the operations people?

Diskin: Yes, we talk to them. I talked to them quite a bit during those difficult years. In general, the amount of operations we carried out during those years was very large. People accumulate both physical fatigue and mental fatigue. There's a lot of tension. In the end, there's nothing you can do, we're human, and humans get burned out on this stuff. I have no doubt that our people and those in other systems have paid and maybe still presently pay a price for those periods. Humans ultimately can't just let that stuff pass them by, unless they're not human.

In the case of Sha'alavim, in one of the cars we did manage to locate the suicide terrorist with the explosive belt or the explosive bag, I don't remember right now exactly what he was carrying, but of course this drama captivated the Israeli media, and they applauded the Shin Bet and gave us all kinds of accolades. It was really nice to read it in the papers, but within the organization, I gave the instruction to conduct a very thorough investigation, because as far as we're concerned, we should have blocked him long before he entered Israeli territory. And the fact that we stopped him in the last minute in Sha'alavim, we perceived it as failure on our parts. Not as success. Let's say that same suicide bomber, instead of turning on Highway 1, would have said—hold on, why should I drive all the way to the Check Post in Haifa? I'll go into Jerusalem here and blow myself up on King George Street, exactly in the middle of the city. . . . We couldn't have prevented the attack.

As far as the public is concerned, what's more dramatic than our good men from the Shin Bet and the Yamam catching a terrorist before he reaches his destination? They really are good men from the Shin Bet and the Yamam, and they did do a fantastic job, only we should have done it fifty kilometers (about thirty miles) earlier. And it's not the problem of those good men, but ours, the decision makers in the organization, who were a little rusty, as I said, and it took us too long to reach a decision to summon our special team, and to take all required action. That's why, in a lot of management courses, I also tell the people in the Service, "Don't believe what they write about you in the papers. Believe what you really know about yourselves."

What goes through your mind when you hear that a terrorist with a belt of explosives is on his way?

I'm going to surprise you: these aren't the really difficult parts in our lives. I mean, you're so adrenalized and so focused on the intelligence and the operation and the decisions, that that's the "aquarium" we're used to swimming in, and we feel relatively good and comfortable there. You're focused, you're sharp, you understand, you know what your toolbox is, you know which actions you have to take, you're tense because you want things to happen, and on time, and you hope you've made progress and made contact with the suicide bomber or with the terrorist where you wanted to. Of course sometimes, along the way, things don't happen exactly according to what you want, but the feelings usually come later. Whether you succeeded or failed.

I can't describe everyone's experiences. I can describe my experiences. Sometimes there's a transition from a feeling of high elation—if you really succeeded in your mission and you understand what was actually prevented at that moment—to a feeling of deflating. As if all the air has gone out of your body. Suddenly you feel you can break free, and then you become like a balloon that's been emptied out. You don't feel anything. And if, God forbid, we failed and a terror attack took place, and that has also occurred, unfortunately, it's a terrible feeling. You can't describe our disappointment, especially in cases where we had intelligence and despite everything, we couldn't carry out the actions. People take it very hard. Definitely the decision makers.

The hardest day I remember from my point of view in the Second Intifada was a day where we simultaneously dealt with six terror attacks; on the same day, in parallel, we dealt with six fronts, terror attacks racing toward our territory, in one day. And essentially, from 5:00 a.m. to almost midnight, we sat there, a large group of people, and just like the Dutch, every time we ran to plug the leak somewhere else in the dam. By the way, we ended that day entirely successful, but I can't remember a day like that in terms of what we went through in one day.

Six terror attacks were launched on that same day?

Six terror attacks ran at us in different directions on one of the hardest days of the Second Intifada. I remember the night before, Bogie was deputy chief of general staff then, I was deputy Service director, and I remember summoning Bogie here, we met in this room. And I told him: Bogie, listen, these are the things that are going to happen. We see an accumulation of very hot warnings here, and we have to be ready with a lot of capabilities and tools and units and so on. And we sat here and together we decided on the actual plans and how we work in real time and just conducted a general recruitment of all the tools and the capabilities, ours and the Army's, and in simply amazing cooperation that day, we managed to prevent it. But it was a really very, very stormy day. It's . . . I can't remember a day like that.

How can you even imagine something like that. . . . You watch that series, *24*. . . . And here, six terror attacks in one day.

Diskin: There are also other difficulties. When I was deputy Service director, one of the commanders from the operations unit, who had taken part in a lot of operations during this period, came to me and asked to talk to me in private. And then he told me, "Listen, Yuval, I'm in some situations I'm having a very hard time with. We're chasing after fugitives with a lot of blood on their hands, and in the end we find a terrorist like that in a residential house. Sometimes it's an apartment building with multiple stories. Two, three, four, in the city it can even be more. You don't always know where he is, in which apartment. You know he's armed and sometimes you know he has a belt or belts of explosives with him. How do you handle a situation like that? How do you start to get the people out of the house? And usually these operations aren't conducted during the day, but in the wee hours of the night, and down come old people, women, adults, babies, and sometimes it takes hours to handle an event like that. And suddenly there are people standing on the sidelines who have needs, and they want to rest, or want some corner to go pee in or do other things. With all of our dealing with these things, it's like you insulate yourself too much against what's going on in the sidelines. Against people."

And he told me, "Listen, I'm bothered by the feeling that we, with all our running around every day and every night, again and again, people get tired and stop being sensitive to little things. Ultimately,

I'm human. It doesn't matter if I'm in the Shin Bet, in the army, I'm ultimately human. I understand why it's important to do what we do, but you have to make people here wake up to this situation." Following that, we conducted a series of very deep conversations in order to tell people, "Okay, you have to carry out these missions, but don't be insensitive. Take a look at what's going on around you." These situations aren't easy, especially when they last not a week or two but months and years.

I can tell you that in the Service, we didn't have a story like the Pilots' Letter and the insubordination that took place in the Air Force. I've always been wary and asked myself, could something like that happen in the Service, where people would stand up and say, "We don't want to do what we're doing"? And it's not because I had doubts regarding the rightness of our path. It was very easy for me to justify the actions we were taking. Your question as a commander or as a manager is, do your subordinates really understand what you understand? Do they have enough tools to deal with these very complex situations in which they find themselves? And at least according to what I've heard from people, the fact that we all sat down, including the commanders of that executing force, and discussed in depth all aspects of the operation—not just the operational ones but also the ethical and moral aspects—and clarified and sharpened the "do and don't do" rules, this very process was very helpful to people in dealing with the very complex situations they were in. According to what I understood from a lot of people, the fact that they're a part of the deliberations and the dilemmas, and state their opinion, and also hear the decision maker debating on these questions, helped them deal with this matter and maintain their mental health in the midst of very tough situations and very dangerous conditions.

Usually, in hierarchical organizations, such as the army, a command "comes down" and you have to carry it out.

I don't want to make comparisons to other organizations. I can say that with us, that's how it was conducted and is conducted. Even in very busy, rough days.

When I was a graduate student at the University of Haifa, after I'd finished my deputyship in the Service, one day I saw a poster in the University about a symposium on ethics and war. It said there would be a panel with the participation of part of the group of insubordinate pilots, including that guy, Yonatan Shapira. I told myself, interesting, I'll go watch that. Now I'm an anonymous person, sitting in the audience there with a few more of our guys who studied at the university with me, and listening to the very fascinating discussion that took place there. First of all, it was a difficult experience. You're sitting there in the audience and hearing things you know a hundred times more thoroughly than those participating in the panel, because, unfortunately, a majority of those insubordinate pilots didn't even take part in those things they were opposing, but they portrayed themselves in the media as if they had their finger on the trigger who knows how many times. I looked into it personally with authoritative people, and it turns out most of those who were there, including their main speaker, weren't even fighter pilots at that stage, certainly didn't take part in operations like that, and all the dilemmas they described unfortunately didn't characterize them personally. . . .

I sat there at that debate fuming. Because on the one hand, I had a burning desire to stand up and say some things, and on the other hand, I decided to maintain my silence. When the debate ended, some of the pilots approached Dr. Shmuel Gordon, who was in Iftach Spector's legendary squadron.* And he actually opposed their behavior during the symposium. He did support some of the things, but said, "You acted incorrectly." His main message was that even if the Air Force control cell tells you you can shoot, ultimately the pilot is the one who decides whether to pull the trigger or not, based on what he sees. Therefore, he added, "I don't accept you shifting the blame to someone else, and I don't accept the path you chose—insubordination."

Some of the people approached him later and talked to him outside. I tried to approach him and talk to him, too. I came closer, and saw them already around him. I waited and heard parts of the conversation. And my feeling was that it was a few young guys who weren't equipped with the means of dealing with that mental pressure. And when they talked to him, he asked them something like, "Did they talk to you? Did they sit down with you and try to

---

* Spector was credited with eliminating twelve enemy planes, and is considered one of the best pilots in the Israeli Air Force.

conduct a discussion, to analyze this thing?" And they said, "No." You could see their hunger, with some of them. Maybe if they had talked to them and dealt with the situation differently, it could be that some of them, at least, would not have been among the insubordinates.

If there's something I'm proud of regarding the way we dealt with these very complex situations in the organization, it's the fact that through the processes of plan authorizations, decision making, we apparently knew how to discharge a large part of people's pressures, and to share. People felt they weren't just thrown forward to deal with situations, but that these are dilemmas that decision makers within the organization are also debating about in a very intense, very deep way. I'm among those who believe that the way is often more important than the destination. Because sometimes you can do something and attain the goal once, twice, three times, five times, but you're destroying yourself, you're destroying the organization, and you're destroying your people. So it's important that the way is one whose implications you can live with, sometimes more than with the results.

You've actually said that at critical points, ultimately what matters is the person in their entirety. Isn't that a dangerous thing? Because you said that every person is composed of the personal baggage he carries. You're not like Dichter, and the person who will replace you is not like you. Isn't that dangerous?

Dangerous, of course. That's just an indication why in places like the Service, like the Army, like the Mossad, like the police, you primarily need quality people. Quality not just in terms of their professional and operational abilities, but in regard to education and values and norms. Good people. Now, it's perfectly clear that mistakes also happen, and sometimes less appropriate people show up, or they're appropriate but don't end up in the situations they're qualified for, and then mistakes can happen. But because this world is ultimately run by people, and no one has come up with some other trick to manage things, apparently that's what will continue to happen in the future, too.

I'm taking your experience, of the guy who tells you—I'm getting burned out, I feel that my heart is starting to coarsen and I'm burning out. The preventions become a kind of method. The question is whether this burnout he's describing isn't dangerous, and

how do you refresh, because we're constantly conducting activity over there.

After my deputyship, when I was studying toward a master's at the University of Haifa, I had a very interesting conversation with the university president, Professor Aharon Ben Ze'ev, who's a philosopher who has conducted some studies in the realm between philosophy and psychology. I asked him exactly those questions, ethical, moral questions, and he told me one very simple thing. He told me, "Look, there's no way to resolve a great many ethical and moral situations. You'll think like this, the person next to you will think another thing, sometimes the number of opinions equals the number of people in terms of what you should and shouldn't do. But the best way to deal with it is to discuss it with the people."

And that's actually so simple and so true. When you authorize a plan in preparation for a very complex operation, you try to analyze all kinds of scenarios in which you could find yourself during the operation, and that's where the ethical dilemmas also come in: will he be alone or won't he? Will there be another person or two with him? Will there be more people with him who are definitely terrorists but I don't know their names? Will they be armed or unarmed? All kinds of very complex questions. Now, you can say, okay, I resolved it really quickly. . . . I authorized matters. People see, go, work. . . . But if you pause in these situations, and discuss and analyze and debate, people also see that it doesn't just bypass you. It's something that's difficult for you, that it bothers you, you have doubts about what to do in the matter, and they cooperate with you on that matter. It also helps them deal with it.

I've gotten through plenty of situations like that, and my conclusion is that there are no clear answers to many of them. What was right or what wasn't right. There are no "classroom solutions." There's no math book that provides you with some equation that solves these things. Ultimately, these are very complex human situations, and it's you and the situation. You're mostly dealing with counter-prevention, and now you have a terrorist you've been looking for for a very long time, who launched a terror attack against you where a great many people were killed. Several terror attacks. And now you can hit him, but he's driving in a vehicle. And in the vehicle there's another person or two with him, and you don't know with certainty whether they're members of his cell or not. So what do you do? Do you shoot or do you not shoot? It's a very difficult question. And in the end you have to decide whether, in our way of speaking, you "issue an 'approved'" or "don't issue an 'approved,'" and what is a reasonable or unreasonable price? I don't know if anyone has come up with any kind of answer to this. I can only say we've dealt with it a lot, including with our legal advisors.

Legal professionals can help here, but they can't solve the problem for you. Because in a lot of these situations, you're ultimately with yourself, not with the law book and not with the legal advisor and not with anyone; it's you with the decision. And there are no clear answers here. At least I haven't found clear answers. Maybe there are people who have clear answers. I've heard some people say, "Guys, don't quibble, if you've got him—hit him." I've also heard the other heroes who say, "No way, you don't shoot in situations like that." So I can't say where the truth is located. I can say where my dilemmas were located.

When you get to these situations, usually it comes down to one person and funnels down to him. He doesn't have the ability to stop and conduct ethical, value-oriented, and philosophical debates with those around him. In the end, as I've said, it's you and the situation, and a lot of forces are acting upon you, as the result of the command position you're in, of the environmental pressure you're under sometimes, because people expect you to make a decision. And usually they mean a decision that states, "Do it"—because that's a "decision." Saying you won't do it always looks easier, but sometimes it's a lot harder. And you actually have to deal with the full impact of these pressures, and there's no time here. A lot of times these situations last between several seconds and a few minutes, and during that time you have to process a lot of data, continue to track the situation, process all the pressures around you, and make the decision. And I say, apparently they still haven't invented a brain that knows how to do all these things in such brief intervals, so it's a lot of intuition, and intuition doesn't come out of nowhere. Intuition, at least the way I see it, is built on experience and exposure and knowledge you've accumulated, and on a lot of other things like values, education, the sum total of things that build you up as a human being.

And sometimes, even after you've carried out a "super-clean" job or operation—no one was hurt except the terrorists themselves—even then there are sometimes situations where later you, or at least

I, stop for a moment. It doesn't happen to you during the events themselves because you have no time to think while it's going on, but suddenly life stops during the night, during the day, while you're shaving, on vacation, everyone has their own story. You suddenly tell yourself, okay, I was in this situation, I made a decision and X people were killed, three or four terrorists who were definitely on their way to carry out a brutal attack were killed. No one was harmed around them, the most "sterile" you can get, supposedly, and still, when an operation like that ends, and actually successfully, you say to yourself, there's something unnatural about this situation. And that unnatural thing is actually the power you have to take from three people—terrorists, right?—but to take their lives like that in one second in that situation.

Where do you discharge these things? You personally?

I share some of these things with Etty. Not everything, because I'm not sure she can process and understand the whole situation, the one I was in. A lot of times it's mostly with myself. And I, personally, have two kinds of therapy. In recent years, I've gone back to exercising. There are days when I push myself into very high effort, and those are the stages where I discharge tension like that. I finish something like that, and I already feel a little more balanced. The second thing is I write poems for myself, usually poems about exactly those kinds of situations. That's my private therapist. I discharge a lot of those experiences and pressures there. There was a period when it was at a level where I would write them and I had a kind of ledger, like I'd walk around with the therapist right next to me, it was with me all day. When I'd ride in the car, when I'd be sitting like this, when no one would see, I'd open it, read it, sometimes write all kinds of things to myself, but that was my method. That's where I'd let out all these pressures.

Because the meaning of these things sits very heavily.

Yes. I'm sure that when I leave the job and have more time, these aren't things you just leave behind. I assume what happens to most of us is that we put it in some kind of closed box somewhere in the brain. You can repress some of the things or bury them in some corner, because otherwise, if you walk around all day with these thoughts, you stop functioning. I assume at some point I'll have to deal once again with a lot of more positive and less positive experiences I've had over many years here.

In the poems you describe the situations. . . .

Yes. My feelings about all kinds of situations, which are hard for me. There were periods where I wrote a lot and periods where it suddenly went dormant. It's some kind of internal need. It's the psychologist. Apparently my clinical psychologist is poetry.

Can we see the poems?

No.

Days of Disengagement

"The planned evacuation: twenty settlements in the Gaza Strip and on the West Bank within a year or two."

"This vacuum situation, caused due to the Palestinians, can't go on. Therefore I have instructed, as part of the disengagement, to carry out an evacuation, pardon me, a relocation of 17 settlements, including their 7,500 residents, from the Gaza Strip to Israeli territory," Prime Minister Ariel Sharon said in a comprehensive conversation with *Ha'aretz*, yesterday morning at his official residence in Jerusalem. "The goal is to relocate settlements from locations that cause us problems or from places we won't be in under the permanent accord. Not just settlements in the Gaza Strip, but also three problematic settlements in Samaria," Sharon added.

(Yoel Marcus, *Ha'aretz*, February 2, 2004)

"The director of the Shin Bet met yesterday in secret with the leader of religious Zionism, Rabbi Avraham Shapira, in order to prevent violence."

Yesterday Shin Bet Director Yuval Diskin arrived for a covert meeting at the home of Rabbi Avraham Shapira, leader of religious Zionism and of those opposing settlement evacuation. Diskin arrived for an "acquaintance meeting," and the two agreed that tensions should be decreased and violence avoided during the evacuation. The rabbi asked to release soldiers for whom evacuation is unconscionable from that duty, and claimed, "It's like anti-religious persecution." The rabbi also expressed his firm opposition to those pouring oil and nails on roads. The rabbi claimed the religious public feels it is being shoved aside, and Diskin replied, "That's wrong in my opinion. I'm not Shin Bet director for the left-wingers, but for everyone."

(Guy Mei-Tal, Haim Levinson, *Yediot Ahronot*, July 5, 2005)

Avi Dichter: When the subject of disengagement came up, we began to get information about intentions to carry out an attack on the Temple Mount. And an attack on the Temple Mount is not a new thing; we're familiar with it since the days of the Jewish Underground. There were reports on the purchase of a drone that they planned to fly toward the mosques. The purchase of anti-tank weapons, a LAW missile that was supposed to be fired at the dome. They'd started the process of purchasing and choosing a location from which they planned to fire it. Both those terror attacks were thwarted. And I remember driving to a meeting with rabbis in the West Bank, actually the more difficult rabbis. I chose to sit at their place and not in a neutral location, but in their home in Samaria, and I told them to take one thing into account: "An attack on the Temple Mount, in Israel—we'll know how to deal with it. Unfortunately, we already have experience with riots and so on; we can handle it. But in the Jewish world, in Marseilles and Paris and in Buenos Aires and in the United States and in South Africa and in other countries as well, Jews will fall prey to Muslims. After an attack on the Temple Mount, the Jews would just be subject to pogroms, and the blame for this will be on the hands of rabbis who didn't act, at least according to their rhetorical ability, to discourage the thought that the solution lies in an attack on the Temple Mount."

We understood at the time that right-wing nuts were talking about two ways to stop the disengagement: hitting the Temple Mount or harming Prime Minister Sharon. And once we conducted the intervention with the rabbis, we said that if it was effective, we'd only be strengthening the threat to the prime minister. I think that was the first time in the history of the Service that the operations unit was recruited to work on protecting the prime minister.

The prime minister traveled almost every day to his ranch from Jerusalem. Arik Sharon didn't like to fly in a helicopter to the ranch and always preferred riding in a vehicle. You try to make adjustments in accordance with the person being secured, and try to disrupt the routine, but between you and me, how much can you really break up the routine in the route between Jerusalem and Shikmim Ranch in the south? We activated our operations unit to secure the motorcade from the outside. Including using planes occasionally. And we invested in a lot of new, creative measures in order to give this bubble called "the prime minister's convoy" much greater security. The thought was that the closer you get to the disengagement date, the more the threat to the prime minister gradually increases.

You assume the job of Service director in 2005, three months before the disengagement. Arik Sharon has a close affinity with the settlers. What do you find there?

Yuval Diskin: I'm very disturbed by the environment around the disengagement, and mostly by the possible implications. So my big fear is where it could take us. It also introduces you to very hard questions regarding what's legitimate and what isn't. What is the Shin Bet's role in a period like that.

In that period, I had a monumental meeting with the members of the Shin Bet's Jewish branch. It was one of the first meetings I had immediately after I'd started the job. We had an evening of a few hours in Jerusalem. I talked to all of the people and asked to understand how they saw the situation, the period, what we should do. And I discovered there was confusion among the people. We approached some very interesting questions regarding the role of the Shin Bet in a democratic country, and later established a think tank that investigated what we should and shouldn't do.

At the same time, Moshe Feiglin,* for instance, is standing out in public with a megaphone and saying, "You should block intersections, you should do this. . . ." and so on. Should the Shin Bet deal with Feiglin or not? My answer is no. Why? Because he did it in public. He expressed his opinion. Even if it's not entirely legal, there are things that in certain situations are still in the legitimate outskirts of the law, and a democracy needs to have the patience to pay certain prices. Because if people can't let off steam, there'll be a very serious problem. So I think that in that case it's definitely not the Shin

---

* Moshe Feiglin co-founded the Zo Artzeinu ("This Is Our Land") movement, along with Shmuel Sackett, to protest the Oslo Accords. In August 1995, the movement initiated the blocking of eighty intersections throughout the country in an act of civil disobedience protesting the Oslo process.

Bet's role, and if someone thinks it's not proper, then there's the state attorney, there's the police, to deal with him.

I believe the Shin Bet should have dealt mostly with covert activity. Because if he's doing it covertly, apparently he has something to hide, and I'd better know what it is. If my impression is that it's nothing, he's just hanging up posters in the streets, then fine. But if he wants to cause harm, to hurt people, to harm regime infrastructures, to hit the Bezek phone company, electricity lines, to hit the Temple Mount, to perform acts that stop the diplomatic process, then that's where I, as the Shin Bet, have to be.

When Avigdor Eskin performs a "Pulsa diNura" curse ceremony before the prime minister's residence, do you have to issue an alert?

I don't believe in "Pulsa diNura," so I don't get excited. Also, I don't have to deal with what's done on the public level. But I do have to know about it, because sometimes it starts with events like this and switches to other tracks.

Were there concrete threats on Sharon's life during the disengagement period?

There was a certain atmosphere. I don't remember that we had anything on an operative level, where someone was really going to carry out an action. There was talk. My fear was that someone would veer out of control. I remember that on one of the meetings on the eve of the disengagement, then–prime minister Sharon said to me, "Listen, Yuval, all of you have to do everything to ensure that the country can keep on functioning." So I told him, "What do you mean, Mr. Prime Minister?" By the way, I take great care that my people and I don't address ministers and Knesset members by their first names. Always by their titles. It's both a matter of respect, because he's a publicly elected official and I'm a public employee, and that's not the same thing, but it also maintains a proper distance between me and them. The person who sharpened that issue for me was Ami Ayalon when he was Service director, and I identified with that very much, and I think today it's entrenched very deeply in the Service.

Anyway, as I said, I answered, "What do you mean, Mr. Prime Minister?" And he said, "Everything, do everything you can so that it doesn't happen." I told him, "Mr. Prime Minister, of course we'll do everything we need to do, but understand that there are things we apparently won't do."

He asked, "Like what?"

I told him, "Look, the intersections are blocked by a lot of people, not necessarily terrorists. There are a lot of people who oppose the disengagement, including even in your party. Some people oppose it, and they block intersections. So do you want the Shin Bet to start conducting surveillance on party branches in Netanya, in Ramat Gan and in other places? It doesn't seem legitimate or right to me that we do such things. We can't do everything. Some things we apparently won't do, because it's not democratic and I'm also not sure it's legal. And there's always the dilemma there." And Sharon accepted that.

The Shin Bet is one of the tools the state and the government have to deal with expressions of extremity, but this is significantly beyond its capabilities. I can deal with the most out-there, harsh, dark edges of this problem. Okay. But I don't know how to handle the public atmosphere. The atmosphere needs to be handled in a social context. That means dealt with by educators, by "spiritual" authorities. When those aren't there, that's a problem.

And if we're talking about people of faith, especially after the disengagement, there's a dramatic disintegration of leadership. There are no longer those great rabbis who would utter their decree, and everyone would fall in line accordingly. Today when they say, "Find yourself a rabbi," it doesn't mean to find a rabbi and listen to what he says, but find yourself a rabbi who will fall in line with your stance, and if he doesn't fall in line with your stance, then we'll look for someone else. . . . Meaning, rabbis are falling in line with the public atmosphere, and not trying to create a different public atmosphere. But when they stand facing their public instead of leading it, then they turn from shepherds into sheep.

For example, there are many rabbis within religious Zionism who think the insubordination story is not legitimate, and they don't dare say it openly, because they're afraid. I sometime read media you're not really familiar with, [not the] publicly published press, but by extreme factions. There's an online newsletter that's also handed out for free. It's called *The Jewish Voice* and it apparently expresses the opinions of a very extreme group of [right-wing nationalist] "hilltop youth" in the Yitzhar area, but not only there. And they reference [West Bank activist] Pinchas Wallerstein's resignation from the Yesha Council two weeks earlier. In the article, they supposedly treat him with respect and address the fact that he resigned, among other reasons, because of his criticism of the insubordination, and the Price Tag policy* that these factors carry out. And they tell their readership there: that's exactly what should actually happen. They say: it's very good that Pinchas Wallerstein paid the price and that others won't dare say what he said. There are other people who think like Pinchas Wallerstein, but they know saying it would be political suicide as far as they're concerned. And that scares me. It sounds silly, but to me that's a very serious crack in society. A democratic society where people are scared to state their piece, that could lead to problematic places.

What do you tell them in the meetings you conduct with them?

I was in a pre-military preparatory program in Eli in 2006. I faced four hundred people there and told them very harsh things about how I perceive Jewish terrorism, for example. I said that in my eyes, a Jewish terrorist is dozens of times worse than a Palestinian or Arab terrorist. Because it's a cancer in our society. There's no reason for a Jew to go carry out a terror attack. He has a state, he has an army, he has the Shin Bet, he has the Mossad, he has the police, he has all the apparatuses, and he controls this country. So why would you go carry out a terror attack? How do you even get to that place? A Palestinian, I'm not justifying it, anyone who hurts innocents, that's wrong, but you can understand where he's coming from. There's conflict. He feels conquered by another people. He wants his land. A Jew? How did you get there? And I say this openly. Unfortunately, I don't hear public figures in communities from which Jewish terrorists sometimes originate sounding that statement openly. Loudly. Not with insinuations and indirect, roundabout statements. That's cowardice to me.

We didn't learn our lesson from Rabin's murder?

I don't think we did.

Could another political murder happen?

Yes. Because I think Israeli society doesn't know how to internally handle events like that. It couldn't create a process of deep social

* The term "Price Tag policy" refers to acts of violence aimed randomly at the Palestinian population and Israeli security forces, perpetrated by settlers on the extreme right, in retaliation for any action taken against the settlement enterprise.

discussion that analyzes these things and tries to redefine the common denominators between sectors of the public, the lessons that must be learned in order to change these things. Unfortunately, it didn't happen after Rabin's murder, and not after the disengagement, which was an event that shook things up.

From our perspective, Israeli society didn't properly handle the issue of disengagement. Those who supported disengagement returned to their cafés, and, as far as they're concerned, it was a logistic operation where eight thousand or nine thousand people were displaced from their homes, and that's it. For those who opposed disengagement, whether they live on the Gaza Strip or elsewhere, it was uprooting people from their homes. And there was no dialogue between the different sectors in Israeli society. That's not a dialogue that the Shin Bet is supposed to create. The Shin Bet can't be in those places. That's a dialogue which maybe should be formed from the bottom up, from the people themselves. It's possible that political factors should create that conversation, but there has to be willingness to create a dialogue. To understand this was a difficult trauma for a lot of people, and to analyze it in depth, if we're really a people that sees itself as one people, even if there are political differences between us in this regard. And that didn't take place. So I think that at least our, the Shin Bet's, impression is that there are still a lot of people bleeding as a result of the disengagement, and therefore they would also apparently be willing to oppose future acts of evacuation in a much more significant way.

And the reason for that is not religious?

It's not religious, it's ideological. Because what religion has to say about it is subject to interpretation. It depends which religious stream you belong to. But there's an ideological matter here. You can't argue the fact that a very significant part of Jewish history developed in the West Bank. That's a historical fact. For those people, going back there was closure. And suddenly pulling out of there again, it shakes them up in a very harsh way. So I can't say what the solution is. I know there's one thing I definitely recommended, and will also recommend in the future to the government in these situations—to try and speak and negotiate, before taking aggressive action.

With no negotiation, if and when these kinds of issues are on the agenda, for example if there's diplomatic negotiation and if they discuss the evacuation of some of the settlements, I think we might reach very dangerous situations, and realize the lesson was not learned. I think that what was inconceivable then has become a lot more legitimate in many people's view in situations of returning parts of the Land of Israel, evacuating communities, settlements. Many people means tens, hundreds, who think it's legitimate. Of those, dozens might be willing to pick up weapons and take certain actions, and of those, all you need is one or two who would even want to assassinate. You don't need more than that. You don't need to anticipate thousands who would do it. As the threat of people having to leave their homes increases, we'll see more and more people, and not on the outskirts, supporting or joining actions which ultimately might lead to use of force—including against the army, including against the police—and this could also lead to another political murder.

A civil war? Professor Yeshayahu Leibowitz said the best remembered of US presidents is ultimately Abraham Lincoln, and the reason is because he said there were things that justify a civil war.

There are situations in a people's life where the option is either to split up—establishing the Kingdom of Judea and the Kingdom of Israel—or to go for a situation where one side enforces its opinion and defeats the other side fully and absolutely.

And if one day we do enter diplomatic negotiations where the price is evacuating the settlements, what's your scenario? What will happen there?

A diplomatic action, if it's enforced and they try to enact it quickly by force, there's no chance of it working. It will blow up very quickly. It's our fate, whether we like it or not, for the process to take time. I mean years. The optimists say two or three years, I think more. But I believe the fact that it will take a few years can help the process of internalizing it within Israeli, Jewish society. At least with most of the public.

Ultimately, living within a society, a community, is a matter of many compromises. The most extreme can't make compromises, so I think for the most part our discussion within the country should not be aimed at the fringes. The out-there Kahane supporters on one side or the out-there anarchists on the other side of the political map, apparently there's no talking to them. Why? Because usually those people are at such a level of brainwashing that you can't create any sort of dialogue there. But what's in between, the center, which is also spread out along a certain spectrum, but does seek the common denominator, that's where I believe the discussion should be aimed. And my claim is that despite the religious and ideological tenets, you can actually find common denominators and somehow find bypasses for those unsolvable problems.

As Shin Bet director, can you today envision someone who manages to carry out the step of evacuating Kiryat Arba, or evacuating Ofra, and for them to accept it? As a result of the dialogue?

Obviously it's going to be very difficult. It depends to a large extent on when it happens and what the situation is.

But the feeling is that the more time goes by, it just causes radicalization. At the moment, it seems they're becoming more and more extreme, including statements referring to burning mosques.

One of the things I don't feel comfortable with is when I see the group suspected of burning down a mosque. That's a bunch of pretty pathetic punks, at least in my view. If those are the people dictating terms to us as a country, this big, strong country called the State of Israel, if they're the ones ultimately determining what happens, and they're the ones dictating the rabbis' agenda—what they say and what they don't dare say—then we're doomed. I think we all have to sober up a little. All of us. Including the Shin Bet, in this regard. There's no way that group will dictate the state's actions. Just like the state shouldn't accept that some group of Palestinian punks or terrorists would be those who determine whether a peace treaty does or doesn't happen.

The Hamas Coup:* We Didn't Believe It Would All Be Over in a Week. Neither Did They.

"Hamastan."

"Bloodbath in the Gaza Strip: Hamas forces control all areas following battles which claimed another 24 casualties."

(*Yediot Ahronot*, June 14, 2007)

* In June 2007, after a short military conflict, Hamas fighters took control of the Gaza strip, ousting rival Fatah officials. The battle resulted in the dissolution of the Palestinian unity government, leaving Gaza in the hands of Hamas, while the Fatah-led Palestinian National Authority maintained control of the West Bank.

Yuval Diskin: The Service is sometimes perceived, mostly by our colleagues, as an organization that sees everything "through a drinking straw," and some have said "through a keyhole." Some have defined us as a tactical, micro-tactical organization. Even though I can tell you, from discussions at the more significant decision crossroads, definitely in the last decade, that I've also seen the organizations that consider themselves big strategists, when they come to the dramatic decision-making crossroads, sit down with us and with other agencies, and their recommendations turn out to be completely contrary to the course of history. In contrast, our "keyhole" organization, in spite of everything, was able, in the moment of truth, to put out a recommendation which proved itself later on.

When I commenced my job, I found myself repeatedly conducting very complex discussions with the prime minister or in another forum, when on the way there I have to prepare myself, between the phone calls, the fatigue, the pressure. I told myself there was no reason for it to happen like that. I can take the professional people within the organization and build a unit here which can provide this thing in a better way. We put together all the research components that were spread out in the Service in all kinds of areas, established one unit, and beside it we also established a unit responsible for integrating recommendations for positions and policy by the Service to the political echelon, which is one of our areas of responsibility according to the Shin Bet Law. I believe today we do it much better than in the past, much more professionally and also much more responsibly.

Does the research unit let you anticipate large processes?

Good question. That's our biggest challenge. We always make a distinction between situational surprises, to use a professional term, and basic surprises. A situational surprise is some tactical event that happened and I didn't manage to predict it. A basic surprise is a dramatic turn of events for which I had no indicators or ability to provide advance warning. By the nature of things, the whole predictive field in research is complex, because that's already prophecy. And usually we lean on past experience and hope the future will unfold similarly. Today we try to develop more innovative models and more sensitive sensors, in order to really be able to monitor dramatic changes. I can say we have yet to go through a real, major test.

In my period as Service director, there were two events like that. One was the Hamas victory in the January 2006 elections, and the second was the coup that Hamas carried out in the Gaza Strip in June 2007. I'd define both of those as events after which we carried out investigations in order to examine ourselves and the quality of predictions we handed in to the political echelon. Actually, for the first event, the Hamas win in the elections, we were pretty much in the right direction. It wasn't as sharp as I'd like us to be on that matter, but I can say I sat with Prime Minister Sharon on the eve of his trip to the UN, after the disengagement, and it was clear that he was going to meet senior American administration officials there. I told him, "Mr. Prime Minister, you have to convince them not to apply pressure on us to carry out elections in the Authority. That has to be taken off the agenda, because I don't like the direction it's going in." I thought I'd convinced him, but later, probably due to heavy pressure applied on him by the [George W. Bush] administration, he went with the election thing. We anticipated Hamas would attain significant achievements in the elections, but we didn't anticipate the scale of the achievement. I have to say that we could have done better there, in my estimation.

At the moment it might sound like an excuse, but one of the things that makes it very difficult in general in the Palestinian front to forecast election results, for example, is the amount of undecided voters. In initial surveys, you get a picture that tells you what about fifty or sixty percent of the public will do, but forty or fifty percent of the public define themselves as undecided voters, or refuse to even say how they're voting. So, if I discount that limitation—we weren't far, but we weren't close enough.

Regarding what happened in June 2007, the Hamas coup in the Gaza Strip, it wasn't a basic surprise, because we'd seen how Hamas was in effect gradually gaining control over the Gaza Strip, and we reported it constantly, and it was clear to us that Fatah was gradually disappearing there. On the other hand, when the chain of events started that week, we still didn't see it going toward a total, absolute coup. After two or three days, we already understood that. But I have to say that we can state with certainty that Hamas also did not intend to carry out a coup yet. When they started applying pressure, they saw that the whole thing was coming apart, and then it was a local decision by some senior members in the local branch of Hamas, without the agreement of their superiors, and no doubt without the agreement of those in Damascus. So everyone was surprised, including military Hamas leadership abroad. So it's not exactly a basic surprise, because it's not something that knocked our socks off or that we didn't foresee at all. We understood very well what was going on, but we didn't believe they'd finish the whole thing in a week.

Avi Dichter: The event of Hamas's military coup is on a scale without any precedent. Think about it, sixteen thousand [Palestinian National Authority] security personnel in Gaza in June 2007; within three days they lose the Gaza Strip, but mainly all their assets, the archive. Do you know what that means, the archive of an entire organization passes, as is, into the hands of Hamas? Think about it, their [version of] Shin Bet transfers its archive, their Mossad transfers its archive, the police transfers its archive . . . what losers. I don't know how to define it, just lack of leadership. When in June 2007, none of the security apparatus commanders in Gaza are in Gaza. You understand, that's a total lack of faith of every command level in the level above it. They lost Gaza. Lost it because they didn't care about themselves, because of considerations of "every man for himself." I come first, and then the state or the agency.

Yuval Diskin: In the middle of 2007, after the Hamas coup in the Gaza Strip, the Palestinian Authority in the West Bank does almost nothing, is incapable of functioning. Not as a government and not as security apparatuses or a defense system. The field is actually controlled by two factors—IDF and the fugitives. When IDF is present, the fugitives hide. When IDF is not around, the fugitives are in control. The whole territory is in a state of total anarchy, with every bully with a weapon actually enforcing a reign of terror over the neighborhood, the city, the village. And we recognize that we have more than five hundred fugitives from all kinds of Fatah sectors and factions in that territory who are actually responsible for that anarchy, and occasionally for launching terror attacks. We also understand that it'll take a very long time until we get our hands on every one of them. We also tried a few times to offer the Palestinians the option of entering into an agreement where we would enable the fugitives to live securely with certain limitations, subject to them leaving the cycle of terror and handing over their weapons to the Palestinian security apparatuses. We looked for the right timing, when we could leverage it and turn it into as sweeping an action as possible.

The Hamas coup in the Gaza Strip came along, and, as they say, every cloud has a silver lining, because the coup in the Strip made the Authority in the West Bank come to its senses, and understand that if they don't come to their senses now, Hamas will also take the West Bank from them. That's how they felt, and they wanted to take control of the territory. [Palestinian Authority Prime Minister Salam] Fayyad really wanted to do things, but they understood they didn't have the capabilities to deal with these fugitives because these were actually their friends, their collaborators, the Fatah people. They had difficulties enforcing the law upon them and detaining them, interrogating them. And then we approached them with this offer. We also talked with the heads of the apparatuses. I talked with Fayyad. And we offered them the opportunity to enter this course of action. We said—let's start group by group. We'll decide who enters this agreement, and if we see every time that it's working, we take it further. We'll include more groups. Those who will really fulfill the conditions we've set within the time frames we've set, we'll give them more rights until they can normalize their lives, even though we made it clear this wasn't a pardon. Legally, we could, at any given moment, exercise the full extent of the law against those who carried out terror attacks and so on. It was examined by legal professionals and also by the state attorney and by everyone. And they did actually start this course of action. Initially there was a great amount of suspicion, but gradually more fugitives started to join in, and they saw that really, nothing happened to them, so others also wanted in, and the ball started rolling and gathered momentum.

Two and a half years after this step, about 450 of these 500 fugitives exited the cycle of terror. There were little missteps. This agreement survived Operation Cast Lead,* which we thought would shake it up due to Palestinian solidarity. Survived it in a way that was even better than good. Some of the fugitives who violated the terms—a handful, not many—were arrested and paid the price. Without that

---

* A three-week Israeli-Palestinian battle in the Gaza Strip in December 2008 and January 2009, sparked by the firing of rockets into Israel and smuggling of weapons into Gaza.

agreement, we'd still be chasing those same five hundred fugitives to this day. By the way, even the fifty others who aren't a part of the agreement, the great majority of them are sitting quietly because they want to give themselves the opportunity of joining the agreement. An incentive was formed here, because you created some kind of light at the end of the tunnel. When there's light, there's a purpose, there's hope, there's also a chance of changing courses of action. When people don't see any light around them, then their only path is to continue with what they're doing.

Thanks to the agreement, the Authority gradually succeeded in re-establishing the law. Security was returned to the Palestinian residents in cities in the West Bank, and both sides benefited. We benefited on a large scale, and the Palestinians benefited on an even larger scale. Despite that, the agreement is still fragile. It's not something irreversible. If certain situations occur, we might see this agreement fall apart. So both sides have major interest in maintaining it and making sure it succeeds, and everyone understand it's a very crucial key to success and to the relative quiet in the West Bank. I believe it's a crucial terror-thwarting action, different in its approach from the actions we're usually familiar with. You could take it from the small scale to the political level. On the political level, too, if you don't create purpose and hope, it's very hard to resolve conflicts.

When you decide, for example, to recommend that someone merits targeted prevention, do you also use political considerations?

There were periods when we didn't do it so well, because we were very overloaded, but I believe one of the things included in our duty in regard to the political echelon is analyzing in a far-reaching way the implications of an operation before it's carried out. To come and say to the political echelon, "Listen, I've got the capability to do a certain thing, but I'm going to present to you several possible scenarios of what could happen as a consequence. It could succeed from this aspect, it could fail from that aspect, you might evoke angry reactions from this or that country, there might be public criticism, it's possible that Abu-Mazen will decide to freeze negotiations with Israel. . . ." Because if the operation led to complications or failed, before they come and ask why the prime minister or the minister of defense didn't ask this or that question when he authorized a certain plan, I think it's necessary to check whether we, the heads of agencies, presented all these things to them. Because if we don't present the whole picture to him, the prime minister, with all his duties and within the time at his disposal to authorize things, could never ask all the questions. So it's part of your integrity and professionalism as the head of an organization to come and present the other side of the picture as well, even if you really want to carry out the operation.

One of the problems of the political echelon, all over the world, is that they usually really like binary options. They don't like you to come to them with three or four alternatives. They want you to tell them 0 or 1. "Do" or "don't do." When you present them with four alternatives, it takes time, they need to analyze them, read them, think. Almost all prime ministers prefer not to deal with too many alternatives. Come with a binary option: 0 or 1. "Just tell me, and we're done." That's the reason why I'm among those who think that beside the prime minister there must be a staff that can create those options for him. If you like, the National Security Council. At the moment it exists in theory, but doesn't really do these things.

And how does the political echelon treat your assessments?

Look, I don't like to grade myself or the organization. I can honestly say that we, in the areas we're responsible for or tangential to, have a very large influence on the political echelon. We don't do it "up front." Even after we've exerted influence, we don't run and reveal it in the press. What's important to me is that we were a good influence in the right direction. People, including those who don't like us, appreciate us as a discreet and professional organization. We do it a lot of times in places civilians would be surprised by if they knew we were there. But we've dismantled quite a few mines in recent years in the State of Israel.

Does it bother you when disagreements with the head of state are exposed?

Yes. I, for example, can say that I was wrong when, after the Second Lebanon War, I protested the way the government dealt with Israeli citizens in the north. I didn't go to the media with it, but I appeared in a certain forum outside of the Service, which was supposed to be closed to the media, and I should have anticipated it would leak from there. I voiced criticism. During that event, I was apparently under the impression of my personal experiences of all kinds of things that happened in that period, and, as they say, I "let loose" that criticism. And I think I shouldn't have done it. I think it's not right that a Service director, a chief of general staff, the chief of police, the head of Mossad, will come out with public criticism against the political echelon. Not because I'm submissive when dealing with the political echelon. I think that's just not a correct relationship between public employees and publicly elected officials. Obviously you, as a member of the media, have a hard time with that.

I have a hard time with that as a citizen. Because you, supposedly, represent me. You're my representative. You were appointed by the prime minister, but you protect me, and I trust you as a citizen a lot more than I trust the political echelon. Because the political echelon, one day it's here and the next day it's there, and you're supposedly the professional echelon that serves me, and I want to hear you. If you think mistakes are being made, I want to hear it.

I understand, and I can identify with your feelings. Because if I was sitting in the citizen's seat, I, too, would be very curious to know what the Shin Bet director is thinking and what the chief of general staff is thinking about the functionality or the decision making or our performance in regard to this or that issue. And yet I still think it's not right for it to happen in that way. I was appointed by publicly elected officials, and I think my criticism should take place between me and them, and not over the newspaper pages or TV channels.

You said you'd dismantled quite a few mines. Can you give me a concrete example?

I'll take it to a place where it might seem strange to you or to people that the Shin Bet even deals with it—the subject of privatization in Israel. It turns out the Shin Bet does have something to say on the subject, because what is it we're privatizing? Usually you privatize national infrastructures that are very important to the country. And today there are international crime organizations in the world and countries that have an interest in taking control of infrastructures in order to have the ability to dramatically influence all kinds of things. Sometimes, if you dig deep in regard to the person who's going to purchase the company, behind him you discover a country or a superpower that wants, for example, to control the global energy market, through various shell companies, or oligarchs that represent it, so you need an organization that's able to examine it. There were a few cases of "almost" where, if we hadn't been there, you would have found factors that you really wouldn't want to see in control of the privatized infrastructures in the State of Israel. We did a very thorough job, and following that, de facto changes have taken place in the process, and I hope de jure changes will soon follow. It's something that in the past, the Shin Bet didn't even consider dealing with.

When you come to a prime minister, you're aware of who you're facing. Ehud Olmert isn't the same as Benjamin Netanyahu, and Ehud Olmert isn't the same as Ariel Sharon. Does the Service's recommendation change in accordance with the understanding of who the prime minister is and which opinion he represents?

I can't say that I don't think about it sometimes, but I really try not to let it disturb me. One of the things I think we excel at as an organization is our ability to state our professional opinion unsparingly, even if it doesn't look nice to whomever and even if, in regard to certain issues, it could bring on a clash, which has happened in recent years. The bottom line is, although those weren't easy situations, the political echelon appreciates you for saying what you think and not what they want to hear.

Ami Ayalon: During Yuval Diskin's term, there was a case where the media reported that the Shin Bet director reported something and the prime minister stopped him and prevented him from reporting signs of moderation in Hamas. I thought that was unequivocally part of a Shin Bet director's role. I thought a prime minister can't prevent a Shin Bet director from making a report like that. No one is allowed to prevent cabinet members from hearing every opinion.

When you say that Hamas is showing initial signs of willingness to negotiate . . .

Yuval Diskin: That's a professional opinion. I have no problem, if I'm giving a professional opinion that states: I believe Hamas—for example, I'm saying something hypothetical at the moment—wants to reach a true, just peace agreement with Israel, and the political echelon says: I'm not even willing to hear about Hamas, I have no problem saying that because that's not a criticism of the political echelon. But to say, for example, the prime minister and this or that minister made incorrect decisions on this or that matter, that's not my job. You, as the public, can grade them on Election Day or in the criticism you write about them in the papers.

You've worked with three prime ministers. How does a Service director maintain independence without getting swept up in "the spirit of the commander," as it's called?

Diskin: It's not easy, but it ultimately goes back to your personal resilience as the head of an organization. If you have enough personal resilience, and if you also receive similar appreciation from the political echelon, then you can deal with these situations. If you're not like that, then apparently you'll go flying in the wind every time the political echelon blows on you.

Were there crossroads where you felt the political echelon was aspiring to a particular policy from you that you didn't feel wholehearted about? Did you face situations like that?

Yes. Quite a few. There were situations where I felt or got the impression that the political echelon was pulling towards places that to the best of my understanding were dangerous, or might lead to complications. And I also had the understanding that no serious discussion had been conducted on the matter. And there were cases where I openly opposed the political echelon, to the extent that things stopped and there was even a crisis later, but in my view things were prevented in that way. I discovered that politicians have much thicker skin. . . . That's apparently one of the capabilities required to be a politician. They have an amazing ability to get through this thing. There could be stress, a crisis, a month goes by, two months, three, and sometimes it's as if nothing happened. Sometimes there's also a residue.

Is it always in the direction of restraining, or also in the opposite direction?

The more dramatic examples are in the direction where you have to restrain. To prod into action is usually easier. Restraining is usually the stage where you have to oppose movement by the political echelon. Not to push it forward but to oppose it. It's a stage that requires lots of mental strength, and also paying the price for it. Because it might have a price. The political echelon, at least the people I'm talking about, they're not people who really like to have you disrupting their ideas, their plans, and opposing them. Of course, it's also a hard step psychologically. You feel the loneliness at its most intense. You understand you're alone. Ultimately it's you butting heads with the political echelon, and of course that's not a simple feeling. I think a lot ultimately depends on you, on your personality, on your seniority, and on the basic attitude you bring to things.

I can testify about myself. I really wanted to be Service director. I can't hide it. I thought that I had grown and was ready for this thing. But the day when I sat in the chair, or even before that, in many conversations with myself but also with Etty and with a few of my close friends, I said I really want to be Service director, but not at any price. The minute it clashes with a principle I couldn't live with, I had no problem getting up and leaving. I think it's my public duty. I decided that there wouldn't be a situation where my position was more important to me than my personal truth, or my professional truth. And if you believe that, you tell yourself, "Worst comes to worst, I won't be the head of Shin Bet, but I'll stand up for my truth opposite the political echelon," and that makes things simpler. You're less scared, and you also assure the political echelon that your mouth and your heart are equal. You say what you think. Whether they like it or not—that's what you do.

Of course, it's the sort of thing that's easy to say and hard to implement, but I think that's how I acted throughout my term, and I was willing to pay the price. Once or twice it came pretty close to that, when matters of principle brought me to harsh confrontations. Ultimately I believe they ended the way they should have ended. It wasn't an easy step. This friction is very hard. Look, it's still a hierarchical system. You're a public clerk, and they're publicly elected officials. I wasn't elected by the public. I was chosen by them. And you're arm-wrestling over a certain topic with the authority in charge of you. It's not like you and me sitting and talking. They don't greet you with open arms and a welcoming attitude. Sometimes it gets to a level of arguments where you forget who the prime minister is, and there's shouting and things that aren't very nice. Finally you tell yourself, "I'm head of the Shin Bet, and I'm standing and yelling at this or that prime minister. . . ." I really don't want to name names.

Ultimately there's a stage where you stand with your professional truth opposite those who are in charge of you, and you and they just don't agree. Now the question is, will you have the courage to say things in the clearest, truest, most blatant way possible, and insist that they discuss them and take them into account, or will you tell yourself: "Why should I make life complicated for myself? He wants to do that, let him do that. How is this my business? Let me finish my term in peace." There are heads of systems who chose that path, and others chose an uncompromising path in regard to these things. And I believe that that's what a true Service director has to do.

Ultimately, if the prime minister decides to take an action that's in opposition to the opinions of the Mossad director and the Shin Bet director, is it his right to make that decision?

Not his right, but the government's right. A large part of the decisions you deal with are not just the prime minister's alone. The prime minister decided, the prime minister released. . . . It's not the prime minister. The prime minister conveyed a proposition that the government authorized. But where's the government's collective responsibility for its decisions or its successes or its failures? Where?

So, okay, apparently that's how politicians are all over the world. The problem is that with us, tactical events can have strategic implications. You can't have mistakes here, certainly not big mistakes. This country is really so sensitive to things happening within it or in the region around it, that if anywhere in the world the political echelon needs to be good, in Israel it has to be excellent.

When you look at the upper political echelon, if you don't want to talk about Netanyahu and Barak personally, what kind of leadership do you see? Do you see leadership that can steer the ship?

I see a whole lot of very good people in Israel who are afraid to approach the political system because of the way it functions. That means there's a lot of potential in the Israeli public, but a lot of very good people are just afraid of going near that system, because they're afraid it will corrupt them, and I can understand that feeling.

Last Conversations, After the May 2011 Retirement

What's it like being on the outside?

Yuval Diskin: A pleasure. I have a lot of empathy for the place, for the organization. But that's it. I've finished my part, and I'm currently looking ahead.

Thirty-three years, that's your whole professional life.

It's thirty-seven years with the army, a lot.

You don't miss anything?

No, no. I also don't regret anything. There was already a hunger in me to get out, to do other things.

There was talk of you replacing the Mossad director.

So there was talk. I didn't ask for it, despite what they say in the media, quite the opposite. I was very much waiting to get out. This story came up—I think it was a politicians' game—and I told them that if I was asked, I wouldn't say no. They told me, "Listen, how many people can say on their résumé that they were both Shin Bet director and Mossad director?" I can't say that that's something to dismiss, but really, deep inside me, I already felt an immense desire to get out, and I'm glad it didn't materialize. As odd as it sounds.

What did you discover on the outside?

I don't know. It's too early. In the meantime, all I've discovered is that I can get along well with myself. And I discovered, if you can call it that, my family, and some of my friends, whom I've unfortunately neglected in the last six years, maybe even earlier, simply out of lack of time.

Has something in your perspective changed when you look today at the areas for which you were responsible, from outside the system?

It's too early to say.

You opposed the Shalit exchange* as it was proposed, and suddenly Yoram Cohen came and replaced you, and the exchange was carried out.

That's not accurate. I oppose all exchanges. In principle, I believe deals where we exchange hundreds or thousands of prisoners, terrorists, for IDF soldiers are unworthy. They harm the State of Israel, harm the country's image and its deterrence ability. I think that's where all the prime ministers went wrong. That's my basic opinion. From the moment there's a decision about making an exchange, it should be done at the lowest possible price in regard to the damage to Israel's security. But still, the Shin Bet

---

* The 2011 prisoner exchange between Israel and Hamas involved the release of Israeli soldier Gilad Shalit in exchange for 1,027 prisoners, mainly Palestinians and Arab-Israelis, including 280 prisoners sentenced to life in prison for perpetrating terror attacks against Israeli targets.

director—and it doesn't matter if his name is Yuval Diskin, Yoram Cohen, Avi Dichter, or whoever—has no advantage over any other person in the State of Israel in determining the deep, far-reaching question of the price of security in relation to the ethical, moral, public price. It's every person's right to express his opinion, and I don't think I know more than some Moyshele who's walking down the street whether it's right or not. I can comment regarding the price in terms of security, whether it's worthy or not, but it's not my decision. Not mine and not my predecessor's and not that of the person who replaced me.

I had an opinion about where the reasonable price ends in terms of security, and where it begins to become too much, and I expressed it very clearly, both to previous prime minister Ehud Olmert and to the current prime minister. On a personal level, I think prisoner exchange deals are unworthy, and I say that as someone who has a son in the army in a combat unit and two more sons who are about to be recruited into the army, and as a father who worries about his children very, very much. Despite everything, I think it's unworthy. I think these exchange deals encourage the next abduction, and that's clear. Look at what's happening now after the Shalit exchange. Already there's some Saudi billionaire who offered $900,000 in return for abducting the next soldier, and all the organizations announce that of course they'll keep on abducting soldiers, because, obviously, why not? If you release a thousand or more than a thousand in return for one soldier, really, why not do it?

But if Israeli leadership was strong enough—and I say the leadership, first of all, not the public. Because the leadership could have also affected the public. Only a weak leadership is dragged after the public—if the leadership was strong enough and knew how to say openly, "We'll agree to exchanges of one for one at most," the more you insist that there's a red line, the more you increase the chance that the price will be lower, and also that in the future, the hunger for carrying out abductions will decrease. That's my rationale, and I know the subject better than most people, because I know how many abduction plans we manage to thwart. It's true we didn't manage to thwart the attack during which Gilad Shalit was kidnapped, but every year we manage to prevent at least twenty or thirty abduction plans in various stages. So I'm familiar with the motivation, believe me, and therefore I think the rationale is not good, not healthy at all.

Beyond that, obviously it harms Israel's image, and Israeli deterrence ability. And they can come and tell me it empowers the public. I don't know who exactly it empowers. I don't feel that the public is empowered. I'm also not impressed when the media says that in surveys that this or that Internet site conducted, eighty percent of the public say they support the exchange. I'm among those who say that sometimes the leadership knows better than the public what's good for the country in the long term, so I think this thing is unworthy. Just like that.

I'm not making light of the claim about mutual responsibility, on the contrary. Mutual responsibility? That's fine. We'll exchange one soldier. Why did Israel carry out a prisoner exchange for Ilan Grapel,* who was arrested in Egypt, and release dozens of Egyptian detainees, in exchange for a man who was arrested through no fault of his own? What happened there? Later it's portrayed as a strategic achievement that improved our relationship with Egypt, or as if the Shalit exchange strengthened the State of Israel. We displayed strength. I don't accept those claims. Unfortunately, that's not how we're perceived by those around us, or by ourselves. Those around us perceive us as a country that's gradually weakening, headed by a weak leadership that can't withstand pressure and tell the public, "There's a line I won't cross." That's what would reduce the number of future soldier abductions. It would also decrease the price of these deals.

Personally, as the father of a son who's a soldier and sons who are going to be soldiers, I was very happy that Shalit returned home. But what's with this festival and the buses that came to Mitspe Hila to watch? Okay, it's a soldier released from imprisonment, and that's that. It's not really such a heartening event in the state's history, and it's without a doubt not comparable to someone like Meir Har-Zion,**

* Grapel was arrested by Egyptian authorities on charges of fostering unrest in Egypt as a Mossad agent, although no substantiation for the allegations was ever specified. Israel and Egypt agreed on the release of Grapel in exchange for twenty-five Egyptian prisoners held in Israeli jails, and the exchange was carried out in October 2011.

** Har-Zion was an Israeli military commando fighter and a key member of elite Unit 101, whose conduct on the battlefield was highly praised by former Chief of General Staff Moshe Dayan and by Ariel Sharon.

or some mythically heroic character, or someone like Uri Ilan,* who committed suicide in prison. That's not the story. Not that I expect Gilad Shalit to do that, but let's not blow it out of proportion. This is a PR country, a country of publicists running events, and unfortunately many dedicate themselves to this thing and abide by these rules and laws, and that's very sad.

Why did Prime Minister Netanyahu, when he announced the exchange, need Shin Bet director Yoram Cohen standing next to him?

That's a display of weakness. If you're the prime minister and you made the decision, why do you need the Shin Bet director next to you? Say, "I made the decision," like Arik Sharon did in the Elhanan Tannenbaum affair,** or Yitzhak Rabin did with the Jibril agreement.*** I believe they both made a mistake when they made those deals, but they at least said, "We made the decision," and didn't hide behind the shoulders of the Shin Bet director or the Mossad director or anyone else. That reminds me a little of Ami Ayalon, who was also brought along at the beginning of his term in the Western Wall tunnel events, when Bibi conducted the press conference and placed him next to him. What happened? Where's the claiming of responsibility?

It's not a secret that Ehud Barak and Benjamin Netanyahu wanted to appoint Yoav Galant as chief of general staff. For legal reasons, Benny Gantz was ultimately appointed. Yoram Cohen was appointed as Shin Bet director, and Tamir Pardo as Mossad director. Does the political echelon appoint people so that it can conveniently pass decisions with no resistance?

---

* Ilan was an Israeli soldier who committed suicide in a Syrian prison in 1955, after being captured and tortured.

** Tannenbaum is an Israeli businessman and former IDF reserve colonel who was kidnapped in 2000 in Dubai and held for more than three years by Hezbollah. He was released in January 2004 as part of a prisoner exchange in which 435 prisoners held by Israel were freed.

*** The Jibril agreement was a prisoner exchange deal which took place in May 1985 between the Israeli government and the Popular Front for the Liberation of Palestine–General Command (PFLP-GC). As part of the agreement, Israel released 1,150 prisoners in exchange for three Israeli prisoners of war captured during the First Lebanon War.

I don't want to talk at the moment about the appointments made. I ultimately look at who was appointed under the system by which I and my predecessors were appointed and ask, is this a good system or not? I think it's not good. I also include myself in the story. If the prime minister appoints his candidate, of course he'll appoint people he approves of.

In recent years we're constantly faced by the Iranian question. It's not a secret that the prime minister and the minister of defense encountered opposition from you, Chief of General Staff Ashkenazi, and Mossad Director Meir Dagan, as well as from the head of Aman and the Air Force Commander, to action in Iran. And eventually all these heads of systems were replaced.

I'm not sure the opinions of the current heads of systems on this or that issue are different from ours. They've also not withstood a real test yet, so there's no point in judging them before they do. The thing is, in games like this, there are no second chances. And that's the problem. The first mistake could be a strategic mistake. I really want to hope that the current professional echelon, which is subordinate to the prime minister and the minister of defense, knows how to stand its ground on the essential subjects, and states its professional opinion and not another opinion. They shouldn't feel like they owe anyone anything. Their debt is only to the Israeli people and to their professional truth. If you see they're trying to evade the debate, don't give up. That's the hard part. The thing is to be really determined right up to the line of confrontation, something like, "If you don't raise for discussion this or that matter, which I believe is crucial, I'm taking another step forward. I might also get up and resign."

Do you think the public debate over the Iranian nuclear issue is irresponsible, and accompanied by too much loose talk?

The amazing thing about this discussion is that the people who took the debate to the open, public sphere are the prime minister and the minister of defense. The minister of defense did it in an event broadcast on television. And later they ask why there's loose talk. . . . From the moment you open discussion on a certain topic, what exactly are you complaining about? You may have opened it up on purpose. A prime minister who's going to give a speech in the Knesset's winter session, does he not think about the things he's about to say? And doesn't he know what's going to happen after he expresses himself on the subject? He knows it very well, so this seems very ridiculous to me. The covert threat we received through the prime minister's office leak to Al Jazeera, that Dagan and Diskin "recruited reporters"*. . . the whole thing's just amusing. But I know the system well, and how it works, I've seen it laid bare in this matter, and I'm making what might be a harsh statement here: some people comment on your conduct, and you've got respect for them and you take it to heart, you clearly care what they say, and with some people, you don't.

As Service director, you were one of the most appreciated people in the State of Israel, in terms of fighting terror. Suddenly, today, you're a public enemy.

Why "public enemy"?

In the media, suddenly you're leaking information along with Meir Dagan to *Al Jazeera*. . . .

That's what the prime minister's office said. Okay, so they said it. Does that mean I'm a public enemy?

It wouldn't be surprising if you were summoned to a Shin Bet interrogation.

I told you earlier, there are things that, other than evoking mild amusement, I wasn't even insulted by. It's just funny. What caused me to address the subject is the fact that throughout the time when they were talking about the Iranian issue, they mainly asked whether it was or wasn't smart to attack Iran. Do we or do we not have the operational ability? I have an opinion on that, too, of course, but I think the more complex and more crucial thing, about which it's very important to me to raise public discussion, is the question whether those steering the country are capable of managing an event on a scale of that kind.

It's relatively easy to go into an event like that; all you have to do is decide, "Let's attack Iran." But from the moment we've entered such an event, will those two, Bibi Netanyahu and Ehud Barak, actually

---

* According to an anonymous *Al Jazeera* story, former Mossad director Meir Dagan and former Shin Bet director Diskin are responsible for leaking details regarding planned Israeli action against Iran. The story claims Dagan and Diskin recruited several prominent Israeli journalists and gave them mostly false information in order to politically harm Prime Minister Netanyahu and Minister of Defense Ehud Barak.

be capable of extracting us from it with the desirable results for the State of Israel? Since I've seen these people at quite a few plan authorizations, operations, various events, during their current term and in the past, I and quite a few of my colleagues did not feel secure regarding their ability to lead such a move. We didn't feel confident about these people's motivation.

The feeling many of us shared during sensitive discussions that took place, both during Olmert's era with Barak's participation and later in Netanyahu's era with Barak's participation, was that the question "who'll get the credit" for certain things might sometimes push them into surreal decisions or recommendations. I can't get any more specific than that. But those recommendations left the participants in those exclusive discussions with their mouths wide open, not once and not twice.

In a report broadcast in Amnon Levi's TV show regarding the attack on the Syrian reactor, they interviewed a foreign reporter who says that when Barak replaced Peretz in the Ministry of Defense, there were already plans to attack the reactor, and Barak opposed them. No one could understand why, and then the theory emerged that he believed Olmert would topple following the Winograd Commission report on the Second Lebanon War, and that he himself would be elected prime minister, and then the credit for destroying the reactor would be his. Now, there was fear that in the meantime the reactor would become active. If that's true, then it means Barak wanted to wait and risk attacking the active reactor, which might pollute the Tigris and Euphrates rivers, just to get credit?

I won't address that specifically, but I told you earlier that there are people who in certain situations are willing to give precedence to considerations of credit they'll earn, or that someone else will earn, over other, primary considerations. Enough said. . . .

Including radioactively contaminating a river?

I told you I don't intend to address this whole story. But we always had the feeling that at the moment of truth, they were more motivated by their personal agenda. Now, does that affect or did it affect us when we had to consider embarking on all kinds of operations, missions, or grandiose plans, of this or that variety? It definitely did.

It's known that in terms of security I'm a "hawk," out of a deep awareness that there's no place for weakness and wimps in the region where we live. But, in fact, after all those years when I fought terror, and saw so much death and carnage in battlefields, in the streets of Israeli cities, in the alleys of refugee camps and villages in the Bank and in the Gaza Strip and in Lebanon—there's a moment where you understand that you have to do everything, and I mean everything, to find another way, a way of negotiation and compromise, in order to attempt to ensure a better future for our children. And what I'm saying is completely free of political considerations, right or left.

As long as I was in the system and running the Service, or I was in those or other high-ranking roles, I was mainly busy with the endless day-to-day level of dealing with threats, warnings, terror attacks, and operations, managing things, commanding them, making sure they happen and succeed. Even though I dealt a lot with strategic thought and complicated policy matters, it was actually after I retired and started spending a lot of time with my family that the question started to bug me more and more, what kind of country will my children and grandchildren have—did I really contribute to making that country into a place they would want to live, a place they'll be proud of?!

Today, when I see the current leadership, I'm worried about what we'll leave for them here. In a few more days I'll have two kids in the army, and in a year I'll apparently have three kids in the army simultaneously, so obviously I'm very concerned.

In an episode of the TV program *Uvda* ["Fact"] on the subject of Iran, Ilana Dayan described a situation where Netanyahu and Barak, in the end of a meeting of "the eight" [the prime minister's defense advisory group], trigger the system in preparation for impending war.

It wasn't "the eight forum," it was a meeting I participated in. I didn't want to address this topic, but since things have already been made public in one way or another, I'll say there was a meeting, in a very exclusive forum, in which they tried to pressure us into triggering the military and defense system in preparation for commencing the operation. Obviously, an operation like that means entering into a war. And that's where the three of us had to stand up and make a very sharp statement against the instruction and against its appropriateness, and there was a very intense argument with Bibi and with Barak.

Who's "the three of us"?

The head of the Mossad, the head of the Shin Bet, and the chief of general staff. I think the head of Aman was there, too. We got up and said it was an illegal decision. You can't give us an instruction like that, because its meaning is that you're actually preparing the army to go to war. And declaring war is already a decision that only the government is authorized to make. We had a feeling that this was an attempt to steal something behind the scenes. Under the radar. That's exactly what I meant earlier when I talked about the feeling by the heads of organizations in the defense system that they have to be on their guard.

Barak says it was within their authority.

If you're telling the army to be ready within X hours for "go time," meaning embarking on an operation, those are not preparations made in meeting rooms. The army has to carry out all kinds of active steps, from recruiting reserve forces and preparing equipment and going through those or other maneuvers and other things that are very significant and prominent. It's very hard to keep things like that secret over time. When you prepare such a large system, it's a high-profile event which might have implications. It's not like I pick up the phone and call some commando guys and say, "Get ready." We're talking about triggering a whole system for a step which everyone agrees has a very high probability of leading to war. Neither the minister of defense nor even the prime minister has the authority, on his own, to issue an instruction like that.

Therefore, it was a very harsh confrontation, exposed to the rest of the ministers of "the eight," and then it became a lot harsher, because the ministers also felt there had been an attempt to steal it behind their backs. Why weren't they invited to take part in the advisory forum, in which, supposedly, the most sensitive things are discussed? Why was this all of a sudden not discussed in "the eight" forum? Something about this smelled very fishy.

And what happened in the end?

The fact that's hard to argue with is that this action was canceled. Apparently there was something inappropriate about it. You could also say that maybe this was a manipulation aimed at the international community, but I didn't see anyone from the international community sitting at that classified debate, so I don't know how to explain it. And that's one of the reasons why I'm afraid there are stages where these people's ego, and all kinds of imaginary and more or less messianic ideas, might drag us to places we didn't mean to go. Maybe even they didn't mean to get there, but suddenly you could find a whole country getting sucked into this story.

The fact that people who were Shin Bet directors or Mossad directors or major generals in the army, or held other senior positions in the defense system, suddenly acquire this kind of "dove" image after they leave their jobs is not because we've suddenly changed. We were simply intimately involved with these problems, we repeatedly exercised force so this country keeps functioning, but we understand the limits of force very well. So, over the years you become more measured when making decisions, definitely those involving exercising force.

The Future

I want to read you something that Professor Yeshayahu Leibowitz said in 1968: "A country that controls a hostile population of a million foreigners will by necessity be a Shin Bet country, with everything that stems from that, with consequences in regard to the spirit of education, freedom of speech and thought, and the democratic regime. The corruption typical of any colonial regime will also stick to the State of Israel. The administration will have to deal with suppressing an Arab uprising movement on the one hand, and with acquiring 'Quislings,' Arab traitors, on the other hand, and there's also a risk that IDF will atrophy by becoming an army of occupation."

What do you think about what he said at the time, considering the way the State of Israel looks today?

Yuval Diskin: I agree with every word. Every word he said here is rock-solid. I believe that's an accurate description of the reality that has developed from '68 to this day. I wouldn't go as far as saying Israel has become a Shin Bet state, but the situation we're in in regard to the Palestinians has, without a doubt, created a reality that's quite similar to what Yeshayahu Leibowitz was describing.

When you send soldiers or Shin Bet people to territory you occupy, which you've conquered, it influences you and influences society. For children who grow up in a period of terrorist attacks, as far as they're concerned, from a young age, a Palestinian and an Arab is a terrorist who kills Jews. That's ultimately the banal perception that is etched in their minds. And it's apparently similar to the way a Palestinian child perceives us. You see it in behavior, in thought, in the way of thinking, in the style of expression. Look at fans' cheers in Beitar Jerusalem's soccer games. It infiltrates a lot of places in our lives, and I believe it's a very heavy price we're paying unaware. Look at surveys conducted today and published in the media about aspects of racism in Israeli society. As a father to children, and I hope that at some point also a grandfather to grandchildren, I'm very bothered by the fact that my kids are growing up in this environment.

Avraham Shalom: You put most of our young men and women in the army, and they see an oxymoron there. On the one hand, they see it strives to be the people's army, and aspires to be like the Nahal, and on the other hand, a brutal occupying army that's similar to the Germans during World War II. Similar. Not identical. And I'm not talking about their behavior toward the Jews, which is an unusual thing with its own unique aspects. I'm talking about the way they treated the Poles and the Belgians and the Dutch and the Czech and all of them. We're slowly becoming professional conquerors, and from that stems very dangerous behavior among ourselves.

It's behavior that ultimately becomes a part of your character. And that's what scares me. You're standing in a roadblock, and if one Arab gets tired of standing in line, and he has an outburst, then you hit him with the butt of your gun. That's not an unusual thing. It becomes a norm for you. And in the end you also go home after your military service, and you have a wife and you have kids, and you yell at them like a commander at his soldiers. And then the kids become like that, too. That's a very negative trait we've acquired, to be cruel—toward ourselves as well, but mostly toward the ruled population—using the excuse of the war on terror.

We've been swept into a situation where we won't be able to forgive ourselves and fix it. What will happen? A few people will refuse to serve in IDF, some people will leave the country, and most will get used to the new situation and act accordingly, and then we're in trouble. And look what happened to the Americans in Iraq; the fact that here and there, they put some American who hit an Arab on trial, that's nothing. Luckily for them, they don't stay there for long; they stay for a year or two, and then they're relieved. Over here, everyone's the same all the time. I have a grandson who was halfway a "Peace Now" supporter; he served three years in Hebron, and became less "Peace" and less "Now." Today he's in reserve duty, so he came to his senses a bit, I think. I talk to him about it. Ultimately, we won all the battles and no wars.

You said you saw Hitler in Vienna, that you personally experienced the racism there. Is the humiliation really the same humiliation?

Shalom: The same type of humiliation. It's a humiliation where they tell you you're nothing. I can do anything I want with you. Stand in line, shut up. Open your mouth and you'll be slapped. And if you don't open your mouth, you'll also be slapped, and there's nothing you can do about it. That's humiliation. We're like them in that way.

By the very fact of our being occupiers, conquerors, there's almost no way to avoid this matter of humiliating others.

Shalom: No way to avoid it? If we were educated like they do in Norway, maybe there'd be a way to avoid it. But even then, not for long. After three, four, five years, not to mention forty-two years, there's no way to avoid it. We shouldn't have stayed there so long.

Carmi Gillon: We cause millions of people's lives to become impossible. Turn them into one ongoing human misery. And we leave the decision of what is proportional and what isn't proportional in the hands of a soldier who's only been in the army for a few months, and a year earlier—at best—he graduated from high school. And he's standing there facing a father with a baby girl, and has to decide if he does or doesn't search him, whether that father is allowed to go through or not. It kills me, I want you to know. It destroys my heart, this story. The everyday things—the roadblocks in the West Bank, the exposure of young children, maybe not actual children but young guys, youths of eighteen or nineteen, to confrontations with human suffering that they don't know how to deal with. That's what bothers me—the social price we pay. And believe me, I'm not just relying on what I read in the papers.

Ya'akov Peri: You get to a house in the middle of the night, knock on doors, wake up a sleeping, cuddling family. The harsher the winter is, the denser and more suffocating things are. And the mother's tears, or the moments of parting from that suspect you take from the arms of his family—are not easy moments, and that's an understatement. All in all, you see the suffering family, the difficult moments between parents and children, between children and parents. Those are the moments that ultimately leave a deep impression on you. And when you retire from the Service, you start leaning a bit to the left, since in some way you're not only meeting the focused population, which was the reason you were appointed for the job. You generally see the whole population. And you see that finally, seventy percent, eighty percent of the population is a population that wants to live in peace, to make a living, to feed itself, to feed its children. You know that about the same percentages, if not higher, are also the case on your side. And you start feeling some anger at the regime or the state that can't ultimately make an arrangement, reach an agreement, and start living a more peaceful, healthier life, which is what the majority on both sides wants. I think these images, and the feelings you experience, whether it's during arrests, whether it's in interrogation rooms, whether it's in all the situations you live through when you're at a place like the General Security Service, definitely have a crucial weight.

How is it that the all the heads of the Service leave the Service and suddenly say—we support two states, we support an arrangement? What's out there that's not inside? Why is this revealed only when you get out?

Peri: I think the great majority of those who have served—whether it's in the Service, whether it's in the Mossad, whether it's in IDF or in other military organizations—ultimately reach the conclusion that you can't win this conflict through Shin Bet–ian or military measures. There's no alternative to a diplomatic process. All measures which are military-intelligence-operational measures are good for the fight against terror, for a focused war on those who rise up to kill you. But you ultimately need a diplomatic outline, a diplomatic process, in order to reach the results which both sides want.

Now, people who are in this mess, who live in it for numerous years, who see the most terrible, the most horrifying, the most tragic sides of this system, the Israeli-Palestinian conflict, understand it better since they've experienced it on their own flesh. Only those who were there understand that ultimately we're fated to sit in the same part of the world that God Almighty has brought us to, and we can't change that historical reality unless we make territorial changes. And the minute we're fated to live in this part of the world, we're mostly the ones who have the possibility of changing that reality. And if we don't change reality, the probability of reality changing by itself is practically zero.

Carmi Gillon: We all appear right-wing during our service and look left-wing to the public after we retire. But it comes from a very sober perspective. Not a political one. We don't learn things from the papers; we manufacture the stories in the papers.

What characterizes a head of Service—and not just the head of Service, but a Service employee after twenty-five to thirty years—is that you become the most realistic thing I know. Those who work in the Service are very realistic people who actually suppress their politics, because we're supposed to be an apolitical organization. When you go to the dining hall in the Service, there are no political debates; it's a subject that doesn't exist. You live the field all the time. For so long, you live information about Mohammed and Yousouf and Abdullah and so on, and on the other hand you live the Jewish side, and you live the information you receive from foreign countries and so on. You're not just an intelligence man, you're someone whose feet are very firmly planted on the ground.

So how is it that all of you, all Shin Bet directors, actually say yes today to a two-state solution, agree to a return to the borders of '67? Where does it come from?

Gillon: You interview Service directors, you meet Service directors, but let's try another exercise. Go to the coordinators. To the hundreds and thousands of former Service coordinators. We're talking many thousands. Some of them with knit skullcaps, and some of them with black skullcaps,* and some of them with no skullcaps, some from the right and some from the left; go ask them. They'll give you the same answers you get from Service directors and from heads of Service branches and from heads of Service departments. The Shin Bet, due to its constant contact with the field, knows you can't achieve any positive result for Israel by preserving this conflict. And that it's in our distinct interest, and we're not doing the Palestinians any favors; we're doing ourselves a favor by trying to reach an arrangement.

Time and again, we ask ourselves what we're conceding to the Palestinians, what the Palestinians are gaining, and we're less concerned with the question of what we're gaining. Does anyone think the economy—the economic boom we had here for years until the last crisis—would even be possible if we were a recusant country? It wouldn't have happened. Can you imagine a Wall Street investor coming and investing in the Israeli high-tech industry when he isn't sure whether in half a year, there won't be a war, or something else, here?

---

* Knit skullcaps are usually associated with more moderate religious believers, while black skullcaps characterize the more extremely religious.

You know what motivated Yitzhak Rabin to go for the Oslo process? You've probably heard a thousand versions. I'll add another one. Every Friday, I'd take part in what's called "the Territories forum," headed by the prime minister and the minister of defense. And every Friday, the heads of IDF Central Command and Southern Command would get there, and demand to recruit more and more reserve forces because they don't have enough forces to maintain security in the Gaza Strip and in the West Bank. It came to an average of one hundred reserve companies serving. I'm talking about a short time ago, '93. Those were the years when a hundred reserve companies were permanently out of the workforce. People went on reserve duty every three months. For officers it got to ninety days a year. And it wrecked Rabin. He was constantly thinking about it, about the economic price, about the educational price, all these things. And he'd tear out what remained of the hair on his head in every one of those discussions. The prime minister runs a country, he has to see the whole complex. He can't just see the agenda of the chief of Central Command or the chief of Southern Command. He also has to think about what it does to Israeli society, what it does to the Israeli economy, and so on. And that really pushed him to give some kind of chance to escaping from this thing, which could have gone on like that for many generations to come.

And I look at all these things and tell myself, the West Bank today doesn't contribute anything to the State of Israel's security by virtue of the settlements existing there. It's very important to leave it demilitarized, but for that you don't need to hold two hundred to three hundred thousand settlers there. We have to get out of there, and take all the money and everything we've invested there, and not destroy the fantastic roads we built there, leave them for the Palestinians, and take and channel all those energies inside, into Israel.

Ami Ayalon, in September 2000, on the eve of the outbreak of the Second Intifada, you told the journal *Nekuda*, "I claim that in the 1987–1993 Intifada, we lost, and I claim we'll lose in every Intifada, and I claim it's a good thing we'll lose, because the price of victory in a phenomenon like the Intifada is losing our humanity. As someone who was a major general in IDF, I tell you that our control over an Arab population in the territories of the West Bank and Gaza causes us to do things which are unconscionable."

Ami Ayalon: What's the question?

Explain it to me. A statement like that, two or three months before the Intifada erupted. . . .

Look, the only thing that bears discussing is the concept of victory or defeat. You're an Israeli citizen. What's victory? Define it.

When the other side accepts what I want, that's victory.

Can you define what you want?

As an Israeli citizen?

Yes.

I want to live in peace and happiness. Too simplistic?

Let's put it like this. [Prussian military theorist Carl von] Clausewitz, who was a smart man, even though he wasn't Jewish or at least we have yet to uncover his Jewish roots, said more than two hundred years ago, "Victory is simply creating a better political reality." That's victory. Meaning, victory doesn't necessarily dictate that we have to conquer Gaza or Ramallah or Nablus or Hebron. I think my son, who served three years or almost three and a half years in the paratroopers, participated in conquering Nablus at least two or three times. Did that bring us victory? I don't think so. The question is whether it brought us closer to a better political situation. Now, I define a better political situation in a very simple way. We're actually here so that the State of Israel will be the democratic, safe state of the Jewish people. That's our goal. And from there we also want to build an economy and a society and an education and welfare system, but, ultimately, under the definition of "a democratic, safe Jewish state," we include everything. Did the Intifada bring us closer to that? My claim is it didn't.

By the way, this situation is so frustrating that other nations which encountered it experienced a major threat to their democracy. I'm telling you that the French in Algeria won a sweeping military victory. But they paid a price which, you know, in current terms is impossible. But they won. Did they really win? Ultimately, they won from a military standpoint, and were defeated politically until de Gaulle came and, with an act of political leadership, brought them to a different reality.

You know, in the beginning of the Intifada, when a situation was created when the foreign affairs minister was trying to lead a policy of political negotiations, with the prime minister's approval, and the chief of general staff came out against him and said he was obstructing IDF from winning the war, can you imagine a situation like that in a healthy democracy? When then–Chief of General Staff Bogie Ya'alon comes out and says the ministry of foreign affairs is obstructing IDF from winning the war? That was the situation at the beginning of the Intifada. So you have to understand that we didn't define the concept of victory for ourselves in a sufficiently apt way.

Sometime in 2002, when I was no longer Shin Bet director, I came to London following an invitation from the London School of Economics. The Intifada is raging, Israeli citizens and Palestinians are being killed on both sides of the no-border, a real hell, and we leave for London, a group of Israelis and a group of Palestinians, to see whether anything can be done. Like the whole peace industry, something pretty naïve. In London, they say everything is more convenient; even this discussion is more convenient.

At some point I make myself a cup of coffee, and a Palestinian acquaintance walks over to me; his name is Eyad Sarraj, a doctor of psychiatry. I knew him when I was in the Shin Bet, even though he wasn't really involved with terror. He's a psychiatrist who deals with and treats children suffering from shock. In the journalistic editorial articles he writes, he talks about the next generation of violence, which is built into the Palestinian childhood in Gaza during the Second Intifada. Very harsh articles, by the way, to an Israeli eye. He served time in Palestinian prison because he opposed Arafat and his corruption. He's one of the authentic people who led the nonviolent resistance, but really led the struggle against Arafat's regime, with everything implied by that. And he walked over to me and told me, "Ami, we finally beat you."

I say to him, "Tell me, are you nuts? What do you mean, you beat us? Hundreds of your people are being killed, at this rate it'll be thousands. The little bit of state you have, you're going to lose, and you'll lose your dreams of statehood. That's victory?"

He says, "Ami, I don't understand you. To this day, you don't understand us. Victory for us is to see you suffer. That's all we want. And the more we'll suffer, the more you'll suffer," he says. "Finally, after fifty years, we've achieved a balance of power, a parity. Your F16 opposite our suicide bomber."

And I, usually pretty sharp and witty, was speechless. That statement by Eyad Sarraj created a very clear insight in me. Suddenly I understand the suicide phenomenon. Suddenly I understand our reaction in a whole other way. How many operations have we carried out because we're in pain? Because when our buses explode, it really hurts us and we want to see revenge? How many times have we done that?

We support IDF, even when we know the operation or the achievement actually sets us back. We've lost the meaning of victory. We're in a cycle of terror which is gradually escalating. We keep thinking that "what isn't achieved by force will be achieved by even more force. . . ." so when I tell you we won or lost, it's not in military terms. The tragedy of the public debate in Israel regarding security is that we don't understand the very frustrating situation where we do indeed win every battle, but we still lose the war.

Avi Dichter, I'll read you a sentence from the book *Boomerang* [by Raviv Druker and Ofer Shelah]: "IDF and the Shin Bet attained many operational achievements during the seventies . . . but all of them did not help Israel attain achievements in the war, because a war without purpose is unwinnable." I quote Avraham Shalom: "Since '48 we've been winning all the battles but losing the wars." Do you understand these statements?

Avi Dichter: Listen, I know these statements—"We won the battles, we lost the war," or "We lost the battles, we won the war"; "A nation which rules the sea has never been beaten"; "The tank is the iron, the man is the steel." I don't know the exact meaning of the sentence you read from *Boomerang*, about the war without purpose being unwinnable. I don't know what a "war without purpose" is. The war against terror has a very worthy purpose to me, which is ensuring normal life for people in Israel. I don't know a more purposeful purpose than that. And Israel has shown that it can fight terror.

Ami Ayalon said we're defeating terror, it's true, but the question is whether it's bringing us to a better place.

Dichter: I look sixty years back, to what those who established the state were imagining, and think the State of Israel is a significantly better, healthier, and more developed state than what they imagined. I also don't know exactly what it means that we're not thinking how to develop a more productive relationship opposite the Arabs, opposite our neighbors, opposite the Palestinians, or how to get to know them more deeply. It always reminds me of those Palestinians who would say to us, "If you Israelis don't deal with us, you'll be dealing with Hamas. . . ." I said, "Sure, what do you propose so that we are dealing with you?" They said, "Guys, a little patience, don't build, don't shut down, don't put up roadblocks, don't attack us, let us get organized a little."

In one of the meetings, I asked them, "Tell me, how many casualties do you need us to have in order for you to get organized?"

I don't think we need to beat ourselves up over what we're missing by not understanding the other side. I don't know how much the other side understands itself, and Gaza is just one example of the lack of understanding that led them to where they ended up. So what? Now we have to do the same thing in the West Bank? Why?

And I'll tell you again: the barrel of terror has a bottom. Sometimes it's unpleasant getting there, it's a long way, but there is a bottom. And that barrel, unfortunately, fills up from time to time. It's not a barrel that you empty and that's it. There are other barrels, alas. There was the barrel of before the Six Day War. There was the barrel of the '60s, the early '70s, there was the barrel of up to '93, and later there's the barrel of this Intifada, and I hope there'll be no other barrels, but I'm not so sure.

The four Service directors who preceded you called for a political solution to the conflict in an interview in *Yediot Ahronot* published during your term. Do you identify with what they say there, or is there really no partner to speak to?

First of all, we're different people. The fact that we're Shin Bet people doesn't mean that even in running the organization, we share a similar view of things. Each of us managed it differently, and needless to say, our political stances are far from identical. Ami Ayalon joined one party and I joined another party. But to come and say there's no partner on the Palestinian side, and that there won't be a partner, that's a statement I can't support. It's true that since the beginning of the Intifada, the Palestinian side has just avoided dealing with the problem of how to actually build a state for themselves. Not on the back of the State of Israel—beside it. If they don't understand this fact, they won't have a state. And in order to build a state beside Israel, it's required to have the ingredients that every state has—a hierarchy of law enforcement. So that Israel understands that the Palestinian side understands that a terrorist from Nablus who acts in Israel is their problem just as much as it is ours. This mutuality appears reasonable to me between two states who want to live next to one another.

We also know the Palestinians. We know the characters; it's not just names. You know, in Syria or Lebanon we don't know the characters except through reading and intelligence collection. Here we know the people, we've sat down with them, we've joked around with them, we talked to them, we've gotten angry at them, we worked with them, we worked against them. We know them, believe me, like we know ourselves. And what surprises me is how what should have happened with them, to the best of my understanding, didn't happen. I told you—once we sat in a meeting with the Palestinians and the Americans. And one of the senior Palestinians says during the small talk, the idle chat between discussions, that Yasser Arafat is the Palestinians' Ben Gurion. Listen, we didn't have time to answer, and another, very senior Palestinian jumps up and tells him in Arabic, "We wish he was our Ben Gurion." Why do they wish that? Because they could analyze exactly where Yasser Arafat didn't make the decisions that were required of him. Not required by Avi Dichter, required by them, in order to really start building the infrastructure for a Palestinian state.

Is there a chance?

Look, the greatest advantage is the fact that there was a very significant leap in the standard of living both in Gaza and in the West Bank in the last thirty years. I started working in Gaza thirty-three years ago, so I can say—I know Gaza fairly intimately. There's no similarity between today's Gaza and Gaza in those days. In terms of standard of living, education, people's insights, and so on. And it doesn't matter if it's Hamas or other people. The West Bank—certainly so. And my claim is that with people who can foresee an improvement to their standard of living, to their quality of life in general, opposite those people, there's hope. Now, we know these characters. They're not people with horns, they're not people whose culture we can't understand. We more or less understand their issues, and they understand our issues very well. So I think there's definitely a chance. The chance will rise or fall over characters, over leaders.

Do you support talking to whomever it's possible to talk to?

Avraham Shalom: Anyone whom you can talk to. Even if he answers impudently, I support continuing. There's no alternative.

Including Hamas, Jihad?

Shalom: Including everyone. I said everyone, so that also includes [former Iranian leader] Mahmoud Ahmadinejad. I always support talking. In general, that's one of the traits of an intelligence professional. Talking to everyone. You want to know what's going on. You can't know what's going on if you don't talk.

Even if it's Hamas, which is unwilling to acknowledge the State of Israel's right to exist?

Shalom: I don't even care what he thinks; if he talks, then he talks. He may not want to talk to me, in which case I can't make him. But if someone's willing to talk, even if it's someone junior, and even if it's on that subject or on this other subject, on anything. When you talk, things become clearer. I see you don't eat glass, you see I don't drink gasoline. . . . That's how it is.

But we don't know how to talk. With us, there are no options. It's "wham," Palestinian state, no Palestinian state. Destroying Hamas, not destroying Hamas. Can you destroy Hamas? What kind of nonsense are you talking? Where will these guys with those clear-cut opinions bring us?

Dummies—us and them. We could already be in Switzerland here. We thought we were coming here because, two thousand years ago, someone gave us this country. That's true and that's nice, and I accept the logic that the Jews need a country. It's very important that they have a country, otherwise they'll go through another Holocaust, but two thousand years is a lot of time. . . . It doesn't work like that. You have to know your limitations, and your limitations are five million opposite a billion and a half. That's not funny.

Ultimately, the Arabs don't understand us. I wouldn't understand, either. State, no state. Why is it okay to establish settlements even though you're saying "two states"? If you can't follow through, don't promise. I don't see a solution, because I believe that even if there are two states for two peoples, there'll still be terror. Maybe on a different, smaller scale. Then it depends how we choose to behave. The other side has problems, too. They're not real saints, either. They're very cruel. And until we escape this "schmaltz," I don't see how you can even reach a solution. Two peoples, two states—you'll have terror. Two peoples, one state—there's no Zionism. You have to take into account that it's a terrible dilemma, that will ultimately be built on mutual trust. Not on force.

Yuval Diskin, should we talk to everyone?

Yuval Diskin: We should talk to whoever represents the other side. Whoever the legitimate representative of the other side is, that's who we should talk to.

Hamas?

Diskin: I don't think the State of Israel should talk to Hamas. I think the Palestinian Authority currently has a representative named Abu-Mazen, and behind him is a party which is still the majority, which led the Oslo Accords, with the goal of creating the solution of two states for two peoples here, and he's the one we should talk to.

I have a serious problem with Hamas. Maybe it's a result of my and the Service's over-familiarity with Hamas, but it's a national radical Islamic movement which has very clear religious goals. And its goal is to re-establish the Islamic caliphate in the area and in the world. I have a hard time envisioning a situation where Hamas becomes flexible and willing to compromise on those stances. The only thing they might well become flexible about, and quite a few people disagree with me there, is the time frame. Meaning, they'll be willing to say, "We're not solving the problem now, we're willing to wait another ten years, another twenty years, but our ultimate goal is to swallow the State of Israel and establish a caliphate here." Not only the State of Israel, by the way; they also want to swallow some of the Arab states around us, because to them, the regimes of those states are not legitimate, either. So I think talking to Hamas is all good and well, but it will only postpone the problem.

In one of the government sessions during your term under Netanyahu, you said you recognized initial signs of a willingness to talk on the side of Hamas.

Hamas constantly wants to talk, because it wants legitimacy. On the one hand, it gained a very large achievement—it took control of a piece of land called the Gaza Strip, which is an achievement that none of the other Islamic Brotherhood movements has attained for many years. But on the other hand, it's besieged, surrounded, it has no achievements which it knows how to sell to its public. It stands a very large chance of additional confrontations with us. Hamas tries every means of escaping from the complex situation it's in, so, as far as it's concerned, talking is fine. There's an Arabic proverb: "Kiss the dog on the mouth in order to get what you need from it." In Islam, a dog is one of the most unclean things in existence. That means "Take what you need to take from it." And in my view, even if they don't say it, that's the logic guiding them.

Carmi Gillon: My opinion is that you should talk to everyone, including Hamas. Not that they'll acknowledge us, and they'll never sign the Balfour Declaration* or anything else, but in Israel, it's too much of a luxury not to talk to our enemies. So, as long as they decide not to talk to us, I don't have a choice, but when we decide not to talk, I think we're making a mistake. I think we're holding Hamas by the balls a lot more than they're holding us, and we're not reaping the advantages we could be getting from it, because we're sulking and refusing to talk. Regarding Abu-Mazen personally, I have my doubts. In contrast, the Palestinian Authority is actually growing stronger in the West Bank, and I hope that process continues.

Ami Ayalon: If we don't create a political framework and define for ourselves what we really want, and whether we're willing to pay the price, the State of Israel will not experience a diplomatic victory in the foreseeable future. And I'm telling you that the price is to pull out of the majority of the territories of the West Bank, in order for Israel to be Jewish democratic, not because the Palestinians deserve a state, not because of some bleeding-heart leftists, not because we have compunctions for being conquerors—that's a different debate that needs to be held. The price that must be paid is only so that the State of Israel will be the democratic country of the Jewish people. A political treaty is more important to our security than another F-15 squadron or two divisions.

But to this day, ministers in the Israeli government come and say that Homesh [a West Bank settlement dismantled by Israel in 2005] should be rebuilt and that all settlements are legal, and that there's no intention of evacuating them. On the one hand, the prime minister talks about two states for two peoples, and on the other hand the ministers of the Israeli government inform us day and night that this is basically almost completely insincere, and is only due to succumbing to the American agenda. Do I have to come to a political

---

* The 1917 British government statement declaring support for a Jewish state in Palestine.

arrangement because the president of the United States is applying pressure on me? Do I have to uproot people from settlements or put a halt to construction that is essential to their everyday lives because the president of the United States wakes up in the morning and decides that it's part of the American agenda? My answer is "no" with three exclamation points. I have to do it because it's in Israel's best interest. And that's what the prime minister isn't telling us clearly. He lets us understand through his body language that he's doing it to gain something opposite Iran, that he's doing it due to American pressure; and because it's being done in that way, it won't happen. Because it's being done in such a way that if it does happen, we'll encounter a much higher level of violence.

In the West Bank there's a third and fourth generation of settlers whom we sent there. Most of them, including their rabbis and their public leaders, would be willing to take their homes, and their grandchildren, and their dead and their Torah books, and go back to what I call the State of Israel. Contrary to their ideology. They would be willing to do it only if they understand it's in Israel's ultimate interest. It's an essential condition in order for Israel to be Jewish and democratic, and for us not to hurt each other. If they don't understand that, it won't happen. Not politically, and not in terms of the level of violence we'll encounter along the way.

So the future is grim?

Ayalon: The future is not grim. I think at the very end, if we act correctly, if we don't treat the settlers like "propellers,"* if we show them that it's in Israel's best interest, if we do it as a dialogue and a discussion, but also with determination and clarity about where we're going, I believe the great majority of them, including their leaders, will know how to live with it and also provide themselves with the theological explanations that I can't give.

In some discussion, a rabbi once told me, "Look, the problem isn't the theological debate. I have the explanation. The Land of Israel isn't ours, it belongs to God Almighty, and he grants it at his will." So there may be a situation where the decision isn't mine. Ultimately, the principle that "all Jews are responsible for one another" supersedes, for

---

* In a 1993 reference to protesters from the Golan Heights, Yitzhak Rabin said the protesters can "spin like propellers."

the great majority of them, for almost all of them, the holiness of the land. The real problem is that the discussion doesn't even approach those areas. Everything is perceived as political manipulation. They really feel they're being cheated. They feel that they elect a prime minister, whether it's Arik Sharon once or Benjamin Netanyahu a second time, who swears to them on everything that's holy that he won't retreat, he won't contribute to the establishment of two states for two peoples, under no circumstances will he let it happen, and the moment he becomes prime minister, he changes his stance.

They can't explain to themselves why they pulled out of Gaza. I can say why we did it, even though it's completely obvious that the security situation is worse, and despite the fact that it's completely obvious we did it in the worst way possible. Because, despite all the problematic aspects, the State of Israel today is slightly more Jewish and slightly more democratic. But so long as they feel that everything that's happening is a result of political manipulation or a result of American pressure, they won't cooperate with it.

And you believe that a leader who will do it will emerge?

Look, Rabin didn't believe in political processes. His worldview wasn't "security-conscious," it was "security-centric." Rabin gave the instruction to "break the Palestinians' bones" because in 1989 he believed that if we break their bones, they'll understand. And Rabin got it. He got it and became a leader of stature nationally and historically, and I believe internationally, as a result of taking his understanding and using his political power and the diplomatic opportunity in order to change direction in Israeli politics. So I can't tell you whether the next leader has already been born or whether he's already been elected. I'm an optimistic man. I can tell you that under certain circumstances even today's leadership could, against its will, or against its previous perceptions, lead actions which will bring the Israeli people closer to the place that you and I want them to be.

Avi Dichter: I think the public in Israel, including the religious public, knows where Israel is heading in terms of its final borders. When that reality is presented to Israeli residents, in concrete terms—that this is the peace accord we're going for, these are the borders, these are the terms—I think it'll be a completely different reality than the one we see today, of hobbling around from place to place, from line to line, from this settlement to that settlement. There's no sense today that what's happening is really leading to some final arrangement. We're dealing, I'd say, with the outskirts of the outskirts. I'm convinced that when we confront the dilemma, that this is the ultimate border and the evacuation process is now inevitable, it will be a completely different reality.

My optimism stems from my conviction that the Palestinians' best interests are not different from our best interests. Listen, I know them. They want to live. They know how to live. They love to live. They don't like to die. Not in terror attacks and not in terror-attack prevention. But, as in many other cases, sometimes a small group can drag you into the abyss. The same is true for us in Israel. Look at our history. How many times have we been toppled into the abyss? Not by large groups. By small groups. So we have to be very careful.

Yuval Diskin, you, the heads of Shin Bet, might be the biggest experts on the Palestinian front. Why, after so much time, can't we resolve this story?

Yuval Diskin: First of all, the fact that we're experts is not enough. We're not always sufficiently experts on these things. We're not always involved enough where we should be involved. But if you ask me, in order to resolve a conflict that is a historical, national, religious conflict and a conflict over land, which I believe is the most complex conflict you could think of, all the expertise in the world won't be enough if there isn't leadership on a very, very high level on both sides simultaneously, at a given time. That's why it's so difficult.

Meaning, ultimately it's the leadership? On both sides?

To me, real leadership that is really capable of leading nations in this case, with a true willingness to solve a problem, can provide a chance to solve a problem, even on this scale. I believe we didn't succeed. We were very close to it. I have an immense feeling of missed opportunity about Oslo, for example. I look at it as someone who saw from the inside what was happening with the Palestinians and what was happening with the Israelis. In the beginning of the process there was real enthusiasm from those involved. There was even, I'd say, romance. Not on the level of mutual love, but in the feeling that an actual historical event is taking place here. But the minute it got to practical implementation, the leadership wasn't good enough and didn't enable this venture to succeed.

I'll take you to South Africa, which everyone mentions as a classic model. There they had really impressive leadership by Nelson Mandela on the one hand and [F. W.] de Klerk on the other, who sat and decided to change the course of history in South Africa. De Klerk apparently understands the price he and the whites of South Africa are going to pay, and Mandela understands that he supposedly won, but on the other hand understands the importance of a conciliatory approach so that the country doesn't fall apart. Very impressive. But when you look at it from a historical perspective, if you go to South Africa, I'm not sure that from a perspective over time, it's really that successful. Because it's loaded. There's very significant baggage between the two sides. According to my understanding, whites in South Africa currently live in ghettos. You see their houses, and it's pretty scary to see, with barbed-wire fences and means of deterrence, and they're afraid to leave their houses at certain hours. I really wouldn't want us to live like that, even if it solves the problem. So my claim is that it's a lot more complicated than it looks.

Or take Northern Ireland. It's also portrayed as a success story, and I think there really was a process there of an attempt to make up and achieve some sort of new co-existence. As far as a lot of people are concerned, the story in Northern Ireland is over, but I tell you, it's not over, because in the last year there were quite a few terror attacks by the IRA. For some reason, the media has already closed this file, and it looks like the British government has also closed this file, and it already has been branded as a success, but apparently the actual situation is a lot more complex.

So how does this pertain to us?

I don't want to compare us to these other places. I think the solution of the Israeli-Palestinian conflict is a lot more complex than it's perceived. The only chance for a solution is if both sides have very strong leadership based on a very significant political majority, and with a real desire to solve the problem, accompanied by willingness to compromise.

What do you recognize in Palestinian society today, in the context of the peace process? Are we heading toward a third Intifada? Is there hope, in terms of public atmosphere?

Look, I think the Palestinian public has grown tired and weary of the Second Intifada. It's very disappointed by the achievements after everything that happened in the Intifada, and I believe the

Palestinians paid an even greater price than the price we paid. I think the Palestinian public is tired out, and would very much like peace. On the other hand, the disappointment and the sobering up that we've all experienced in the last sixteen years, from Oslo to today, undermine the confidence of quite a few people on both sides regarding the ability to really attain peace.

There are many shades in the Palestinian public, but let's focus on the average Palestinian citizen—not the most extreme Hamas supporter or peace supporter. I think he's like me or you. Everyone wants quiet first of all, wants personal security for themselves and their family members. It doesn't matter what their country or their religion is. And a citizen like that would be very happy if he had some quiet and he had freedom of movement and freedom of trade, and if he could do what he wanted professionally. And of course the only way to achieve that is peace. But to get to peace, you need to solve some very weighty essential problems between us and the Palestinians. You have to get over a lot of people's ego on the way. On both sides. And without very strong leadership on both sides, with a lot of surrounding pressure from a lot of elements who would make it move forward, there's no chance of solving the weighty problems on the agenda. This solution won't happen by itself.

Do you sleep peacefully at night?

Diskin: No. I sleep well because I'm tired from my riding practice, but do I actually sleep peacefully in that sense? No.

Why?

Because I think this country is really dealing with a very, very large quantity of challenges, which, in order to be managed correctly, require first-class leadership ability. I don't feel we have that. If there's no leadership to lead Israeli society to different places, and which can tell Israeli society with no fear and hesitation what needs to be done and where to go, then we're heading for a bad place. Israeli society will be a lot more polarized and divided than it is today, and it's already in a bad place today. And a large part of the chasms will grow wider and wider over time; that's my assessment.

In order to handle these things, first of all you need strong, authentic, worthy leadership, whose words reflect what's in its heart. The personal example it conveys to the public also needs to be in accordance. The hour of decision isn't here yet, but when it comes, these things will erupt onto the surface more and more.

And is there such leadership on the horizon at the moment?

No. At the moment I don't recognize it.

Ya'akov Peri, what do you think a realistic permanent agreement with the Palestinians might look like?

Ya'akov Peri: That's a difficult question. We'll have to give up, and I think that about this there's near-agreement, all of the territories of the West Bank. We'll have to maintain some sort of capabilities for ourselves in our borders with Jordan, and we'll have to find an adequate solution to the problem of Jerusalem. Ultimately, in my eyes, the easiest thing to do is international supervision of the holy sites. And we'll have to grant some powers for Palestinian sovereignty over what Itzik Mordechai would call "the outskirts of Jerusalem." I think a solution can be found.

A Palestinian East Jerusalem?

Not all of it. I wouldn't include the Jewish neighborhoods in that. Regarding the settlements, I'd build blocs and let every settler, as happened in Yamit in Sinai or in the Gaza disengagement, to receive compensation if he evacuates from there. And those who want to stay in an island, let's call it Ariel, within the Palestinian state that will be established, we'll give them access into Israel through east-to-west roads.

Refugees?

The right of return,* no way. That needs to be bought with money. I don't think that will be the obstacle. The Palestinians have understood on their own that the great majority of Jerusalem and the subject of the right of return are topics the State of Israel is very firm on. You can reach a consensus about a certain amount of people who can return to their previous residences. You can settle the matter in a more business-like way, but no one in Palestine will step up and say they've relinquished the right of return. That's a topic that will be with us through the years.

---

* The concept of the Palestinian right of return asserts that Palestinian first-generation refugees and their descendants, displaced as a result of the wars in 1948 and 1967, have a right to return and to reclaim the property they or their forebears left behind in Israel and the Territories.

Ultimately, I think there's still a majority in the Israeli public that supports an agreement with the Palestinians, because people are tired of the current situation. People want their peace of mind, the quiet. I have to warn and come out and say that that's also an illusion. Since with every kind of treaty, even the kind most convenient to Israel, there will always be opposition groups on the Palestinian side, and to some extent or other on our side as well, which will try to harm it. Many generations have to pass here—I don't know whether decades or centuries—until the two nations both learn how to sit under their own grapevines and fig trees and stop bothering the other side.

Where there moments during the last few years when you thought differently, that it was nearer than decades or centuries?

Yes. There were moments, not too many, the nearer I was to the subject of the negotiation. For example, immediately after the Oslo process. But since then, unfortunately, not too many times.

And why aren't you optimistic today? Because there's no leadership on both sides?

I don't know if there's no leadership. There's leadership, but it has to make very hard decisions, some of which are opposed to its political outlook. I can say in a pretty firm way that those who led, or some of those who led, the negotiations with the Palestinians weren't the most qualified in Israel to do so. Not in terms of their knowledge of Palestinian society, not in terms of intimate familiarity with the mentality, with the way to talk to Arabs, with the way in which a relationship of trust is created. Some of them were excellent professionals in their fields, whether it's lawyers or various kinds of go-betweens, and might have been highly acceptable to those who sent them, but they also have to be acceptable to the other side.

Meaning, we failed in bringing in the right people to lead the negotiations?

Among other things. Without a doubt.

Carmi Gillon, is there a chance that a Palestinian president or an Israeli prime minister will agree on withdrawal, and it will actually happen? With everything that's happening on the ground?

Carmi Gillon: Yes. I'm sure it will. Whether we want or don't want it to happen. I think the settlements will be evacuated. Not the big blocs, not Ariel and Ma'ale Edomim and Gush Etzion, whose continuing existence I support, in return for territorial exchanges, but all the settlements are going to go away. There'll be resistance, but the violence level won't be that of two hundred thousand people. You have to remember, the vast majority of settlers will go home quietly. A large part of them will demonstrate, fight for their home, but won't go beyond the boundaries of permitted behavior. A small minority of a few hundred definitely could take very harsh actions, but I think we know where they are and can gain control over them.

And why haven't we been able to make a decision like that up to now?

Because our political system is messed up. Because since Yitzhak Rabin, we don't have leadership that can rise above the current political accounting.

What was it about Rabin's, and Sharon's, generation, that they could make those decisions and we can't?

Look, Rabin and Sharon and Begin, these are people who arrived with a record of decision making. They grew up as leaders. The younger generation is a generation of "technocrats." Ehud Barak is a technocrat. Bibi Netanyahu is a technocrat. He's not a leader. Look, I remember that at camp in the Scouts, we were all asked, "What do you want to be when you grow up?" I didn't think I'd be Shin Bet director, but Bibi said, "I'll be prime minister." At the age of fourteen. And we believed him. Meaning, he was certainly a natural leader with charisma even then. But he grew up as a technocrat. He wasn't qualified to be a leader. He was a clerk. A senior clerk, but a clerk. The same was true of Ehud Barak in the army. He didn't elevate himself to the level of leadership of someone who comes and says, hold on, I'm not just serving myself, I'm serving my people. I'm willing to pay a personal price. Maybe I'll lose these elections, but I'll win the next elections.

What you saw, both with Ehud Barak as prime minister and with Bibi Netanyahu during his previous term, is a kind of survival battle—how do I get through the day. What kind of trick do I make up now to preserve my status as prime minister. And with Rabin you didn't see that. You didn't see that with Sharon, either. He probably made those calculations to the same extent they did, a lot better than them, but before the public, he appeared as a man of decision. He makes decisions, tears apart a party, establishes a new party, all for disengagement. All for the people of Israel. I'm sick of the Likud Central Committee, so I don't bow down to it, I take the whole thing apart and leave Bibi in the opposition with twelve mandates. If he hadn't gotten ill, you'd have a completely different reality now, in my estimation. And believe me, I'm not a big fan of Sharon. But he was a leader, no doubt about it.

Is there a leader like that on the horizon?

Not that I know of.

Avraham Shalom, can you see a leadership on the horizon that could do this?

Avraham Shalom: Not that I know of. All the prime ministers I worked with were afraid to lose majority in the government. To them, that was more important than the political structure of the Israeli people, or its very future existence. The State of Israel could fall apart over this. If not in a year, then in ten years. And they actually understand it, too. It's not that they don't understand, but they think the country is less important than the party. Golda was one of the first to express it. She said: first the party, then the country.

There's no Israeli leader who was a strategist?

Shalom: Only Ben Gurion. I think that Arik Sharon, out of all the "hawk" politicians, was the first to understand it wouldn't work without a separate Palestinian state, and that they were a people under occupation, that they couldn't live with it and neither could we. I claim we're the ones who can't live with our occupation of them. I don't really worry about the Arabs. But today the whole Israeli political spectrum is right of center. There's still some left, but they're a small minority. It might be we just don't have good people. I did reach that conclusion, but I can't make that judgment. I'm not any better myself.

Our politicians don't have the ability to look thirty or fifty years into the future and see the Jewish people in a sea of Muslims. Leaders lose their nerve. You need a healthy amount of nerve to fight terror. It doesn't end in one day. And in the end you already know today that you won't win. You won't lose, but you also won't win. A leadership that's responsible for these things ultimately loses its orientation, its nerve, its senses. We lose our discernment, our proportions. No other country, including those whose existence is threatened, thinks in terms of genocide. Only here every soldier who's killed, who's wounded, is like half a holocaust to us, because on some level we haven't left the Diaspora. I don't know why, but it's a fact. Everyone who comes to Israel for the first time, where do they take him? Yad Vashem [the Holocaust memorial museum], of course. And immediately afterward to some other Holocaust thing. I know, the Ghetto Fighters' House Museum. It can't be like that. You can't raise a whole nation, three generations, if not three and a half generations, constantly on disasters—Holocaust. Holocaust, that's a matter of worldview, of perspective, of proportions.

You're eighty-one today. What do you think the State of Israel should do? If I gave you the cards, and told you, Avraham Shalom, the cards are in your hands. . . .

I'd give them back to you. What is this, punishment?

But if I insisted. What do you think Israel should do?

Talk to everyone. Start talking and change the tone. Talk to everyone all the time. All the time. Anywhere they want to talk to us, on any topic they want to talk to us about. I think the stronger party should yield. But we're losing the position of strength. That's what worries me. Yesterday's strongest is no longer today's strongest.

INDEX

Film director Dror Moreh had a vision: to seat all the heads of the Shin Bet, the Israeli intelligence organization, in front of the camera for a conversation on the Israeli-Palestinian conflict, the battle against terror, the leadership losing its way, the missed opportunities, the blood spilled. But even as he embarked on shooting his award-winning film *The Gatekeepers*, he never imagined that Avraham Shalom, Ya'akov Peri, Carmi Gillon, Ami Ayalon, Avi Dichter, and then-current Shin Bet director Yuval Diskin would bare their scars to him, convey their personal story with riveting honesty, and contradict some widely accepted assumptions.

The book *The Gatekeepers* collects the original interviews which served as a basis for the eponymous movie and television series, but also includes many stories which have never been previously revealed, confessions which haven't been previously voiced, and insights for which the right words have never been found before.

The Gatekeepers is a unique document in examining the relationship between the security system of any country and its citizens. A moment of honesty. The heads of Shin Bet are exposed here as flesh and blood. Six people who have dedicated their lives to the war against terror now look, some of them for the first time, directly into the mirror.

Will we dare to look there as well?